# CLASS AND SOCIETY IN
# CENTRAL CHIAPAS

# CLASS AND SOCIETY IN
# CENTRAL CHIAPAS

ROBERT WASSERSTROM

University of California Press

BERKELEY   LOS ANGELES   LONDON

University of California Press
Berkeley and Los Angeles, California

University of California Press, Ltd.
London, England

© 1983 by
The Regents of the University of California
Printed in the United States of America


1 2 3 4 5 6 7 8 9

Library of Congress Cataloging in Publication Data

Wasserstrom, Robert
    Class and society in central Chiapas.

    Bibliography: p.
    Includes index.
    1. Indians of Mexico—Chiapas—Social conditions.
2. Indians of Mexico—Chiapas—History. 3. Tzotzil
Indians—Social conditions. 4. Chiapas (Mexico)—
Social conditions. I. Title.
F1219.1.C45W37    1983            305.8′97′07275            82-11126
ISBN 0-520-04670-6

# CONTENTS

|  | PREFACE AND ACKNOWLEDGMENTS | vii |
|---|---|---|
| ONE | INTRODUCTION | 1 |
| TWO | THE CONQUEST AND COLONIZATION OF CHIAPAS, 1528–1590 | 11 |
| THREE | SPANISH SOCIETY IN COLONIAL CHIAPAS, 1590–1821 | 32 |
| FOUR | NATIVE SOCIETY IN THE CENTRAL HIGHLANDS, 1590–1821 | 69 |
| FIVE | THE LAST FRONTIER: REBELLION AND REVIVAL IN THE LIBERAL CENTURY, 1821–1910 | 107 |
| SIX | END OF THE DIASPORA: CATTLEMEN AND TENANT FARMERS IN CENTRAL CHIAPAS, 1910–1975 | 156 |
| SEVEN | "OUR FATHERS, OUR MOTHERS": DOMESTIC LIFE AND RELIGIOUS CHANGE IN ZINACANTAN, 1910–1975 | 216 |
| EIGHT | CONCLUSIONS | 240 |
|  | APPENDIX: INDIAN SURNAMES IN ZINACANTAN, 1749–1855 | 253 |
|  | GLOSSARY | 261 |
|  | NOTES | 267 |
|  | BIBLIOGRAPHY | 315 |
|  | INDEX | 331 |

# PREFACE AND ACKNOWLEDGMENTS

I am aware that another book on highland Chiapas will not be regarded as much of a novelty by anthropologists and historians. Within the past few years, literally dozens of works on the region have appeared in print, mainly in the United States but also in Mexico and Europe. Still, I have decided to proceed with the work for a variety of reasons. Primary among these is the fact that until Murdo MacLeod's monumental book *Spanish Central America: A Socioeconomic History, 1520–1720* appeared in 1973, the history of Chiapas remained shrouded in the vapors of time and—what was worse—feverish imagination.

The urgency to correct this situation arose in the early 1970s, when native organizations in Mexico and elsewhere realized that they could not accurately chart their future as long as they did not clearly understand their past. Merely relying upon oral tradition in places like Zinacantan and Chamula did not solve this dilemma: conflicting versions of major events were as plentiful as ethnographies, and suffered from many of the same shortcomings. With such problems in mind, I decided to complement my own fieldwork on religion and economic change with archival research. MacLeod's book (which arrived as I was writing my doctoral dissertation) provided much information about Central America in general and a few working guidelines for Chiapas in particular. Thereafter I found myself caught in the unrelenting tension between field and archive, a tension which I was never completely able to resolve. The book at hand reflects this difficulty: it is not quite history and not quite anthropology. If, however, it helps to connect the present with the past, I will have achieved my purpose.

Naturally a project of this sort proceeded through several stages. Fieldwork in Zinacantan began during the summers of 1969, 1970, and 1972, and then continued from mid-1973 to mid-1975. At this point I conducted biographical and autobiographical interviews (in Tzotzil) with Indians from half a dozen villages. For about 18 months my wife and I lived in one hamlet (Petztoj) and traveled extensively in the Grijalva river valley. This research was supplemented with two large economic surveys, in Na Chij and Elan Vo', and smaller household surveys in Salinas and Nabenchauk. During the first half of 1975, I carried out another economic survey to provide comparable information on household income and employment in Chamula. Additional interviews were also collected in surrounding Tzotzil communities: Mitontic, Chenalhó, Santa Marta, San Andrés. From then until June 1977 (when we returned to the United States), I served as a research fellow at the Centro de Investigaciones Ecológicas del Sureste in San Cristóbal. In that capacity, I was able to follow the Chamula diaspora to such places as the Soconusco and the Lacandón jungle. As the question of class structure came more sharply into focus, I also compiled a series of autobiographies from *mestizo* politicians, plantation owners and administrators, ranchers, former policemen, bodyguards, and others. These interviews were extremely valuable in reconstructing the events which influenced native communities after 1936. Finally, my archival research was undertaken for the most part between 1975 and 1977 and continued sporadically until 1980. In the United States, this research was combined with another set of interviews which focused upon social scientists who had conducted their own fieldwork in Mexico before 1955.

Throughout these years, I have come to regard my work as something of a collective enterprise. Anthropologists are helpless without the forbearance and aid of the people among whom they live, and I hope that this book in some measure repays that kindness. Without the patience of my *compadre* Lorenzo Santis Velio, for example, I might never have learned Tzotzil and would certainly have found it more difficult. A similar debt of gratitude is owed to Salvador López Guzmán, who ran the Chamula survey and must take much of the credit for its success.

In Zinacantan and Chamula, our lives were enriched by conversation with Domingo Santis Velio and Manuel Sánchez, among many others. In San Cristóbal, we came to value especially the friendship of Janet Marren and Marcey Jacobson, Jan and Diane Rus, Ron and Kippy Nigh (who also drew many of the maps in this book), Bob and Mimi Laughlin, Chip Morris, John Burstein, Kees Grootenboer, Naomi Brickman and her son Ari, and Jim Nations. At the Centro de Investigaciones Ecológicas del Sureste, I received considerable support and encouragement from my boss, Dr. Fernando Beltrán, and several of my colleagues. I also received excellent assistance from Juana Carmona, Lydia Prieto, María Antonieta Alcázar and, in later years, from María Elena Fernández Galán. During our short breaks in Oaxaca, we found sympathetic refuge with Marc and Cicely Winter, Stéfano and Linda Varese, Martin and Wilunya Diskin, and Miguel and Alicia Bartolomé. In Mexico City, we enjoyed the hospitality of Emma Cosío Villegas and Rafael Ortíz (who also provided financial support for most of the Chamula project), Sergio and Cynthia Alcántara, and Herminia Grootenboer and Jorge Contreras. I am especially grateful to Arturo Warman for the interest which he took in my work and the suggestions that he offered.

In the United States, I received critical guidance and advice from John Womack, Murdo MacLeod, Sandy Davis, and Albert B. Lord. At various times, a number of people have nursed me over the rough spots: Eric Wolf and Sydel Silverman, Eleanor Leacock, Peter and Jane Schneider, (Waldemar) Richard Smith, David Freidel, Mike Hughes and Nancy Scheper-Hughes, Georganne Chapin (who also helped me prepare the manuscript), Robert Alvarez, William Taylor, Leith Mullings, and Carter Wilson. Throughout the entire undertaking, I have benefited from the close collaboration and friendship of Jan Rus, with whom I shared the heady joy of rediscovering native history.

Many of the ideas presented here probably originated with him, and in any case it would be pointless to separate what is his from what is mine. Similar thanks are due to my parents, William and Rose Wasserstrom; my brothers, Andy and Jim; my in-laws, William and June, Robert and Lauren Poplack; and Sue Kelly and Patrick Hallinan. Finally, perhaps my largest debt is owed to my wife, Janice, and to my son, Eric. More than anyone else, they have borne the difficulties of this venture with relative good humor and have enabled me to pursue my strange obsession with a certain peace of mind.

# INTRODUCTION

Perhaps more than any other social group in recent memory, native people in highland Chiapas have been subjected to prolonged and continuous anthropological scrutiny, an unrelenting examination of the most intimate details of daily life. The outpouring of scholarly literature on such topics has been correspondingly prodigious: during the past quarter-century, no less than 30 books and monographs on Indian communities in the area have been published; perhaps 20 of these have appeared in the last dozen years alone.[1] Despite great diversity of authorship and emphasis, however, virtually all of these works share a number of common themes—or perhaps more accurately, they represent a set of variations on a single theme: the community-as-tribe, the town as social (or moral) universe. Notwithstanding Eric Wolf's early injunction that such towns must be considered as part of much wider and more complex social systems, anthropologists in Chiapas seem to have followed quite a separate agenda, one set out most clearly by Sol Tax and his collaborators in *The Heritage of Conquest.*[2] In this view, ethnic divisions coincide with local boundaries; what takes place beyond these boundaries is of little consequence or interest to people who share the "cultural trait of indifference" toward members of other ethnic groups.[3] And if such indifference characterizes the relationship between inhabitants of adjacent Indian *pueblos*, how much more

1

indifferent these people must feel when they confront *mestizos* or members of other social "castes"!

Ironically, this picture of native society, though it was original- ly inspired by Robert Redfield's views on folk society, represent- ed a particularly conservative interpretation of those views. From his correspondence with Tax, we now know that Redfield accepted such ideas only with great reluctance and considerable misgiving.[4] After all, on the subject of progress, he remained a staunch Victorian, imbued with the conviction that things neces- sarily changed—most often for the worse, to be sure, but some- times for the better. Ambivalence of this sort is most transparent- ly illustrated in the rather extraordinary way in which he concluded his first major article on culture change (1934):

> I have found it convenient to speak of [rural] society as Culture, and the [urban] type as Civilization. If this terminology be adopted, the study we are now engaged upon is one of deculturalization, rather than of acculturalization. But as there are objections . . . to denying the term "culture" to the life-ways of the city man, it may be more acceptable to describe this study as that of the change from folk culture to city culture.[5]

In contrast, for Tax and his disciples, change invariably meant degeneration, the catastrophic rupture of communal bonds and social ties:

> It may well be that what is defined here as the "civilized world- view" is something that developed only once in the world—in our civilization—and now will never be given the chance to develop independently again. . . . If such a thesis be acceptable, we may also treat the civilized world-view as we do any other cultural invention, and we can conveniently speak of its diffusion to other peoples.[6]

As for the nature of such diffusion, Tax was measurably less sanguine than his mentor about the possibilities for voluntary accommodation and peaceful amalgamation:

> It might be possible to distinguish two kinds of acculturation. In one kind, both our world-view and our type of social relations are

imposed on native peoples. In the other, only our world-view is imposed on a people who have independently . . . developed an analogous kind of social relations.[7]

In either case, he concluded, acculturation was synonymous with culture loss, with the displacement of *their* mental culture by *ours*.

With these facts in mind, it is perhaps easier to understand why anthropologists who shared Tax's distaste for studies of social change were led to focus upon native communities in central Chiapas. As in highland Guatemala, such communities appeared to offer an almost unique opportunity to test anthropological tools and concepts, to observe Indian society in a virtually uncontaminated setting, to develop paradigms for application and extension to other regions and problems. In fact, it is not unfair to say that these communities quickly acquired the role which in previous years had often been played by so-called tribal groups in the United States and Canada: they permitted ethnographers to imagine how indigenous life might have been organized and conducted before the intrusions of Europeans.[8] To this end, Tax and his followers soon devised a unique style of anthropological writing that (in keeping with professional standards of the day) placed heavy emphasis upon the ways in which local beliefs and practices reinforced communal solidarity. As a result, community studies in the region tended to concentrate upon a relatively narrow and stereotyped range of topics: kinship and family organization, *fiestas* and other "ritual behavior," civil–religious hierarchies, witchcraft and shamanism, subsistence farming and handicrafts. By the 1960s, such topics had received more or less official sanction in the *Handbook of Middle American Indians;*[9] thereafter, instead of producing generalized monographs which touched on all of these subjects, investigators directed their efforts toward increasingly specialized and restricted fields of inquiry.

Under these circumstances, it is appropriate to ask what we have learned from such an undertaking, or indeed whether the consensus on native society which has existed for nearly half a century must finally be revised. Let us consider, for example, the concept of equilibrium, which underlies virtually all anthropological scholarship on Chiapas. In Tax's hands, this concept served to explain how Indian communities managed to isolate themselves from external disruption and perpetuate their way of life almost intact over hundreds of years. Although subsequent researchers revised Tax's quasi-biological (or genetic) view of culture, it was precisely the notion of equilibrium that led Frank Cancian to examine the relationship between corn production and ritual service in Zinacantan—and thereby to provide a model for anthropological research throughout Mexico.[10] In effect, Cancian suggests that Zinacantecos have responded to economic and demographic pressures by expanding their religious system; in so doing, they have maintained the essential balance between self-preservation and social peace upon which ethnic identity is based. More recently, George Collier has extended this argument to the neighboring community of Chamula, where he claims that even destructive agricultural practices have been enlisted as a means of reinforcing communal bonds.[11] Common to both of these discussions is the conviction that ideological harmony—not disunity or conflict—informs cultural behavior and sets the pace of agricultural production. But Cancian admits that during the past generation Zinacantan has become deeply divided over questions of land and wealth. Inevitably, then, one must question whether all Zinacantecos (or Chamulas) now occupy the same moral universe, whether this common sense of community has not become a convenient anthropological fiction.

Similar questions arise when we consider the rather substantial body of writing on the subject of native world-view and epistemology. In *Gossip, Reputation, and Knowledge in Zinacantan*, John Haviland argues that by examining the ways in which Zinacantecos talk we may understand not only how they think but indeed what fundamental premises underlie all of their actions and behavior:

> Gossip always draws our attention immediately to the important facts and it never fails to draw appropriate conclusions. . . . Furthermore, [it] continually alludes to generally inaccessible bodies of native theory and belief. . . . Gossip leads the ethnographer to (and draws on the native's knowledge of) pieces of such native theory.[12]

Implicit in this view, of course, is the notion that speech itself may serve as a proxy for other forms of social action: "What we cannot talk about is irrelevant, or at least unavailable for scrutiny. For the outsider, it is talk that leads directly to what is relevant, on native theory."[13] What is most striking about such assertions, however, is the extraordinary importance they attach to the "conventions and rules" of Zinacanteco culture, and the rather naive faith which they place in the ability of native theory to explain a range of complex phenomena. After all, how many Americans understand the Federal Reserve System, the interbank lending rate, or the Toxic Substances Control Act, which are surely not irrelevant to their lives? Moreover, as Francesca Cancian has recognized in her book *What Are Norms?*, there is the problem that people often say one thing and do another; justifications for such behavior can readily be invented after the fact, but their value as testimony must necessarily remain quite limited.[14]

Absent from all of these discussions is the problem of history, of how Indian communities in Chiapas and elsewhere became what they are today and how the past has determined their present position in national society. And it is here that we encounter in its most graphic form the double standard of scholarship which constitutes Tax's most unfortunate legacy in the region: Indians have no relevant history because they are culturally (genetically) programmed to respond in a certain limited fashion to outside stimuli—to live in patrilineal compounds, for example, and to practice pre-Columbian religion in the guise of Catholicism. So deeply have such ideas become ingrained in the anthropological consciousness, in fact, that some authors (most notably E. Z. Vogt and Gary Gossen) continue to search among modern-day Zinacantecos and Chamulas for keys to the mysteries of classical Maya civilization.[15] Of course, it is true that other researchers like Henri Favre and (to a lesser extent) Victoria Bricker have made selective use of historical information to interpret ethnographic data.[16] But efforts of this sort have invariably been marred by an undue willingness to accept anthropological wisdom more or less at face value; at best, history is invoked to endow these interpretations with a proper pedigree, with the air of respectability so often missing from strictly ethnographic accounts. In contrast, no such account of non-Indian Mexico would be entertained by any serious scholar unless it made at least an honest attempt to understand how colonialism and civil warfare have influenced modern institutions and sensibilities—just as we insist upon a proper respect for American constitutional history when we read about our own political affairs.[17] Or are we saying that Indians in Chiapas (and Oaxaca and Yucatan) are somehow different—that *their* history, in Vogt's phrase, is just another point of view?

In the following pages I have tried to raise precisely these questions and to conduct a historical examination of how ethnic distinctiveness and modern social relations have emerged in central Chiapas. Naturally, an undertaking of this sort is fraught with difficulties, not the least of which involves my own reluctance to accept much of the anthropological evidence upon which previous accounts have drawn. As a result, I have been forced to start broadly and to end narrowly—that is, to begin by examining the organization of colonial society in general, and to concentrate upon two communities, Zinacantan and Chamula, as these have come more sharply into focus. Such a procedure, I believe, is justified for two reasons. First, by the late 16th century most of the differences which may have characterized native *señoríos* (principalities or fiefdoms) before the conquest had disappeared under the combined pressures of demographic catastrophe and political collapse. For the next two centuries, these communities remained quite homogeneous in both their internal structure and their position within the colonial order. Only after independence, it seems, and in fact toward the end of the 19th century, did such towns acquire the distinct ethnic identities which later fired the imaginations of anthropologists. Second, as my inquiry has approached the present, I have used only that ethnographic information in which I have a high degree of confidence—primarily the research of investigators who did not set out to confirm what they already knew. In so doing, I hope that I have made a case for the need to see anthropology and history not as complementary activities but as a single enterprise—one which begins with those forces and pressures that are continually reorienting the coordinates of Indian life itself.

## CENTRAL CHIAPAS BEFORE THE CONQUEST

Colonial Chiapas extended from the borders of present-day Tabasco and Oaxaca southward to the Sierra Madre mountain range, which separated it from the province of Soconusco (MAP 1). To the east, Chiapa (as it was then known) was bounded by an uncharted jungle, the Lacandón rain-forest; to the west, it spread across a dry, windy plain that joined Oaxaca and the Soconusco at the Isthmus of Tehuantepec. From May to October each year, when the rains fell, this arid desert was transformed into a verdant subtropical savanna. Such accidents of climate and geography divided the entire region into a number of distinct ecological zones which facilitated intraregional exchange among its early inhabitants. Of primary importance, the Grijalva River basin (which bisected the province between the Sierra Madre range and the central highlands) provided fertile ground for such crops as cotton and later sugarcane. It was here, in fact, that Chiapaneca invaders from central Mexico established their own political hegemony among Zoque natives around 900 A.D.[18]

> Spanish Chiapa was thus an inland province.... The descent from the Sierra Madre to the Río Grande is gradual, through wide alluvial valleys, while on the northeast there is a sharp rise to the Meseta Central. The latter, with elevations of 1,500–2,000+ m, is a series of rugged limestone ranges and peaks alternating with a gently rolling surface.... There is extreme variety of climate and vegetation. The valley of Chiapas [i.e., the central depression] is relatively dry and hot.... The higher parts of the plateau are quite cold, with heavy seasonal ... rains and a good deal of forest.[19]

Toward the northwest, too, the central highlands tapered off until they merged with the coastal plains of Tabasco. In these foothills, exotic commodities like cacao and cochineal abounded. And finally, to the northeast, highland forests of pine and oak gave way to a network of temperate valleys in which indigenous settlers produced maize, beans, dyestuffs, spices, tobacco, and other important goods.

Political organization in the area was quite complex. According to Edward Calnek, "at the time of the Spanish conquest

## Map 1.
## Early Colonial Chiapas

highland Chiapas was divided into small, warring principalities or petty states, called *provincias* in early accounts."[20] Like other minor fiefdoms in this part of Mesoamerica, such provinces were apparently governed by local nobles aligned with the resurgent Chontal dynasty on Cozumel.[21] Under their guidance, towns like Zinacantan and Ixtapa became important ports-of-trade between Guatemala (including the Soconusco) and central Mexico. Capitalizing upon this trade, such towns had been transformed by the late Classic period into major commercial centers.[22] "In this province of Zinacantan," wrote Bernardino de Sahagún, "[the Indians] make amber and also large feathers called *quetzalli* ... and the rare skins of wild animals. All of these things are obtained by [Mexican] merchants known as *nahualoztomeca* ... who use them for rings which are worn by men of special valor."[23] Commerce of this sort was complemented by a lively regional market for labor and goods of various sorts which were sent off to cacao plantations in Soconusco.[24]

> The valley of Ixtapa served as a point of exchange for the western highlands and the Chiapa area ... [and] participated in a single cultural tradition which spread from the lowlands into the highlands, culminating in the terminal Classic in a continuous net of contact and exchange.[25]

By the 14th century, however, rivalry between Chiapaneca *caciques* and nobles in Zinacantan had deprived Ixtapa of its role in this exchange and had displaced the center of economic activity to Zinacantan alone.[26]

What Spanish soldiers found when they arrived in Chiapa, then, was a mosaic of "ethnic states" which occupied distinctly different territories and environments. To the west and north of the Grijalva River, Zoque people dominated the province's production of cacao and cochineal. Along their southern margin, these men and women were constantly harassed by the Chiapanecas, who had strategically founded several towns in the river basin itself, at the precise point where the Ixtapa valley meets the central depression. According to Bernal Díaz del Castillo, who joined the first Spanish expedition into this region, the Chiapanecas were quite bellicose and made war on their neighbors . . . and robbed and pillaged wherever they might take captives. Moreover, they maintained fortified posts at narrow places along the road to Tehuantepec where they assaulted Indian merchants who traveled from one province to another, so that at times this commerce was entirely interrupted. . . .[27]

Unlike either the Zoques (who were related to Mixe people in Oaxaca) or the Chiapanecas, Indians elsewhere in Chiapa participated in more generalized patterns of Maya culture which extended into neighboring Guatemala. In the western highlands, these men and women (normally called *quelenes* in colonial documents) spoke various dialects of Tzotzil and were divided among approximately seven distinct political entities. They shared the area with speakers of Tzeltal (called *Zendal* by Spanish settlers), who occupied the towns which spread east to Comitán. Between Comitán and the Guatemalan border lay several communities inhabited by people who spoke a language known as Coxoh, which may be the same as present-day Tojolabal. Finally, along the northern edge of the Tzeltal region, Spanish armies encountered a few people who spoke Chol, a language which they shared with unpacified Lacandones in the eastern jungles.

# THE CONQUEST AND
# COLONIZATION OF CHIAPAS,
## 1528–1590

The arrival of Diego de Mazariegos in 1528, unlike Luis Marín's unsuccessful invasion of Chiapas four years earlier, signaled the definitive colonization of lands and territories which until that moment had formed the unquestioned patrimony of such extensive pre-Columbian *cacicazgos* as Chiapa and Zinacantan.[1] As in other parts of Central America, the *conquistadores* who subsequently took possession of these lands soon left off their search for silver and gold—treasures which, they hoped, overflowed in Chiapas' rivers and streams. True enough, the area possessed its riches. Not gems and minerals (although small amounts of gold were extracted near Copanaguastla)—but Chiapas contained such scarce or valuable commodities as cacao, cotton, and dyestuffs. More important, perhaps, the Grijalva River basin (where these first Spaniards made their homes) abounded both in fertile lands and—no less valuable—a stable and well-organized native labor force. No sooner had Mazariegos established the province's first *cabildo*, therefore, than he divided Chiapaneca communal territories into agricultural properties which he distributed among his followers.[2]

For Indians in Chiapas (who in 1528 may have numbered as many as 200,000), the conquest brought not only the twin afflictions of *encomienda* and *repartimiento*, but also within a short time spelled the end of their traditional political authority. Unlike Oaxaca, for example, where both the Marqués del Valle and royal officials maintained local *caciques* and *principales* in positions of responsibility, the *encomenderos* in Chiapas decided almost immediately to brook no interference from native chieftains or their clerical supporters.[3] Ironically, it may well have been Fray Bartolomé de Las Casas, the famous Defender of the Indians, who inspired such intransigence among his avaricious countrymen. For in his zeal to preserve the *república de indios* against encroachment by Spanish settlers, Las Casas provoked local authorities to attack autochthonous social and political institutions without quarter—an onslaught against which his subsequent maneuvering in Spain proved largely unsuccessful. Naturally, this lesson was not lost upon the missionaries who followed him. Only a few years after Las Casas had threatened to excommunicate many of Ciudad Real's most prominent *vecinos* (Spanish residents) for holding Indian slaves, his hand-picked successor, Tomás Casillas, prudently limited his remonstrations with provincial officials on this delicate subject to a few well-chosen words of disapproval.[4] In fact, Las Casas' original efforts to shield Indians in Chiapas from unlawful treatment soon gave way to a period in which both civil and ecclesiastical authorities hastened to consolidate their hold over native lands, bodies, and souls.

Despite their early assault upon indigenous social life, Spanish *encomenderos* did not greatly modify the existing system of agricultural production and trade. In contrast to Baltazar Guerra, first *encomendero* of Chiapa, most settlers did not rush to construct *ingenios* (sugar mills) in their new bailiwicks nor compel their Indian charges to cultivate such exotic new crops as sugarcane. On the contrary, like their counterparts elsewhere in Central America, they chose instead to usurp local trading for their own enrichment. As in the adjacent province of Soconusco, cacao frequently played a prominent role in such machinations— not the cacao grown along the Pacific coast, but rather that cultivated by Zoque people near the Tabasco border.[5] In this way— according to the Dominican chronicler Antonio de Remesal— Pedro de Estrada, *encomendero* of Zinacantan until mid-century and a half-brother of Mazariegos, pursued a double strategy in accumulating a larger personal fortune. On the one hand, royal regulations notwithstanding, he soon built an *ingenio* within his grant and obliged the Indians there to plant and grind cane. On the other hand, he also demanded that they pay part of their tribute in cacao from distant Zoque plantations.

> Their tribute numbered 120 loads, while today even the entire province of Soconusco, which is the heartland of cacao, does not give to the King more than 200; so that . . . all Sevilla would have difficulty in paying it. And although many other things also helped, one of the principal matters which moved the *audiencia* to . . . remeasure the land was this excessive tribute which the Zinacantecos paid. When the *encomendero* learned this . . . he demanded the tribute for the whole year before the accustomed time had arrived. . . . And in his cleverness, he sold it very dearly to the Indians, so that they might return it to him [in payment].[6]

By mid-century, however, this situation had already begun to change. As in New Spain and Guatemala, *encomenderos* in Ciudad Real soon realized that indigenous markets and traditional commodities did not offer the means for acquiring great fortunes. New avenues of enrichment had to be explored, new industries developed, new crops put under cultivation. Like their neighbors in other provinces, then, these settlers turned their attention to cattle raising, to the production of cotton and cotton cloth, and to an expanded sugar industry. In some cases, as with cotton and cochineal, these crops were simply demanded of Indian tributaries, who subsequently bore the risks and difficulties of cultivation. But as the native labor force declined and Spanish settlement grew, many colonists began to create their own *estancias de ganado* (cattle ranches) and sugar plantations—primarily in the fertile Grijalva valley and adjacent areas. As a result, Indians who were already hard-pressed to pay their tribute in cacao, chickens, and maize found themselves forced to move their *milpas* (cornfields) onto difficult mountain slopes of uncertain productivity. Perhaps it was this adverse combination of circumstances which so weakened Zinacantan's population that in 1565 all but 50 of its inhabitants succumbed to an epidemic which left other communities virtually untouched.[7]

Royal officials in Gracias a Dios and later in Guatemala could not ignore these problems, nor were they entirely unsympathetic to the plight of Indian communities. In 1545, the colonial court (*audiencia*) commissioned one of its judges, Juan Rogel, to revise tribute lists in Chiapas and to investigate the behavior of local functionaries. Although Rogel proved reluctant to punish the province's *encomenderos*, he nonetheless saw fit to

> abolish much of the personal service which Indians performed in mines, *ingenios*, and cattle *estancias*. . . . He ordered under threat of severe penalties that no Indian might serve within any *ingenio*, nor in any sugar press, nor in any other such thing, but that they might be employed only outside [these buildings] to carry firewood and cane. He also abolished most of the *tlamames*, or Indian bearers, which tributary towns gave to carry the merchandise that entered and left the region, and ordered that [these Indians] might not be sent out of their own land more than 15 or 20 leagues.[8]

In Las Casas' eyes, however, even these measures were insufficient to protect Indian communities from the mounting pressures to which they were subjected. Together with his principal collaborators, he lobbied steadfastly—both in Guatemala and in Spain—for a second *visita* (inspection), by which involuntary servitude and unlawful seizures of native territory would be ended forever in the region. Four years later this campaign appeared to be on the verge of success; the *audiencia* dispatched one of its officers, Gonzalo Hidalgo de Montemayor, to Ciudad Real in the capacity of *juez real* (special judge), with instructions to free all Indian slaves and "measure the land once again."[9]

Unlike his predecessor, Hidalgo did not hesitate to hold individual settlers responsible for the excesses which they had committed and to enforce his decisions with strong legal sanctions. Reserved and almost secretive during his *visita*, he surprised and horrified Spaniards in Ciudad Real by depriving 16 prominent *encomenderos* of their tributary income.[10] Simultaneously, and over the concerted opposition of the province's aspiring *hijos-dalgo* (gentry), he permitted the Dominicans to condense dispersed Indian hamlets and households into highly organized *pueblos*, "sociable republics," so that "with greater speed they might come together for mass or for sermon, and for all that which may be propitious for their governance." [11] Yet in spite of Hidalgo's unabashedly pro-Dominican attitude, it would be extremely shortsighted to ascribe his actions to simple piety or even to an overly zealous enthusiasm for legal principle. For it must be remembered that royal authority in Chiapas was as yet extremely uncertain and would remain weak for many years more. Knowing that settler communities in both Peru and Nicaragua had rebelled over similar matters, Hidalgo may well have felt that the Crown's interests in Chiapas might be much more safely entrusted to the area's missionaries than to Ciudad Real's hotheaded and belligerent Spanish gentry. In any case, as Murdo MacLeod has pointed out, Hidalgo's efforts to enforce the New Laws quickly came to grief at the hands of less honest or more timorous judicial superiors.[12] Nevertheless, he established a relationship between the *audiencia* in Guatemala and the Dominican Order in Chiapas which was to last—not without difficulties, of course—throughout the colonial period.

One can only imagine the havoc which this relationship worked upon the principles and purposes of missionaries in Chiapas. Originally numbering around 40 members, Las Casas' band of Dominican apostles initiated their labors by defending indigenous communities against *encomenderos* and officials alike.[13] In the early days of missionary work, they agitated vigorously for enforcement of the New Laws (which effectively abolished Indian slavery and prohibited Spaniards from interfering in most aspects of Indian life), and at the same time refused to minister to the spiritual needs of local colonists. Similarly, in explaining royal ordinances to their native followers, they instructed these men and women about their rights and duties as Spanish subjects. In this way, for example, the Chiapanecas first learned (from Fray Pedro Calvo in 1545) that they owed fealty and obedience not to Baltazar Guerra but to the King of Castile, of whom— it was reported—neither Guerra nor any other Spaniard had ever spoken to them.[14]

Within a few years, however, such militancy among missionaries gave way to a more cautious, more moderate attitude toward Spanish settlers and administrators. In large measure, changes of this sort reflected both the Order's growing interest in land-ownership after 1572 and its fear that the *Consejo de las Indias*, influenced by the Council of Trent, would replace regular clergy with secular (diocese) priests in New World parishes. Threatened with the secularization of their "benefices, curacies, and *doctrinas*" (in a *real cédula* of 1583), Dominicans in Chiapas tactfully modified their stand on the twin issues of restitution (the obligation faced by Spaniards to restore whatever land, goods, or labor had been illegally extorted from Indian communities) and administering the sacraments to colonists. In return for such concessions, the Council dictated a series of measures which, beginning in 1567, permitted regular clergy to ignore many of the more distasteful regulations devised at Trent. As a result, by 1590 Dominican missionaries had lost much of their original concern for Indian welfare, and preferred instead to devote their energies to such secular concerns as cattle production and sugar planting. It is this process, and the polarization of ethnic relations to which it led, that will be examined in the following pages.

## LAS CASAS AND NEW WORLD THEOCRACY

Any discussion of missionary activity in early colonial Chiapas must inevitably begin with Fray Bartolomé de Las Casas, the famed *defensor de los indios*. A former *encomendero* in Cuba, Las Casas in 1514 renounced his rights to Indian tribute, to enter the Dominican Order and "transform himself into a committed fighter on behalf of the Indianist cause."[15] By temperament and training he was anything but a starry-eyed philanthropist: his experience in Cuba had acquainted him with the realities of conquest and colonization, which he ultimately perceived as an unmitigated disaster for native peoples. Although his views were at first quite moderate, he soon became convinced that royal policy itself was highly questionable—on both moral and political grounds. Fortunately, Las Casas was far from alone in his efforts to reduce or eliminate altogether the rights which Spanish colonists claimed over Indian lands and labor. On the contrary, "the surprising rise which this simple cleric, unaffiliated with the dominant class, enjoyed within high ecclesiastical circles in a few years' time demonstrates ... that the ground on which he walked had already been prepared by an entire movement, both within the state bureaucracy and within the Church."[16] Las Casas' specific contribution to the cause of Indian defense, therefore, did not lie in proposing that, as vassals of the Crown, America's native people enjoyed essentially the same responsibilities and privileges as any other Spanish subjects. But Las Casas did bring to this discussion a new tone of urgency, a harsh insistence upon the awful realities of conquest, and a willingness to call royal policy radically into question.

Out of these discussions emerged the New Laws. Propagated by Charles V in 1542, this code of colonial administration (which took its inspiration from Las Casas' own political views) gave judicial form to two closely related legal concepts. First, as the future bishop himself had contended, the conquest "did not abolish the *natural right* of [subject] peoples to preserve their internal organization [the preeminence of their *caciques*], their customs (insofar as these did not run afoul of Church teachings), and their culture."[17] It followed that royal authority within such regions might be carefully controlled and limited to "the reconstruction of local governments ruled by *caciques,* responsible directly to the Crown."[18] Obviously, America's *repúblicas de indios* had no need for the wave of Spanish soldiers of fortune, bureaucrats, and merchants which quickly flooded the hemisphere. Of course such people, too, enjoyed certain rights in the New World; but these rights, Las Casas felt, should be restricted primarily to that universal freedom which poor men enjoyed to labor on unoccupied lands (perhaps with the aid of black slaves) or to engage in some other honest occupation. Reflecting these notions, the New Laws decreed that neither *encomenderos* nor any other Spaniards might live in Indian *pueblos,* nor indeed reside there more than a few days. And finally, they instructed royal authorities that *encomiendas* should be granted only for the lifetime of their initial (or current) holders, after which the Indians involved were to become direct tributaries of the Crown.

Who, then, might oversee the affairs of these "associated republics," administered at least in theory by native *caciques* and *principales?* Certainly not the colonial civil service, for which Las Casas showed unconcealed contempt.[19] He remained pro- foundly suspicious of royal officials, who lived principally by selling their influence, exploiting indigenous labor, and specu- lating in Indian lands. Let them govern the *república de españoles,* he declared, those unruly colonists (the epithet is his own) who in any case required more governing than did Ameri- ca's peaceful natives. As for the *república de indios,* Las Casas looked to his monastic colleagues for those qualities of disinter- ested charity and uncompromised principle which such a task required. After all, he contended, their vows of poverty, their discipline, and their unquestionable evangelical purpose would keep them true to the spirit of duty which had brought them to the New World.

However naive or self-deceiving such notions may appear today, it must be remembered that they reflected quite accurate- ly the political situation in Spain during the 16th century. For in those years, imperial administrative posts were filled with priests and monks, many of whom occupied positions of considerable authority and standing. Furthermore, this relationship had found formal expression in the *patronato real,* by which the Pope had conferred upon Charles V the power to appoint or discharge Spanish prelates and even minor curates at his own discretion. Under these circumstances, Las Casas argued that Spanish cler- ics were admirably suited to serve simultaneously as spiritual ministers and officials of the Crown, subordinate only to the Council of the Indies. Although he never suggested that Indian affairs should become the exclusive concern of the religious or- ders, nonetheless he most certainly did demand "nothing less than the establishment of a theocracy which, through its author- ity over the area's Indians, would have held in its hands the fate of the colony."[20]

Determined to put these ideas to the test, then, in 1543 Las Casas accepted the bishopric of Chiapas and the following year traveled to Ciudad Real. In fact, this journey—which removed him for two years from the heat of political debate and intrigue at the court—nonetheless proved to be of major (and largely unrecognized) significance in the lives of native people. Until that moment, as Remesal writes, *encomenderos* in Chiapas had successfully suppressed missionary activity in the province and had usurped for themselves alone the rights and privileges which Christianity conferred upon Spanish subjects.[21] In large measure, this situation reflected their desire to preserve an artificial "state of war" between Spaniards and Indians in the area, a condition which permitted them to enslave native people without interference from high-minded clerics or other authorities. Among the first regulations propounded by the *cabildo* of Chiapa in 1528, for example, local settlers declared that against "those Indians who refuse to give provisions to the Spaniards, war shall be declared, and those who are taken prisoner shall become slaves."[22] Similarly, in 1537—that is, seven years after the Crown had abolished all forms of native slavery in the New World—the *ayuntamiento* (town council) in Ciudad Real nevertheless saw fit to pass four laws restricting the rights of colonists who were not *vecinos* of the province to meddle in local slave-trading.[23]

Not only did these settlers wish to command native labor, but like British plantation owners two centuries later, they also set out with considerable single-mindedness to unravel the social fabric in which Indians lived. Their efforts to destroy indigenous culture assumed two forms: first, interfering decisively in local marriage patterns, they compelled native men and women to break the rules of alliance upon which indigenous society was based. In this way, for example, Baltazar Guerra obliged Chiapaneca *caciques* and *principales* to marry women from inferior lineages—in the obvious hope of discrediting them and rendering them unfit to retain high office.[24] Second, both he and other colonists installed native *caciques* and removed them when it suited their convenience. In this way, Guerra selected one Chiapaneca *principal,* Pedro Notí, to become the town's main governor shortly after the conquest. When Las Casas arrived, however, Notí promptly befriended the friars and in so doing aroused Guerra against him. As a result, Notí soon found himself cast into irons in Ciudad Real, his *cacicazgo* now occupied by a more compliant relative. It was only after Las Casas had returned to

Spain in 1547 that Notí was released from prison by royal order and restored to his former position. Faced with this unforeseen *dénouement*, Guerra observed ruefully that

> I made him *cacique* against the common will and desire, and in so doing I violated several of your laws and ancient customs such as that which holds *Let no man become cacique who has not first held some position of honor in the republic*—of which I am now truly repentant.[25]

Little wonder, then, that Indians in Chiapas accepted with utmost sincerity the ministrations of Las Casas and his colleagues, to whom they looked for deliverance from many of the humiliations of conquest. As in Oaxaca and Guatemala, these missionaries consciously and deliberately supported native *caciques* such as Notí and Bartolomé Tzon of Zinacantan, whom they enlisted in the missionary effort.[26] In many ways, it was an alliance made in heaven: after all, Las Casas' view of evangelization obliged his collaborators to receive converts on the most generous possible terms. For their part, indigenous people in Chiapas regarded conversion to Christianity as the most direct and effective means of asserting their rights as Castilian subjects and reclaiming the ground they had lost to Guerra, de Estrada, and other *encomenderos*. In other words, as Remesal writes, they welcomed the friars precisely because these foreigners, unlike their insatiable compatriots, offered to end the monopoly which Spanish settlers held in matters of both faith and citizenship. As Remesal put it:

> They understood that to be baptized was to become a person of Castile, and to enjoy sufficient favor with the Spaniards to be relieved of the ill treatment which was continuously inflicted upon them and which they deeply regretted ... and even today there are old men who say "when we bought baptism"—and many bought it two or more times, for if they forgot the name which the cleric gave them on the first occasion, they came a second time to be baptized. . . .[27]

But the outcome of such collaboration and cooperation was not always felicitous for native chieftains. In most of highland Chiapas, the *cabildo* of Ciudad Real imposed its will upon Indian communities. Possessing only the least pretense of legal authority, it ruled on all but the most trivial questions of village administration.[28] Protesting that native *alguaciles* (*principales* whose judicial and political powers had been confirmed by the *audiencia* through Dominican intercession) were "forcing themselves upon the wives of common *macehaules*," for example, this body unilaterally and without authorization from any superior tribunal abolished the position of *alguacil* in 1546.[29] As might be expected, this action could be traced to the close relationship which one particular *alguacil*, Bartolomé Tzon, had developed with the friars. Moreover, because the Dominicans had built one of their principal houses in Tzon's *cabecera*, Zinacantan, this town had been converted into something of a battleground between *encomenderos* and missionaries. In fact, at one point, several months before the *cabildo*'s resolution to suppress native authorities in the highlands, Tzon had disobeyed an order from de Estrada to deny the friars food or sustenance until these high-minded clergymen agreed to hear confession and grant absolution to Spanish settlers. In the end, Tzon paid dearly for his loyalty to the Fathers: not only was he deprived of his office, as the resolution specified, but he also found himself banished from the region.[30] And more significantly, indigenous government in the town remained suspended for several years, until late in the century when native *cabildos* were organized throughout Chiapas.[31]

## "THE ROOT OF EVIL WAS EVER HIDDEN"

By 1546 it had become clear to Las Casas that, as long as he remained in Chiapas, he could not pursue his struggle to enforce the New Laws with any hope of success. Four years earlier, in Spain, he had scored his greatest triumph. Now he understood that if such victories were to be achieved in the future, he must return to that arena which had served him so well before: the court. Upon his departure for Spain, he commissioned his band of adherents to maintain faith in the vision of a theocratic Indian republic over which they would preside. For their part, settlers in Ciudad Real, having rid themselves of that "antichrist of a bishop," breathed an audible sign of relief—and promptly began to make amends with their Dominican neighbors. Whereas previously they had shown themselves to be intransigent, prideful, and uncompromising, they became transformed virtually overnight into the very picture of Christian generosity and magnanimity. Were the Fathers tiring of their rude little house in Zinacantan? Then the *cabildo* of Ciudad Real offered to construct a convent more worthy of Their Paternities in the city, where they might also enjoy more frequent commerce with their own countrymen. And without further hesitation, the city council "promised for it 16,000 Indians, and declared that when those were spent they would give more. And the Fathers accepted, because the convent was to be founded for the good of the Indians."[32] By the time Hidalgo arrived in 1549, then, *encomenderos* in Chiapas had taken a second major step toward limiting Dominican influence: they had enticed the Fathers away from Zinacantan and established them beneath the vigilant eyes of their own secular authorities.

Given these facts, it might be useful to ask why the missionaries accepted such an obviously corrupting proposition, one clearly intended to undermine their integrity. Would Las Casas have welcomed the idea of "spending" 16,000 Indians to build himself a convent? Certainly not; and yet, even before his ship had reached Spain, his closest associates—consoling themselves with the thought that such a wanton waste of indigenous lives and labor would in the end benefit Indian souls—did so eagerly. In order to explain this apparent paradox, it is important to consider that such friars bore a theological vision charged with contradictions and complexities. On the one hand, they realized that their hopes for the peaceful conversion of native people in Chiapas depended upon the tolerance and even-handedness with which they conducted themselves—even as they coaxed their followers away from superstition and idolatry. On the other hand, as they readily admitted, their experiences in Spain had not prepared them for the task of explaining Christianity's mysteries to "rude and uninstructed" Indians. In their estimation, it was sufficient that native Americans, like Spanish peasants, learn to glorify and revere these mysteries, that they behave in proper and pious fashion. It might be said, too, that these missionaries responded to the exigencies of life in the field—that is, that they assumed with much greater enthusiasm the difficulties of baptizing the unbaptized, of increasing the number and extension of Christian communities, than of deepening and broadening the faith of their indigenous converts. In effect, therefore, the fathers grant-ed Indian followers only the narrowest and most limited partici-pation in religious life, and restricted their education to a few essential points.[33] If native Christians wished to earn salvation, the friars reasoned, let them do so with the work of their hands, let them win God's favor by building churches and convents throughout the province.

Despite the enthusiasm with which these people received the missionaries, despite the energy and goodwill with which they labored to memorialize their new faith, they soon realized that they in fact enjoyed no greater religious and social equality than in Mazariegos' day. On the contrary, like the area's first *enco-menderos*, Spanish friars jealously guarded Christianity's deep-est secrets and preferred to dole out instruction only where their political ambitions might best be served. To this end, they worked with unstinting zeal to organize within the province a rudimentary system of ecclesiastical governance and administra-tion. Beginning with the churches in Ciudad Real and Copana-guastla, they soon founded additional houses in Chiapa, Comi-tán, Tecpatán (among the Zoques) and later in Ocosingo (Map 2). From these towns (which served as *doctrinas* or parish seats), the friars ventured forth to baptize and preach and to construct new chapels—in short, to recreate the pageants and institutions upon which, in their eyes, Christian orthodoxy depended. In this way, between 1553 and 1588, the Portuguese missionary Fray Pedro de Barrientos transformed Chiapa into a model of theocratic law and orderliness more or less along the lines that Las Casas had laid down in 1546. Not only did Barrientos introduce such novel-ties as religious *cofradías*, but in order to assure his colleagues

MAP 2.
Doctrinas in Chiapas, ca. 1590

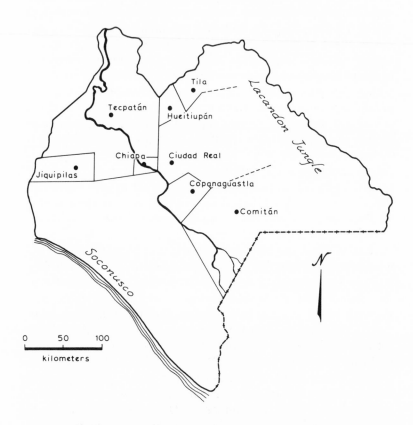

their sustenance he also constructed a sugar *ingenio* in the area. Even after his death, Fray Pedro's success in these endeavors moved one Spanish judge to describe the town with an enthusiasm that bordered upon pure rapture.[34]

It is only in this light that we may understand the scandal which erupted in Chiapa in 1584, that "relapse into idolatry" which caused Pedro de Feria, the investigating bishop, such profound anguish and consternation. Among all native chieftains, it seemed, *principales* in Chiapa had converted to Christianity with the most genuine sincerity and eagerness. Not only had they

submitted to Barrientos' ministrations with exemplary obedience, but the friar himself enjoyed an apparently unshakable
friendship with Juan Atonal, "one of the noblest Indians of that
town," a man who for 30 years had confessed regularly and
taken communion. Despite his loyalty to Barrientos, however,
and despite his position as *alcalde* of Chiapa, it was revealed that
Atonal had organized several of his followers into a *cofradía*
which, according to de Feria, worshipped the devil. "In the
aforementioned town of Su-chiapa," wrote the bishop in his report,

> there existed a *cofradía* of 12 Indians who styled themselves the
> 12 apostles, and they walked abroad at night and traveled from
> mountain to mountain, and from cave to cave . . . and they took
> with them two women, one of whom they called Santa María, and
> the other Magdalena, with whom . . . they undertook certain cere-
> monies, saying that by these means they . . . became spiritualized
> and transformed into gods. . . .

To make matters worse, the *corregidor* of Chiapa (who greatly
prized their services in collecting the town's tribute) refused to
punish these apostles with the severity they so plainly merited.
In consequence, the bishop complained, they "are now saying
that all Christendom is a mockery, except for the *corregidor* of
Chiapa and the King, and that the bishops and the friars have
deceived them with their churches and with their laws."[35]
   In contrast to de Feria, who portrayed this incident as an
isolated case of religious backsliding, it appears that Atonal's
new faith found considerable sympathy among a wide range of
native people. For one thing, his ceremonies involved not the
area's "new Christians" (for whose sake de Feria wished to make
an example of the apostles), but rather, precisely those loyal and
devoted Indians who had for many years served the friars.[36] Like
Atonal himself, such chieftains had in general converted many
years earlier to Christianity. For another thing, these rituals drew
interest and support from Christian nobles as far from Chiapa as
Ocotepeque (Zoque) and Ocosingo (Tzeltal), many of whom traveled to Chiapa from their communities in order to participate in

*cofradía* functions. Even more intriguing, Atonal's activities seem to have earned him the close friendship of such long-time enemies as the *principales* of Zinacantan, with whom he had engaged only a few years earlier in a long and bitter legal dispute over community lands.[37] Under these circumstances, modern scholars must reject the views of commentators who, following Remesal and Francisco Ximénez, have sought the source of such practices in the Chiapaneca god *Maviti*. For as de Feria himself admits, *cofradía* rituals took their ideological coloring from elements of Christian worship which Indians throughout the province had almost universally acquired. In the King's name, Atonal seemed to declare, they would rescue their new religion from that cabal of deceitful prelates and tyrannical friars into whose hands it had mistakenly fallen. And once that urgent task had been accomplished, once they had attained both God's grace and Saint Mary's favor, then as loyal subjects of the Crown they would govern their new kingdom in their own right.

Although these men and women failed in their efforts to create an autonomous Christian republic, they nonetheless bore witness to the seriousness with which they had accepted many of Las Casas' ideas. A more important result of their reaction to Barrientos' heavy-handedness is especially worth mentioning. What these quarrels disclose is a series of profound changes which had occurred within the Dominican Order itself during these years. Whereas in 1545 the friars had arrived in Chiapas as true mendicants, determined to share the poverty of their native followers, by 1590 they had acquired a substantial number of cattle ranches, sugar *ingenios*, and other valuable properties.[38] In fact, as the century drew to a close, they regularly devoted so much of their time to such matters that in 1589 they were ordered to sell their holdings in both Chiapas and Guatemala—an order which did not inhibit in the slightest degree their growing appetite for land. In this respect, they were not unlike the province's Mercedarians, who had arrived in Ciudad Real eight years before Las Casas. Choosing to concern themselves exclusively with their own enrichment, these monks avoided altogether the travails of evangelization. Beginning in 1539 with a single plot of land in the city, their superior, Marcos Pérez Dardón, quickly amassed a variety of urban properties to which he subsequently added "houses, and a church with ornaments and adornments, together with several cattle *estancias,* which he founded near Copanaguastla, where he also built a country house and a sugar *trapiche.*"[39] In the same fashion, therefore, Dominican monasteries, which even as late as 1572 "owned in the province not one handsbreadth of land," were by 1580 deeply involved in the area's expanding agricultural economy.

Why as the 16th century drew to a close did the friars deviate so profoundly from their original purposes and intentions? First, such transformations coincided quite readily with Dominican theology of the day. Clerical acquisitiveness traced its origins directly to that vision of evangelization which measured divine grace in the ostentation and ornamentation of churches and convents. In addition, however, the friars now found themselves confronted with two new and potent adversaries—disease and political isolation—which threatened to shatter their fragile empire among America's native people. In 1565, for example, an epidemic of unknown origin carried off half of Zinacantan's population. Similarly, three years later, in Comitán, "Divine justice sent a plague so terrible . . . that it seemed as if the whole town would disappear, losing each day 20 or 30 people."[40] In Chiapa, Indian mortality was even more horrifying: of the 21,000 Chiapaneca tributaries registered by Mazariegos in 1528, only 3,411 of their descendants were alive in 1600.[41] As the number of native people in the province declined, of course, those who remained "could no longer be so liberal with their alms." Consequently, the friars "began to ask His Majesty for lands or pastures . . . and filled them with mares and cows, which multiplying with time served the community greatly."[42]

But these measures, though they assured that convents in Chiapas would enjoy steady revenues for years to come, did not yield sufficient income to maintain the friars in their day-to-day activities or to provide them with working capital. Beginning in 1559, then, they organized *mayordomías* and *cofradías* in indigenous communities throughout the region. So successful did this system prove to be in augmenting clerical stipends that within a century virtually all Indian men served the greater part of their lives in such organizations (Table 1).[43] And yet the popularity which *cofradías* enjoyed among Dominican missionaries cannot be attributed exclusively to their utility in collecting alms and fees. On the contrary, these institutions, over which parish priests maintained extremely tight control throughout the following centuries, also lent themselves quite readily to Dominican theological purposes.[44] Faced with the spectre of Lutheranism in Europe, Dominican missionaries launched a revitalized campaign to defend the mysteries of the faith. In this sense, *cofradías* and ceremonial functions proved to be particularly useful: by extolling and glorifying such mysteries (e.g., the Eucharist, the Virginity of Mary), they lent themselves ideally to the Dominican struggle against New World heterodoxy.

Beginning in Santiago de Guatemala, therefore, these missionaries decided to organize *cofradías* throughout the province in honor of Mary (principally of Nuestra Señora del Rosario) and of the *Santísimo Sacramento*—a decision which they solemnly reiterated 15 years later in the annual chapter meeting.[45] To this end, they also dedicated their convent in Copanaguastla to Rosario. Thereafter they proclaimed that the image in their chapel possessed powers to cure the sick and relieve the afflicted. Over the next century and a half, no less than 27 miracles were attributed to this image, which in 1617 accompanied the friars from Copanaguastla to the neighboring community of Socoltenango. When the town of Comitán was saved from a terrible plague through the wondrous intercession of San Nicolás (1561), these monks insisted that henceforth Comiteco *cofrades* bring this saint each year to their monastery to celebrate the Virgin's titular feast.[46] And finally, in Ciudad Real, Fray Pedro de Santa María, a Dominican mystic and visionary of the day, came to be regarded as something of a saint because "this Lady favored him frequently throughout his life by visiting him and by attending to his devotion and principal desires."[47]

In contrast to these issues of cult and doctrine, the problem of secularization could not be resolved with such ease and dispatch. In Guatemala, Bishop Francisco Marroquín, a Dominican, had been replaced by Bernardino Villalpando, a secular priest who wasted little time in depriving the mendicant orders of Indi-

TABLE 1.
Indian Cofradías in Chiapas, 1561–1799

| Nuestra Señora del Rosario (and de la Asunción) | Santísimo Sacramento | Santo Domingo, San Pedro, San Sebastián |
|---|---|---|
| Acala | Acala | Aguacatenango |
| Aguacatenango | Aguacatenango | Amatenango |
| Amatenango | Amatenango | Chilón |
| Chiapilla | Chiapa | Comitán |
| Comitán | Chilón | Ocozocuautla |
| Huistán | Comitán | San Bartolomé |
| Huitiupán | Copainalá | Tecpatán |
| Ixtapa | Ocosingo | Tenejapa |
| Ocosingo | Teopisca | Teopisca |
| Ocozocuautla | Zapaluta | Tuxtla |
| Quechula | Zinacantan | Zinacantan |
| San Bartolomé | | |
| San Felipe | | |
| Socoltenango | | |
| Soyatitán | | |
| Tenejapa | | |
| Teopisca | | |
| Tuxtla | | |
| Yajalón | | |
| Zinacantan | | |

| Santa Cruz | | De las Animas[a] |
|---|---|---|
| Aguacatenango | San Bartolomé | Aguacatenango |
| Amatenango | Sibacá | Comitán |
| Chiapilla | Tenejapa | San Bartolomé |
| Comitán | Teopisca | Tecpatán |
| Copainalá | Tuxtla | Tuxtla |
| Huitiupán | | Zapaluta |
| Ixtapa | | Zinacantan |
| Ocosingo | | |

Sources: "Libros de las Cofradías," various years, AHDSC; Francisco Ximénez, Historia de la provincia de San Vicente de Chiapa y Guatemala, vol. 2; Eduardo Flores Ruíz, "Fundación de la parroquia de Comitán," Biblioteca Fray Bartolomé de las Casas (1956); Juan Morales Avendaño, Rincones de Chiapas (1974), pp. 32–37.

[a] Including Benditas Almas de Purgatorio.

an benefices. Similarly, in 1584, de Feria, complying after 20 years with orders from the Council of Trent, asked his Dominican colleagues to vacate "several towns in which [secular priests] might serve and maintain themselves."[48] Realizing that their protests would only aggravate this situation, the friars discreetly conceded a Zoque parish (Jiquipulas) and within a few years also permitted a *clérigo* to be installed in the Chol town of Tila.[49] As it turned out, the monks' tactful compliance with episcopal orders forestalled further mishaps of this sort for almost half a century. But by that time, both the Crown and higher Dominican officials had also taken measures to remind the friars of their original purpose and obligations. In 1587, the King issued a royal *cédula* in which he declared that

> the ownership of property or of personal goods contradicts the rigor of their institutions, precepts, and vows of poverty.... [It is therefore ordained] that nothing ... which is given in payment to the monks in Indian districts or *doctrinas* may enter their personal possession, but must be conveyed to their superiors or convents.[50]

And finally, modifying his famous decree of 1567 (in which he had restored to the religious orders their pre-Trent prerogatives), the King demanded immediate secularization of all "benefices, curacies, and *doctrinas*" for which non-mendicant clergy could be found.[51]

## CONCLUSIONS

Clearly, Christian evangelization in Chiapas at the end of the 16th century had changed dramatically from the days when Fray Pedro Calvo, filled with visionary zeal and fervor, promised the Chiapanecas that faith in Christ would deliver them from the grasp of Spanish *encomenderos*. In place of this messianic creed, which continued to haunt native imaginations for centuries to come, the cult of Nuestra Señora—festive, impersonal, mechanical—spread throughout the area. Simultaneously, other *cofradías*, honoring such Dominican favorites as Saint Peter, San Sebastián, and of course Saint Dominic, made their appearance in the province.

And yet, despite this decline in evangelical idealism, it would be an error to claim that Las Casas' militant and uncompromising views, so dangerous in their implications for colonial policy, disappeared in Chiapas without a trace. Henceforth, it would be native people who in the privacy of their own lives would shield and nurture this vision, even as their pastors pursued secular wealth and fortune. Originally, such tasks may have fallen to native *caciques* and *principales,* who enjoyed both a Christian education and great political influence. As these chieftains succumbed to the greed and ambition of Spanish settlers, however, they were replaced by men whose authority and experience derived not from their noble birth, but rather from their membership in *cofradías* and native *cabildos.* As a result, these men became the bearers of a faith in God and community over which even parish priests exercised little control. For the next 200 years, therefore, they struggled actively to protect this faith from the depradations of colonial prelates, and to defend their right to remain Indian in a Spanish world.

# SPANISH SOCIETY IN
# COLONIAL CHIAPAS
## 1590–1821

The English-born Dominican monk Thomas Gage, fleeing from
missionary work in the Philippines, arrived in Chiapas in 1626
on his way to Guatemala and eventually Europe. Twenty years
later, in his memoirs, he described his impressions of that little-
known area of the Spanish Empire:

> This country is divided into three provinces, to wit, Chiapa, Zel-
> dales, and Zoques, whereof Chiapa is itself the poorest. This con-
> tains the great town of Chiapa of the Indians, and all the towns
> and farms . . . toward Macuilapa, and . . . the priory of Comitán,
> which hath some ten towns, and many farms of cattle, horses, and
> mules subject to it. . . . Besides the abundance of cattle, the chief
> commodity of this valley is cotton, whereof are made such store of
> mantles for the Indians' wearing that the merchants far and near
> come for them. They exchange them in Soconusco and Suchitepe-
> quez for cacao, whereby they are well stored of that drink.[1]

Furthermore, he continued, "for Spaniards and such as cannot
live without it," wheat was brought to Chiapa from Ciudad Real
and Comitán. In this way, "poor Spaniards and some Indians
who have got the trick of trading from them do gain not a little in
bringing . . . biscuits of wheaten bread." And finally, he noted,

> Two or three leagues from the town, there are two ingenios or

farms of sugar, the one belonging to the cloister of the Dominicans of the city of Chiapa; the other unto the cloister of Ciudad Real. These contain near 200 blackamoors, besides many Indians, who are employed in that constant work of making sugar for the country.[2]

What is most striking about Gage's description is not that it characterized a brief and ephemeral moment in the province's history, but rather that it remained accurate almost until the end of colonial rule. By the time Gage arrived in Chiapas, Spanish *encomenderos* and settlers were locked in struggle with the region's *alcaldes mayores*, royal governors who purchased their office for a term of five years. Ambitious and avaricious, these officials busily set out to monopolize trade in such lucrative commodities as cacao, cotton, and cochineal. Naturally, *vecinos* in the area did not accept such interference lightly, nor did they relinquish their control of native labor without a fight. Throughout much of the previous century they had governed Chiapas from the *cabildo* in Cuidad Real; now they enlisted the support of bishops like Tomás Blanes and Juan Sandoval Zapata to limit and contain rival authority. In 1619, for example, Sandoval complained to the Council that royal *jueces de milpa* had mistreated native subjects and sharply disrupted the legitimate activities of local *encomenderos*, and he protested that the *presidente* and *oidores* obtained ecclesiastical office for their relatives and retainers to the detriment of native-born *hijosdalgo*.[3] A few years later, in 1624, Bishop Bernardino de Salazar y Frías, alleging that civil officers had exceeded their mandate by removing a black slave from church, excommunicated the provincial governor.[4] For his part, in 1627 and 1628 this *alcalde mayor* and his successor petitioned the Crown for the right to name their own *tenientes* (assistants) in such important towns as Chiapa.[5] Such a measure was necessary, they claimed, in order to protect local Indians from the Spanish community in Ciudad Real and inattentive or timorous *oidores* in Guatemala.

By 1634, royal authorities in Spain had worked out a compromise. Thenceforth, they declared, *alcaldes mayores* in Chiapas might select their own *tenientes* from among the city's *alcaldes ordinarios*—that is, from among its leading settlers. Needless to say, few governors were pleased with this arrangement, which permitted their erstwhile adversaries to share handsomely in the spoils of office. Upon taking up his post in 1636, for example, one such official, Francisco Dávila y Lugo, complained that local Spaniards refused to accept even this moderately subordinate role. "After hearing my proposal that we all abide by royal law and Your Grace's order," he wrote to the Council,

> Don Cristóbal de Velasco, a rich *encomendero*, whose nephew (the son of his sister) is *alcalde*, whose brother-in-law is *alférez mayor*, whose brother and son are *regidores*, and who is creditor or ally to the rest of them, rose up and said, "If the law must be kept, men cannot carry on their affairs, and if the *alcalde mayor* wishes to enforce the law, then the city may rise up against him. . . ."

At issue, Dávila y Lugo continued, was the simple fact that

> These provinces contain more than 100 Indian towns, and in them live more than 22,000 tributaries. . . . Your Grace gives the *encomenderos* more than 80,000 pesos each year which are paid in the form of commodities . . . [including] 4,000 pounds of cochineal . . . and 25,000 pounds of cotton which is harvested, spun, woven and given to Spaniards to resell. . . . [6]

With such prizes at stake, neither he nor local *vecinos* cared to abide by any compromise. Indeed, within a few months, the *alcalde ordinario* of Ciudad Real did lead an angry mob against him.[7] And two years later, when Dávila tried to enforce an order for this man's arrest, he was forced to abandon the province altogether.

Despite their success in this matter, Spanish settlers in Chiapas could not ultimately prevent provincial governors from dominating most aspects of economic and political life. By 1693, in fact, one *alcalde mayor*, Manuel de Maisterra, was able to appoint *tenientes* who were not functionaries—a state of affairs which persisted for nearly a century afterward.[8] But even in Gage's day, such authorities conducted their affairs with a degree of efficiency and ruthlessness which few settlers could emulate. "The merchants' chief trading," Gage wrote,

> is in cacao, cotton from adjacent parts of the country, peddlers' small wares, some sugar from about Chiapa of the Indians, and a little cochineal. But commonly the Governor (whose chief gain consisteth in this) will not suffer them to be too free in this commodity, lest they hinder his greedy traffic. . . .
>
> The Governor's place is of no small esteem and interest, for his power reacheth far, and he tradeth much in cacao and cochineal, and domineers over both Spaniards and Indians at his will and pleasure.[9]

Using capital supplied by wealthy partners in Spain and Guatemala, these men proceeded over the next hundred years to organize a system of agricultural production based upon *repartimientos*—that is, in exchange for goods like dried beef or knives, they compelled native communities to grow indigo or to transform cotton into finished cloth (Table 2). Pressed by these circumstances, many local Indians sold their entire corn crop in order to purchase cacao from Zoque growers many miles to the north, which they transported at their own expense to Tabasco or Guatemala.[10] In much the same fashion, Zoque growers themselves were often obliged to sell their harvest directly to royal officers at a price which did not permit them to purchase maize for domestic use.[11] So successful did such arrangements prove to be that between 1636 and 1780 these officials nearly tripled the amount of cacao which they shipped to Spain. Not surprisingly, Indian communities suffered grievously under these *repartimientos*: throughout the 18th century, native men and women experienced both constant hunger and intermittent famine.[12] And despite periodic denunciations and royal prohibitions, such abuses persisted until 1790, when the *alcaldía* system was finally abolished.

Although Spanish *hacendados* and merchants played a secondary role in provincial affairs, after 1680 ecclesiastical authorities—and even individual priests—created important enterprises of their own. Like civil officers in Chiapas, clerics such as Bishop

Table 2.
Principal Commodities Obtained in Chiapas
Through Repartimientos, 1546–1784

| Product (pounds) | 1546 | 1636 | 1760 | 1768 | 1784 |
|---|---|---|---|---|---|
| Cochineal | | 4,000 | 20,000 | 16,700 | 10,000 |
| Cotton | | 25,000 | 100,000 | | 85,000[b] |
| Cacao | 3,000[a] | | 30,000 | | |

Sources: Antonio de Remesal, Historia general, vol. 2, p. 73; "Informe del juez real Francisco Dávila sobre la residencia del alcalde mayor de Chiapa, Juan Ruíz de Contreras," (1636), Hermilio López Sánchez, Apuntes históricos, p. 651; "Repartimientos del alcalde mayor de Ciudad Real," AGGG, Boletín 2, no. 4 (1937): 476–478; "Producción de la grana en 1784 entre los pueblos zoques de la provincia de Chiapa," AGCh, Boletín 1 (1953): 59–86.

[a] Tribute paid by Zinacantan to its encomendero, Pedro de Estrada.
[b] Estimate.

Juan Bautista Alvarez de Toledo (1710–1713) dedicated themselves to the pursuit of wealth and riches. The Dominican chronicler Francisco Ximénez has provided us with an extensive and highly disparaging portrait of Alvarez, upon whom he places much of the blame for the 1712 rebellion.[13] Not content with his share of Indian tribute and limosnas, Alvarez undertook a succession of annual visitas which left native communities even more devastated and impoverished. In so doing, however, he merely perpetuated a tradition of episcopal acquisitiveness which had already become well established in Gage's day. The bishop's place, Gage wrote,

is worth at least 8,000 ducats a year. . . . Most of this bishop's revenues consisteth in great offering which he yearly receiveth from the great Indian towns, going out to them once a year to confirm their children. Confirmation is such a means to confirm and strengthen the Bishop's revenues, that none must be confirmed by him who offer not a fair white wax candle, with a ribbon and at least four reals. I have seen the richer sort offer him a candle of at least six-pound weight with two yards of twelve-penny broad ribbon, and the candle stuck from the top to the bottom with single reals round about.[14]

In much the same fashion, Dominican friars created a network of sugar plantations and cattle *estancias* throughout the province. And finally, by 1680, a sizable group of secular priests, excluded from highland parishes by their mendicant colleagues, clamored for the right to occupy native benefices. Eventually these men, who came into conflict with both local monks and provincial governors, organized *repartimientos* and purchased *fincas* of their own. In the remainder of this chapter, I shall examine the ways in which such events transformed social life in central Chiapas and set the stage for unrest in the following century.

## THE SETTLERS' WORLD

Unlike New Spain, Chiapas did not enter a period of economic depression after 1580, at least not in the usual sense. Sustained at first by *encomiendas* and regional trade, Spanish settlers in Ciudad Real (who in 1555 numbered around 50) increased to more than 250 by 1620.[15] Unfortunately, the native population did not fare so well: decimated by wave after wave of *peste*, it declined from around 114,400 in 1570 to 74,990 a century later (Table 3).[16] As a result, Indian towns maintained a bleak and attenuated existence or were abandoned altogether.[17] Faced with a serious decline in native tribute, most *encomenderos* found themselves progressively unable to make ends meet.[18] In fact, as Gage noted, by 1620 such people lived in extremely modest, indeed often penurious circumstances.

> It is a common thing among them . . . to come out to the street-door of their homes to see and be seen, and . . . to say: "Ah, señor, qué linda perdiz he comido hoy!" . . . whereas they pick out of their teeth nothing but a black husk of a dry turkey-bean. . . .[19]

To bolster their sagging fortunes, then, as early as 1530 enterprising *vecinos* began to produce sugar and cattle on *haciendas* in Zinacantan and the fertile Grijalva river valley. By 1660, such

TABLE 3.
Native Tributaries in Chiapas, 1595-1817

| District | 1595 | 1611 | 1678 | 1761 | 1806 | 1817 |
|---|---|---|---|---|---|---|
| Ciudad Real | 3,362 | 2,716 | 3,079 | 3,770 | 4,918 | 5,139 |
| Ocosingo | 2,559 | 2,899 | 3,027 | 1,385 | 1,514[a] | 1,939 |
| Chiapa | 3,412 | 2,610 | 2,882 | 771 | 267 | 256 |
| Tecpatán (Zoques) | 4,822 | 4,655 | 4,112 | 3,779 | 2,793 | 1,545 |
| Comitán | 3,391 | 2,472 | 1,317 | 1,006 | 1,104 | 1,042 |
| Copanaguastla (Llanos) | 2,488 | 1,742 | 1,412 | 1,577 | 1,686 | 1,573 |
| Huitiupán | 684 | 1,011 | 701 | 310 | 876 | 823 |
| Jiquipulas | 718 | 905 | 637 | 704 | 403 | 355 |
| Tila | 617 | 766 | 959 | 1,158 | 1,195[a] | 1,831 |
| laboríos | | | 810 | | | 519 |
| mozos | | | | | | 1,162 |
| Total | 22,053 | 19,776 | 18,936 | 14,460 | 14,756 | 16,184 |

Sources: Peter Gerhard, The Southeast Frontier of New Spain, p. 159; Manuel B. Trens, Historia de Chiapas, pp. 177-180; "Estado de curatos del arzobispado de Guatemala, 1806," AGGG, Boletín 3, no. 2 (1938); 225-228; "Padrón de los tributarios de Chiapa" (1816-17), AGGG, A3.16.3.

[a] These figures probably undercount a substantial number of tributaries in Ocosingo and Tila. Adjusting them in appropriate fashion (Ocosingo, 1,700; Tila, 1,650), the total may be estimated at approximately 15,300.

properties had spread as far as Ixtacomitán (among the Zoques) and to Jiquipulas, near the Oaxaca border.[20] Throughout the colonial period, these haciendas, which ranked high among the region's most valuable and successful agricultural enterprises, enjoyed a ready market for their products in Tabasco.[21] Similarly, between 1590 and 1600, local settlers received permission from the Crown to raise horses, mules, and wheat on land taken from native communities in the altiplano.[22] And finally, after 1750, the fertile Ocosingo valley (where in 1627 the Dominican convent in Ciudad Real established its own haciendas and trapiche) underwent extensive settlement (Table 4).[23]

Throughout this period, however, Spanish landowners faced the unresolved difficulties which scarce credit and uncertain conditions imposed upon them. Cattle diseases, unsteady labor supplies, high transportation costs, and laboriously slow commu-

TABLE 4.
Fincas and Estancias in Chiapas, 1611–1817

| District | 1611 | 1774–78 | 1816–17 |
|---|---|---|---|
| Ciudad Real | 2 | 7 | 8 |
| Chiapa | 7 | 6 | 25 |
| Zoques | 0 | 2 | 12 |
| Comitán | 12 | 13 | 53 |
| Llanos | 13 | 16 | 19 |
| Ocosingo | 0 | 2 | 9 |
| Huitiupán | 0 | 0 | 0 |
| Jiquipulas | 0 | 12 | 18 |
| Tila | 0 | 0 | 1 |
| Total | 34 | 58 | 145 |

Sources: E. Pineda, "Descripción geográfica ... de Chiapas"; Juan Manuel García de Vargas y Rivera, "Relación de los pueblos que comprehende el obispado de Chiapa"; Francisco Polanco, "Estado de los vasallos que tiene Su Majestad en este obispado de Ciudad Real de Chiapa," (1778); "Padrón de los tributarios de Chiapa."

nications—all these factors restricted agricultural expansion and prevented the growth of new *haciendas*. After 1700, too, many landowners became heavily indebted to local religious orders, and these debts limited their economic reach. Drawing upon large cash reserves, such orders (which acquired their capital through donations, *cofradía* payments, and their own investments) granted mortgages on both rural and urban property at 5-percent interest. By the end of the 18th century, for example, the Jesuits and Mercedarians of Ciudad Real together had lent almost 30,000 pesos to local *vecinos*.[24] One result of such policies was revealed in 1803, when the Hacienda de Nuestra Señora del Rosario in Ixtacomitán (one of the region's oldest cacao and cattle plantations) was sold for the impressive sum of 14,000 pesos. It was discovered upon examining the estate's records that 8,606 pesos (62 percent) of this amount was owed to the cathedral in Ciudad Real, the Dominican monastery in Tecpatán, and a variety of lesser clerics.[25] Faced with such difficulties, many Spaniards chose to seek their fortunes elsewhere. By 1684, according to the city council, half of these people had left the province.[26] And within another 50 years, their number had declined to its lowest point since the conquest: of the 49 families who remained, only 35 resided in the town; the rest eked out a marginal livelihood on their isolated *fincas* and *labores*.[27]

Like private *hacendados*, religious orders in Chiapas quite early took up cattle and sugar production to counteract the effects of declining native populations and public revenues. Beginning with modest gifts of royal lands (*realengas*), they soon established sugar plantations in the Grijalva and Ocosingo valleys. Among ecclesiastical landowners, the Dominicans distinguished themselves for both their resourcefulness and their greed. As in Oaxaca, their early interest in landowning gave them a strategic advantage over later arrivals in the area. In 1620, for example, the convent in Comitán had already established its famous *haciendas de la frailesca*, 10 profitable cattle ranches in the upper Grijalva valley. Simultaneously, the convent in Chiapa organized its own *ingenio* and *haciendas* in the same region—as Gage's description indicates.[28] Ever mindful of their investments, these friars continued for nearly a century and a half to acquire *estancias* near Ixtapa and Soyaló. As for the monks in Ciudad Real, they soon realized that the Grijalva area offered few additional possibilities for development and exploitation. Instead, they turned their eyes toward the temperate zone around Ocosingo. There, in 1626, they began to cultivate sugarcane and to raise cattle. A few years later, they acquired still more land, this time among the Zoques in northern Chiapas and southern Tabasco. For the next half-century, while Dominican cattle in Ocosingo grew fat on such estates, local Indians watched their maize supplies diminish to an insignificant trickle. Small wonder, then, that in 1712 Tzeltal armies razed and ruined these *haciendas*. In the end, of course, native efforts to destroy Dominican properties came to nought: within 50 years, the intrepid friars had not only restored their original landholdings, but in the vicinity of Tenejapa and Huistán they had even added additional farms (Map 3).[29]

In contrast to Dominican monasteries, native *cofradías* did not possess large amounts of land. Only in Ixtapa and Huistán did

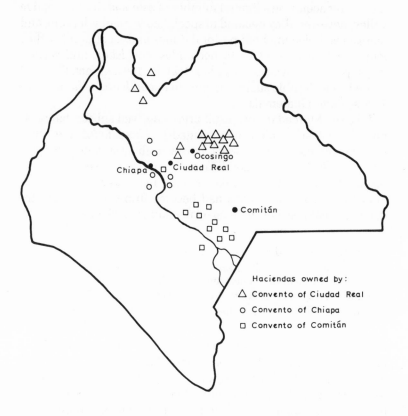

MAP 3.
Dominican Landholdings in 1778

Haciendas owned by:
△ Convento of Ciudad Real
○ Convento of Chiapa
□ Convento of Comitán

such organizations maintain cattle *estancias*, which local *hermanos* and *mayordomos* operated at their own risk and expense.[30] In reality, such properties, over which parish priests exercised absolute control, represented a form of ecclesiastical ownership and tenancy. In this way, the Mercedarians (who reestablished their monastery in Ciudad Real after Las Casas' departure) received a modest but useful income from three *cofradía* estates. Like their Dominican colleagues, these friars also took an early interest in landowning and in sugar cultivation. Their *trapiche de la Merced*, established in the mid-16th century, represented one of the earliest ventures of this sort in the province. After acquiring a limited number of *estancias* in the Grijalva valley, however, they decided to specialize in money-lending and mortgages. Rejecting both pastoral duties and local politics, they lent over 20,000 pesos to 15 *haciendas,* one *labor,* and several urban property-owners in Ciudad Real. By 1803, in fact, they had loaned considerable sums of money to *hacendados* as far away as Tabasco and Guatemala.[31]

Like the Mercedarians, Jesuit priests derived substantial revenues from loans which they granted to *hacendados* and other wealthy clients. In many ways, however, their situation differed from that of the area's mendicants. For unlike these monks, the Jesuits did not arrive in Chiapas until 1667—that is, until well after their mendicant rivals had become firmly established. Indeed, 40 years earlier, in 1626, Gage had remarked that

> The city of Ciudad Real is one of the meanest cities of all America. . . . The fact that the Jesuits have got no footing there (who commonly live in the richest and wealthiest places and cities) is a sufficient argument of want of gallant parts and prodigality in the gentry . . . and so poor Chiapa is held no fit place for Jesuits.[32]

But by 1660, after over half a century of life in the countryside, at least some members of Chiapas' gentry had acquired a sufficient number of "gallant parts" to endow a Jesuit *colegio* in Ciudad Real. Beginning with four donations—two cacao plantations near Ixtacomitán, a "lot and houses for the school's treasury" in Ciudad Real, and a thousand silver pesos—Chiapas' Jesuits added to their possessions a cattle *hacienda* in the Grijalva valley and a *labor* (which produced wheat) near the city.[33] Thereafter, they did not attempt to expand their landholdings. Instead, following the example of their Mercedarian colleagues, they directed their resources into loans and mortgages, which they divided equally between urban and rural estates. By 1767, therefore, when they were expelled from the New World, they had granted over 8,000 pesos in loans that produced an annual income of 462 pesos. By planning these investments carefully, they had obtained liens not only on three of the province's leading sugar *ingenios* but also on several important cattle ranches—primarily those which lay close to the Oaxaca border.[34] And finally, each year they received a sizable *limosna* from the province's Indian parishes.[35]

Unlike the religious corporations, provincial governors set out to organize a network of commercial enterprises based not upon direct ownership of land but upon the intensive exploitation of native labor. At first, they simply demanded that indigenous communities pay their tribute in commodities such as cacao, cloth, or corn; when such imposts were not met, these officials paid themselves with funds from local *cajas de comunidad*. In 1594, for example, one Spanish judge, Juan Pineda, wrote that the Indians of Chiapa

> possessed two cattle *estancias* and other fertile lands where they planted maize, *frijoles, chile*, cotton, and dye plants. In the town reside many artisans, such as carpenters, tailors, and blacksmiths, shoemakers, sandal-makers, and other craftsmen. The *vecinos* of this settlement also manufactured white cotton cloth called *tol-dillo* which they used to pay their tribute. The administration of the sacraments and other religious offices was in the hands of Dominican friars, and these monks also managed the town's *caja de comunidad*.[36]

But in the following years, income from tribute alone plummeted—from 80,000 pesos annually in 1636 to 11,000 in 1663 (Table 5). Finally, by 1734, the *alcalde mayor* was moved to complain that "one of the main reasons for the reduction in tributaries is the lack of a regular count of the Indians. . . . Because diseases like *sarampión, viruelas*, and similar contagions are frequent in these villages, it is not uncommon for them to lose many people, and particularly the very young."[37] As a result, he continued, in towns such as Huitiupán, Oxchuc, and Huistán, those few men and women who survived were required to pay the Crown as much as 7 pesos a year. And despite their constant petitions for redress and relief, in times of scarcity such people endured not only famine but the undiminished rapacity of provincial officials who sold them corn and beans at inflated prices. Indeed, it was precisely such unequal commerce which precipitated the 1712 rebellion.[38]

Interestingly, after the uprising such arrangements underwent

TABLE 5.
Native Tribute in Chiapas, 1663

| District | Tribute |
| --- | --- |
| Ciudad Real | 3,748 *tostones* |
| Ocosingo | 4,433 |
| Chiapa | 3,071 |
| Zoques | 4,486 |
| Comitán | 1,932 |
| Copanaguastla | 1,748 |
| Huitiupán | 1,134 |
| Jiquipulas | 541 |
| Tila | 1,132 |
| Total | 22,225 *tostones* = 11,112½ pesos |

*Source:* "Certificación del escribano real comprensiva del tanto que cada pueblo de esta provincia ha pagado de tributo" (1663), AHDSC.

significant modification—though they did not culminate, as Henri Favre has claimed, in a relaxation of Spanish authority.[39] As the native population began to recover, local *alcaldes mayores* became increasingly jealous of their right to control Indian trade. Faced with the possibility of producing augmented quantities of cacao, cotton, cochineal, and other products, they readily paid the Crown higher fees for the right to hold office in Chiapas (Table 6). Consider the letter which Bishop Jacinto de Olivera y Pardo wrote in 1716 to the King:

Your Grace has asked me to report on the corn, beans, and chile which the Indians of this province pay in tribute, and which the *alcaldes mayores* purchase by means of third parties at prices which prevailed four or six years ago. . . . I understand that for many years now in the month of February a public auction is held in which corn and other products paid by the Indians are offered to the highest bidder, and that these products are bought by third parties for the *alcalde mayor* without competition . . . because the *vecinos* are reluctant to arouse his ire. . . .[40]

TABLE 6.
Amount Paid for Alcaldía Mayor
of Chiapas, 1683–1738

| Year | Amount |
|------|--------|
| 1683 | 4,000 pesos (and loan of 200 pesos) |
| 1685 | 5,000 pesos |
| 1711 | 6,000 pesos (and 6,000 pesos at end of term) |
| 1722 | 200 ducados |
| 1738 | 8,000 pesos |

*Sources:* "Real cédula a favor de don Martín de Ur-
dániz" (1683), López Sánchez, *Apuntes Históricos*, p. 677;
"Real cédula a favor de don Manuel de Maisterra y
Atocha" (1685), ibid., p. 679; "Real cédula a favor de don
Pedro Gutiérrez de Mier y Terán" (1711), ibid., pp. 695–
696; "Título de alcalde mayor de Chiapa concedido a
don Juan Guatista Garracín Ponce de Leon" (1738), ibid.,
p. 795.

So single-mindedly did such officials pursue their own enrichment, in fact, that they even insisted upon supplying meat to the
public market in Ciudad Real—an office which the local *cabildo*
had previously auctioned off among its own members. Naturally,
Spanish *vecinos* protested against such measures—first to provincial authorities, later to the *audiencia* itself. By way of response, Gabriel de Laguna, who became *alcalde mayor* in 1732,
refused to certify the election of municipal counselors, and
thereby in effect suspended the city's *ayuntamiento*.[41] Freed
from the interference of this body, Laguna and his successors
proceeded to amass considerable fortunes which included money embezzled directly from the royal treasury or from municipal
funds.[42] And until 1781, despite repeated instructions to the contrary, they refused to reconvene the city council.[43]

Let us now consider in more detail how these *alcaldes
mayores* managed their affairs. Having overcome organized re-
sistence to their authority, provincial governors nonetheless selected their *tenientes* from among the better class of Spanish

residents—that is, from among those men who possessed the experience and the skill to administer complex *repartimientos*. In so doing, they neatly divided the area's proprietors and merchants into two incompatible and mutually hostile factions: on the one hand, a few prominent *comerciantes* abandoned independent enterprise and shared in the spoils of royal office; on the other, the majority of traders and landowners found themselves compelled to fill minor roles as suppliers and agents. In 1760, for example, one governor, Joaquín Fernández Prieto, named an important settler, Pedro Tomás de Murga, to the post of *teniente*. A few years earlier, Murga—who held the rank of colonel in the provincial militia and had served as *regidor decano* in the city council—had been active in the fight against Laguna and his successor, Juan Bautista Garracín.[44] Now, however, he dutifully took up the task of administering Prieto's far-flung enterprises; indeed, in 1767, when Prieto was subjected to a *residencia* (judicial review), Murga filed a financial statement—largely perjured—in which he attempted to exonerate his former patron of any wrongdoing.[45] Ironically, it is from this document that we may gain a valuable (albeit incomplete) idea of how the *repartimiento* system functioned at midcentury (Table 7). In the words of one unsympathetic observer,

> The Indians' vexations, nudity, idiocy are born of and propagated (in the main) by the excessive *repartimientos* and general commerce which the *alcaldes mayores* undertake with the Province's fruits. . . . This commerce . . . consists of buying and selling cacao, cotton, maize, cochineal, dyes, indigo, cattle, horses, mules, bulls, beef, wax, iron, steel, bolts of cloth, hats, wools, mats. . . . In some towns the *alcaldes* distribute more of these than the Indians can pay for, in which case they are forced to buy on prejudicial terms to meet their obligations. In this way, although the *alcaldes* pay only 10 pesos for a load of cacao, the Indians, if they do not harvest enough to repay him for his goods, must buy it from him at 18, 20, or more pesos.[46]

Rather than correct such abuses, however, royal authorities in Guatemala, anxious to enhance public revenues (and to enrich themselves in the bargain), chose instead to turn a blind eye or

Table 7.
Profits Earned by the Alcalde Mayor of Ciudad Real
on Repartimientos, 1760–1765 [a]

| Activity | Profit |
|----------|--------|
| Spinning 500,000 lbs. of raw cotton into 100,000 lbs. of thread (in central Tzotzil and Tzeltal region) | 27,500 pesos |
| Forced production of 100,000 lbs. of cochineal (Zoque region) | 16,000 |
| Forced production of 150,000 lbs. of cacao (Zoque region) | 10,000 |
| Forced production of 12,000 bunches of tobacco (northern Tzotzil region) | 3,750 |
| Others (largely involuntary sales of trade goods to native communities) | 13,475 |
| Total | 70,725 pesos |

*Source:* AGGG, *Boletín* 2, no. 4 (1937): 476–478.

[a] This information is taken from testimony given by the *alcalde's* personal assistant (*teniente*), who claimed that Indian producers were paid in all cases to transport their goods to Ciudad Real or Chiapa. Because such labor was generally uncompensated, however, we may estimate that the *alcalde's* profits approached 100,000 pesos.

even to encourage them. By 1760, *repartimientos* of cacao and cotton had become so lucrative that they proposed to divide central Chiapas into two separate *alcaldías,* a measure which effectively doubled the exactions to which many native people were subjected.[47] Pursuing this mandate, the new *alcalde mayor* of Tuxtla, Juan de Oliver, wasted little time in reorganizing the cacao trade. Upon assuming office in 1768, he appointed a *teniente* in Ixtacomitán, that is, in the center of the Zoque region. In turn this man, Salvador Esponda, named a series of *cajeros* and *mayordomos* who utilized both forced sales and public whippings to increase cacao production. Traveling from one town to another, they compelled native people to abandon altogether their small plots of corn and beans in order to plant this commodity.

For their part, members of the *audiencia* willingly overlooked such excesses—at least until a particularly devastating plague of locusts threatened to destroy agriculture in the province entirely. In June 1770, these insects made their appearance in Zoque fields; by August, according to one local priest, maize and beans had become so scarce that virtually none of his parishioners could afford them. Moreover, he charged, the origins of this dreadful situation could be traced less to capricious nature than to official greed:

> A legion of devils in the guise of *tenientes* has sprung up upon this earth: a sect of exacting Herodians who by unscrupulous means lay waste to, sack, destroy, and annihilate the province. . . . To establish their violent monopoly, they have set a thousand traps . . . so that buyers must purchase cacao from them by whatever method, and sellers must sell it to them. . . .[48]

And although the locusts had complicated such matters, he concluded, clearly the blame for this state of affairs lay with Oliver and his minions.

Within a few months, similar complaints were voiced in other quarters. In January 1771, Bartolomé Gutiérrez, treasurer of the cathedral in Ciudad Real, wrote to the *audiencia* that "Civic duty obliges me to mention the notorious epidemic of hunger experienced in the city and throughout the province last year, and which assuredly will occur again in the present one, despite a copious harvest, because many private individuals have withheld their fruits with the intention of selling them at more than one ear of corn per *medio real.*"[49] Furthermore, these officials were told, native people themselves often engaged in speculation. "If Your Lordship will send a special judge," wrote one parish priest to Bishop Juan Manuel García de Vargas y Rivera in a letter which Gutiérrez forwarded to the *audiencia*, "I will show him the fields which have been planted in this town [Oxchuc] so that the Indians may be compelled to sell their produce in the city. Merely offering to purchase it is useless, because they have told me and other Spaniards that they have none, and will only sell it to Indians in other towns at a price of 18 pesos per *fanega*."[50]

In response, the royal *fiscal* ordered Chiapas' governors to require all *vecinos* of Ciudad Real, Tuxtla, and Comitán to sell their stores "at moderate prices which, taking into consideration the current conditions of scarcity, nonetheless afford them a modest and equitable profit." Those *ladinos* who refused to comply with such orders, or who insisted upon cheating in other ways, were to forfeit their merchandise. As for rural communities, the *audiencia* asked Bishop García de Vargas to ascertain how much corn, beans, and chile were currently available for commercial use—although it cautioned him not to "allow the Indians to perish in order to provision the city." And finally, convinced that native sloth and indifference, rather than excessive *repartimientos* and poverty, had prompted indigenous families to reduce their plantings, García in turn commanded his priests to undertake a *vista de ojos* (visual inspection) of native fields in the company of local *justicias* so that they might "stimulate the Indians to plant larger *milpas*... and take measures to extinguish or contain the plague of locusts."[51]

The results of this exercise, which continued throughout February and March 1771, provided a desolate and startling view that gave royal authorities great cause for alarm. In contrast to the curate of Oxchuc, most highland priests did not uncover great stores of hidden grain in their districts. On the contrary, what they found in almost every case was a condition of endemic starvation. "These towns are in such a state," wrote the *cura* of Ocosingo, "that most of the inhabitants have abandoned their houses, taking refuge in the hills and living on roots or dispersing themselves among other *pueblos*. And although they have planted the corn they call *sijumal* [sweet corn], the Lord our God has punished us with a lack of spring rains and an abundance of sun, for which reason the corn has dried up or become stunted."[52] Similar accounts were forthcoming from virtually every town along the lower slopes of the *altiplano*. In Chilón, the local priest found only one man, a *ladino* named Lorenzo de Vera, who possessed a small surplus of corn—a surplus which he was very reluctant to sell. As for preventive measures, this *cura* continued, only Divine Providence could overcome the plague, "which becomes stronger every hour, wasting the strength of the miserable Indians who remain in their fields day and night to protect their crops, contracting incurable fevers from the fatigue and exposure to which they are subjected. In this way, most of the people of Yajalón, Petalcingo, Tila, Tumbalá, and Chilón have perished, a fact which makes it impossible to collect the locust eggs or larvae."[53] Such discouraging opinions were shared by the priest in Tila, who reported that "They declare that they do not possess sufficient corn even to sustain themselves. . . . And I assure you that the *pueblos* in my parish are in such a miserable state that many of the Indians have abandoned their homes and fled to the forests in search of wild roots, and others have gone to the province of Tabasco."[54]

Faced with a crisis of such proportions, royal authorities were forced to take bold and dramatic action. Already in 1754, men and women from Tumbalá, afflicted by an earlier outbreak of pests, had established a series of settlements in the Lacandón jungle.[55] Although they continued to pay tribute and serve municipal office in their original community, they remained largely beyond the control of provincial governors in Ciudad Real. In order to prevent other highland Indians from joining these refugees, on October 31 the *audiencia* relieved native *pueblos* in Chiapas of most of their obligations; in a few cases, they canceled tribute payments altogether.[56] Even so, highland communities recovered slowly from the devastation which both natural disaster and human avarice had wrought. On November 27, 1773, for example, royal judges in Guatemala were informed that these towns "have been successfully restored because of the good harvests which they have enjoyed, except for the districts of Tzeltales and Guardianías, consisting of 25 *pueblos* that have not experienced the same good fortune . . . given the continuous waves of locusts which afflict them."[57]

Then, too, there was the question of ecclesiastical imposts: between 1737 and 1750, Church revenues had stagnated at around 10,500 pesos a year; in the following years, this figure declined to about 8,000 pesos—that is, to the amount received a century earlier.[58] In order to offset such losses, of course, local bishops had customarily undertaken annual *visitas* and collected those *derechos* to which they were entitled. In 1677, for example, Bishop Marcos Bravo de la Serna Manrique embarked upon a *visita* which lasted 35 days and raised episcopal income from 5,000 pesos to more than 8,000.[59] But when García de Vargas announced that he intended to conduct a similar enterprise, Juan de Oliver, *alcalde mayor* of Tuxtla, protested to the *audiencia*. Episcopal extravagance, he claimed, not legitimate investment or unkind nature, had brought the province to the edge of ruin.[60] As competition for native revenues grew, therefore, as the Church placed greater demands on men and women already exhausted by burdensome *repartimientos*, the stage was set for a major confrontation between the province's civil and religious authorities.

In order to understand these events, it is necessary to consider briefly how the Church itself had become divided during the previous century. As we have seen (Chapter 2), in 1584 Pedro de Feria, fearful that his superiors might secularize New World *doctrinas*, persuaded the regular clergy in Chiapas to relinquish two minor parishes. As for other native towns, these remained by and large under Dominican control. By 1656, however, resentment against the friars had become so widespread among other clerics that the local bishop, Mauro de Tovar, attempted to install secular *clérigos* in several vacant benefices.[61] Predictably, Dominican superiors responded to this challenge by appealing to the *audiencia* in Guatemala. Asserting that they alone possessed the experience and linguistic training to administer Indian curacies, within a few months they had recovered their lost towns (Map 4). Undaunted, a succession of bishops and their retainers pressed for secularization, and indeed in 1680 they obtained a *cédula* which permitted them to serve in seven important native towns.[62] By this time, too, such measures had gained considerable urgency: not only had native tithes declined, but the first graduates of Chiapas' new seminary, founded in 1678, were preparing for ordination. Even so, the Dominicans refused to retire to their monasteries. On the contrary, by mobilizing their allies in

MAP 4.
Dominican Curatos in Chiapas, 1650

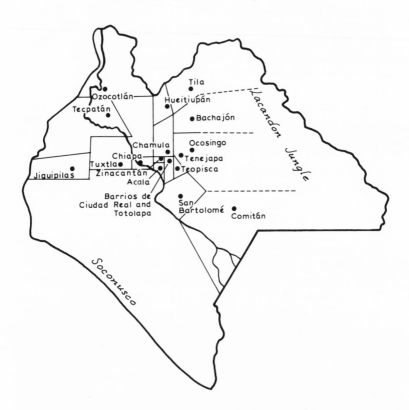

Spain, they obtained a second *cédula* which allowed the *audiencia*—always a bastion of support for the mendicants—to postpone definitive action. And in the kind of compromise which made consistent administration all but impossible in the colonies, in 1682 the Council directed subordinate authorities to replace aging friars with qualified *presbíteros*.[63]

As one might expect, hostilities between the Order and Chiapas' *cabildo eclesiástico* remained muted during the incumbency of Bishop Francisco Núñez de la Vega, who was himself a Dominican, and of his successor, Alvarez de Toledo. Invoking once again the unfitness of secular priests to serve a savage and barba-

MAP 5.

Curatos and Anexos in the Central Highlands, 1712

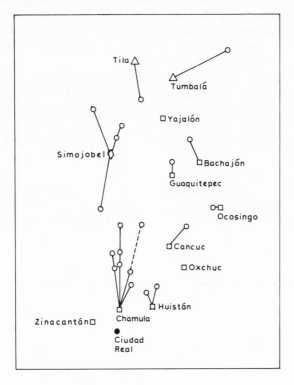

☐ Dominican Curato

△ Secular Curato

◊ Franciscan Curato

—O Anexo

---O Anexo of unknown affiliation

rous race, the friars turned violence and rebelliousness in 1712 to their advantage and reasserted their hold over native benefices (Map 5). But not for long: as the number of jobless *curas* in Cuidad Real grew, as episcopal emoluments remained inadequate and began to decline, local prelates and their retainers became even more anxious to limit the power of mendicant friars in the diocese. In 1732, therefore, they obtained a new *cédula* which instructed the civil *ayuntamiento* of Ciudad Real to determine whether qualified secular clergymen were available to serve in Indian parishes.[64]

As we know, this order was never carried out: the following year, Gabriel de Laguna, anxious to curtail the freedom of local *vecinos,* dissolved the city council. In order to remedy this situation, in 1735 the cathedral chapter interviewed 20 prominent men and compiled its own report on the subject. Not content to extol the virtues of provincial *clérigos* (to whom in many cases they were related), these men provided a lengthy and detailed description of Dominican misconduct. Manuel de la Tovilla, a former *alcalde* of Ciudad Real who owned several *haciendas* near San Bartolomé, declared that "There is one town in the province of Los Llanos where it is common knowledge that at Easter the friars demand an *arroba* of cotton or half a *fanega* of corn to hear confession, and in this town there are 3,000 Indians."[65] In much the same vein, another local landowner testified that

> He had once asked Miguel de la Torre, a literate Indian and *escribano* of San Bartolomé, if it was customary to give cotton or money at Easter, and this Indian told him, "Señor, several years ago the native *cabildo* of this town sent me to the priest with a message that the Indians here could not fulfill their spiritual obligations because they did not each have an *arroba* of cotton to give him every year, and because of this not only could they not fulfill their obligations but they were also fleeing from the town; and since I was the one who brought him this news, he ordered me whipped, and I was given 200 lashes...."[66]

And finally, virtually all of these witnesses claimed that the friars aided and abetted the *alcalde mayor* in the administration of his *repartimientos.*

Despite the highly prejudiced and partial nature of these accounts, they reveal a significant fact about social life in central Chiapas: for many years, Dominican friars and provincial governors had developed a *modus vivendi* which—although it never involved them in common enterprises—nonetheless had coalesced into an overt political alliance. The origins of this alliance are difficult to establish; in any case, I would suggest, it was undoubtedly reaffirmed in 1678 when the *audiencia* dispatched a special judge, José Descals, to investigate accusations of official misconduct in Ciudad Real.[67] Ironically, these accusations had been made by Núñez de la Vega himself and had embroiled the bishop in a series of intrigues with the *alcalde mayor*. After issuing a set of regulations to rectify this situation, Descals turned his attention to the question of Church revenues, and particularly to the large number of *fiestas* which local friars celebrated in native parishes.[68] Infuriated at what he considered to be Descals' treachery, Núñez quickly maneuvered to force him out of Chiapas and then filed a complaint against him with the Inquisition in Guatemala. Moreover, he drafted a new body of *constituciones diocesanas* which called into question the authority of royal officers in such affairs. And although the Inquisition eventually vacated Descals' *ordenanzas*, this controversial document, which clearly violated the *real patronato*, was soon suppressed. Not surprisingly, thereafter the friars sought to resolve their differences with provincial governors in private. Finally, after 1712, this alliance was further strengthened when Dominican superiors, faced with the destruction of their properties in Ocosingo, began once again to rely heavily upon native *limosnas* for both income and capital (Tables 8 and 9). By reorganizing parish administration in the highlands, then, and by collaborating closely with civil authorities, these men hoped with renewed urgency to postpone the day when they would be deprived of such vital resources.

With these facts in mind, it is easy to understand why Dominican *doctrineros* raised few objections when, after 1732, such men introduced new forms of exploitation in native *pueblos*— why, too, Gabriel de Laguna, hearing in 1735 that the cathedral chapter was compiling its report on secularization, quickly elaborated an extensive (and secret) document of his own.[69] Repeating what by then had become a familiar litany, he assured the

TABLE 8.
Dominican Income in Chiapas, 1732

| Convento | Source of Income | Description | Amount per year[a] |
|---|---|---|---|
| Ciudad Real | royal treasury | donation | 1,053 pesos |
| | native parishes | limosnas | 1,800 |
| | hacienda "Poposa" (Tabasco) | unspecified | 800 |
| | capellanías and censos | interest payments | 655 |
| | | Subtotal | 3,708 (4,308) |
| Chiapa | local vecinos | parish fees | 1,955 |
| | native parishes | limosnas | 300 |
| | haciendas | unspecified | 1,013 |
| | censos | interest payments | 60 |
| | | Subtotal | 4,778 (3,328) |
| Comitán | royal treasury and encomenderos | donation | 1,045 |
| | native parishes | limosnas | 1,443 |
| | estancias | unspecified | 500 |
| | censos | interest payments | 354 |
| | | Subtotal | 3,343 (3,342) |
| Tecpatán | royal treasury | donation | 760 |
| | native parishes | limosnas | 2,068 |
| | local Indians | parish fees | 400 |
| | | Subtotal | 3,238 (3,228) |
| | | Total | 15,067 pesos (14,206) |

Source: "Certificaciones de las rentas de los cuatro conventos de Santo Domingo" (1732), AHDSC.
[a] Subtotals are given as they appear in the document. Correct subtotals are shown in parentheses.

Crown that secular priests in Chiapas were few in number, well employed as *capellanes* (chaplains) to Spanish residents, and entirely unsuited for missionary work. For a short time, at least, it seemed as if this *démarche* had been successful: despite the evidence which they had amassed, Church hierarchs were denied permission to secularize native parishes.

TABLE 9.
Dominican Visitas and Limosnas in Chiapas, 1732

| Convento | Personnel | Visitas | Annual Limosnas |
|---|---|---|---|
| Ciudad Real | 10 religiosos sacerdotes | Ixtapa | 80 pesos |
| | 8 doctrineros | Totolapa | 100 |
| | 3 compañeros (for visitas) | Teopisca | 140 |
| | | Oschuc | 200 |
| | | Cancuc | 80 |
| | | Guaquitepec | 80 |
| | | Yajalón | 100 |
| | | Chilón | 40 |
| | | Ocosingo | 100 |
| | | Chamula | 280 |
| | | Subtotal | 1,200 |
| Comitán | 8 religiosos sacerdotes | Comitán | 400 |
| | 1 religioso lego | Esquintenango | 120 |
| | 6 doctrineros | Chicomuselo | 160 |
| | 1 compañero | Socoltenango | 200 |
| | | Soyatitán | 160 |
| | | San Bartolomé | 400 |
| | | Subtotal | 1,440 |
| Chiapa | 8 religiosos sacerdotes | Chiapa | 1,295 |
| | 1 religioso lego | Tuxtla | 400 |
| | 4 doctrineros | Acala | 200 |
| | | Suchiapa | 60 |
| | | Subtotal | 1,955 |
| Tecpatán | 8 religiosos sacerdotes | Tecpatán | 300 |
| | 1 religioso lego | Chapultenango | 192 |
| | 12 doctrineros | Tapisculapa | 720 |
| | 6 compañeros | Ixtacomitán | 192 |
| | | Magdalenas | 128 |
| | | Tapalapa | 192 |
| | | Quechula | 200 |
| | | Copainala | 280 |
| | | Subtotal | 2,204 |
| | | Total | 6,799 pesos |

(continued)

TABLE 9. *(continued)*
Dominican Visitas and Limosnas in Chiapas, 1732

| Convento | Personnel | Visitas | Annual Limosnas |
|---|---|---|---|
| Summary: | 34 *religiosos sacerdotes* | | |
| | 3 *religiosos legos* | | |
| | 30 *doctrineros* | | |
| | 10 *compañeros* | | |
| Total | 77 | | |

*Source:* "Certificación de las rentas de los cuatro conventos de Santo Domingo."

But within a few years the friars again found themselves on the defensive. In February 1753, the Council in Spain, responding to the generalized problem of clerical employment in many parts of America, declared in a new *cédula* that local bishops might fill vacant *doctrinas* with qualified *presbíteros.*[70] As in earlier days, the Dominicans utilized their considerable influence at court to modify this directive, and on June 23, 1757, a second *cédula* ordered prelates in the New World to replace mendicant *doctrineros* with members of the same orders.[71] This time, however, the Bishop of Chiapas, José Vital de Moctezuma, opened up a second line of attack: in 1756, he complained to the Council that episcopal revenues no longer sufficed to maintain the cathedral and its ministers.[72] In order to remedy this situation, he proposed a number of alternatives which included a sizeable donation of royal funds. Rather than take such a drastic step, in 1762 the Crown agreed to attach five important parishes—Chamula, Tuxtla, Oxchuc, San Bartolomé, and Ciudad Real—directly to the cathedral itself.[73] In this way, the bishop or his dean remained nominally in charge of such parishes, which were in fact administered by resident *vicarios.* For their part, such vicars received a fixed salary; all other income was forwarded to the cathedral chapter for its own use. So grateful was this body for the King's largesse that it immediately decided to celebrate a commemorative mass each year at the cathedral's main altar.[74]

Having wrested this small concession from the Council, ecclesiastical authorities were determined to press forward with their campaign for complete secularization. Rather than name Dominican vicars, as the 1757 *cédula* seemed to require, they nominated *clérigos interinos* in those three benefices which had become vacant: Oxchuc, San Bartolomé, and Chamula.[75] In the case of Chamula, their efforts finally bore fruit. But in Oxchuc and San Bartolomé, the friars refused to yield. After deliberating on the matter for several years, in 1768 the *audiencia* instructed secular officials to "make no innovation in the secularization of these *doctrinas*."[76] Once again, it appeared that the mendicants had preserved their empire in Chiapas. Within two years, however, the battle was joined for a third time. Pressed by García de Vargas y Rivera and several leading Spanish *vecinos*, the *audiencia* suddenly reversed itself and announced that it would permit the bishop to appoint interim clerics wherever a vacancy had occurred.[77] On April 10, 1771, the Dominican prior of Ciudad Real, responding to a letter from the bishop, revealed that no less than 22 of the parishes held by Dominicans had effectively lost their curates through death, illness, or promotion—although in several cases such men had been replaced by other friars without episcopal confirmation. Thereafter, between April 15 and June 12, a series of special judges appointed by García de Vargas secularized virtually every parish in the province.[78]

Faced with this renewed and very serious challenge to their authority, Dominican superiors, alleging once again that ordinary *clérigos* were unfit ministers for rude savages, appealed directly to the Crown. Invoking a *cédula* which had been applied two years earlier in Michoacán, they complained that such measures would push them to financial ruin—surely an unfit reward for two centuries of faithful service. Secularization might proceed, they argued, only if the bishop made ample provisions for their welfare—provisions which did not take into account their income from *ingenios* and *haciendas*.[79] In the meantime, they applied to their old ally, Juan de Oliver, to vacate García's orders in parishes which lay within his jurisdiction—a request with which he was only too happy to comply.[80] Then, in order to foment popular dissatisfaction against secular clergymen, they awaited the *fiesta* of Corpus Christi to close the doors of their main church in Chiapa. "In the *cédula* of 1757," they wrote to the *audiencia*,

> it is stated unequivocally that the churches of our monastery and their ornaments may not be included in the order to secularize. . . . From other royal decrees and ancient books, wills, and donations, dispositions of our forebears, it may be deduced that this church has been built and rebuilt not by the Indians but at the expense of the friars themselves, who have also placed in it the appropriate jewels and ornaments. . . .[81]

Despite such actions and allegations, however, native *justicias* appealed to ecclesiastical authorities to appoint a *presbítero* in Chiapa as soon as possible. There was nothing in the monastery, they said in a letter to the *audiencia*, which they or their ancestors had not put there by the sweat of their brows, and they had grown tired of supporting the *Religión de Santo Domingo*.[82] Eventually, of course, the entire matter reached the Council in Spain. Extending the Michoacán directive to Chiapas, on August 23, 1772, it declared that "with our express and deliberate consent, the friars must remain provisionally in their parishes and *doctrinas*. . . ."[83] Moreover, it commanded the *audiencia* to reappoint Dominican pastors in seven communities where secular priests had already assumed their duties. And indeed, this state of affairs might have prevailed until independence had not the arrival in 1774 of a new and particularly ambitious *alcalde mayor*, Cristóbal Ortíz de Avilés, followed the next year by a bishop of strong will and great determination, Francisco Polanco, precipitated a major crisis in relations among authorities of all kinds—a crisis in which, at last, friars and *presbíteros* were forced to make common cause.

As we might expect, the origins of this crisis may be found in the diminished capacity of highland communities to meet the renewed demands of both civil officials and parish priests. Deprived in large measure of the lucrative cacao trade (which belonged primarily to the *alcalde* in Tuxtla), Ortíz quickly developed a system of *repartimientos* so onerous and exacting that most native *pueblos*—which had barely recovered from the plagues of 1770-71—were thrown into a state of chaos. "This illicit commerce," wrote Polanco in one of his numerous complaints to the Crown,

> is the immediate and visible cause for the destruction of the *pueblos*, whose inhabitants are not accorded the rights of other human beings. . . . [Ortíz] buys cotton at a small price and sells it to them at a profit of 200 percent. I will not even discuss here the question of weights, the problem of shortweighting them. The importance of these operations must not be underestimated, because he regularly gives out to the Indians cotton which is yellow and of poor quality, and expects them to return it to him white and well-spun, having sold what they got from him at a lesser price and bought better stock at their own expense. . . .[84]

In much the same vein, by 1776 Ortíz had confiscated most of the *cajas de comunidad,* which he administered according to his own requirements.[85] Without such resources, many of these communities found themselves unable to provide *limosnas* and other fees to their priests (Table 10). Then, too, in many areas indigenous men and women, unable to meet their debts, simply abandoned their towns for the relative safety of peonage on lowland estates—a process which threatened to undermine the very basis of parish organization and priestly stipends in central Chiapas.[86] It was this situation, therefore, which finally made further collaboration between Dominicans and royal governors untenable and which allowed Polanco to forge an uneasy alliance within the Church.

Oddly enough, the controversy between Polanco and Ortíz—a controversy which came to involve almost every important resident of Ciudad Real—arose over the actions of one particularly unsavory curate, Joseph Ordoñez y Aguiar, the vicar of Chamula, a cleric whom even Polanco was reluctant to defend. Like his brother Ramón, Don Joseph (who eventually became canon of the local cathedral) regarded his benefice as a source of income which he invested in private *fincas* and *labores.* Not content with his nominal salary, however, he inflated those fees which his unfortunate flock was compelled to pay for baptisms, confession, and other sacraments.[87] But despite the fact that he often neglect-

Table 10.
Proportion of Priests Residing in Their Parishes,
1650–1778

|      | Total Priests in Chiapas | Priests in Rural Parishes | Percentage |
|------|--------------------------|---------------------------|------------|
| 1650 | 65                       | 17                        | 26%        |
| 1735 | 48                       | 24                        | 50         |
| 1778 | 191                      | 53                        | 28         |

Sources: Ximénez, Historia vol. 2, pp. 288–289; "Estado actual de la cleresía del obispado de Ciudad Real" (1735), AGGG A1.52.285.23; Polanco, "Estado de los vasallos."

ed to share such income with his superiors, his earnings remained relatively modest. In order to overcome these limitations, therefore, he introduced a series of measures which brought him into open and direct competition with Ortíz. According to one ecclesiastical colleague, Vicente Guillén, curate of Zinacantan, "he required his parishioners to spin and weave between 600 and 700 arrobas of cotton . . . and he also sells them mules, hats, cattle, and other merchandise on credit."[88] Similarly, Miguel Trujillo, the schoolteacher in Chamula, complained that "the Indians say they cannot pay their taxes because of the work which they must perform for their priest, and which has become so onerous that they no longer wish to remain in their towns."[89] As for the Indians, they declared that

> The priest has a farm where he sends the children from catechism class to carry rocks, firewood, and to remove the straw from his wheat without paying them anything . . . and he gives out wool to the girls so that they can weave clothes for him, but he gives them so little that they must buy more, for fear that he will whip them if the clothing is not finished. . . .[90]

Ironically, it was to prevent such abuses, Ortíz claimed in 1778, that he had removed the town's caja de comunidad to his own residence.

From these events it becomes clear that the Church in Chiapas might prosper only if provincial governors were compelled to relinquish their control over native commerce: by 1775, even Dominican *doctrineros* complained that highland *repartimientos* had severely undermined their incomes. To this end, Polanco began to court the principal *vecinos* of Ciudad Real, who for nearly 30 years had watched helplessly as local *alcaldes* and their *tenientes* enriched themselves at public expense. On behalf of these *vecinos* (who by that time numbered around 50), he initiated a cascade of petitions which in 1780 and 1781 forced the *audiencia* to reinstate the city's *ayuntamiento*.[91] In fact, acting under orders directly from the Council, colonial authorities took the unusual step of charging the bishop himself with this task.[92] At the same time, in order to assure the sympathy of municipal functionaries, and also to improve the state of ecclesiastical revenues, Polanco utilized a device which his predecessor had introduced into the province: the *remate de diezmos*.[93] Whereas in 1775 not a single person of substance had come forth to bid on the collection of tithes, after 1778 such pledges regularly exceeded 5,000 pesos. By means of such devices, Polanco and his subordinates created a network of merchants and *hacendados* whose personal fortunes became inextricably linked with those of the Church.[94] But perhaps his most dramatic accomplishment involved a lawsuit which in 1778 the *alcalde mayor* initiated against Joseph Ordoñez. Responding to the accusation that priestly avarice, not *repartimientos*, had driven people in Chamula to desperation, Polanco prepared a lengthy set of documents on the subject of forced labor throughout the highlands.[95] And despite the fact that Chamula's *justicias* filed a detailed affidavit in favor of the governor (who had treated them less harshly than their own curate), the *audiencia* enjoined civil authorities from engaging in commerce of this sort altogether.[96]

Of course, it would be naive to assume that provincial governors automatically obeyed such orders, or that they did not continue to organize *repartimientos* wherever they were able to do so. On the contrary, in 1784 Ramón de Ordoñez, acting on behalf of the *cabildo eclesiástico*, complained that the *alcalde mayor* had "distributed among the Indians money or goods for [cacao] at its old price [of 10 pesos per *arroba*] without taking into consideration the paucity of the harvest or notifying the growers that they might sell their product to private merchants. . . . He then sold it himself in [Guatemala] at 75 pesos per *arroba*."[97] But despite such incidents, the *repartimiento* system—indeed, the entire structure of forced production and distribution in the province—was clearly giving way to a more complex set of social relations. Stimulated by the smuggling boom throughout Central America, local merchants and *hacendados*—supported by the Church itself—expanded their enterprises in the Grijalva basin. Between 1780 and 1820, for example, three new plantations were founded in San Bartolomé; a few miles to the southeast, around Comitán, no less than 20 cattle *estancias* came into existence.[98] Moreover, such properties provided much greater returns to their owners than they had in the past: in 1819, mules sold for twice the price that they had brought 50 years earlier; horses had increased 50 percent in value, cattle 33 percent.[99] For their part, secular priests, whom by 1778 Polanco had installed in many native parishes, played an important role in this process: unfettered by membership in monastic orders, they freely extracted both cash and labor from highland communities and invested these in other ventures (Maps 6 and 7).

In effect, then, the replacement of provincial *alcaldes* by a more honorable group of *intendentes* in 1790 merely ratified in administrative form what had already become an established economic fact. Thenceforth the central *altiplano*, rather than providing directly those goods which were traded abroad, was transformed into a reservoir of unused Indian labor, a reservoir which might be tapped during moments of expansion and dammed at moments of contraction (Table 11). Who controlled this flow, and how it was regulated, came to occupy a central position in the area's political life throughout the 19th century.

## Conclusions

Unlike the Indians of Oaxaca who, according to William B. Taylor "were still self-sufficient farmers on the eve of . . . indepen-

MAP 6.
Curatos in Chiapas, 1778

dence," the indigenous people in central Chiapas had by 1821
abandoned their traditional economic and agricultural occupations.[100] Here and there, individual families or family groups
managed to eke out a living from their small *milpas*. Indeed,
throughout the highlands during the 17th and 18th centuries,
land was not a major cause of concern among the Indians. Only
in a few highland valleys—Ixtapa, Zinacantan, Teopisca, and
Ocosingo—did Indians find themselves deprived of their ances-
tral patrimonies. In contrast, taxes, tribute, and the system of
*repartimientos* to which these belonged, brought about profound

MAP 7.
Curatos and Anexos in the Central Highlands, 1778

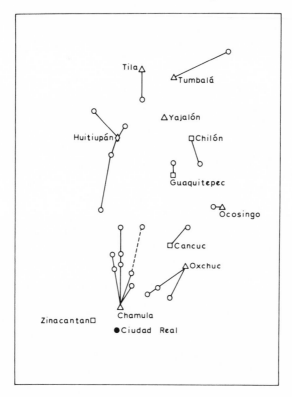

transformations in Indian communities. By means of such devices, provincial governors organized and mobilized a vast native labor force which produced cacao, cochineal, sugar, and cotton cloth. Even as late as 1819, 30 years after such *repartimientos* had been abolished, native people in Chiapas still paid an exorbitant amount of tribute in comparison with Indians in New Spain. Untroubled by serious competition from private landowners, Chiapas' *alcaldes mayores* created a highly sophisticated network of plantations, markets, and manufacturers. And incredibly, they devised this network without purchasing either

TABLE 11.
Indian Population of Chiapas, 1611–1817

| | 1611 | | 1678[a] | | 1778 | | 1817[a] | |
|---|---|---|---|---|---|---|---|---|
| Central Highlands[b] | 36,911 | 39% | 37,410 | 43% | 22,448 | 50% | 39,478 | 67% |
| Comitán | 12,665 | 13 | 6,344 | 7 | 4,716 | 10 | 4,227 | 7 |
| Chiapa | 11,958 | 12 | 13,883 | 16 | 353 | 1 | 1,038 | 2 |
| Llanos | 8,267 | 9 | 6,802 | 7 | 6,061 | 13 | 6,381 | 11 |
| Zoques | 21,107 | 22 | 19,808 | 23 | 10,799 | 24 | 6,207 | 11 |
| Jiquipulas | 4,306 | 5 | 3,068 | 3 | 688 | 1 | 1,440 | 2 |
| Total | 95,214 | 100% | 87,315 | 100% | 45,065 | 100% | 58,771 | 100% |

*Sources:* Gerhard, *The Southeast Frontier* p. 159; Polanco, "Estado de los vasallos"; "Padrón de los tributarios de Chiapa."

[a] Estimated from number of tributaries.
[b] Including Tila and Huitiupán.

a single *vara* of land or beast of burden. Both land and animals remained in Indian hands: they formed the capital which each year native people themselves husbanded and regenerated.

Given these facts, it is perhaps not surprising that opposition to the *repartimiento* system was led by a succession of secular clergymen and non-mendicant bishops. Not that such men were motivated by questions of doctrine or conscience: on that score, Dominicans and *clérigos* alike showed an almost complete disdain for their native parishioners. Instead, opposition of this sort may be traced to the peculiar powerlessness of local *vecinos*, to their vulnerability at the hands of royal governors, their isolation from the *audiencia* and its *oidores*. Lacking both capital and political connections, they were continually impoverished and humiliated by men like Laguna and Garracín. Certainly they could not look to the Dominicans for support: as the clamor for secularization gained in intensity after 1680, friars and functionaries became more tightly bound by relations of mutual necessity and mutual defense. Then too, despite the presence of many native-born monks, to the very end of colonial rule Dominican communities in Chiapas were dominated by *peninsulares*. As late as 1819, for example, their *procurador* asked the *audiencia* to withdraw 10,000 pesos from indigenous *cajas de comunidad* to pay the costs of bringing a new contingent from Spain.[101]

Under these circumstances, we may understand why the cathedral in Ciudad Real (and its seminary) became a focal point of intrigue against both the Order and civil authority, how it provided a political haven for priestly *hacendados* and their disenfranchized relatives. Secularization in 18th-century Chiapas aroused many of the same passions which came into play again a century later at the onset of *desamortización* (disentailment), and for similar reasons: it broke the stranglehold over economic life which for nearly three centuries had been exercised by a small group of monks and administrators. In so doing, it prepared the way for a generation of economic expansion, one dominated in part by clerics who had been reared in the spirit of Joseph Ordoñez and his acquisitive colleagues.

# NATIVE SOCIETY IN THE CENTRAL HIGHLANDS

## 1590–1821

Compared to our view of Spanish society in Chiapas, information about Indian life is much less plentiful and revealing. Most of what can be learned about native communities must be inferred from documents which were composed for other purposes or which deliberately set out to misrepresent the facts. Beginning in 1584 with de Feria's report on Juan Atonal, a succession of Dominican prelates, inspired by European superstitions of the day, set out to denounce indigenous heresies, expose witches, and represent native religious expression in the worst possible light. In this way, they hoped to persuade the Council that only they and their minions remained fit to occupy native benefices. For their part, bishops such as Mauro de Tovar (1655–1666) and Marcos Bravo de la Serna y Manrique (1674–1680), anxious to augment parish fees and to advance the cause of secularization, eagerly embraced such tactics, which they directed against the friars themselves. Hence the origins of a very tenacious, indeed almost indestructible kind of Black Legend: native people merely feigned conversion to the new faith, it was said, in order to deceive their priests and to practice their old religion in secret. And if the mendicants had not yet succeeded in converting Chiapas' heathens, these bishops suggested, then perhaps it was time for less incompetent pastors to step in. Ironically, perhaps, ideological repression of the sort which became commonplace after

1650 did not intensify so much during periods of widespread heterodoxy, but rather at those moments when controversy within the Church, combined with declining revenues, reached a particularly critical level.

By way of contrast, contemporary evidence indicates that Indians converted sincerely and with great devotion, that they elaborated a set of rituals and institutions which originated in the late 16th century within native *cofradías*. Faced with augmented repression, indigenous communities responded with increased resistance and stiffened resolve—a response which local priests and civil officials alike were quick to interpret as sedition. And indeed, when other alternatives were unavailable, when all avenues of appeal and legitimate protest were exhausted, native people did occasionally rebel. In 1693, for example, over 300 Indians in Tuxtla, infuriated by the onerous *repartimientos* to which they had been subjected, killed the province's *alcalde mayor*, Manuel de Maisterra, in the public plaza.[1] Similarly, in 1722, when native men and women in Ocozocuautla refused to perform unpaid labor for their pastor, Sebastián de Grijalva (illegitimate son of the Dominican *cura* of Copainalá), they were accused of idolatry and *nagualismo* (spiritism). Rather than pay for their services, Grijalva railed at them from the pulpit until he was forced to flee for his life.[2]

Of course, *motines* (riots) of this sort were common enough throughout Spanish America; indeed, a few years earlier, in 1660, Indians in Tehuantepec had revolted against provincial administrators over much the same issues. And as long as they were directed against specific abuses, as long as their ringleaders might be isolated and detained, such outbursts remained both relatively circumscribed and easily contained. But when economic injustice was combined with the kind of inquisitorial and self-serving onslaught against native life which took place in Chiapas in the years preceding 1712, protest gave way to open rebellion and to the creation of an Indian church—in which native pastors prophesied an imminent end to "the rule of the Jews" in Ciudad Real.

## THE SOULS OF RED FOLK

In late 1649, during the course of his annual *visita,* Bishop Domingo Villaescusa y Ramírez de Arellano (a Hieronymite friar) arrived in the Tzotzil *pueblo* of San Andrés. Summoning the local *mayordomo,* he demanded an accounting of *cofradía* funds, from which he expected to collect 7 pesos. To the bishop's dismay, the *mayordomo* declared that such funds were virtually depleted; indeed, only 4 pesos were available to pay the bishop's fee. Undaunted, Villaescusa y Ramírez required the hapless Indian to borrow 3 pesos from his neighbors. After all, he explained, it was their responsibility to support him and to maintain the cathedral in Ciudad Real.[3]

By 1630 such incidents occurred with considerable regularity in many highland towns, where renewed waves of disease had drastically reduced the number of men available for *cofradía* membership (Tables 12 and 13). Then, too, Spanish settlers, anxious to establish *trapiches* and cattle ranches of their own, persuaded the Crown to grant them labor drafts which included Indians from precisely these communities.[4] Pressed by such circumstances, as Kevin Gosner has recently shown, it is not surprising that nearly half of these people married outside their own *pueblos*—a fact which made stable administration even more difficult.[5] Deprived of both members and money, native *cofradías* often suspended their activities or ceased to perform religious functions altogether. As a result, episcopal revenues, which were derived largely from *limosnas* paid by these brotherhoods, remained stagnant. And as the number of unemployed secular priests rose toward the century's end, provincial bishops were faced with the urgent task of devising new sources of income.

Under these circumstances, it is not surprising that such bishops employed virtually the same mechanisms which Dominican missionaries had used a century earlier—that is, they reorganized *cofradías* which had become defunct and required Indians to celebrate more numerous and elaborate festivals. Adapting a device employed frequently by the Crown to raise its own income, they also added a new body of religious officials—known

TABLE 12.
Epidemics and Famines in Chiapas, 1529–1818

| Date | Description | Extent or Effect |
|------|-------------|------------------|
| 1529–31 | plague and famine | general |
| 1532–34 | measles | general |
| 1545–48 | *cocoliztli* | general |
| 1565 | *peste* | killed half of Indians in Zinacantan |
| 1576–81 | *matlazahuatl* | general |
| 1600–01 | *peste* ⎫ | killed one-third of the Indians in |
| 1607–08 | *peste* ⎭ | Comitán and Copanaguastla |
| 1631 | *peste* | general |
| 1693 | *peste* | general |
| 1733 | *peste* | Jiquipulas, San Felipe, Bachajón |
| 1769 | locusts | famine in Yajalón |
| 1771–73 | locusts | generalized famine |
| 1786 | *peste de la bola* | unknown |
| 1788 | unknown | famine in Zinacantan |
| 1795 | *viruelas* | unknown |
| 1798 | leprosy | unknown |
| 1800 | *garrotillo* | various towns |
| 1802–3 | *viruelas* | entire highlands |
| 1803 | *tabardillo* | various towns |
| 1806 | *viruelas* | Zoque region |
| 1808 | locusts | unknown |
| 1818 | famine | Huitiupán |

Sources: Gerhard, *The Southeast Frontier*, pp. 158–159; Remesal, vol. 1, p. 380; López Sánchez, vol. 2, p. 651, 679–680; 813; AGCh, *Boletín* 4 (1955): 27–68, 113–115; "Autos en que consta la despoblación de varios pueblos de la provincia de Chiapa" (1734), AGGG, A1.1.3.1; "Los nativos de Yajalum informan de que sus sementeras han sido destruidas por la langosta," (1769), ibid., A1.1.10.1; "Informe del alcalde mayor de Ciudad Real de Chiapa acerca de que en su jurisdicción ha aparecido una peste nombrada de la bola..." (1786), ibid., A1.1.18.1; "Autorización a los indios de Zinacantan para que del fondo de sus comunidades tomen lo necesario para el fomento de sus siembras" (1788), ibid., A3.40.4343.334; "Informa el gobernador intendente de Ciudad Real sobre haber sido invadidos los pueblos por la peste de viruela" (1795), ibid., A1.4.7.22.2; "El obispo de Ciudad Real solicita licencia para que el naturalista José Mocino parmanezca en Chiapa el tiempo necesario para combatir la lepra" (1798), ibid., A1.14.302.21; "Informes acerca de la aparición de la peste de garrotillo en varios pueblos de Chiapa" (1800), ibid., A1.4.13.636.58; "La audiencia de Guatemala pide informes a las autoridades de Chiapa acerca del estado de peste de viruelas aparecida en Chamula" (1802), ibid., A1.1.28.2; "Informe del estado de la peste de viruela que ha invadido Chamula" (1802), ibid., A1.1.29.2; "Acerca de la epidemia de fiebres que hay en Ciudad Real" (1803), ibid., A1.1.30.2; "Informa el gobernador intendente de Ciudad Real haber peste de tabardillo" (1803), ibid., A1.4.9.30.2; "Medidas tomadas en el pueblo de Solistaguacán para evitar la propagación de la peste de viruela" (1806), ibid., A1.4.7.651.58; "Los oficiales reales contra el convento de Santo Domingo de Ciudad Real sobre el pago de cierta suma invertida en la extinción de la langosta" (1808), ibid., A1.15.587.25; "Los naturales de Santa Catalina Huitiupán piden dinero del fondo de comunidades para comprar géneros" (1818), ibid., A3.40.4380.336.

TABLE 13.
Native Tributaries in Central Chiapas, 1595–1817

| Town | 1595 | 1611 | 1761 | 1816–17 |
|---|---|---|---|---|
| Abasolo | — | (with Oxchuc) | 27 | (with Oxchuc) |
| Aguacatenango | 194 | 131 | 110 | 126 |
| Amatenango | 233 | 113 | 108 | 167 |
| Bachajón | 476 | 457 | 113 | 399 |
| Cancuc | 151 | 255 | 232 | — |
| Chalchihuitán | 52 | 42 | 87 | 188 |
| Chamula | 270 | 219 | 567 | 1,947 |
| Chenalhó | 41 | 23 | 153 | 450 |
| Chilón | 335 | 323 | 53 | 90 |
| Guaquitepec | 158 | 343 | 155 | 244 |
| Huistán | 204 | 161 | 116 | (with Tenejapa?) |
| Huitiupán | 196 | 70 | 43 | 67 |
| Ixtapa | — | 269 | 150 | 141 |
| Magdalenas | 89 | 70 | 115 | 185 |
| Mitontic (and Pantelhó) | (with Chamula) | 21 | 49 | 219 |
| Ocosingo | 481 | 315 | 178 | 577 |
| Oxchuc | 168 | 174 | 404 | 782 |
| Petalcingo | 107 | 106 | 258 | 218 |
| San Andrés | 140 | 42 | 191 | 587 |
| San Lucas | 30 | — | 102 | 113 |
| Santiago | 98 | 34 | 28 | 71 |
| Sta. Marta | 104 | 75 | 57 | 75 |
| Sibacá | 270 | 243 | 321 | 116 |
| Simojovel | 90 | 246 | 148 | 218 |
| Sitalá | 164 | 327 | 68 | 256 |
| Tenango | 186 | 167 | 26 | (with Tenejapa?) |
| Tenejapa | 117 | 129 | 206 | 1,025 |
| Teopisca | 366 | 259 | 165 | 155 |
| Totolapa | 235 | 175 | 295 | 96 |
| Yajalón | 170 | 388 | 239 | 257 |
| Zinacantan | 422 | 205 | 306 | 603 |
| Total | 5,547 | 5,382 | 5,070 | 9,372 |

*Sources:* See Table 3.

as *alféreces*—whose primary responsibility consisted of providing *limosnas* for extra masses. What is perhaps more surprising is the way in which royal *oidores*, and especially the Council, were persuaded to accept such measures, were persuaded in fact that such measures had become necessary to save Indian souls from imminent damnation. In 1664, for example, Bishop Mauro de Tovar received papal license to exercise a number of extraordinary powers and to bring some order into the spiritual affairs of Spanish colonists. As for the area's Indians, these subjects had apparently given the Holy See no great cause for concern: it merely gave Tovar permission to "read the works of heretics and pagans wherein they speak of their religion."[6] Similarly, ten years later, the *audiencia* sent a royal *visitador*, Jacinto Roldán, to regulate relations between Spaniards and *naturales*. In his *ordenanzas*, which extended to almost every aspect of life in the region, Roldán felt compelled to mention native religion in only two minor instances.[7]

Within three years, however, this state of affairs had changed radically. Moved by a sudden conviction that idolatry had spread throughout the province, Bishop Bravo de la Serna y Manrique published an elaborate series of regulations in which he dramatically limited native religious expression. Particularly reprehensible, he declared, were practices "such as the dance of Bobat, when they jump and shiver as if from the cold—but at midday, and around their fires, through which they pass without the slightest injury."[8] And finally, armed with a revised schedule of ecclesiastical fees, Bravo de la Serna set off on a *visita* in which he almost doubled the amount that indigenous *cofradías* paid to the *sagrada mitra* (Table 14).

Having set in motion this campaign against native superstition, the bishop proceeded to attack more familiar targets. In 1678, he arrested a man from Tenejapa for witchcraft and then asked the Council for permission to suspend Dominican *doctrineros* in seven Tzeltal parishes.[9] By the time his request was granted, however, Bravo de la Serna had died. His successor, a Dominican bishop, Francisco Núñez de la Vega, took up the cause of eliminating heresy with equal enthusiasm and zeal. In

TABLE 14.
Episcopal Income in Chiapas, 1668-1808
(pesos/year)

| 1668 | 1675 | 1677 | 1737-50 | 1759 | 1783-86 | 1803-06 |
|------|------|------|---------|------|---------|---------|
| 9,000 | 5,000 | 8,000 | 10,500 | 8,000 | 23,750 | 13,925 |

Sources: Orozco y Jiménez, Collección de documentos inéditos, vol. 2, pp. 209–211; "Informe del obispo de Chiapa, Dr. don Marcos Bravo de la Serna y Manrique, al rey" (1677), López Sánchez, pp. 664–665; "Una representación hecha por el cabildo al rey de España sobre la necesidad de esta santa iglesia agregando cinco curatos" (1759), AHDSC; "Informe rendido por la Sociedad Económica de Ciudad Real sobre las ventajas y desventajas obtenidas con el implantamiento del sistema de intendencias" (1819), AGCh, Boletín 6 (1956): 16–17.

1684, arguing that his colleagues were both worthy and effective, he persuaded the Council to rescind its order regarding the seven *doctrineros*; thereafter he conducted a public *autillo de fe* in which he burned "a painting of the *nagual* Tzihuitzín or Poxlón" that had allegedly been found inside the church in Oxchuc.[10] Núñez de la Vega also commissioned the first of several manuals in Spanish, Tzotzil, and Tzeltal to guide Dominican *curas* in their pastoral duties.[11] Before administering the sacraments or performing other such tasks, for example, the priests were instructed to ask their flocks the following question: "Have you paid your dues to the Church, as all faithful Christians must?" And on the subject of redemption, they were encouraged to reiterate that message which Bravo de la Serna had first devised, stressing the unusually heavy price that Christ had paid for Indian sins. "Listen, my children," began one Tzotzil sermon:

Where you go at the world's end depends upon whether you do penance; you must also do good deeds during your lives, because when you die your soul can do nothing, it receives its reward for what it did here on earth. For this reason you must be good, you must pray with the holy rosary in front of Our Holy Mother St. Mary, so that she will act upon your hearts, so that you will do only good deeds, so that you will desire to go into God's sight in heaven. . . .[12]

By 1690, then, Núñez de la Vega had successfully used the question of idolatry to postpone secularization and to strengthen his hold over parish administration. According to Manuel Trens, native *cofradías* celebrated no less than 35 annual festivals, for which they paid augmented *limosnas* and *derechos*.[13] Moreover, between 1684 and 1706 (when he was succeeded by Juan Bautista Alvarez de Toledo), Núñez conducted three *visitas* throughout the province, during which he collected additional fees. In fact, it was precisely to rectify this state of affairs that in 1690 José Descals, another visiting magistrate, issued his own regulations. After prohibiting the local clergy from engaging in a variety of enterprises, Descals ordered them "to eliminate several of the *fiestas* which now take place during the year, because the Indians spend much of their time drunk and idle."[14]

In response, in 1692, Núñez drafted his monumental *Constituciones diocesanas*, in which he reiterated that such practices were necessary to prevent the Indians in Chiapas from lapsing hopelessly into heresy and paganism:

> There are many bad Christians of both sexes who, enveloped by the darkness of error, shirk the light of truth. . . . In all the provinces of New Spain, these people are called *nagualistas*, and cannot in truth be distinguished from those superstitious astrologers . . . who with false science seek to know divine will. . . . To the Indians, these infernal teachers are saints, and they are sought out to tell the future.[15]

Not content to expose such errors, however, Núñez proceeded to compose an elaborate and highly fanciful description of native religion—one which, ironically enough, has provided a model for similar documents in the centuries that followed.[16] And finally, protesting that Descals had overstepped his bounds in regulating the Church, Núñez prevailed upon the Inquisition to restore the *status quo ante*.[17]

Behind these quarrels and intrigues, we vaguely perceive the outlines of an indigenous religious experience which sought both to understand and to transcend the tragedy of colonialism. Out of the spiritual disorder which 16th-century evangelization had inflicted upon Indian communities, native *cofrades* labored to create an orderly and coherent ceremonial life of their own. Individual salvation, far too precarious an idea in those years of early death and sudden flight, remained in their minds strictly a Spanish notion. Among the Indians, men and women might attain salvation only if their villages outlived individual members, only if their descendants lit candles for them and wept over their graves on the Day of the Dead. As for their souls, these became absorbed into that collective soul commonly called "our ancestors." To the memory of these righteous forebears—who, as Christ had promised, would one day rise again and live for a thousand years—and to the village saints, native men and women addressed their prayers and lamentations. For had not the Fathers told them that the souls of good Christians live forever at God's right hand? Inspired by the ideal of communal survival, then, they surrounded their *pueblos* with shrines and crosses. Beyond these limits, they seemed to say, lies a hostile world, a world of *ladinos* and untamed beasts. Inside, they declared, our ancestors watch and wait, ready to speak on our behalf when the Day of Judgement arrives. And periodically, as if to reaffirm their faith, native *mayordomos* and *alféreces* carried their saints, flags flying, trumpets sounding, to the far corners of this animate landscape—there to recall the past and to contemplate their future deliverance.

Naturally, ecclesiastical attacks on native superstition were not limited to *autillos de fe* and demonstrations of public piety. By 1670, the insouciance with which local clerics had treated their pastoral responsibilities had created far greater doctrinal problems which called for direct and decisive action on the part of Church authorities. "If you only knew how Christ suffers when you celebrate unworthily," Bravo de la Serna had written to his priests in a rare moment of vision, "and the ways in which you crucify Him, how you would weep with pain and sorrow for your misdeeds. . . . For more priests will be condemned at the altar than ever common rogues and highwaymen were hung on the gallows!" Rather than correct such abuses, however, Bravo de la Serna then directed his fire against native liturgical practices. "It is hereby ordered," he wrote, that no priest may permit flags and pennants to be unfurled as the Host and chalice are raised, both because those who hold such flags irreverently turn their backs upon the divine sacrament and cover themselves, and because of the disturbance which they cause, diverting attention from the Sovereign Mystery. . . .[18]

Similarly, church ornaments and banners were not to be employed by "private persons or even legitimate officials of inferior grade, since no distinction is made regarding the position or rank of His Majesty's officers." Finally, he added, "out of reverence for the Divine Mysteries," only "consecrated priests, lords or nobles of Castile, presidents, judges, governors, and *alcaldes mayores*" might remain seated in church during mass. However corrupt and unworthy these officials might be, he seemed to say, however many of them might be condemned at the altar like common thieves on the gallows, Indian subjects must respect and obey them.

Then one day, after almost two centuries of Spanish domination, they decided to wait no longer. In 1712, a young Tzeltal girl—who later called herself María de la Candelaria and claimed to be inspired by the Holy Virgin—told her followers in the highland town of Cancuc that both God and King had died. The time had come, she declared, for *naturales* in the province to rise up against their Spanish overlords, to avenge their past sufferings and reestablish the true religion. Within a week, word had spread to native *pueblos* as far away as Zinacantan, Simojovel, and San Bartolomé. According to the *alcalde mayor* of Tabasco, for example, a band of Indians "showing signs of rebelliousness" arrived three days later in the Chol town of Tila to take possession of the community's religious ornaments. Then, he continued, these men—who appeared to be acting as public heralds—stated their message:

It was God's will that [the Virgin] should come only for His native children to free them from the Spaniards and the ministers of the Church, and that the Angels would plant and tend their *milpas*, and that the sun and the moon had given signs that the King of Spain was dead, and that they must choose another.[19]

Despite their protestations of surprise and horror, Spanish authorities had received ample warnings that something more serious and deadly than a grain riot was afoot. For several years, miracles had abounded and prophets who proclaimed the end of the world had appeared on the very outskirts of Ciudad Real. In March 1711, for example, Fray José Monroy had interrogated a young girl in Santa Marta (a Tzotzil *pueblo* in the parish of Chamula) who told him that

> Arriving one day at my *milpa*, I found on a fallen branch this Lady who, calling to me, asked if I had a father and a mother, and when I answered No, she told me that she was a poor woman named Mary, who had come down from Heaven to give aid to the Indians, and she ordered me to inform my *justicias* that they should build her a chapel at the entrance to the town.[20]

Like other priests in that region, Fray Monroy had become alarmed at the growing signs of restiveness which, three years earlier, had appeared among the highland Indians. Perhaps, too, he felt uncomfortable about the increasingly strident tone which his colleagues introduced into their sermons, and the increasing disrespect which native people showed for their pastors.

Fray Monroy recalled several years later that one day in 1708,

> About two o'clock in the afternoon, some Indians from the town of Santo Domingo Zinacantan arrived ... and told me that on the road to that town, inside a tree-trunk, an inspired hermit was exhorting them to repent, and that inside the same tree-trunk one could make out a statue of the Holy Virgin which, having descended from Heaven, emitted beams of light, giving them to believe that She had come to offer Her favor and aid.[21]

Upon being questioned by Bishop Alvarez de Toledo, this hermit (who proved to be a *mestizo* from New Spain) explained simply that he was "a poor sinner whom they will not allow to love God." Judging him to be insane, the bishop locked him away in the Franciscan monastery in Ciudad Real.

For two years the matter was forgotten. Then in 1710, Church officials discovered this man again in Zinacantan, where he had built a chapel. By that time, word of the hermit's activities had reached native people as far away as Totolapa, and Indians throughout the area ceased to attend mass in their parish churches. After burning his chapel, therefore, Alvarez de Toledo banished him permanently from Chiapas. All to no avail: within a few months the Virgin reappeared in Santa Marta, where for half a year native authorities hid her effigy from prying clerical eyes. And no sooner had Monroy confiscated this statue than he learned of still another and more impressive miracle:

> The inhabitants of San Pedro Chenalhó . . . arrived to give notice that several days ago they had constructed a chapel for Señor San Sebastián in their town, because his image had sweated on two occasions, . . . and that one Sunday they had seen beams of light coming from the Image of San Pedro and from his face, and that the next Sunday the same thing had occurred again.[23]

Despite Monroy's moderation, native people refused to be calmed. In June 1712, a group of Indians from the Tzeltal town of Cancuc informed Alvarez that a miraculous cross, descended from heaven, had appeared in their *pueblo*. To celebrate this event, Cancuc's civil authorities had constructed a chapel to which Indians from surrounding communities daily brought offerings and gifts. The town's pastor, Fray Simón de Lara, immediately went to investigate. To his horror, he found that such a chapel had indeed been built—not to honor the cross, but rather to house the image of yet another Virgin. Like the effigy in Santa Marta, this image had been discovered in the forest by a young Indian girl. De Lara's consternation was increased when he learned that this girl, surrounded by a group of *mayordomos* and religious officials, remained continuously in the Virgin's company and interpreted aloud her otherwise silent will. Infuriated by such sacrilege and nonsense, de Lara arrested the town's *alcaldes* and *regidores,* whom he sent to Ciudad Real. After replacing them with Indians he trusted, he attempted to destroy the chapel—an act which almost cost him his life. To make matters worse, at that moment the *regidores* whom he had jailed returned to Cancuc, where they declared "that they alone were true friars and that only those whom they elected were *alcaldes.* . . . [They ordered] that the chapel, which was the work of their hands, be maintained, that other *pueblos* be called to defend it, and that the Indians count not their trials, for soon they would be relieved of all toil."[23]

By July 1712, when Alvarez de Toledo notified indigenous *ayutamientos* of his impending visit, native people had already rejected the spiritual authority of Spanish clerics and had taken steps to free themselves from ecclesiastical domination. Although Alvarez did not create this situation, he undoubtedly provided the catalyst—"the spark which ignited the powder," as one Dominican official later wrote—which brought highland Indians to the point of open rebellion. In anticipation of his impending visit, the Virgin summoned native *justicias* from throughout the highlands to Cancuc (now renamed Ciudad Real) where, She proclaimed, they were to celebrate a grand festival in her honor:

I the Virgin who have descended to this Sinful World call upon you in the name of Our Lady of the Rosary and command you to come to this town of Cancuc and bring with you all the silver of your churches and the ornaments and bells, together with the communal funds and drums and all the books of the *cofradías,* because now neither God nor King exists; and for this reason you must come immediately, for if you do not you will be punished for not coming when I and God called you.[24]

The Spanish God, She declared—that leering caricature of Our Lord, draped in episcopal finery—that God had died. In His place, a true Redeemer had appeared, an Indian king of kings who had come to reward native people for their sufferings and trials. And finally, She proclaimed, Indians must arm themselves, they must rise up against the "Jews in Ciudad Real" who even at that moment were preparing to kill Her and reestablish once again their unholy rule over Christendom.

On August 10, five days after Alvarez departed from the city to begin his *visita,* civil and religious officials representing nearly 25 Tzeltal, Tzotzil, and Chol towns gathered in Cancuc to venerate the Virgin. Under the leadership of a Tzotzil prophet, Sebastián Gómez, they and their townsmen were divided into military divisions and placed under the command of native captains. These *capitanes generales,* who in previous years had frequently served as assistants and *mayordomos* to parish priests, seem especially to have despised the Dominican Order. For Gómez instructed the native *alcaldes* "that no one was to give food to the Fathers, under pain of death, an order which was punctually fulfilled."[25] Within a few days, Indian leaders took even more militant steps. First, they attacked the Spanish settlement in Chilón and killed all the town's adult non-Indian men. Spanish women and children were taken to Cancuc, where they were called "Indians" and compelled to serve native authorities as domestics. A short time later, indigenous armies stormed Ocosingo, where they destroyed the Dominican *haciendas* and sugar *ingenio.* Thereafter they proceeded systematically to capture whatever hapless friars fell into their grasp. By late November, they had wrought havoc upon the Church in central Chiapas.

We naturally wonder about the form of worship which these men and women preferred to Spanish religion. And in pursuing this question, we must examine in detail the attitudes and activities of Sebastián Gómez. Arriving in Cancuc in July 1712 from Chenalhó (where he led the unsuccessful movement to build a new chapel for San Sebastián), Gómez proceeded to organize an indigenous Church which, he hoped, would replace the "Church of the Jews": "He brought a small image of San Pedro wrapped in cloth, which he placed in the chapel, and said that this saint had chosen him to be his vicar, and had granted him the power to ordain and appoint other vicars and priests who would minister to the towns." One month later, following the execution of Spanish clergymen, Gómez summoned Indian *fiscales* from 17 Tzeltal towns to appear in Cancuc. After ascertaining which among them could read and write, he ordained several of them into the new priesthood:

> The method of ordination was to compel each *fiscal* to remain on his knees for 24 hours with a candle in his hand repeating the Rosary, and then, in view of the whole town, Don Sebastián de la

> Gloria [as he called himself] sprinkled him with water which, they claimed, had been blessed. . . . Having been ordained and assigned to their parishes, they began to exercise their office like very correct pastors, preaching, confessing, and administering [the sacraments].[26]

At first, Gómez seemed content to dispense with the elaborate hierarchies which characterized the Spanish Church. In establishing a system of authority, he appointed one of his priests, Gerónimo Saraes, to the office of vicar-general—a common enough post in colonial dioceses. At the same time, Saraes and another native priest, Lucas Pérez, became secretaries to the Virgin. And in the true spirit of Christ, who as we recall washed His apostles' feet, Gómez named to the "See of Sibacá" an old man who "had spent his life making *tortillas* for the Fathers."[27] Soon, however, he expanded this primitive hierarchy until it had assumed alarming (and familiar) proportions. Thus Saraes, too, was granted an episcopal throne, while two Indian friars—both of whom enjoyed the title of *predicadores generales*—became vicars-general. Little by little, Divine Justice became obscured behind a battery of new prelates and patriarchs.

Meanwhile, Gómez turned his attention to the difficulties and problems of civil administration. For in his vision of a theocratic state, he regarded Chiapas' *república de indios* as a New Spain, a second empire in which Indians had become Spaniards and Spaniards Indians. But if God and king were dead, if native people no longer owed their obedience and loyalty to the *audiencia* in Guatemala, who would rule the republic in San Pedro's name and the name of his earthly vicar? Within Indian *pueblos*, of course, native *cabildos*—appointed by the movement's leaders—continued to govern in local matters. But such elementary and primitive forms of government, he felt, were ill-suited to an Indian empire—especially an empire that was at war. In order to rectify these problems, as Ximénez tells us, "in order to dispense justice to those who required it, and to reward those who merited it," they would found an *audiencia* in Huitiupán. "With this in mind, they styled the town Guatemala with its president and judges. . . ."[28] And finally, Gómez and other lead-

ers promised at least one military commander, Juan García, that
if the rebellion succeeded he would be crowned king of Cancuc.[29]

To be sure, Gómez's state was not universally admired. There
were many Indians who refused to accept these measures, who
even lost their lives in defense of the colonial order. The *fiscal* of
Tenango, Nicolás Pérez, who remained loyal to Fray de Lara,
was whipped to death in front of the chapel in Cancuc. Similarly,
the inhabitants of Simojovel and Palenque chose to abandon
their homes and hide in the mountains rather than join the rebellion.[30] Indian *pueblos* along the periphery of highland Chiapas
(San Bartolomé, Amatenango, Aguacatenango, Teopisca, and
Comitán) and Zoque towns to the northeast of Ciudad Real refused to support the Virgin. More important, however, Gómez's
empire-building, his careful imitation of Spanish administrative
and ecclesiastical forms, soon provoked disenchantment even
among many Indians who had at first followed the movement
with enthusiasm. In particular, they demanded an end to tribute,
to tithes, and—above all—to the Order of Saint Dominic. Instead, as one witness wrote, Gómez reprimanded them sharply:

> Because there have been complaints among the subjects to the
> effect that [the Virgin's] word has not been fulfilled with respect to
> the abolition of tribute, of the Order of Santo Domingo, of the
> King, and of the rule of the Jews, let it be known that Señor don
> Pedro told his chosen emissary Señor don Sebastián Gómez de la
> Gloria that he could not preserve the world without earthly bonds-
> men. Our Father Señor San Pedro has offered himself as our
> bondsman before God, and thus, according to the heavenly word
> which is not of the earth, there must be in each town a priest who
> will serve as bondsman before God by means of the mass, because
> without them, as the world is filled with sin, the world will end,
> and for this reason the masses which these fathers celebrate will
> calm God's anger. . . .[31]

In the end, it may well have been this theocratic bent which
brought the Cancuc rebellion to a quick end. To be sure, Spanish
authorities possessed sufficient military power to vanquish the
Virgin's poorly-armed and ill-disciplined legions. But colonial

forces, taken by surprise, had found themselves completely un-prepared to defend Spanish settlers. During those weeks when Ciudad Real's meager militia, entrenched in Huistán, stalled for time, Indians in Zinacantan and Chamula, sympathetic to the Virgin, enjoyed ample opportunity to attack and subdue the city. Why did they not do so? Certainly their love of Spanish bishops and governors was no more intense than that of other Indians elsewhere in the highlands. On the contrary, because of their service as porters and their proximity to Ciudad Real, Zinacante-cos had suffered even more acutely than many Indians at the hands of colonial authorities. Did they then fear the punishment which these officials would surely inflict upon them? Apparently not, for they prepared and organized themselves to march against the city. No: their reluctance to pursue this venture does not appear to have been inspired by fear or timorousness. In-stead, they allowed themselves to be dissuaded by Fray Mon-roy—who, we must presume, convinced them that the Virgin was a fraud. And in the days that followed, such key towns as Chenalhó and Chalchihuitán also defected from Her cause. Why, they seem to have asked, should we exchange one earthly kingdom for another?

Indeed, Gómez himself, it would seem, anticipated such oppo-sition. In his order to disgruntled tributaries, he declared that even in the New Age, Indians would continue to sin and would therefore require the services of their priesthood. Otherwise, he wrote, the world would end. This vision of the Day of Judgement, however well it served his purposes, must in the end have in-spired little enthusiasm among men and women who yearned for justice and an end to exploitation. For it violated that sense of community, that sense of promise, which since the days of Las Casas had become the cornerstone of their spiritual and political lives. The feelings of discontent and expectation which swept Chiapas between 1708 and 1712 reflected a desire to realize those old ideals in modern form, to transform the multitude of isolated *pueblos* into a single native community founded upon faith, equality, and divine law. For this reason—according to Herbert Klein—the movement's leaders declared at one point that their Spanish captives must marry Indians. From such a union, they claimed, there would spring a new race—neither Spanish nor Indian—which would truly merit salvation. And despite the movement's failure, these feelings continued to stir native imaginations and to hang in the air like incense—while colonial authorities, jubilant at their victory over the forces of darkness, resumed their unfinished business of capricious law and systematic graft.

Given these motives, it is not difficult to understand the Church's response to this cry for moral regeneration. As might be expected, the rebellion only confirmed those opinions, common among clerics of the day, which held that Indians suffered from a special variety of original sin. "The points upon which our sermons concentrated," wrote Ximénez, who preached to the subdued defenders of Cancuc,

> were, first, the hardness of their hearts, because in 200 years of instruction God's law had not taken hold in their hearts; . . . second, how much better they lived under the rule of the King of Spain than in pagan times under Moctezuma; . . . fourth, their origins, descended from the Jews whom God had punished for their idolatry and who later came to these lands by unknown routes. . . . [32]

Moved by such convictions, Spanish priests intensified their efforts to suppress native religiosity and ritual. In his Tzotzil catechism (1735), for example, Fray Manuel Hidalgo took great pains to impress upon his listeners that their own earthly travails—however great and painful these might be—paled to insignificance beside the agonies which Christ had suffered on their behalf. "Your price is a great one," Hidalgo wrote, echoing his predecessors of 50 years earlier, "and for this reason He suffered terribly while here on earth." [33] In order to assure that the Indians heard and understood this message, the number of priests and parishes doubled, then tripled. And whatever other lessons these clerics may have learned from the rebellion, they remained as committed as Bravo de la Serna and Núñez de la Vega to the legend of native apostasy.

## NATIVE LIFE AFTER THE REBELLION, 1713–1821

It has been suggested by Henri Favre and Herbert Klein that the 1712 uprising coincided with a temporary relaxation of civil authority—that in the years which followed, Spanish officials "were never again able to restore completely their former prerogatives."[34] And yet, as we have seen, there is little question that economic injustice and exploitation became even more intense during the second half of the 18th century.

Within a few months of Gómez's defeat, Indians in Chamula and San Felipe (encouraged by the *alcalde mayor*, who as ever was eager to limit the activities of local *vecinos*) complained that they had been compelled by the province's *sargento mayor*, Pedro de Zabaleta, to carry heavy loads of iron and other goods between Tabasco and Ciudad Real—a task for which they had been paid in worthless trinkets.[35] A few years later, the *audiencia* found that Zabaleta had indeed committed substantial "excesses, vexations, and ill-treatment" against these people, and ordered him imprisoned in Guatemala.[36] Naturally, Zabaleta—who shortly thereafter escaped to Spain—appealed his case to the Council. In 1721, this body placed him under house arrest in Madrid while it reviewed the matter.[37] Several months later, sustaining the *audiencia's* judgment, the royal *fiscal* determined that Zabaleta had in fact "defrauded the Indians of that province by falsifying the tribute list and census which he drew up, and in the assessment of maize, chile, and beans."[38] But the *fiscal* contended that in all of these enterprises Zabaleta had acted in concert with the area's governor, who in 1715 had himself come under investigation for similar offenses. Unwilling to decide which official had committed the greater crime, the Council therefore in 1722 released Zabaleta and declared that, in effect, he had done nothing wrong.[39]

The results of this situation, as we know, became eminently clear in the years after 1720. Having subjugated their Spanish rivals, functionaries such as Joaquín Fernández Prieto and Juan de Oliver expanded their own commercial activities and demanded more Indian labor. So, too, did the Church: as Table 15

Table 15.
Cofradías in Highland Chiapas, 1712–1790

| Town | Cofradías | Capital | Comment |
|------|-----------|---------|---------|
| Aguacatenango | Santísimo Sacramento<br>San Sebastián<br>de las Animas<br>Santa Cruz | | |
| Amatenango | Santísimo Sacramento<br>Santa Cruz<br>San Pedro Martir<br>Nuestra Señora del Rosario | 40 pesos | 2 mayordomos<br>2 mayordomos<br>2 mayordomos |
| Chilón | San Sebastián<br>Santo Domingo<br>Santísimo Sacramento | | |
| Guaquitepec | Santísimo Sacramento<br>Santa Cruz<br>Santa Ana<br>de las Animas<br>Nuestra Señora del Rosario | 21<br>52<br>27½ | |
| Huistán | Nuestra Señora de la Luz | | finca de ganado |
| Huitiupán | Nuestra Señora de la<br>Concepción | | |
| Ixtapa | Santa Cruz | | finca de ganado,<br>2 mayordomos |
| Ocosingo | Santísimo Sacramento<br>San Sebastián<br>de las Animas<br>Santa Cruz<br>Nuestra Señora del Rosario | 21½<br>21<br>15½<br>23<br>26½ | |
| San Felipe | Purísima Concepción | | |
| Sibacá | Santa Cruz | | |
| Teopisca | Santa Cruz<br>San Sebastián<br>de las Animas<br>Nuestra Señora del Rosario | | |

(continued)

TABLE 15. *(continued)*
Cofradías in Highland Chiapas, 1712–1790

| Town | Cofradías | Capital | Comment |
|------|-----------|---------|---------|
| Tila | Santísimo Cristo de Tila | | |
| Yajalón | Santísimo Sacramento | 28 | |
| | Santa Cruz | 24 | |
| | Santo Niño | 20 | |
| | Vera Cruz de Mayordomos | 27 | |
| | San Sebastián | 19 | |
| | Nuestra Señora del Rosario | 62 | |
| Zinacantan [a] | Santísimo Sacramento | 162½ | |
| | Santa Cruz | 184 | |
| | Nuestra Señora del Rosario | 240 | |
| | Santo Domingo | 203½ | |
| | Benditas Almas de Purgatorio | 200 | |

*Sources:* "Libros de las Cofradías," various years, AHDSC; "Informe de la parroquia de Zinacantan" (1793), AHDSC.

[a] In 1793.

suggests, ecclesiastical authorities wasted little time in reorganizing native *cofradías* and reinstituting public festivals. By 1769, in fact, the number of celebrations had risen to the point that royal officials once again felt compelled to intervene.[40] Furthermore, in order to insure that Indians understood their place in the social order, on three separate occasions (in 1735, 1782, and 1804) these prelates revised and published their Tzotzil-language manuals on doctrine and matters of faith.[41]

Faced with the unabated deterioration of their lives, native people were forced to choose between two equally distasteful alternatives: either they spent precious resources to petition the Crown for relief, or they abandoned their *pueblos* altogether. As early as 1729, for example, the mayordomos of *Santísimo Sacramento* in Amatenango, unable to pay their *limosnas,* simply ran off to lowland *haciendas* and were never heard from again.[42] A few years later, the Crown was told that a number of important communities, including Jiquipulas, Coneta (which in 1540 had formed part of the large *corregimiento* of Comalapa), Guaquitepec, Bachajón, San Andrés, Istapilla, and Zacualpa, had all but disappeared;[43] and Indians in Zinacantan asked the *audiencia* to reduce their tribute, which in any case they could not pay.[44] ⸱Responding to their request, royal *oidores* in 1749 directed local authorities to conduct a new census of native towns throughout the central highlands—a census which revealed that many Indians had already fled the region in despair.[45] Furthermore, as Spanish landowners expanded their holdings in the Grijalva basin after 1750, a growing proportion of native people found permanent refuge as *laboríos* (sharecroppers) and *mozos* (Table 16).

Given this state of affairs, it is useful to examine the ways in which such events shaped and transformed the lives of Indians in two important Tzotzil communities, Zinacantan and Chamula. Because of its strategic location along the royal highway between Ciudad Real and Chiapa, we know that Zinacantan attracted Spanish settlement from the very beginning of colonial rule. As early as 1540, Pedro de Estrada had already established both a *trapiche* and an *estancia* (called El Burrero) there; by 1600, his descendant, Luis Alfonso de Estrada, was raising 30 mules and 200 horses on the property.[46] By that time, too, Cristóbal Arías, an Indian from Zinacantan, had obtained permission to create his own *estancia* on lands which had formerly belonged to his unfortunate community.[47] As for the value of such farms, in 1651 El Burrero was sold for 1,000 pesos, half of which was paid to the monastery of San Francisco (where Luis Alfonso's son Luis had founded a *capellanía*).[48] Thereafter, as the demand for mules and wheat grew during the following century, the number of *labores* in Zinacantan rose from two to five.[49] And when in 1750 one of these properties was sold to the *alférez* of Ciudad Real, it brought the respectable sum of 2,314 pesos—payable, of course, in the form of *censos* (mortgages) held by various convents and religious groups.[50]

By contrast, Chamula escaped direct settlement and loss of territory. True enough, after 1590 various settlers had obtained *composiciones* and had created several *estancias de ganado* on communal lands. But altitude and unfavorable terrain conspired

TABLE 16.
Laboríos and Mozos in Chiapas, 1817
(number of families)

| District | Mozos | Laboríos |
|---|---|---|
| Zapaluta (Comitán) | 140 | 100 |
| La Frailesca (Comitán) | 9 | 0 |
| Comitán | 0 | 467 |
| Cuxtepeques (Llanos) | 0 | 111 |
| Ocosingo | 103 | 85 |
| Cintalapa (Jiquipulas) | 90 | 181 |
| Jiquipulas | 14 | 18 |
| Ixtapa and Bochil (Ciudad Real) | 0 | 42 |
| Chiapa | 0 | 32 |
| Zoques | 0 | 72 |
| Total | 356 | 1,108 |

Source: "Padrón de los tributarios de Chiapa" (1817).

to frustrate such ambitions, and by the late 18th century, only a single *estancia*, Yalchitóm, continued to function; the others had effectively been reincorporated into the town's *fundo legal* (public land).

Deprived of their more fertile lands, Indians in Zinacantan turned to a variety of occupations in order to meet their *repartimientos*. Although they continued to grow maize and beans on rocky hillsides, contemporary reports suggest that by 1750 they survived primarily as *cargadores* (bearers) and *arrieros* (muledrivers) in the employ of Spanish merchants and landowners. More occasionally, they seem to have accepted merchandise on consignment from *comerciantes* in Ciudad Real, which they then peddled throughout the province.[51] Even so, poverty was the general rule: in 1749, the town's *justicias* asked the Crown to grant them a portion of their tribute to repair the local church, which several years earlier had collapsed.[52] Such petitions, in fact, were frequent during the late 18th century: in 1788, community officials once again solicited royal aid to reconstruct their

TABLE 17.
Cofradías in Zinacantan, 1793

|  | Capital | Number of funciones | Contribución |
|---|---|---|---|
| Santísimo Sacramento | 162½ pesos | 7 | 35 pesos |
| Santa Vera Cruz | 184 | 9 | 42 |
| Nuestra Señora del Rosario | 240 | 7 and 12 monthly masses | 44 |
| Santo Domingo | 203½ | 5 and 4 monthly masses | 33 |
| Benditas Almas de Purgatorio | 200 | 2 and 12 monthly masses | 31 |
| Total |  |  | 185 pesos |

Source: "Informe de la parroquia de Zinacantan" (1793).

cabildo and mesón; in addition, they requested (and received) permission to use funds from their caja de comunidad to ward off imminent starvation.[53] By way of contrast, parish priests took special pains to ensure that the town's cofradías possessed sufficient capital to yield a good income. As in other highland pueblos, Zinacanteco cofrades were required to borrow these funds at 5 percent annual interest, which they repaid each year to support public festivals. By 1793, therefore, five such cofradías, each headed by four mayordomos and endowed with around 200 pesos, functioned in Zinacantan (Table 17). Whatever difficulties they may have encountered in making ends meet, these cofrades (and their wives, the prioras de taza) paid their cura a handsome stipend of 185 pesos for 58 masses and processions celebrated in their honor.

It is perhaps surprising that domestic life in Zinacantan was organized largely around small family units which for the most part functioned in semi-isolation from their neighbors. Not that such people were separated by great physical distances; on the contrary, with the exception of a few families who may have worked the salt springs at Salinas (located about half-way be-

TABLE 18.
The Population of Zinacantan, 1611–1816

|  | 1611 | 1749 | 1778 | 1816 |
|---|---|---|---|---|
| Number of inhabitants | 1,130 | 1,169 | 1,188 | 2,269 |
|  | 1637–41 | 1689–93 | 1736–40 | 1786–90 |
| Crude birthrate ($\%$/year) | 5.6[a] | 3.8 | 7.1 | 8.1[a] |
|  |  | 1611–1749 | 1749–78 | 1778–1816 |
| Net growth rate ($\%$/year) |  | .02 | .06 | 1.72 |

Sources: E. Pineda, "Descripción geográfica"; "Padrón y nueva cuenta de los tributarios del pueblo de Zinacantan, provincia de Chiapa" (1749), AGGG, Serie Chiapas, A3.16.4509.353; Polanco, "Estado de los vasallos"; "Padrón de los tributarios de Zinacantan," (1816), ibid., A3.16.3.4169.309.

[a] Estimate.

tween Ciudad Real and Ixtapa on the *camino real*), virtually all Zinacantecos lived within the main town.[54] Nonetheless, household heads (usually married men) bore primary responsibility for tribute payments and *repartimientos*; if they defaulted, the entire *pueblo* (not individual relatives) bore the additional burden. Furthermore, access to land and other resources was determined not by family membership, but rather by communal residence— a fact which placed sharp limitations on the value of family ties. Strained by early death and sudden flight or prolonged absence, such ties in any case were difficult to maintain. Then, too, throughout most of the colonial period the town's population remained fairly small and grew very slowly (Table 18).

The effects of such pressures on family organization were clearly visible in the 1749 *padrón*. Of the 450 households recorded in this census, most consisted of married couples with one or two children (Table 19). Unlike modern Zinacantecos, such people do not seem to have maintained close bonds even with near

TABLE 19.
Zinacanteco Households, 1749

| | Number of Households | Percentage | Number of Children (average) |
|---|---|---|---|
| Married couples | 397 | 85% | 1.6 |
| Widows | 27 | 6 | 1.6 |
| Widowers | 11 | 2 | 1.6 |
| Unmarried men and women | 14 | 3 | |
| Orphans | 10 | 2 | |
| Huidos[a] | 10 | 2 | |
| Total | 469 | 100% | |

Source: "Padrón y nueva cuenta de los tributarios de Zinacantan" (1749).

[a] Households of men who had fled the community.

relatives or immediate ancestors: only a small number of adults (2.6 people on the average) shared the same pair of surnames (Spanish and Tzotzil); in practice, this number ranged narrowly from one to six. In effect, therefore, such groups included perhaps two or three siblings (Indian women inherited both of their paternal surnames, e.g., Pérez Icaltzi: "Pérez Blackdog") or a father and two married children. But within a single generation, these children apparently emigrated or acquired new Tzotzil names—probably in order to distinguish them from older domestic units. And finally, a significant proportion of these families (6 percent) were headed by women—usually young widows who had outlived their husbands.

Interestingly enough, beginning around 1780 this situation underwent a dramatic, indeed a radical change. As the demand for native workers on lowland fincas rose, Zinacantecos who might otherwise have abandoned their community established new settlements on uninhabited land overlooking the Grijalva basin.[55] At the same time, as Figure 1 suggests, epidemics and excessive repartimientos had taken their toll of at least one major source of native laboríos: the Chiapanecas. As the number of

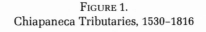

FIGURE 1.
Chiapaneca Tributaries, 1530–1816

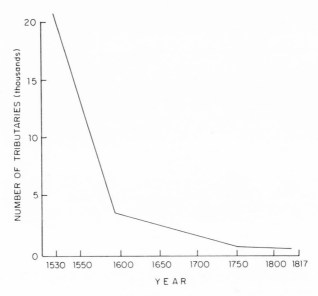

new estates in Chiapa and Acala (i.e., the area adjacent to Zina-cantan) grew from 6 to 25, then, Zinacantecos found ready em-ployment as sharecroppers, tenants, peons, and *jornaleros* (day laborers). In this way, for example, men and women from Sali-nas moved to Muk'ta Jok', where they obtained work on ranches in Chiapa and Ixtapa. By 1819, in fact, more than half of the local population lived in such hamlets (Table 20). Among those fam-ilies which remained in the *pueblo,* many men worked as *ar-rieros* and traders rather than fieldhands.

Naturally, changing patterns of work and residence also brought about substantial modifications in family structure and organization. As mortality rates among *laboríos* and seasonal workers rose during these years, the proportion of households headed by women tripled. Even so, most Zinacantecos, like other Indians in the relatively remote *tierra fría* part of the highlands (which included those communities closest to Ciudad Real), ex-

TABLE 20.
The Population of Zinacantan, 1819

| Locality | Inhabitants |
| --- | --- |
| *cabecera* (main town) | 1,102 |
| Na Chij | 63 |
| X'ukun | 68 |
| Gur | 27 |
| Sagchaguo | 82 |
| Hacienda de San Pedro | 25 |
| Trapiche de la Merced | 19 |
| Hacienda de San Antonio | 27 |
| Hacienda de Nandayageli | 49 |
| Potogtig | 93 |
| Jok' Ch'enom | 90 |
| Topolguó | 18 |
| Muk'ta Jok' | 381 |
| Jitogtig | 59 |
| Nichim | 30 |
| Ycalum | 20 |
| Jipuyum | 53 |
| Apas | 63 |
| Total in community | 2,269 |
| Total outside of *pueblo* | 1,167 |

*Sources:* "Sobre reducir a poblado a los oriundos de la zona de Zinacantan que viven dispersos por los montes," (1819), AGGG, Serie Chiapas, A1.12.274.19; "Padrón de los tributarios de Zinacantan" (1816).

perienced less disruption than did their counterparts in places like Ocosingo and San Bartolomé—that is, in towns where the native people were incorporated directly into the landless labor force (Table 21). In such places, fully one-third of the Indian households were without adult men.

In contrast to Zinacantan, native people in Chamula did not lose their most valuable lands during the 17th and 18th centuries. Land in Chamula, except in a few places, did not lend itself to commercial farming or animal husbandry. Even so, beginning in

TABLE 21.
Proportion of Households Headed by Women in Central Chiapas, 1778

| Zone | Town | Total Households | Headed by Women | Average Number of Children per Household |
|------|------|------------------|-----------------|------------------------------------------|
| *tierra fría* | | | | |
| (highlands) | Cancuc | 107 | 26.2% | 3.53 |
| | Chamula | 375 | 20.5 | 2.30 |
| | Huistán | 125 | 14.4 | 1.80 |
| | Oxchuc | 335 | 17.6 | 2.80 |
| | San Andrés | 176 | 22.7 | 1.26 |
| | Magdalena | 92 | 21.7 | 1.84 |
| | Santa Marta | 44 | 15.9 | 2.57 |
| | San Martín | 68 | 30.9 | 2.04 |
| | San Miguel | 84 | 22.6 | 3.99 |
| | San Pablo | 99 | 22.2 | 2.93 |
| | San Pedro | 207 | 16.9 | 2.61 |
| | Santiago | 37 | 24.3 | 2.05 |
| | Tenejapa | 346 | 11.8 | 2.29 |
| | Tenango | 46 | 23.9 | 1.87 |
| | Zinacantan | 276 | 19.9 | 2.52 |
| *tierra caliente* | | | | |
| (lowlands) | Aguacatenango | 66 | 27.3 | 1.64 |
| | Amatenango | 159 | 39.1 | 1.98 |
| | Bachajón | 129 | 26.3 | 1.60 |
| | Chilón | 34 | 26.5 | 1.44 |
| | Guaquitepec | 69 | 31.8 | 1.19 |
| | Ixtapa | 68 | 38.2 | 2.03 |
| | Ocosingo | 244 | 29.9 | 2.58 |
| | Palenque | 35 | 24.4 | 1.00 |
| | Petalsingo | 87 | 27.6 | 2.83 |
| | Pinola | 129 | 31.8 | 2.07 |
| | San Bartolomé | 1,031 | 31.8 | 2.57 |
| | San Lucas | 81 | 38.3 | 2.75 |
| | Sibacá | 100 | 32.0 | 1.98 |
| | Sitalá | 93 | 30.1 | 1.53 |
| | Socoltenango | 101 | 34.6 | 2.37 |
| | Soyatitán | 90 | 40.0 | 2.54 |

(continued)

TABLE 21. *(continued)*
Proportion of Households Headed by Women in Central Chiapas, 1778

| Zone | Town | Total Households | Headed by Women | Average Number of Children per Household |
|------|------|------------------|-----------------|------------------------------------------|
| | Teopisca | 105 | 31.8 | 1.57 |
| | Tila | 358 | 34.3 | 2.28 |
| | Totolapa | 102 | 36.3 | 1.97 |
| | Tumbalá | 323 | 31.9 | 1.88 |
| | Yajalón | 182 | 33.0 | 1.04 |
| Average of all towns | | | 27.9% | 2.14% |
| Average of highlands | | | 20.8% | 2.42% |
| Average of lowlands | | | 32.7% | 1.99% |

*Source:* Polanco, "Estado de los vasallos."

1763 the people of Chamula were afflicted with a particularly onerous burden in the person of their acquisitive and unscrupulous vicar, José Ordoñez y Aguiar. Within a year of his arrival, Ordoñez had persuaded the *audiencia* to grant him a *repartimiento de indios* in order to set up a *trapiche* in the Grijalva basin,[56] and he vastly inflated the fees that native *cofrades* and *alféreces* paid for public festivals (Table 22). Not content with these measures, however, or with his modest salary of 300 pesos (plus 6 *reales* for each mass that he celebrated), he also required local men and women to pay for services which—in theory at least—were exempt from such charges.[57] As if such imposts were not enough, he also demanded that everyone in the community—not just local officials—provide him with corn, beans, lambs, chickens, eggs, and extra money to supplement his living allowance (Table 23). So determined was he to use these *contribuciones* for his own purposes, in fact, that for a number of years he concealed his true income from his ecclesiastical superiors. When he was caught, he argued coolly that he had used the money to buy such items as wax and sacramental wine—items which his parishioners had in reality purchased.[58] Eventually, of

TABLE 22.
Old and New Schedule of Parish Fees in Chamula, 1779

| Fiesta | Old Fees Cash[a] | Other | New Fees Cash[a] | Other |
|---|---|---|---|---|
| San Sebastián | 15 | | 30 | 5 lambs |
| Semana Santa | 100 | | 240 | 16 lambs |
| San Juan | 50 | 12 lambs | 100 | 6 lambs |
| Santa Rosa | 15 | | 30 | 6 lambs |
| San Nicolás y San Mateo | 30 | | 60 | 1 hen |
| San Pablo | 5 | | 11½ | 1 hen |
| San José | 0 | | 3 | 1 hen |
| San Pedro Martir | 0 | | 3 | 1 hen |
| Santa Cruz | 0 | | 3 | 1 hen |
| Santisima Trinidad | 0 | | 3 | 1 hen |
| San Antonio | 0 | | 3 | 1 hen |
| San Pedro Apóstol | 5 | | 13½ | 1 hen |
| Santa María Magdalena | 0 | | 3 | 1 hen |
| Santiago | 0 | | 3 | 1 hen |
| San Cristóbal | 0 | | 3 | 1 hen |
| Santa Ana | 0 | | 3 | 1 hen |
| San Jacinto | 0 | | 3 | 1 hen |
| San Bartolomé | 0 | | 3 | 1 hen |
| San Agustín | 0 | | 3 | 1 hen |
| San Miguel | 0 | | 3 | 1 hen |
| San Dionisio | 0 | | 3 | 1 hen |
| San Lucas | 0 | | 3 | 1 hen |
| Santa Catalina | 0 | | 3 | 1 hen |
| Santa Lucía | 0 | | 3 | 1 hen |
| San Juan Evangelista | 0 | | 3 | 1 hen |
| Todos Santos | — | 60 lambs | 0 | 400 lambs 46 sheep |
| Total | 220 | 72 lambs | 539 | 433 lambs 46 sheep 21 hens |

Source: "Instancia de los indios de Chamula de la provincia de Ciudad Real sobre que su cura, don Josef Ordoñez, los grava con derechos y contribuciones excesivas," (1779), AHDSC.

[a] Tostones.

TABLE 23.
Limosnas and Contribuciones Received by the Vicar of Chamula, 1789

| Town | Misas de cofradías | Fees (pesos) | Festividades de alféreces | Fees (pesos) | Other Cash[a] | Total (pesos) | Lambs | Hens | Maize (fanegas) |
|---|---|---|---|---|---|---|---|---|---|
| Chamula | 47 | 108½ | 53 | 220½ | 312 | 641 | 80 | 71 | 30 |
| San Miguel and Sta. Catarina | 12 | 28¾ | 15 | 82¾ | 43 | 154½ | | 10 | 24 |
| San Pedro | 19 | 36¼ | 18 | 70½ | 83½ | 190¼ | | 15 | 44 |
| San Pablo | 25 | 47 | 18 | 94¼ | 139 | 280¼ | | 18 | 27 |
| San Andrés | 22 | 44¼ | 44 | 166¼ | 184½ | 395 | | 32 | 56 |
| Santiago | 11 | 25¾ | 11 | 42½ | 51 | 119¼ | | 12 | 19 |
| Sta. Marta | 19 | 43¾ | 14 | 56½ | 79½ | 179¾ | | 11 | 21 |
| Magdalena | 19 | 42 | 17 | 76 | 93½ | 211½ | | 12 | 41 |
| Total | 174 | 376¼ | 190 | 809¼ | 986 | 2,171½ | 80 | 181 | 262 |

Source: "Estado que manifiesta las festividades que se celebran al año en los pueblos del curato de Chamula," (1789), AHDSC.
[a] Semana Santa, sustento, mantas, frijoles, wine, and candles.

course, he was ordered to share his dubious gains with the cathedral chapter in Ciudad Real—but not before he had appealed the matter to both the *curia metropolitana* (archbishop's court) and the *audiencia* in Guatemala.[59] And finally, as we know, Ordoñez also organized a system of forced labor which was so exacting that it brought him into direct conflict with the *alcalde mayor*, Ortíz de Avilés. Little wonder, then, that by 1779 Ordoñez's possessions included not only the *trapiche* which he had built in 1763 but two highland farms and four *haciendas* as well.[60]

Naturally, Indians in Chamula and its *anexos* protested against this treatment and petitioned to have Ordoñez removed. Led by their *gobernador*, they even succeeded on two occasions in expelling him from the *pueblo*. Rather than permit such a precedent to be established, however, Bishop Polanco at first urged and later required that they take him back. Reluctantly, they agreed—but not before they had stolen the priest's *cuadrante* (parish accounts) and then dispersed into the surrounding hills.[61] For his part, having reinstalled himself in his vicarage, Ordoñez played what he knew was his safest card: in 1778, he arrested a number of civil and religious officials in San Andrés for idolatry.[62] Naturally, Polanco was forced to take some action in this matter, which threatened to provoke a major reaction throughout the region. Preferring discretion to an intemperate display of zeal, he appointed Tomás Luis de Roca, a Dominican friar who was not fond of Ordoñez, to investigate the charges. Roca began his inquiry by questioning the local priest, Nicolás Morales, Ordoñez's deputy in San Andrés, from whom he learned that the Indians in several towns, apparently hoping to avoid Ordoñez's burial fees, had for some time interred their dead in a cave known as Sacumchen. Furthermore, Morales declared, "In this cave they have hidden an idol or statue which they worshipped in pagan times, and which was mentioned by the illustrious Sr. Núñez in his ninth pastoral letter, by the name of *Poxlom, Potolán, Tzihuitzin,* or *Hicalahau,* all of which [Morales] had been told by the person who led him there."[63] As for the prisoners, they admitted only that they had prayed there from time to time for aid and good fortune. Satisfied that nothing particularly heretical had transpired, Roca asked Morales if he cared to amend his previous testimony. In fact, the priest replied, he did: as it turned out, he had never heard of *Poxlom* or *Hicalahau* until Ordoñez had read to him from an old copy of Núñez's *Constituciones.*

From this incident, it becomes clear that by the late 18th century, native forms of worship had diverged almost completely from Spanish practices, that two distinct forms of Christianity coexisted in the highlands. On the one hand, parish priests like Nicolás Morales and José Ordoñez utilized their churches as tax-collection posts, warehouses, and even debtors' prisons; on the other hand, native *cofrades* and *alféreces*, charged with the nearly irreconcilable tasks of supporting these pastors and obtaining divine grace, sought a special kind of saintly intercession. Listen, for example, to the testimony which one young official, Lorenzo Hernández K'elpixol, gave to Roca:

> Five or six years ago, when I was *alférez de pasión*, I went to the cave and asked the angel of Sacumchen for good luck, because that is the custom in this town. Sacumchen is like the head of our *pueblo*: it sustains us, second only to God Himself. In Chamula they have a *paraje* called Calvary, where they do the same things. . . . I lit two candles and burned some amber and a few small pine branches, and then I prayed, "Help me, divine spirit, saintly captain, so that I will have good weather during my *fiesta!*" Everyone who is responsible for the *fiestas* does this.[64]

Similarly, another witness, Lucas López Nikaxlan, declared that one of his neighbors, Felipe Díaz (who also served as *alférez* of San Andrés),

> continued to pass on the teachings of Diego González (now dead), which are the teachings of our ancestors. Once he took me to the cave with him and we beat ourselves 30 times with whips. . . . On several occasions we lit candles and incense, and when we did this we took the cross which is kept inside the cave and placed it outside or . . . set it apart from us. . . .[65]

Upon taking up such matters with Morales, in fact, Roca was

informed that activities of this sort occurred throughout the region. "In this town alone," Morales told him,

> there are two more *adoratorios* that I know of . . . and another in Santiago which I haven't seen; in Santa Marta there is a *paraje* which is also quite well known to the superstitious, and two other places which the *padre vicario* has already searched, as well as one in Chamula which he has not. . . . When I was a seminarian I used to go to Zinacantan, where in a place called Niguoó [Ni Vo'] they light candles and incense and sacrifice chickens; in Salinas, and at a spot called Large Rock (above the road to Ciudad Real), they do similar things. . . .[66]

Far from trying to abolish such practices, it seems, Morales and his colleagues had learned to tolerate and perhaps even to encourage them—except in times of political uncertainty.

## CONCLUSIONS

In 1790, a series of *cédulas* abolished the position of *alcalde mayor* in Chiapas and established a new form of civil administration, the *intendencia.* Unlike their predecessors, *intendentes* did not purchase public office, nor did they engage in trade or commerce. Instead, they supervised the collection of taxes and tribute, acted as appellate judges, and engaged in routine affairs of government. Similarly, their deputies, the *subdelegados,* relieved local *ayuntamientos* of their responsibilities as tax collectors.[67] Naturally, such measures brought about the total collapse of commercial crops like cacao and cochineal, which had been produced largely with forced labor. In 1819, for example, the Sociedad Económica de Ciudad Real (a sort of merchants' association) complained that "with the establishment of *intendencias,* the . . . *alcaldes mayores* were dismissed and the *repartimientos* were abolished. For want of such devices, the Indians have now sunk into backwardness and inactivity."[68] For his part, upon arriving in Ciudad Real, Agustín de las Cuentas Zayas, the province's first *intendente,* declared that

> Within a short time I recognized the decadence into which these
> provinces had fallen, filled with poverty, wanting for industry and
> commerce. . . . Virtually all of the churches in the [Tzotzil] district
> . . . need general repairs, not only of their buildings but also of
> their ornaments and other indispensable things. In the Tzeltal
> area the same thing is true. . . .[69]

In these passages, repeated in countless official documents of the
day, we recognize the origins of a second Black Legend, a legend
which characterized official attitudes toward highland communities for generations to come: removed from the mainstream of
economic life, such *pueblos* were condemned to eternal isolation
and impoverishment—a state of affairs which might end only
when native labor could be put to more gainful use.

What de las Cuentas saw, of course, was not a region that had
remained outside the mainstream of economic life, but rather a
region that for nearly 300 years had been systematically pillaged
and decapitalized. Consider the case of Yalchitóm, the *estancia*
in Chamula. After milking this property until it would produce
no more, its owner, a prominent *vecino* in Ciudad Real, arranged
with provincial authorities to sell his worn-out and dilapidated
ranch to local Indians for twice its assessed value.[70] By the time
de las Cuentas arrived in Chiapas, however, compulsion of this
sort had given way to an economic order which placed much less
emphasis upon direct coercion and relied to a much greater degree upon wages and tenancy. For instance, commenting upon
the reasons which had led many Zinacantecos to abandon their
town, in 1819 their parish priest wrote that "they do not possess
enough land in the *ejidos* and unclaimed areas around their
*pueblo* . . . because those which they own are absolutely ster-
ile. . . ." As a result, such people fell easy prey to lowland ranchers "who desire to have *mozos* on their *haciendas* and farms, as
well as *baldíos* to work as day laborers; these *baldíos* are attracted by offers of housing and other things which convince them to
stay and increase their number every day."[71]

Driven by landlessness or unemployment, men and women
from communities overlooking the Grijalva basin—communities
like Teopisca, Amatenango, Totolapa, and San Bartolomé—ac-

cepted their new fate with resignation. Within a generation or two, they were no longer counted as Indians: in 1778, Polanco had found only 527 *mestizos* in this area; by 1819, this figure had risen miraculously to over 2,800.[72] Similarly, in Ocosingo (where fully two-thirds of the indigenous population worked as *mozos* on private estates), the number of people listed as *mestizos* or *mulatos* had increased between 1778 and 1797 by 150 percent![73] Thereafter, all such people were referred to simply as *ladinos*; they spoke Spanish, organized their own *cofradías*, and formed a distinct ethnic and social category.

As for Indians in *tierra fría*, they performed quite a different role in the province's economy. Permitted in most cases to retain their land, they produced many of the children who subsequently moved onto lowland plantations. Even in 1778, families in the highest communities were significantly larger than their counterparts in *tierra caliente*, and fewer of them were headed by widows. Beneath the shift in ethnic affiliation, therefore, beneath the emerging divisions among Indian towns at different elevations, we may clearly discern the emergence of a new social class, a class of agricultural laborers bereft of all communal ties.

Of course, it would be a mistake to suppose that native people everywhere in the highlands were incorporated into this new workforce. On the contrary, in places such as Chamula, Tenejapa, Oxchuc, and Huistán—that is, in areas which lay outside the major zones of commercial expansion—these people turned not to wage labor but to subsistence farming, small-scale horticulture, or itinerant peddling. Not surprisingly, they also rejected whatever novel forms of exploitation provincial authorities devised for them. In 1791, for example, Bishop Olivares y Benito founded a school of spinning and weaving in Teopisca so that local girls might make profitable use of their idle hours. To his great consternation, most Indians refused to send their children to the school. "For a piece of *manta*," they told the *subdelegado*, "our daughters will not be made slaves to the *señor obispo*."[74] In matters of religion, too, they insisted on less meddling from colonial officials. As a result, ecclesiastical authorities modified their views of native *fiestas*, which they had labored so diligently to organize and against which they now inveighed with equal piety and zeal. "This is the ruination of the Zinacantecos," wrote one priest to Bishop San Martín y Cuevas in a passage which might have referred to any highland town,

> living dispersed about the world, their *pueblo* in ruins. Each day they encounter more hardships or contract more debts because of the continuous *fiestas* which they celebrate during the year and which involve indescribable costs, principally for liquor. There are Indians who by virtue of their position as *alférez* must provide food and drink for most of the town during each function of the saints . . . and who purchase 10 or 12 barrels a year. . . .[75]

As long as these *alféreces* continued to pay their alms and dues, however, Church officials begrudgingly accepted such excesses. And finally, when intervention in local affairs became too heavy-handed or clumsy—as it did in Yajalón in 1819—native people responded by moving away or by forming an angry mob.[76] Indeed, it was the likelihood of these two events, which occurred with almost unbroken frequency throughout the following years, that colored class relations in the region and gave them their peculiar tone.

# THE LAST FRONTIER
## Rebellion and Revival in
## the Liberal Century
### 1821–1910

Like the conquest, Chiapas' independence from Spain and its subsequent incorporation into Mexico (1824) left deep impressions upon native life and society. By 1821, the edifice of colonial domination, grown topheavy and weak, was unable to withstand the forces which closed in upon it. Preferring a creole monarchy to a Spanish republic, the country's clergy eagerly embraced the notion of an independent Mexico—a decision which they soon regretted. For the next 50 years, Liberals and Conservatives— both members of the landowning aristocracy—jockeyed for control of native land and labor. In fact, it was precisely this state of affairs which discouraged the American traveler John L. Stephens (who visited Chiapas in 1840), from proceeding to San Cristóbal. "War was again in our way," he wrote, "and while all the rest of Mexico is quiet, [the southeast was] in a state of revolution."[1] From his description, it becomes clear that independence from Spain did not immediately alter the conditions in which indigenous people lived. By the time he arrived in Chiapas, the province had experienced both nationhood and annexation to Mexico, empire and republic, federalism and centralism—all without modifying the creole-dominated social order. In those euphoric days after the Treaty of Córdova, Liberal politicians throughout the country had declared that all Mexicans were—in principle at least—equal. To the north and west, in Yucatán and central Mexico, they even spoke of transforming the *castas* into true social classes. In Chiapas too, though they accepted the existence of special privileges among their own kind, the Liberals appeared anxious to apply such measures to Indian society. And to insure the means to carry out their program, they continued to collect a sort of native tribute (the head tax or *capitación*) and to favor indigenous servitude.

Not surprisingly, these new creole rulers soon enclosed and entitled the choicest Indian lands, on which they created vast *haciendas* and cattle ranches. Freed from the interference of greedy governors and supported by British, French, and later American investors, they cultivated export crops which toward the end of the century reached 15 million dollars in value.[2] In matters of local administration, too, they introduced dramatic and wide-ranging reforms. Enunciating a secular version of the Black Legend, for example, the priest in Chamula observed in 1830 that "All of these towns are governed by *ayuntamientos* composed exclusively of Indians who, although one may find a scribe with the title of secretary who knows how to read and write, possess no other element which qualifies them to enforce the laws and the duties which these impose." More reprehensible still, such difficulties revealed the state of degradation and moral torpor into which his flock had fallen:

> Surely it is for this reason that [these towns] are now in a state of complete neglect, though we may not blame them entirely for this situation, since they have been raised from a very early age in an environment of general ignorance and stupidity, without recognizing any other authority than that of their depraved customs, inherited from their elders, which in themselves reveal why they are incapable of greater progress and are apt for all manner of vices which degrade and bestialize them more and more, leading them to their complete ruin.[3]

Inspired by civic duty and a natural concern for orderly government, therefore, by 1840 Liberals and Conservatives alike had succeeded in imposing their own system of administration upon native communities.[4] And despite the fact that such *municipios* supposedly enjoyed some measure of autonomy or indepen-

dence in local affairs, in reality their officers were closely supervised by non-Indian *secretarios* and *jefes políticos* who governed
the area's numerous political districts.

Like their civil counterparts, clergymen in Chiapas quickly
learned to live with the new ideologies and institutions. During
the state's first federalist regime (1824–1835), for example, the
cathedral chapter published a vigorous defense both of Mexican
independence and of Governor Joaquín Gutiérrez's economic
program. By 1830, too, all but a few of the area's parishes had
been secularized.[5] In place of the regular orders (which remained politically conservative until they were abolished 30
years later), worldly priests such as Padre Solís, whom Stephens
met in Sotaná, occupied these benefices. In many cases, such
priests had openly enlisted in the Liberal cause: the *cura* of
Palenque had been chastized by his superiors in the hopes that
he would recant his distasteful views; and his colleague in Yajalón, a prominent federalist politician, had served as Chiapas'
deputy to the national congress.

> He had bourne an active part in all the convulsions of the country
> from the time of the revolution against Spain, of which he had
> been an instigator, and ever since, to the scandal of the Church
> party, stood forth as a Liberal; he had played the soldier as well as
> the priest, laying down his blood-stained sword after a battle to
> confess the wounded and the dying; twice wounded, once chroni-
> cled among the killed, an exile in Guatemala, and with the gradu-
> al recovery of the Liberal party restored to his place.[6]

To be sure, not all local *presbíteros* supported such principles
and took arms in their defense. In particular, the regular orders,
with their enormous landholdings and wide-ranging involve-
ments, became increasingly hostile to federalist administrations.
Liberal politicians throughout the 1840s and 1850s in order to
defuse such opposition, pledged to uphold the Catholic faith
"without toleration of any other." By forswearing the anticleri-
calism which prevailed elsewhere in Mexico, then, they were
able to concentrate upon the more urgent tasks of mobilizing
native labor and exploiting native land.

## THE PLANTERS' PROGRESS

In 1819 the curate of Zinacantan complained that landowners in Chiapa, Acala, and Chiapilla had recruited Indians from his parish to work as *mozos* and sharecroppers on their properties. Ten years later, according to his successor, Zinacantan had lost 400 more inhabitants.[7] During this period the number of *laboríos* residing in Acala and Chiapilla rose from 90 to 300 and seven estates were founded in Totolapa and San Lucas, doubling the population of those nearly-deserted towns.[8] But such changes, startling as they might at first appear, merely set the stage for a much more dramatic series of social and economic upheavals.

Beginning in 1826, and again in 1827, 1828, and 1832, the state government, bankrupt and disorganized, encouraged landowners to denounce and entitle native *ejidos* and common lands.[9] In this way, public officials hoped that they might meet the taxes and levies which national authorities constantly imposed upon them. By 1838, the number of estates within the former Chiapaneca region had risen from about 25 to 41. In the central and southern parts of the Grijalva basin, this figure had increased from around 50 to 167.[10] After 1844, however, surveying procedures were simplified until virtually anyone with the right political connections might acquire such lands. Spurred by these measures, local *hacendados* proceeded to entitle virtually the entire valley. In fact, so successful were they in occupying unused territories that nine years later Santa Anna's own administrator in Chiapas, Fernando Nicolás Maldonado, refused to deprive Liberal opponents of their new acquisitions.[11] And when this task had been accomplished, land-hungry ranchers moved out into the scrubby, unwatered plains to the west and northeast. By the end of the Porfiriato, this area, embracing the departments of Comitán, Chiapa, and La Libertad, contained 2,318 *fincas rústicas*—fully one-quarter of the state's rural properties (Table 24).[12]

What caused agriculture in the Grijalva valley to expand so rapidly during the 19th century, and particularly after 1832? We know that at first cattle ranching, combined with a little sugar production, sustained the region's economy and provided the

TABLE 24.
Fincas Rústicas in Chiapas, 1909

| Department | Haciendas | Ranchos | Others | Total | Percentage in State |
|---|---|---|---|---|---|
| Comitán | 143 | 905 | 72 | 1,120 | 11% |
| Chiapa[a] | 130 | 232 | 528 | 890 | 8 |
| Chilón | 82 | 167 | 264 | 513 | 5 |
| Las Casas[b] | 0 | 348 | 3 | 351 | 3 |
| La Libertad[c] | 77 | 98 | 133 | 308 | 3 |
| Mezcalapa | 19 | 310 | 349 | 678 | 6 |
| Mariscal | 32 | 73 | 116 | 221 | 2 |
| Pichucalco | 208 | 572 | 461 | 1,241 | 12 |
| Palenque | 73 | 318 | 23 | 414 | 4 |
| Soconusco | 240 | 1,568 | 232 | 2,040 | 19 |
| Simojovel | 53 | 170 | 195 | 418 | 4 |
| Tuxtla | 33 | 308 | 1,316 | 1,657 | 16 |
| Tonalá | 30 | 673 | 50 | 753 | 7 |
| Total | 1,120 | 5,742 | 3,742 | 10,604 | 100% |

Sources: Gobierno del Estado de Chiapas, Anuario estadístico, p. 52; Enrique Santibáñez, Geografía regional de Chiapas, pp. 47–49.
[a] Including the municipios of Acala, Chiapa, Chiapilla, Ixtapa, Osumacinta, San Gabriel, Soyaló, Villa Corzo, and Villa Flores.
[b] Including the municipios of Amatenango, Chamula, Chanal, Huistán, Magdalena, Nuevo León, San Andrés, San Cristóbal, San Felipe, San Miguel Mitontic, Santa Marta, Santiago, San Pedro Chenalhó, Tenejapa, Teopisca, and Zinacantan.
[c] Including the municipios of Aguacatenango, La Concordia, San Bartolomé, San Diego la Reforma, Soyatitán, and Totolapa.

capital which local merchants used in smuggling. Significantly, according to Stephens, after independence much of this illicit commerce was redirected from Villahermosa to Comitán. "It is a place of considerable trade," he wrote,

> and has become so by the effect of bad laws; for in consequence of the heavy duties on regular importations at the Mexican ports of entry, most of the European goods consumed in this region are smuggled in from Balize [sic] and Guatimala [sic]. The proceeds of confiscations and the perquisites of officers are such an important

item of revenue that the officers are vigilant, and the day before
we arrived 20 or 30 mule-loads that had been seized were brought
to Comitán; but the profits are so large that smuggling is a regular
business. . . .[13]

As the century wore on, however, the composition of agricultural activities in the Grijalva basin began to change. Increased
international demand for sugar prompted many landowners to
expand their cane fields. By 1909, over 1,000 metric tons of sugarcane (yielding 11.5 metric tons of semi-refined sugar and 1,000
hectoliters of *aguardiente*) were produced in central Chiapas.[14]

But it was not the sugar industry which eventually transformed this area into a prosperous agricultural heartland. After
1875 local *hacendados* turned their attention to another, more
lucrative venture: cotton production. Whereas sugarcane could
be sold at only 1 centavo per kilogram (elaborated sugar brought
2.5 centavos), a kilo of cotton brought 10 centavos. Responding to
such inducements, the area's landowners had by 1909 increased
their production to 1,219 metric tons—93 percent of Chiapas'
total cotton harvest. Similarly, indigo, which a century earlier
could be found only in Tonalá and along the Tabasco border,
enjoyed a renewed burst of popularity among local farmers. In
the early 1900s, as the price of indigo reached 2 pesos per kilo,
they planted 35.5 metric tons of this commodity. Other export
crops, cultivated in abundance, brought them additional profits:
rice (at 15 centavos per kilo), peanuts (at 5 pesos per hectoliter)
and coffee (of which 583 metric tons were harvested in 1909).
Moreover, 46 percent of the valley's surface continued to support
large herds of cattle. All in all, as the 19th century drew to a
close, these enterprises absorbed approximately one-fifth of the
state's total agricultural capital.[15]

But despite such wealth and prosperity, the Grijalva valley
represented only one of several regions which in the final quarter of the 19th century underwent rapid and dramatic expansion.
To the north, in Pichucalco, creole landlords also denounced and
entitled Indian lands on a large scale; by 1909, this area had
almost as many large *haciendas* as central Chiapas. For the most
part, landowners in Pichucalco, like their colonial predecessors,

cultivated cacao—two-thirds of the country's entire crop, according to one contemporary geographer.[16] Between 1883 and 1909, as the price of cacao rose from 370 to 1,000 pesos per ton, they increased their harvests to 514 tons.[17] Then, too, Pichucalco's *fincas* produced one-quarter of the state's maize, as well as significant amounts of *aguardiente*, coffee, rice, and rubber. Three other departments—Chilón, Palenque, and Simojovel—exported large quantities of coffee, sugar, maize, *frijoles*, and (in the case of Simojovel) tobacco. Apparently such activities proved attractive enough to draw foreign capital: on the eve of the revolution, a number of foreigners (Americans, Germans, and Belgians) had invested more than 2 million pesos in Palenque's coffee and rubber plantations.[18] Furthermore, between 1880 and 1910, British, French, American, German, and Spanish businessmen invested 4.3 million pesos in Chiapas' burgeoning coffee industry, concentrated in Soconusco (Table 25). By the end of that period, coffee production had reached nearly 6,000 metric tons per year—a crop which brought foreign investors a 24-percent return on their capital.[19] So important, in fact, did coffee become in the state's economy that by 1910 such plantations, which never represented more than 3 percent of the region's rural properties, absorbed almost 15 percent of its capital.

Under these circumstances, it is perhaps unusual that, for a short time at least, international interest in Chiapas was focused on quite a different kind of crop: rubber. During the late 19th and early 20th centuries, most of the rubber consumed by the world's industrialized nations was collected from wild trees in the Amazon basin—a risky and inefficient venture that kept prices high and made supplies uncertain. As the demand for rubber rose, enterprising men in Europe began to establish plantations wherever local conditions permitted: Ceylon, India, Indonesia, Indochina. By 1905 their efforts had been amply rewarded: Pará rubber from the Amazon accounted for only 55 percent of the world market.[20] Naturally, American businessmen, anxious to share in such rewards, created plantations of their own. In 1900, the Ubero Plantation Company was organized in Boston with one million dollars subsequently invested in 5,000 acres of uncleared land on the Isthmus of Tehuantepec.[21] At about the same time, a

## Table 25.
## Foreign Capital in Chiapas, 1909 (thousands of pesos)

| Department | U.S. | Spain | Germany | England | France | Other | Total |
|---|---|---|---|---|---|---|---|
| Tuxtla | 25.4 | 128.4 | | 400.0 | 1.1 | 3.0 | 577.9 |
| Soconusco | 1,227.1 | 930.1 | 1,373.1 | 469.8 | 355.1 | 79.8 | 4,415.0 |
| Las Casas | | 5.0 | .6 | | | | 5.6 |
| Chiapa | | 16.0 | 184.9 | | | 36.8 | 237.7 |
| Chilón | 11.0 | 792.4 | 19.8 | | | | 823.2 |
| Pichucalco | 11.6 | 132.8 | | | 20.0 | 6.6 | 171.0 |
| Simojovel | | 79.0 | | | 19.2 | 3.1 | 101.3 |
| La Libertad | | .2 | | | | | .2 |
| Tonalá | 545.0 | 361.7 | | | | 1.9 | 908.6 |
| Palenque | 1,614.3 | 36.2 | 229.6 | 869.8 | 375.4 | 266.6 | 3,351.9 |
| Total | 3,434.4 | 2,481.8 | 1,808.0 | 1,739.6 | 770.8 | 397.8 | 10,592.4 |

*Source:* Gobierno del Estado de Chiapas, *Anuario estadístico,* pp. 95–102.

speculator in San Francisco named O. H. Harrison formed the Mexican Land and Colonization Company, which purchased a large tract in Soconusco.[22] But it was in the Lacandón jungle south and east of Palenque, where tropical hardwoods might be cut to repay the costs of planting rubber, that such ventures flourished with unparalleled vigor. In 1883 one local observer complained that "the Department of Palenque is one of the state's most neglected regions. . . . A small amount of sugarcane is grown there [and] . . . a few lumbermen are exploiting its vast and virgin forests."[23] Within 20 years, however, this situation had changed completely. Following the Usumacinta River and its tributaries, nearly two dozen American companies had bought extensive lots (usually of around 5,000 acres each) which they cleared to produce rubber, sugarcane, coffee, and cacao.[24] By 1913, when these activities were abandoned, such companies advertised a dividend of "$100 a month for more years than you can possibly live."[25]

The Lacandón jungle offered another advantage which planters in Soconusco did not enjoy: easy access to highland Indians. Between 1890 and 1910, both lumbermen and plantation owners employed professional labor contractors to recruit native people (and poor *ladinos*) from as far away as Ocosingo, Chamula, Oxchuc, and Tenejapa.[26] At first, these contractors generally resorted to some form of impressment or compulsion to fill their quotas. But in later years, landlessness and population growth in Indian communities rendered such coercion unnecessary (Table 26). By way of contrast, even before the 19th century ended coffee growers in Soconusco began to experience serious labor shortages; indeed, it was this situation which in 1883 prompted the observation that "What is truly lacking there are strong backs and good laws which will civilize the servants or laborers and make capital investment more secure."[27]

In order to provide that civilizing influence, in 1880 the state government enacted a vagrancy law which required Indian workers to remain occupied during specified portions of the year.[28] And when such measures proved inadequate, these authorities raised the head tax (1892) and tightened their administrative control over highland communities (1896).[29] Even so, they

Table 26.
The Population of Chiapas, 1829–1910

| Year | Population | Growth Rate per year |
|------|-----------|---------------------|
| 1829 | 119,829 | |
| 1846 | 147,283 | 1.22% |
| 1851 | 160,301 | 1.71 |
| 1871 | 193,987 | 0.96 |
| 1877 | 219,735 | 2.10 |
| 1884 | 242,029 | 1.39 |
| 1895 | 318,730 | 2.53 |
| 1910 | 438,843 | 2.15 |
| Cumulative Growth Rate | | 1.62% |

Sources: Viviane Brachet de Márquez, La poblac ión de los Estados Mexicanos en el siglo XIX (1824–1895), Instituto Nacional de Antropología e Historia, Departmento de Investigaciones Históricas, Colección Científica, no. 35 (1976), p. 54; Secretaría de Comercio e Industria, Censo general de habitantes, (1924).

were unable to provide a continuous flow of indigenous *jornaleros*: as late as 1896, one planter complained to the San Francisco *Call* that "the worst feature of life there is the difficulty of getting good servants. The natives . . . [whom] we pay from 37 to 50 cents a day in silver . . . are very indolent and inattentive." [30] Like rubber growers in Palenque, after 1900 these growers also hired contractors to procure *peones* from the central highlands. One measure of their success is that between 1897 and 1907 the area's population grew from 10,928 to 36,641; together with temporary laborers, these new residents provided the plantations with almost 10,000 workers each year. [31] In effect, therefore, expanding national and international markets had divided the state into a series of economic zones in which one or two commercial crops set the pace and style of life for *hacienda* workers and Indian villagers alike (Table 27).

Naturally, such events left their mark upon native communi-

## Table 27.
### Agricultural Production by Region, 1909

| Department | Aguardiente (hectoliters) | Cotton (tons) | Indigo (tons) | Rice (tons) | Sugar (tons) | Cacao (tons) | Coffee (tons) | Sugarcane (tons) | Frijoles (hectol.) | Maize (hectol.) |
|---|---|---|---|---|---|---|---|---|---|---|
| Chiapa | 1,000 | 1,150 | 34.5 | 15 | 11.5 | | 25.0 | | 400 | 25,000 |
| Comitán | | | | 1 | | | 9.4 | 498.7 | 3,833 | 53,774 |
| Chilón | 2,230 | | | 0.2 | 35 | .2 | 335.4 | 175.0 | 5,250 | 45,000 |
| Las Casas | 7,895 | | | | | | 2.3 | | 3,489 | 21,888 |
| La Libertad | | 69 | 1 | 104 | | | 228.0 | 825.1 | 5,025 | 9,857 |
| Meacalapa | 258 | | | | 20.4 | 41 | 100.0 | | 1,320 | 4,320 |
| Mariscal | 1,600 | 0.6 | | 2.4 | | | 410.8 | | 49,323 | 93,370 |
| Pichucalco | 1,136 | | | 170.7 | 2.3 | 514.6 | 66.6 | | 27,024 | 226,711 |
| Palenque | 16,439 | | | 29.5 | | .3 | 425.0 | 102.1 | 73,623 | 59,189 |
| Soconusco | 4,000 | 28 | | 15.9 | | 3.8 | 5,849.6 | 5,000 | 1,244 | 48,223 |
| Simojovel | 6,000 | 1.7 | | .9 | .3 | .4 | 973.5 | 101.5 | 5,000 | 108,000 |
| Tuxtla | 5,160 | 20 | 10 | 5.6 | 342.9 | | 156.2 | 1,500 | 10,500 | 173,056 |
| Tonalá | | | | | | | | 440 | 350 | 65,000 |
| Total | 45,718 | 1,269.3 | 45.5 | 345.2 | 412.4 | 560.3 | 8,581.8 | 8,642.4 | 186,381 | 933,388 |

*Source:* Gobierno del Estado de Chiapas, *Anuario estadístico,* p. 52.

FIGURE 2.
Population Growth in Chiapas, 1816–1940

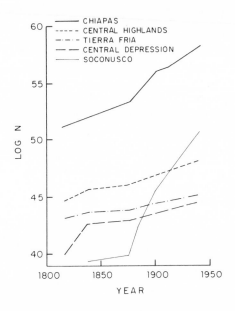

ties, which were transformed in very different ways. Consider for a moment the *municipios* closest to San Cristóbal—*municipios* which lay in the highest part of *tierra fría* and which in previous decades had not experienced direct occupation. Between 1816 and 1838, these communities grew at a very attenuated rate.[32] In this respect, they differed markedly from other highland *pueblos*, which increased at approximately the same pace as the general population (Figure 2). Nor can these differences be attributed to the vagaries of famine and disease, which periodically swept through the entire area (Table 28). On the contrary, such epidemics were much more likely to affect lowland laborers and those who lived in temperate communities like San Lucas, Totolapa, and San Bartolomé. In 1830, for example, the parish priest of Teopisca wrote that "More than 70 people of this town, men in the main, perished [last year] from a malignant fever, and I understand that the cause of this [tragedy] was . . .

TABLE 28.
Epidemics and Famines in Chiapas, 1819–1910

|         | Description | Extent or Effect |
|---------|-------------|------------------|
| 1821    | smallpox    | Zoque region     |
| 1826    | measles     | general          |
| 1829    | fever       | Teopisca, San Bartolomé |
| 1833–35 | cholera     | Tzeltal and Chol regions, San Andrés, and Bochil |
| 1837    | cholera     | general          |
| 1838    | smallpox    | San Bartolomé    |
| 1849    | cholera     | Pantelhó         |
| 1850    | cholera     | San Cristóbal    |
| 1856–8  | cholera     | San Cristóbal    |
| 1862    | cholera     | Bochil           |
| 1883    | cholera     | Soconusco        |
| 1910    | smallpox    | Soconusco        |

Sources: AHDSC, Correspondencia parroquial, 1819–1910; Manuel Trens, Historia de Chiapas, p. 389.

that its poor inhabitants must plant their grains and sugarcane in the lowlands which this *pueblo* owns to the west."[33] In contrast, towns such as Zinacantan and Tenejapa produced a healthy number of new children each year, and many of these children evidently survived to adulthood (Table 29). Thus it seems more plausible that such places now provided the *peones* and *laboríos* who opened new ranches in the Grijalva valley. By that time, in fact, people in the highlands possessed considerable motivation to migrate: using the laws of 1826 and 1832, Conservative politicians in San Cristóbal had reduced nearly one-third of these Indians to the condition of *baldíos*—that is, tenants who owed their new masters four or five days' labor a week in exchange for the right to work their former lands.[34] Little wonder, then, that many men and women chose to become sharecroppers or peons in the lowlands rather than suffer such a degrading and precarious fate.

Table 29.
Population Growth in Highland Chiapas, 1816–1900 (per year)

| Town | Birth Rate | Natural Increase | Net Growth Rate | | |
|------|-----------|------------------|------------------|-------|-----------|
| | | | 1816–38 | 1838–76 | 1876–1900 |
| Chamula | 4.5% | 2.2% | 1.15% | .80% | −.13% |
| Huistán | 4.7 | 2.8 | 1.95 | .16 | 1.81 |
| Oxchuc | n.a. | n.a. | (1816–1900 = −.45%) | | |
| Tenejapa | 3.7 | 1.8 | −.10 | −.15 | .85 |
| Zinacantan | 5.5 | 2.7 | −.03 | .01 | .91 |
| Highland region | | | 1.24 | .18 | .85 |

Sources: "Estados trimestres (bautizos)," (1849–1867); AHDSC; E. Pineda, Descripción geográfica; Flavio Paniagua, Catecismo elemental de historia y estadística de Chiapas; Gobierno del Estado de Chiapas, Censo general, 1910.

As Figure 2 indicates, by 1838 the movement of highland Indians into adjacent lowland municipios had largely abated. After that date, only two areas, Chiapa and Cuxtepeques, continued to attract new immigrants (Figure 3). Nonetheless, between 1840 and 1880 both the highlands in general, and tierra fría communities in particular, lost a great many of their inhabitants. In Chamula, for example, the state's vice-governor, Ramón Larraínzar, in 1846 appropriated a large tract of land which he called Nuevo Edén (Map 8). As a result, Indians in Chamula retained only those small and overused valleys to which their colonial forebears had been confined. Much the same state of affairs prevailed in neighboring towns like Huistán and Tenejapa, which by 1850 had also lost most of their farmlands (Tables 30 and 31). Faced with this unfortunate situation, many native families departed for the new cattle ranches to the northwest. Indeed, as Figure 4 shows, it was not until 1875, when such people found seasonal employment on coffee plantations in Soconusco, that the population of tierra fría communities stabilized and began to grow.

FIGURE 3.
Population Growth in the Grijalva Basin, 1816–1940

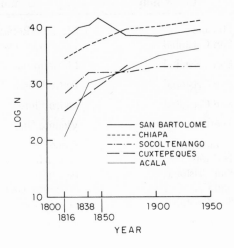

MAP 8.
Municipal Lands in Chamula, 1855

Table 30.
Denuncias in Highland Communities, 1831–1859

| | Community | Denunciante |
|---|---|---|
| 1831 | Huistán | Mariano Robles |
| | San Cristóbal | *varios vecinos* |
| 1832 | San Cristóbal | Mariano Bermúdez |
| 1837 | San Cristóbal | Pedro Flores |
| 1838 | San Cristóbal | Pedro Flores |
| 1838 | Teopisca | Vicente Díaz |
| 1842 | Zinacantan | Ramon Suárez |
| | Huistán | Justo Mijangos |
| | San Cristóbal | Bernabe Aguilar |
| | San Cristóbal | Norberto Ruíz |
| | San Cristóbal | Lino García |
| 1843 | Zinacantan | Leandro Robles |
| | Tenejapa | Domingo José Navarro |
| | | Manuel María Suárez |
| | | (later *cura* of |
| | | Zinacantan and Chamula) |
| | Teopisca | Gloria Navarro |
| | Teopisca | Vicente Díaz |
| | Teopisca | Mariano Esponda |
| | Teopisca | Sabino Antonio Aviles |
| | Chenalhó | Cristóbal Mayor |
| | San Andrés | Mariano Ortíz |
| | Chamula (Milpoleta) | Renugio Urbina |
| 1844 | Huistán | Mariano Ortíz |
| | Amatenango | Sabino Aguilar |
| | San Cristóbal | Ponciano Solórzano |
| | San Lucas | Joaquín Esponda |
| | Acala | Joaquín Esponda |
| | Aguacatenango | Gregorio Cancino |
| | San Andrés | Cayetano de Carfso |
| 1845 | San Felipe | Cristóbal Pérez |
| | Amatenango | Vicente Robles y Cabrera |
| | Teopisca | Catarino Mayen |

(continued)

TABLE 30. *(continued)*
Denuncias in Highland Communities, 1831–1859

|  | Community | Denunciante |
|---|---|---|
|  | San Cristóbal | Emeterio Pineda |
|  | San Felipe | Cristóbal Rúiz |
|  | Huistán | Ramón Larraínzar |
|  | Zinacantan | Francisco Camas de Sánchez |
| 1846 | Teopisca | Petrona Esponda de Coello |
|  | Tenejapa | Emeterio Pineda |
|  | Huistán | Ramón Larraínzar |
|  | Chamula | Ramón Larraínzar |
| 1848 | Santiago, Santa Marta, and Magdalena | Salvador Pineyro |
| 1850 | Santiago and San Andrés | José Hernández |
|  |  | Manuel Ruíz |
|  |  | Antonio Pérez |
|  |  | Martín Pérez |
| 1859 | Teopisca | José María Alvarez |

*Sources:* "Inventario de los expedientes del ramo de tierras que corresponde al Departamento de Las Casas, 1831–1891," AHDSC; "Escritura de venta otorgada por el Lic. dn. Ramón Larraínzar en favor de Santos López Auzel, 1851," Archivo Municipal de Chamula.

TABLE 31.
Petitions for Legal Recognition of Indian Ejidos,
1832–1891

| Year | Community |
|---|---|
| 1832 | Amatenango |
| 1838 | Teopisca |
| 1839 | Teopisca |
|  | Chenalhó |
|  | Barrio de la Merced (San Cristóbal) |
| 1842 | San Felipe |
|  | Santa María Magdalena |

*(continued)*

TABLE 31. *(continued)*
Petitions for Legal Recognition of Indian Ejidos,
1832–1891

| Year | Community |
|------|-----------|
| | San Miguel Mitontic |
| 1843 | Huistán |
| | San Andrés |
| | Chenalhó |
| | San Alonso Tenejapa |
| | Barrio de Mexicanos (San Cristóbal) |
| | Barrio de Santa Lucía (San Cristóbal) |
| | Barrio de San Diego (San Cristóbal) |
| 1844 | Amatenango |
| | Teopisca |
| | Chamula |
| | Zinacantan |
| | Barrio de Santa Lucia (San Cristóbal) |
| | Barrio de San Antonio (San Cristóbal) |
| 1845 | Chanal |
| 1847 | San Andrés (*segunda porción*) |
| | Teopisca (*segunda porción*) |
| | Chamula |
| | San Lucas |
| 1849 | Santiago |
| | Santa Marta (*segunda porción*) |
| | San Miguel Mitontic (*segunda porción*) |
| 1850 | Zinacantan (definitive title) |
| 1856 | Zinacantan (*ejido of* Salinas) |
| 1860 | Amatenango (*segunda porción*) |
| 1866 | Teopisca (division of *ejido* into lots) |
| 1879 | Teopisca |
| 1888 | San Andrés (definitive title) |
| 1890 | San Lucas |
| 1891 | San Felipe (definitive title) |

*Source:* "Inventario de los expedientes" (1831–1891).

FIGURE 4.
Population Growth in the Central Highlands, 1816–1909

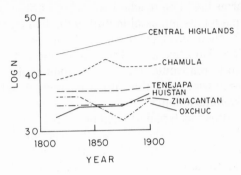

Alarmed by this unforeseen turn of events, officials in Chiapas made a half-hearted attempt to guide local *hacendados* back toward the parallel paths of Liberal economics and free labor. As early as 1849, the state legislature decreed that

> The so-called practice of *baldiaje* which has infected our *haciendas* and farms is hereby expressly prohibited; and from this day forward the owner will be permitted to demand only two days of service each month from those *baldíos* who consent to remain on his lands, in recognition of his direct ownership.

As for peasants who had been evicted to make room for cattle,

> Anyone who by purchasing property has transformed its previous inhabitants into *baldíos* shall demand of them only one day of service each month unless they are subject to the previous article, and he shall not evict them ... unless some individual should prove to be pernicious to him, as certified by the authorities of the nearest town.[35]

Such restrictions, however, were observed mainly in the breach: throughout the century, native tenants continued to work primarily in enterprises that belonged to their landlords. Even more discouraging, perhaps, measures of this sort failed to stimulate commercial agriculture in the central highlands. Along this frontier of *mestizo* settlement, life remained quite primitive, the possibilities for substantial modification almost nonexistent. Often, too, these farms might be reached only over undependable trails which became totally impassable during the five months of summer rains. At such times, even pack animals proved useless for transportation. Paradoxically, then, it seemed that economic progress in this area would depend less upon capital investment and entrepreneurial spirit than upon an increasingly primitive form of indigenous tenancy.

By mid-century, such policies had not only increased the number of landless workers throughout Chiapas but had also fixed the region's social structure within narrow and rigid limits. On the one hand, prominent Conservatives in San Cristóbal extracted rent from native *baldíos* who continued to plant such traditional crops as maize and wheat. In many cases, these landlords also utilized their tenants to grow small quantities of wheat, cotton, and (at lower altitudes) sugar cane on ersatz *fincas* like Nuevo Edén. On the other hand, in the Grijalva basin, Liberal planters and cattlemen, impatient to expand their *haciendas,* became progressively less willing to tolerate such arrangements, which permitted highland *rentiers* to monopolize the Indian workforce. After 1856, when these planters entitled Church properties in Chiapa, Frailesca, and Ocosingo, their need for more fieldhands became truly desperate.[36] In fact, it was this conflict—which transcended much of the debate over political party and economic theory—that divided the creole elite along regional lines and set the stage for 25 years of civil warfare.[37] For its part, the Church, which survived *desamortización* only by inflating the fees which it collected from Indian parishioners, threw its weight behind Conservative landlords who promised to preserve such revenues from the depredations of lowland *hacendados*.[38] Eventually, in 1863, both landlords and ecclesiastical officials followed the path which had been charted by their counterparts elsewhere in Mexico and became fervent *imperialistas*.

Under these circumstances, it is not surprising that native communities, besieged on all sides by Liberals and Conservatives alike, resisted the destiny which *ladino* politicians had chosen for them. In late February 1848, a group of Tzeltal people

gathered near the town of Chilón to conspire against the lives of
mestizo settlers. According to contemporary accounts, the plot
(which eventually included Indians from seven different communities) was to have been carried out in early March, during
the yearly festival of Carnaval.[39] On the very eve of the uprising,
the conspirators were discovered: more than 50 men were incar-
cerated in San Cristóbal. By mid-June, however, most of them
had been released—state authorities, distracted by the Mexican-
American War, could waste no time untangling the byzantine
politics of race in a remote mountain backwater.[40] Predictably,
indifference of this sort precipitated a crisis among the mestizos
in Chilón. Terrified that racial warfare might soon engulf their
peaceful villages and ranchos, many of them migrated to the
neighboring state of Tabasco.

Although local politicians chose to ignore these early signs of
warning, mestizos in northern Chiapas were certainly correct in
their view that violence and disorder had become inevitable. A
few months earlier, Maya peasants in Yucatán had rebelled
against their creole overlords, who quickly found themselves
besieged in the city of Mérida.[41] Fighting on both sides had been
bloody; both Indian and white armies behaved with extraordinary viciousness and cruelty. It would be two full years more
before a ladino victory was assured—and even then, half a century would pass before the last Maya forces accepted defeat. As
in Chiapas, native discontent could be traced to two distinct but
interrelated sources. First, local landowners, encouraged by an
increased demand for sisal fiber and sugarcane, expanded their
holdings at the expense of peasant communities. In so doing,
they undermined the precarious balance between village and
hacienda that had evolved during three centuries of Spanish
rule. Second, in their haste to replace traditional social and political arrangements with more enlightened institutions, Liberal
politicians singled out native religious practices for special ridi-
cule. To the twin curses of dispossession and forced labor, then,
these men added the outrage of blasphemy, a sacrilegious attack
upon Indian life itself.

With such facts in mind, it is useful once again to consider
Stephens' account of his journey through Chiapas in 1840. In

many places, he suggests, *mestizo* encroachment upon native lands had not as yet become unbearable or overwhelming. Only in the vicinity of Comitán had *ladino* landlords established the kind of holdings which existed in Yucatán. One example of such a planter was Padre Solís, a fat old priest whose *hacienda* lay along the eastern edge of Indian occupation. Here, Stephens wrote, "we dined off solid silver dishes, drank out of silver cups, and washed in a silver basin."[42] Nonetheless, such affluence remained the exception among highland settlers. More typical of local *ranchos* was the humble property that Stephens visited a few days later near Ocosingo, in the very center of Tzeltal territory. "It was a mere hut," he declared, "made of poles and plastered with mud, but the situation was one of those that warmed us to country life."[43] To the north of Ocosingo, even such modest signs of civilization diminished to an insignificant trickle. Except for a priest and a subprefect, Chilón was apparently occupied only by Indians—surly, uncooperative people who, Stephens said, "bore a notoriously bad character." It was in this area that the line of *mestizo* settlement seems to have disappeared completely: upon arriving in Tumbalá, Stephens discovered "the wildest and most extraordinary place we had yet seen, and though not consecrated by associations, for unknown ages it had been the site of an Indian village."[44]

Within a few short years, however, this situation had undergone a series of dramatic and irreversible changes. Between 1831 and 1844, three *ladino* landowners established five new properties in Huistán, a Tzotzil community where native *campesinos* had until quite recently grown most of the state's wheat.[45] For their part, Huisteco leaders, unable to make their way through the labyrinth of laws and *licenciados* in San Cristóbal, did not formulate a petition for communal lands until 1843. Predictably, their efforts bore little fruit: after much legal maneuvering, they managed to retain only a small fraction of their former territories. Outraged by this state of affairs, even the local priest was moved to protest what he considered to be a matter of public scandal. "What will become of these Indians after losing their lands?" he asked rhetorically in 1848.

> I would imagine that, lacking the means to support their families, some will beg in the cities and towns, where they will suffer greatly.... To this, one must add that [even those who still own land] find themselves obliged to sell their wheat for a pittance, a situation which forces them to borrow money against their future harvests.[46]

By 1844, as we know, such conditions were not uncommon in *pueblos* near San Cristóbal: not only Huistán, but also Zinacantan, Chamula, Amatenango, Chenalhó, Tenejapa, and Teopisca had all suffered a similar fate.[47]

Despite their relative accessibility, however, these towns did not lend themselves readily to intensive *ladino* colonization. For one thing, they occupied the highest, least productive part of Chiapas' *altiplano* and could absorb only modest numbers of new arrivals. And they already contained large indigenous populations—a fact which discouraged poor *mestizos* from establishing the kind of family *rancho* that Stephens visited in 1840. For such purposes, people of this class turned their eyes toward the temperate valleys near Ocosingo and Chilón, areas where native peasants still practiced independent agriculture on extensive plots of untitled land. By 1848, Chilón, virtually uninhabited in Stephens' day, had acquired a *ladino* community of more than 40 families; in Ocosingo, the number was considerably greater.[48] Remarking upon the effects of immigration on local Indians, the priest of Ocosingo wrote that "Their rebelliousness stems not so much from taxation as from the fact that their lands have been taken over by *ladinos* to such a degree that, lacking any place to build their houses, they are now moving to a hamlet called El Real, 12 or 14 leagues [30 miles] from here."[49] For those men and women to whom escape appeared more attractive than *baldiaje*, therefore, the Lacandón jungle (in which El Real was located) offered a precarious—though inhospitable—refuge. And for those to whom such a remedy seemed worse than the malady it was intended to cure, violent resistance—even against overwhelming odds—now became the order of the day.

Although most of the *mestizos* who migrated into indigenous towns in the early 1840s became farmers, a significant number also turned to an occupation that became known euphemistically as *el comercio:* they sold liquor to the Indians. True enough, commerce of this sort had been common at native *fiestas* and markets since early colonial days; indeed, local priests had complained about it steadily for the previous hundred years. Beginning in the 1820s, however, such complaints acquired a new tone of urgency and authority, a new sense of moral indignation. Typical of such protests were the remarks made by the vicar of Chamula to his superiors in 1830. "Among their principal vices," he wrote, "one must list that of drunkenness, the source of so many evils and of untold catastrophes, which has now taken root among these unfortunates, due to the abuse of liberty, the traffic in *aguardiente* which emanates from the capital."[50] Within a few years, these sentiments were echoed by priests throughout the highlands, not simply those who lived close to San Cristóbal. "What has also contributed to the uprising," wrote the priest of Ocosingo in 1848,

> is that in this town *aguardiente* is sold in such great abundance as to have become a matter of public scandal, since the Indians now buy it with *cincos* of *cacao*, and there is no dearth of *ladinos* who introduce it into this jurisdiction even during the days immediately following the rebellion. Such is the case of don Mariano Zepeda, a resident of this town, who in the company of his wife traveled to Guaquitepec and Sitalá [two communities near Chilón] to sell a large quantity of liquor during the critical days of *Carnaval*.[51]

Apparently, for those *mestizos* who did not relish the prospects of homesteading on backland *ranchos*, the liquor trade offered a more attractive form of livelihood.

Although most clerics were quick to denounce these excesses, they were considerably less inclined to invoke such high moral standards when their own behavior was at issue. Like their civil counterparts, they often conducted their affairs in a spirit of simple venality, as in Stephens' description of the young *cura* in Tumbalá: "the delegate of Padre Solís, a gentlemanly young man from [San Cristóbal] who was growing as round, and bade fair to grow as rich out of this village, as Padre Solís himself."[52] Even when they were relatively honest, such priests frequently became entangled in another sort of controversy: the crisis of spiritual authority to which the conflicting claims of Christian charity and creole racism inevitably gave rise. Examples of this difficulty—which repeated in contemporary form the age-old conflict between white clergymen and native believers—were not hard to find. In 1825, it appears, the first *alcalde* of San Cristóbal was fined 200 pesos for refusing to enforce ecclesiastical sanctions against the *principales* of Chamula. Twenty years later, in 1846, the priest of that town again complained that many of his flock "are ignorant of the most indispensable rudiments of religion"— a situation which they would not allow him to correct.[54] Finally, in 1849, community leaders lodged a formal protest against what they regarded as illegitimate and unreasonable interference in their most Catholic customs and traditions. Responding to these arguments, the curate of Zinacantan defended his colleague on the grounds that

> Although I have ministered to the Indians for more than 34 years, I must confess that I do not understand their extravagance, their propensities and strange customs; in fact, one might say that they form a distinct class of men. . . . Under these circumstances, the Father Vicar of Chamula, wishing only to fulfill the obligations of his ministry, has corrected many errors . . . and for this his parishioners want to get rid of him.[55]

Far from representing a local problem, by mid-century such attitudes seem in large measure to characterize the relations between creole clergymen and their indigenous flocks everywhere in the highlands. On June 10, 1848, for example, the vicar-general of Chiapas sent a circular to all of his priests in which he urged them to report on all matters related to the Carnival conspiracy. Most particularly, he asked them to indicate whether they had noticed "any inclinations, desires, or dispositions among the Indians to rebel against those who are not of their race."[56] The curate of Huistán, Fray José Mariano Guerrero, responded that in many highland communities native inhabitants, "encouraged by a group of *ladinos*," had refused to obey (and support) "higher authorities, their local judges and their priests." But he implied that in both Chilón and Ocosingo his colleagues had actually provoked indigenous leaders to acts of violence.[57] The priest in Oxchuc, Bartolomé Gutiérrez, recounted that on the evening before Corpus Christi, as he finished saying vesper prayers, he had narrowly escaped assassination at the hands of village officers. "As I stood in my doorway listening to the crowd of Indians inside the church," he wrote, "I overheard the *gobernador*, Tomás Chít, who had exited through a small door by the sacristy, say to the *alférez*, Martín Hernández Caña, 'Let him go! He still has to celebrate the *fiesta* and bless the new baptismal fount, and when he does, when he does. . . .' And he smashed his fist into his open hand."[58] And although he failed to find any direct connection between this event and the conspiracy in Chilón, Gutiérrez concluded that "while the soldiers are here I plan to settle my affairs, since I cannot continue to live among my enemies."

From this discussion, it seems clear that the events of 1848 were set in motion not by agrarian legislation alone but by a number of interrelated social and economic forces. True enough, such laws stimulated local *ladinos*—rich and poor—to denounce and entitle native lands, a catastrophe which compelled many Indians to leave the *altiplano* altogether. Equally important, however, the kind of spiritual guerrilla warfare engaged in by creole priests provided a powerful source of native discontent. Freed from the interference of civil authorities, who generally refused to enforce church regulations, native *mayordomos* and *alféreces* consciously elaborated those aspects of Catholic doctrine and liturgy in which priests played only a limited role. The *fiesta*, not the mass, occupied the center of their religious life. In this respect, *ladino* merchants played a novel and unexpected political role. Filled with the spirit of free trade and individual liberty, they often counseled the Indians to ignore traditional habits and institutions—both secular and religious. In so doing, of course, they were motivated less by the desire to enlighten than by the impulse to increase their markets: by stressing such Liberal precepts as the separation of Church and State, they sought actively to loosen the hold which local clerics maintained over their native flocks. Rising to the challenge, parish priests cajoled, threatened, and admonished their parishioners to ignore such ungodly advice.[59] Ironically, then, in their fervor to shield indigenous communities from Liberal ideas, and simultaneously to correct native ignorance and stupidity, these priests perpetuated age-old attitudes and abuses which undermined whatever measure of authority they retained in Indian eyes.

At this point, it is not out of place to consider directly the question of authority, the legitimacy of established order. And here *aguardiente* played a critical, perhaps even a catalytic role. Native *ejidos* were generally inadequate, but they permitted at least a few men to support their families; in addition, a few Indians managed to claim small parcels of private property, on which they raised wheat or maize. As the traffic in alcohol became generalized, these men fell increasingly into debt—a state of affairs upon which several priests commented in their reports. Once in debt, they were compelled either to forfeit their land or mortgage their future harvests at a discount of about 67 percent. What is more, two or three bad years might increase their indebtedness to the point that they could no longer afford to farm. Despite their complaints and lamentations, however, neither local pastors nor state officials possessed the means—or perhaps the will—to intervene. It was much easier to blame such difficulties on the Indians themselves, on the weakness of native character and morality. Hypocrisy of this sort may well have prompted the men and women in Chilón to abandon the avenue of peaceful petition, so assiduously (and fruitlessly) followed at the time by Indians elsewhere. In the end, it was *ladino* society in all its forms that they despised—not (as some alleged) the Christian faith or orderly government. When rebellion occurred, as one might expect, they directed their wrath against the liquor merchants as well as landowners and priests.

From this discussion, it becomes clear that the usurpation of Indian territories did not by itself give rise to violent resistance. Virtually all of the priests who answered the circular of June 10, 1848, indicated that their indigenous parishioners had lost large holdings to *ladino* immigrants; in fact, the curates of Comitán and Teopisca expressed surprise that the conspiracy had not been more widespread. Rather than rebel, highland Indians preferred to explore other means of survival—however unattractive and difficult these might be. For instance, the Zoque people in Amatán, a *pueblo* to the west of Chilón, had also lost virtually all of their land by 1848 and had turned instead to small-scale commerce, an occupation which frequently took them into the neighboring state of Tabasco. There they learned of the uprising in Yucatán, for which they expressed little sympathy. "They speak very poorly of the rebels," their priest reported on June 24, 1848, "and implore God to keep them from the town, for they do not wish to fight with anyone." [60] As long as they could support themselves through trade, they reasoned, why should they risk all—life, liberty, and such land as they still possessed—on a desperate throw of the dice?

And yet, it was precisely the absence of such alternatives, aggravated by the conflicting influences of Liberal merchants and creole priests, that moved Tzeltal people a few miles away to take more drastic action. Hemmed in on all sides by hostile forces, unwilling to migrate into the trackless Lacandón jungle, they chose to stand their ground and resist. [61] In their eyes, one might guess, the established order had become too corrupt, too treacherously evil, to survive. Neither flight nor commerce could save them, far less the living death of *baldiaje* or peonage. No: under these conditions life was not worth preserving; they would take their chances on rebellion. Neither their pastors nor their rulers seemed to learn anything from the experience. When asked if he had noted any strange happenings during those fateful days, the *cura* of Chamula, for example, replied blandly that "far from giving any such indications, [the Indians] have conducted themselves with all due moderation." The stage was set, then, for the true Caste War of Chiapas, a major affair 20 years later in which native people from Chamula and several other Tzotzil towns were massacred by a large force of vengeful *mestizos* from San Cristóbal.

## Life in Zinacantan: The Mayordomos' Travail

Let us now consider how these events shaped the destinies of Indians in Zinacantan. Between 1838 and 1875, approximately half of the town's residents became tenants or laborers on low-land *fincas*.[62] Nor did they migrate exclusively to nearby areas like Acala and Chiapa: as early as 1817, Zinacanteco *mozos* had made their way to Ocozocuautla, near the Oaxaca border.[63] As trade throughout the region rose, however, many Zinacantecos turned away from such employment and chose instead to reside within their community as mule-drivers or itinerant peddlers. Upon such men and women fell the dual burdens of earning a precarious living and paying the parish priest—not to mention the head tax and other official levies.

Of course, not everyone was happy with this arrangement: in 1830, the *cura* of Zinacantan complained that most Zinacantecos spent their lives carrying cacao and other freight between San Cristóbal and Tabasco, "whence they return," he wrote, "only to die."[64] Exaggerated as such claims may seem, nonetheless they are borne out by the fact that in 1832, one-third of the town's families were headed by women; in 1855, this figure had reached 40 percent![65] The source of this imbalance, according to the local priest, was not hard to find. "The main reason why women are more numerous than men in this parish," he reported, "is that the men are constantly engaged in commerce with places whose climate is fatal, such as Tabasco (though now they do not travel there with the same frequency as before), Pichucalco, Ixtacomi-tán, Simojovel, Tonalá, Chiapa, Acala, etc.; another reason is the constant stream of families who leave in search of a way to survive."[66] Throughout the *municipio*, in fact, adult women out-numbered men from the age of 20 onward (Figure 5).

Simultaneously, within the *municipio* itself, many people abandoned older settlements and created new hamlets, which for the most part were located along trading routes to the low-lands. Taking advantage of revitalized commerce between San Cristóbal and Chiapa, for example, three families from Muk'ta Jok'—the Pérez Mochilum, González Caten, and Hernández Co families—refounded the *paraje* of Salinas, which had disap-peared around 1780.[67] By 1856, these people had built a small chapel (dedicated to Nuestra Señora del Rosario); every Sunday their *mayordomo* traveled to Zinacantan and offered his share of the priest's rations.[68] In much the same fashion, Indians from both the main *pueblo* and hamlets like Joyjel, Muk'ta Jok', and

Figure 5.
The Population of Zinacantan, 1855

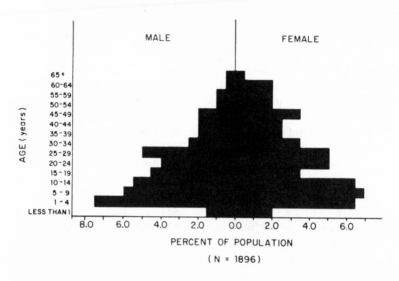

PERCENT OF POPULATION
( N = 1896 )

Sek'emtik moved to Apas, and then established new villages in Nabenchauk and Ibes. Between 1819 and 1855, in fact, a considerable number of people—perhaps as many as 300—left their homes in *tierra templada* and resettled in *tierra fría* (Table 32). Similarly, men and women from the *cabecera* expanded into the upland valleys which stretched along the *municipio's* southern border: Paste', Na Chij, and Elan Vo'. There they planted small *milpas* and raised mules for long-distance trade. Ultimately, two more hamlets—Petztoj and Saklum—grew up a short distance from Salinas.[69] Like their neighbors elsewhere in the community, men in these villages transported wheat and bread between San Cristóbal and such towns as Chiapa and Tonalá.[70]

By mid-century, then, Zinacantan had effectively been split into two demographic zones which possessed their own patterns of labor and domestic organization (Table 33). In temperate *parajes* like Joyjel and Jok' Ch'enom, it appears that most men continued to plant small cornfields and to work as part-time or seasonal fieldhands on neighboring plantations. Although they

TABLE 32.

Population Movement within Zinacantan, 1819–1855

| Settlement | 1819 | | 1855 | | Net Change | |
|---|---|---|---|---|---|---|
| | Inhabitants | Percentage of Households (N = 567) | Inhabitants | Percentage of Households (N = 562) | Inhabitants | Households |
| Zinacantan[a] | 1,350 | 59.5% | 1,217 | 62.5% | 133 | 3.0% |
| Muk'ta Jok'[b] | 671 | 29.8 | 384 | 18.4 | −287 | −11.4 |
| Salinas[c] | 0 | 0 | 167 | 7.4 | 167 | 7.4 |
| Apas[d] | 136 | 6.0 | 267 | 11.4 | 131 | 5.4 |
| Other[e] | 120 | 4.7 | 0 | 0 | — | |
| Total | 2,277 | 100.0% | 2,035 | 99.7% | | |

Sources: "Sobre reducir a poblado" (1819), AGGG, Serie Chiapas, A1.12.274.19; "Padrón del pueblo de Zinacantan" (1855), AHDSC.

[a] Including Na Chij, Xucún, Gur, and Sagchaguó (1819); Na Chij, Laguna, Colomaxtik, and Mecobi (1855).

[b] Including Potovtik, Jok' Chenom, Nichim, and Jitogtg (1819); Joyjel, Gualton, Jok' Ch'enom, Sek'emtik, Ajte'tik, and Manzanilum (1855).

[c] Including Tierra Colorada, Tzub, and Ajil (1855).

[d] Including Icalum and Jipuyum (1819); Ibes, Joc, Nabenchauk, Icalum, and Yalemtaiv (1855).

[e] Including the haciendas of San Pedro, San Antonio, Nandayageli, and Trapiche de la Merced, which are listed only in 1819.

TABLE 33.
Households Headed by Women, 1855

| Locality | Households | Percentage of Households | Percentage Headed by Women |
|---|---|---|---|
| Zinacantan, etc.[a] | 352 | 62.6% | 44.0% |
| Salinas | 25 | 4.4 | 64.0 |
| Apas, etc. | 64 | 11.4 | 24.6 |
| Muk'ta Jok', etc. | 104 | 18.5 | 25.0 |
| Other[b] | 17 | 3.0 | —0— |
| Total | 562 | 100.0% | |

Source: "Padrón del pueblo de Zinacantan" (1855).

[a] Including 13 ladino households.
[b] Ajil, Tzub, and Tierra Colorada, including 3 ladino households in Tierra Colorada.

often died at an early age (about four times more often than in 1749), they nonetheless enjoyed a measure of longevity which must have caused considerable envy among their counterparts in *tierra fría.* It was also from these regions that full-time *mozos* and *laboríos* were recruited—men who renounced highland life and installed their families on lowland *haciendas.* By way of contrast, in places like Apas, Na Chij, and the municipal center, native residents traveled constantly between Comitán and Tabasco or Oaxaca; as their priest noted, these were the men who returned home only to die. In Salinas, which at the time possessed virtually no land suitable for farming, two-thirds of these *arrieros* had actually died or abandoned their families! Only Nabenchauk—a settlement which like Salinas depended in large measure upon *arriería*—does not seem to fit this pattern. This paradox is explained when we learn that Nabenchauk had been founded a few years earlier by immigrants who had generally come from hamlets in *tierra templada,* which for some time it continued to resemble.

Underlying these differences, we may distinguish other, more profound changes in Zinacanteco life. In 1749 the *municipio* contained around 469 households. By 1832, this number had risen to 649; by 1855, it had declined to 562. During this period, it seems, most of these households continued to consist of nuclear families: in 1855, only 8 percent included other relatives or members (Table 34). In the same period, the number of Tzotzil surnames which distinguished these families decreased significantly: from 176 in 1749 to 152 in 1855. But Spanish *apellidos* actually increased from 20 to 25. Furthermore, with two exceptions (Bautista and Mandujano), the new Spanish names involved terms which had previously been appropriated by Zinacantecos to serve as Tzotzil surnames. In this sense, they fell into a somewhat larger class of words which might be used as either first or second names: Bocío (Rojillo), Chailal, Lunes, Patistán, Surian, and Xilón (Girón). Simultaneously, three Spanish *apellidos* (Alarcón, Alvaro, and Díaz) were dropped entirely from Zinacanteco usage. What is more significant, however, is that most surname pairs employed in 1749 (59 percent) had disappeared without a trace (see Appendix). In other words, rather than simply decreasing from 176 to 152, the total stock of such *apellidos* had in fact declined by 113—and then risen again as new terms were added. Nor can we account for this fact by assuming that Tzotzil words remained in use even after their Spanish counterparts were dropped. On the contrary, in only two cases did such terms appear with new partners—although 18 Tzotzil names occurred with more than one Spanish *apellido*. Clearly, the way in which such names were assigned, and the social groups to which they referred, had undergone substantial transformation.

In order to understand such events, we must recall that beginning around 1838, Zinacantecos, like other highland Indians, came to a startling, indeed brutal realization: under the new agrarian laws, their lands and even their houses could be taken from them without recourse. During the next 20 years, in fact, four small ranches—San Pedro Martir, El Carmen, Concepción, and Santa Teresa—were established in the *cabecera* alone; others were founded near outlying *parajes*. By way of response, municipal authorities petitioned the state government to delineate communal *ejidos* and determine which fields might remain inalienable. Finally, in 1844, they were successful: state officials granted them legal title to large tracts of communal land.[71] In-

TABLE 34.
Household Composition in Zinacantan, 1855
[N = 546]<sup>a</sup>

| | Nuclear families | Extended families | | | | | |
|---|---|---|---|---|---|---|---|
| | | With husband's parent(s) | With wife's parent(s) | With other relative<sup>b</sup> | With servant | Other | Total |
| Number | 503 | 4 | 4 | 24 | 7 | 4 | 43 |
| Percentage | 92.1% | .7% | .7% | 4.4% | 1.3% | .7% | 7.8% |

*Source:* "Padrón del pueblo de Zinacantan" (1855).

<sup>a</sup> Excluding 16 *ladino* families.
<sup>b</sup> In the great majority of cases, these households consist of an elderly widow and other family members of unspecified relationship, often other widows (or unmarried mothers) and their children.

stead of resolving their problems, however, such titles simply ensnared them in a web of legal entanglements for which in the end they paid quite dearly. "Far from calming them and quieting their spirits," wrote their priest to his superiors in 1848, "this measure has merely incited them to complain further that they did not have sufficient land, because they saw how no sooner did they occupy their *ejidos* than these were surveyed and sold off to *ladinos*." What is more, whenever he remonstrated with them over unpaid fees and dues, "they excuse themselves by pointing to their poverty, which is common knowledge, and then by invoking the land question, which they claim to be the source of all their misfortunes."[72] Faced with these difficulties, many Zinacantecos decided that private ownership, not common tenure and legal petition, offered them the best opportunity to safeguard their land. Guided by a few enterprising residents, therefore, they soon purchased a large tract from *ladino* ranchers who a few years earlier had appropriated Indian *terrenos*.[73]

Despite the fact that such measures may at first have been intended to deceive the Liberal authorities in San Cristóbal, within a short time they transformed social life in Zinacantan. As in other highland towns, community membership (which included the right to build a house and plant a *milpa*) now depended not upon common residence, as it had in colonial times, but rather upon ties of kinship to legal titleholders and their immediate clients. One way to establish such ties, of course, was to assume the surname of whatever kinsman might possess a more direct claim to ownership. Moved by powerful motives of this sort, men and women in the *municipio* apparently abandoned their earlier practice of taking distinct Tzotzil surnames when they set up independent households. Instead, as they moved from land-poor or marginal areas to *parajes* which enjoyed greater resources, they acquired the names of families whose right of occupancy was less questionable. One indication of this tendency may be found in the fact that the average number of adults who shared a single pair of surnames rose from 2.6 to 8.2; in some cases, such groups included as many as 40 people. By absorbing their dispossessed neighbors, a few large families— about 20 in all—began to crystallize, and eventually included over 40 percent of the town's total population (Table 35). More important, such families were not scattered at random throughout the *municipio*; within each *paraje*, two or three of these groups occupied a position of undisputed preeminence (Table 36). In effect, therefore, changing patterns of land tenure, combined with a shift in the kinds of work performed by most Zinacantecos, gave rise to a series of localized patrilineages which controlled access to land and trade.

Inevitably, changes of this sort modified the *municipio*'s political and religious life. As in other highland communities, Zinacantecos continued to serve both in their *cabildo* and in their *cofradías*. After 1824, in fact, the Church insisted that both sets of officials—*justicias* and *mayordomos*—contribute toward the priest's *sustento* (sustenance) and other costs. In addition, *mayordomos* and *alféreces* were expected to maintain the customary round of *fiestas* and processions—for which their *cura* collected sizable monthly bonuses. According to Patricio Correa, who served in Zinacantan from 1828 until 1851, income from all of these sources averaged around 800 pesos per year.[74] But by mid-century, native *cofrades* apparently accepted such responsibilities with considerable reluctance and misgiving. And little wonder: during most of the year, few men resided within the community; of those who remained, the majority were concentrated in places like Jok' Ch'enom and Sek'emtik, where civil authority was relatively weak. Describing this situation in 1855, their pastor wrote to his superiors that "not all of my parishioners live in the *pueblo*; on the contrary, a large number of them reside in dispersed *parajes* . . . which in the main lie at considerable distance from here. In some cases I have had to make three visits merely to record their names."[75] By that time, too, traditional institutions in the *cabecera* itself had largely collapsed. In 1856, the same *cura* declared that "the 5 *cofradías* which since time immemorial have existed here no longer possess any capital at all. The men elected as *mayordomos* now serve at their own expense, as I have mentioned to you on another occasion."[76] And as we have seen, in the hamlets closest to Zinacantan nearly half of the adult population consisted of widows, who apparently contributed very little to public ceremony. By 1855, then, the

TABLE 35.
Major Name Groups in Zinacantan, 1855[a]
(N = 23)

| Spanish Surname | Tzotzil Surname | Number of Marriages (N = 997) | Percentage in 1855 | Percentage in 1832 | Present in 1749 |
|---|---|---|---|---|---|
| de la Cruz | Chanmul | 13 | 1.3% | 1.8% | yes |
| | Tontom | 10 | 1.0 | 1.0 | yes |
| de la Torre | Cabrito | 21 | 2.1 | 2.5 | no |
| Gómez | Rodrigo | 18 | 1.8 | 1.7 | yes |
| González | Caten | 16 | 1.6 | 2.6 | yes |
| | Lecsim | 11 | 1.1 | 1.0 | yes |
| Hernández | Co | 37 | 3.7 | 2.3 | yes |
| | Gerónimo | 18 | 1.8 | 3.8 | yes |
| | Jolchó | 10 | 1.0 | 1.2 | yes |
| | Rico | 16 | 1.6 | 1.1 | yes |
| | Totom | 11 | 1.1 | 0.6 | no |
| López | Chiuc | 11 | 1.1 | 2.1 | yes |
| | Tzintan | 29 | 2.9 | 2.0 | yes |
| Martínez | Capitán | 11 | 1.1 | 1.1 | ? |
| Pérez | Asiento | 78 | 7.8 | 3.2 | yes |
| | Buluch | 15 | 1.5 | 0.7 | yes |
| | Comyos | 28 | 2.8 | 1.8 | no |
| | Mochilum | 21 | 2.1 | 2.3 | yes |
| | Tanjol | 21 | 2.1 | 2.3 | yes |
| | Xulumté | 13 | 1.3 | 0.6 | no |
| Sánchez | Es | 32 | 3.2 | 3.1 | yes |
| | Pulivok | 12 | 1.2 | 0.7 | yes |
| Vázquez | Xuljol | 43 | 4.3 | 3.0 | yes |
| | Total | 495 | 49.5% | 42.5% | |

Source: "Padrón y nueva cuenta de Zinacantan" (1749), AGGG, Serie Chiapas, A3.16.4509.353; "Padrón de Zinacantan" (1832), AHDSC; "Padrón del pueblo de Zinacantan (1855).

[a] Surname pairs representing at least one percent of the adults who married in Zinacantan.

TABLE 36.
Distribution of Major Surname Groups in Zinacantan, 1855

| Spanish Surname | Tzotzil Surname | Frequency[a] | | | |
|---|---|---|---|---|---|
| | | Zinacantan, etc. | Muk'ta Jok', etc. | Salinas, etc. | Apas, etc. |
| de la Cruz | Chanmul | 1.54 | 0 | 0 | .59 |
| | Tontom | .84 | 2.12 | 0 | .73 |
| de la Torre | Cabrito | 1.12 | 0 | 0 | 2.52 |
| Gómez | Rodrigo | 1.21 | .58 | 0 | 1.27 |
| González | Caten | .63 | 2.67 | 3.80 | .95 |
| | Lecsim | 1.37 | .48 | 1.10 | 0 |
| Hernández | Co | .23 | 2.14 | 4.94 | .41 |
| | Gerónimo | 1.02 | 1.17 | 0 | 1.27 |
| | Jolchó | 1.00 | 2.12 | 0 | 0 |
| | Rico | .94 | 1.96 | 0 | .47 |
| | Totom | 1.37 | 0 | 0 | 1.39 |
| López | Chiuc | 1.21 | .50 | 0 | 1.40 |
| | Tzintan | 1.61 | 0 | 0 | .27 |
| Martínez | Capitán | 1.22 | 1.43 | 0 | 0 |
| Pérez | Asiento | .62 | 2.25 | 1.56 | .59 |
| | Buluch | 1.22 | 1.06 | 0 | .51 |
| | Comyos | .77 | 1.32 | 0 | 2.18 |
| | Mochilum | 0 | 1.51 | 8.71 | 0 |
| | Tanjol | .95 | .25 | 0 | 2.91 |
| | Xulumté | .77 | 2.04 | 0 | 1.17 |
| Sánchez | Es | .73 | 1.32 | 0 | 2.38 |
| | Pulivok | 1.11 | .44 | 0 | 1.91 |
| Vázquez | Xuljol | 1.00 | 1.22 | 0 | 1.42 |

Source: "Padrón del pueblo de Zinacantan" (1855).

[a] Ratio of actual occurrence of surname pairs to their expected frequency under conditions of random distribution.

FIGURE 6.
Average Monthly Income of Parish Priest in Zinacantan, 1855–1905[a]

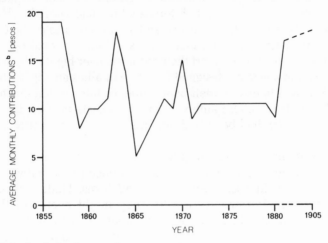

a Excludes fees for baptisms, marriages, masses, etc.
b Basic monthly stipend contributed by civil officials, *mayordomo reyes, mesoneros,* and *mayordomo salinero.*

number of *mayordomos* had decreased from 22 to 12 (two from each *cofradía* and two *mayordomos reyes*), and the amount they paid their curate declined to about half what it had been ten years earlier (Figure 6).[77]

Faced with this situation, local priests pleaded to be relieved of their duties in Zinacantan and sent to more lucrative parishes. In 1857, for example, one curate wrote that "the poverty to which I have been reduced is such that I do not have a *medio* [real] left over to buy myself the necessities of life which by rights I should claim, like clothing, shoes, etc. . . ."[78] Naturally, members of the cathedral chapter rejected these petitions: moral suasion, they counseled, and occasionally outright coercion, might be more effectively employed to maintain clerical stipends. But within a few years, even measures of this sort failed to guarantee a decent living. After a short period of civil war and Conservative rule, in 1861 Liberal politicians again resumed their control of the state government. By that time, of course, animosity between Liberals and Conservatives throughout the country had become much more intense: almost immediately, federal officials requested 1,000 men to fight the French forces which had landed at Veracruz.[79] Alarmed by these events, and anxious to bolster the Conservative cause, Church functionaries in San Cristóbal ordered the area's priests to reassert their authority over highland parishes.[80] And in a gesture designed both to win allies among lowland workers and to extend their own influence into Liberal territory, such priests were also authorized to consecrate the *ermitas* and chapels which had been built for Indian peons on nearby *haciendas*.[81]

Despite these efforts, most native towns remained firmly under the control of Liberal officials, who encouraged native people to withhold ecclesiastical fees and taxes. Under the new constitution, Indians were told, they might even use their churches and conduct their *fiestas* without episcopal permission. Responding to such blandishments, native communities were quick to demand better treatment from their pastors. In March 1862, the *prebendado* of Zinacantan declared that "in order to avoid the foolish nonsense with which the people of this town unjustly importuned the Ecclesiastical Government last year, I have agreed with them to celebrate Holy Week here free of charge and to excuse them from providing the usual large feast."[82] A few months later, in Chamula, this same priest (who had been transferred from Zinacantan) was informed that his new flock possessed no grain with which to pay his rations.[83] Simultaneously, in Bochil and Jitotol, where the local *cura* had obligingly consecrated several new *ermitas*, native workers buried their dead without paying him the corresponding fees—an oversight of which he complained bitterly to the *mitra* in San Cristóbal.[84] And finally, the next year, Indians in Cancuc bluntly told their curate that if he expected to receive food (or anything else), he should be prepared to pay for it.[85]

Denied the cooperation of civil officers, ecclesiastical authorities embarked upon a different and less vulnerable course of action: they permitted clergymen to reorganize ceremonial life and to create novel observances which might provide a better source of revenue. As *cofradía* funds diminished and finally disappeared, these priests in turn abandoned many of the festivals which for nearly three centuries had given shape to native religious experience. In Zinacantan, they ceased to perform memorial masses and other functions which had been supported by the *cofradías*—including such important observances as the feast of Ascención.[86] In place of these *fiestas*, they instituted new celebrations which they assigned to specific *mayordomos* and *alféreces* (Table 37). And in order to assure that such obligations were faithfully discharged, they demanded that municipal *justicias* appoint and supervise these sponsors.[87]

For their part, Liberal authorities, eager to break once and for all the Church's power in such communities, renewed their efforts to disrupt the collection of ecclesiastical dues. Taking advantage of such events, in June 1867, the *ayuntamiento* of Zinacantan decided that they would no longer tolerate the depradations of their priest, Bruno Domínguez.[88] After forcing him to flee from the town, they blandly appeared in San Cristóbal and received a half-hearted scolding from the *jefe político.* Then in November, Liberal officials played their strongest card: they abolished altogether the offices of *mayordomo* and *alférez* in native *pueblos.*[89] Within two months, civil authorities in Zinacantan, accompanied by the town's schoolteacher (a Liberal militant) informed Domínguez that local *mayordomos* and *alféreces* had been dismissed.[90] Unable to function any longer, the aging priest asked his superiors to remove him from the parish. In his place they appointed an ambitious young *cura*, Vicente Anselmo Guillén, whom they charged to restore order in the community's religious affairs. All to no avail: within six months, Guillén declared in desperation that "the *fiscales* and sacristans have abandoned this church to the point that at mass I must serve both as sacristan and celebrant, and to administer the sacraments of baptism and last rites I must enlist the services of women."[91]

Despite these events, Zinacanteco authorities apparently withdrew from the kind of wholesale defiance of religious authority which took place elsewhere in the highlands. Speaking of such resistance, for example, Jan Rus has written that

> From late 1867 to early 1869, letters flooded into the ecclesiastical government telling of communities which spurned the priests'

Table 37.

Fiestas in Zinacantan, 1855–56 and 1873–74

| | 1855–56 | 1873–74 |
|---|---|---|
| January | San Sebastián | San Sebastián |
| | | Santos Reyes |
| February | Purificación de la Sma. Virgen | Purificación de la Sma. Virgen |
| | 1 Viernes | Carnestolendas |
| March | Encarnación del Verbo Divino | Encarnación del Verbo Divino |
| | 2 Viernes | 2 Viernes |
| | 3 Viernes | 3 Viernes |
| | 4 Viernes | 4 Viernes |
| | 5 Viernes | 5 Viernes |
| April | Good Friday | Good Friday |
| | Holy Week and Easter | Holy Week and Easter |
| | | San José |
| | | San Marcos |
| | | San Pedro |
| May | Ascención del Señor | Ascención del Señor |
| | Santa Cruz | Santa Cruz |
| | Espíritu Santo | Pentacostés |
| | | Traslación de Santo Domingo |
| June | Octava de Corpus | Santísima Trinidad |
| | Corpus Christi | Octava de Corpus |
| | | Corpus Christi |
| | | San Antonio |
| July | Triunfo de la Santa Cruz | Triunfo de la Santa Cruz |
| August | San Lorenzo | Santo Domingo |
| | Asunción de María | San Lorenzo |
| September | Natividad de la Virgen | Natividad de la Virgen |
| | Exaltación de la Santa Cruz | Exaltación de la Santa Cruz |
| | | Santo Domingo Soriano |
| October | Nuestra Señora del Rosario | Nuestra Señora del Rosario |
| November | Misa mesal | Todos Santos |
| | Misa de Nuestra Señora del Rosario | Santa Catarina |

(continued)

TABLE 37. *(continued)*
Fiestas in Zinacantan, 1855–56 and 1873–74

|  | 1855–56 | 1873–74 |
|---|---|---|
|  | Finados y Todos Santos |  |
|  | Santa Catarina |  |
| December | Inmaculada Concepción | Inmaculada Concepción |
|  | Nuestra Señora de Guadalupe | Nuestra Señora de Guadalupe |
|  | Navidad | Navidad |
| Total | 28 | 34 |

*Source:* "Cuentas parroquiales de Zinacantan" (1854–1881)," AHDSC.

services and worshipped on their own. . . . If any priest dared to complain, these communities—backed by their own *secretarios*—immediately carried the case to the Liberal government in Chiapa and had him reproved. Such repudiation of the clergy is reported in Oxchuc, Huistán, Tenejapa, Chalchihuitán, Pantelhó, Chenalhó, Mitontic, and Chamula.[92]

By far the most dramatic of these incidents took place in Chamula, where the local *fiscal,* Pedro Díaz Cuzcat, set up his own chapel and *culto* in a hamlet called Tzajaljemel.[93] Within a few months, this chapel had displaced the town's main church as a center of worship for local men and women. Incensed by such blatant disregard for established religion, Conservative leaders in San Cristóbal tried at first to suppress the new cult by detaining Cuzcat and confiscating his *santos.* When these efforts were frustrated by state officials, however, the Church itself decided to intervene.

On May 27, 1868, a commission of three priests was dispatched to reason with the Indians, to talk them back into "paying religion." Finding the masses at Tzajaljemel to be sincere in their beliefs—that is, still Catholic—but nevertheless deluded, the members of this commission blessed a cross for them to worship and cautioned them of the dangers of praying before unconsecrated . . . images. Convinced that their superior theological reasoning had won the day, they then returned in triumph to San Cristóbal.[94]

But throughout the following months, Indians in Chamula persisted in their erroneous ways. Declaring that they were now threatened by a caste war, highland Conservatives then attacked several Tzotzil towns with a militia force of 300 that laid waste to everything in its path.[95]

Given their particular vulnerability, it is not surprising that Zinacantecos took special pains not to place themselves within that path. Unlike other highland communities, which had suffered grievously at the hands of Conservative patriarchs like Ramón Larraínzar, their experiences as laborers and *arrieros* had apparently prepared them to sustain the violent political cross-currents of the day. Seeing what had happened in Chamula, they pioneered a type of reconciliation with Church authorities which soon became generalized throughout the highlands. In 1869 and 1870, they petitioned the *mitra* to remove Vicente Guillén, whose obstreperous efforts to raise Church income there had almost brought the town to the point of open rebellion.[96] Having accomplished this goal, they reinstituted the offices of *mayordomo* and *alférez*. Thereafter, they dutifully paid their curate his rations, bonuses, and other fees—provided that he abstain from meddling in their religious affairs. Already 20 years earlier, the town's *cura* (Correa) had complained that "I find them to be far from fulfilling the Church's commandments, and although they are all Christians because they undertake to receive baptism, they avoid confession and yearly communion except for a small number."[97] Ten years later, in 1856, the man who was then parish priest reported that although resistance to annual communion was decreasing, virtually everyone in the community rejected his religious instruction. Like their forebears, however, Zinacantecos participated most willingly in those public ceremonies over which he exercised the least control.[98] And by 1870 it had become clear to ecclesiastical authorities that they were largely incapable of altering this state of affairs.[99]

Zinacanteco boy selling salt in the San Cristóbal market (1961).

Winding a skein of cotton yarn in Chamula (1960).

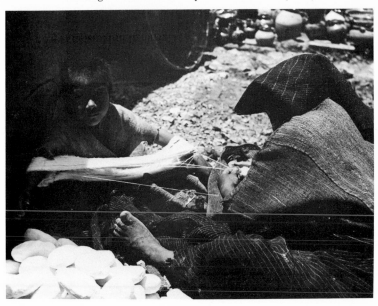

Zinacantecos weaving strands of palm for hats, San Cristóbal (1962).

Procession of the Virgin in San Andrés (1956).

Praying for good fortune in Tenejapa (1961).

Ceremonial combatants in San Andrés (1962).

Boy from Tenejapa bringing flowers to the San Cristóbal market (1961).

Weaving a shirt in San Bartolomé (now Venustiano Carranza) (1966).

Haircut in the Chamula market-place (1962).

*Carnaval* in Huistán (1966).

Wedding in Zinacantan (1972).

Saints from Santiago, San Andrés and Magdalena during the *fiesta* of San Andrés (1965).

Making pottery in Amatenango (1966).

Carnaval dancer in Huistán (1966).

Boy from Oxchuc in the San Cristóbal market (1961).

Chamula farmer selling squash to customers from Tenejapa (1963).

*Toro* leading *Carnaval* procession in Tenejapa (1961).

Bull charging spectator during the *fiesta* of San Pedro in Chenalhó (1966).

Preparing for the *fiesta* of San Juan in Chamula (1965).

Within a few years, too, other factors persuaded them to take a more charitable view of native ceremonialism. Responding to new opportunities for employment in Soconusco, many Zinacantecos abandoned *arriería* and chose instead to work as migratory coffee laborers.[100] By saving their wages, these men were soon able to sponsor public festivals without assistance from other *cofrades*. Now, in fact, with the help of their sons, they might in a few years' time accumulate enough money to take on an important *mayordomía*—and to increase their own worth by embellishing the rituals in which they participated. Naturally, competition of this sort made such positions more expensive; at the same time, it also stimulated Zinacantecos to reorganize religious positions into a hierarchy of ranked offices by means of which their achievements might become a matter of public record. Of equal importance, during these same years many *ladino* artisans and merchants, fleeing the poverty of life in San Cristóbal (which quickly became a highland backwater), installed themselves as shopkeepers and small farmers in Indian communities.[101] By 1890, approximately two dozen of these families had moved to Zinacantan; from their midst, district officials appointed the town's *alcalde* as well as its secretaries and justices of the peace.[102] By performing religious *cargos*, then, Indians not only bought forbearance from the Church, they also asserted their control over the only aspects of public life from which they were not excluded. And although the exact nature of this *arreglo* varied from one community to another, nonetheless in subsequent years the way in which native people organized their ceremonies served as a uniquely sensitive indicator of the political and economic pressures to which they were subjected.

## CONCLUSIONS

By 1910, it was clear that Liberals in Chiapas had accomplished one of their most cherished goals: they had drastically altered both the region's economy and the social relations upon which that economy was based. To this end, they had effectively deprived most native communities of their land, transformed many highland families into lowland fieldhands, and compelled the Indians who remained in their towns to pay rent and the *capitación*. As for life on the plantations, one American admirer wrote that

> The debt worker presented himself to the intending employer and received an advance of wages and a so-called card account, *carta cuenta*, stating the amount owed. This was [often] recognized before a legal authority, before whom was also drawn up a statement of the term—regularly one or two years—for which the man agreed to work every day but feast days. The services of the wife might or might not be included in the laborer's contract. When the laborer wished to move to another farm, he made arrangements with its owner by which the latter would pay the former employer the amount of the laborer's card account. The man was then transferred. The advances on card accounts often reached 500 pesos or more. The wage of the debt laborers in cash was 4 pesos a month, in addition to which they received 500 ears of corn, 20 pounds of beans, salt, house rent, medicines, and two bottles of alcohol.[103]

So successful were these arrangements that by 1910 nearly 24,000 men and women in the central valley alone had sold themselves into permanent bondage.[104]

As we have seen, however, by 1890 devices of this sort could not keep pace with the tremendous expansion of commercial agriculture in more remote areas. Taking matters into their own hands, plantation owners in Soconusco, Pichucalco, and the northern jungle organized a system of labor contracting (*enganche*, or more politely *habilitación*) which functioned independently of state officials. By that time, too, highland Indians, unable to pay their taxes or subsist upon highland *milpas*, reluctantly accepted the work which *enganchadores* offered them. Extolling the virtues of this system, an American publicist, W. W. Byam, wrote that

> These Indians are a mild, inoffensive people, who with proper training, and a reasonable regard for their comfort and well-being, make the best and most devoted of servants. . . . The custom of the country calls the laborer to the field at sun-up in the morning, keeping him there until the sun goes down at night. Through these

long hours the Indian, with only his "machete," will accomplish more at such work as clearing land and "weeding" than will the more intelligent white man with more modern implements.[105]

Of course, not all foreign visitors shared such a benign view of contract labor. In March 1910, one irate rubber planter complained to The India Rubber World in New York about a two-part serial entitled "Three Months in Peonage" which had recently concluded in The American Magazine. "I made a trip to the rubber belt on the Usumacinta River in Chiapas," he declared in a lengthy note filled with indignation, "and I failed to see any signs of slavery." On the contrary, he continued, without proper incentives the native population was condemned to eternal sloth and indifference.[106] "Life was too easy to encourage habits of industry," explained another widely-circulated work on Mexico:

> The great majority of the population were Indians who felt no necessity to work. Only a few of the native towns furnished laborers. The people of the rest of the towns relied on their corn patches and hunting for their livelihood. In the average case, there was little oppression possible on the haciendas, since the Indian could escape and the arm of the administration was not strong enough to hold him to his duty.[107]

As one might expect, throughout this period the myth of the "barbarous Indian," shut off by superstition and idleness from the civilizing influences of ladino society, retained its undiminished popularity among politicians and businessmen of every stripe. Even when Indians voluntarily left their towns to become lowland peons, apologists for both Church and State clung tenaciously to the notion that native customs and beliefs, not the conditions of labor on distant plantations, posed an irrational obstacle to emigration. In a passage which is startlingly reminiscent of Núñez de la Vega's ninth pastoral letter, for example, Byam declared that

> The entire population of Chiapas is Catholic in its religious belief; so, too, in a sense, are a majority of the Indians inhabiting the state. . . . Many of these so-called Christian Indians, particularly

those of Maya descent, are often found to mingle in their private worship certain of their pagan rites. These people have also preserved much of their ancient lore regarding the healing art and the stars. . . . [Their] tutelary deities have, however, taken Christian names, the Red or God of the East having become St. Dominic; the White or God of the North, St. Gabriel; the Black or God of the West, St. James; and the Yellow Goddess of the South, Mary Magdalene.[108]

But now enlightened secular authorities, not incompetent priests and venal friars, had assumed the burden of rescuing these benighted souls. "The school system of the Federal government," Byam concluded, "is being rapidly extended throughout the state of Chiapas and is perceptibly diminishing its rate of illiteracy and gradually melting its superstitions."[109] Within a few years, he assured his readers, these efforts would complete what three centuries of inept preaching and religious instruction had failed to accomplish. Beneath such rhetoric, we perceive a significant and singularly revealing fact: Liberal laws and policies, as important as these may have been, had not strictly speaking replaced feudalism with capitalism in the countryside, as their authors proudly maintained. More modestly, such measures reorganized and extended a system of social classes which had already begun to take shape during the late 17th and 18th centuries. Given the nature of this enterprise—as David McCreery has claimed in the case of Guatemala—politicians in Chiapas assumed a rather ambivalent stance toward much of Liberal economic theory: moved to rapture by the idea of free trade, they nonetheless abhorred the doctrine of *laissez-faire*, which in their view merely encouraged native indolence.[110]

Little wonder, then, that by 1870 highland Indians resented their governors with the same intensity which in the recent past they had reserved for Conservative *caudillos* in San Cristóbal.[111] Nor is it surprising that native towns never fully acquired the closed, corporate structure which later observers ascribed to them—despite efforts undertaken in this direction. Quite the contrary: when *naturales* organized novel religious institutions like *cargo* hierarchies, they did so largely in response to pressure from civil authorities who required that—in principle at least—parish dues be paid voluntarily. Ironically, measures of this sort obliged many Indian families to form corporate groups which in appearance at least resembled pre-Columbian lineages—groups of the kind which Liberal laws were specifically intended to destroy. And finally, caught in the crossfire between warring creole bands, the Indians elaborated a distinctive way of life through which, they hoped, they might soften the bonds of servitude and dispossession that *ladino* prosperity had fostered.

# END OF THE DIASPORA

## Cattlemen and Tenant Farmers in Central Chiapas

## 1910–1975

On September 14, 1914, nearly a century after Chiapas was incorporated into the Mexican Republic, General Jesús Agustín Castro assumed control of the state's public affairs.[1] During the next few weeks, he carefully deployed his 21st Division in garrisons which spread from Salto de Agua to Soconusco. Having accomplished this task, he turned his attention to Chiapas' complicated political situation. Here he faced two major difficulties. First, the area's landlords, especially those who lived in the Grijalva basin, had in previous decades become overwhelmingly Porfirista. Since 1891, in fact, Emilio Rabasa, Porfirio Díaz's proconsul, had governed the state and whipped local planters solidly into line. Unlike their disgruntled kinsmen in northern Mexico, these *hacendados* remained loyal to the *ancien régime*—even after 1911, when Francisco Madero replaced Díaz as President of Mexico. Consequently, they viewed Castro with the utmost distrust and regarded his 21st Division as an army of occupation. Second, another group of landlords, primarily those who resided in San Cristóbal, had watched their fortunes decline under Rabasa's administration; led by Bishop Francisco Orozco y Jiménez (who a decade later as Archbishop of Guadalajara played an active role in the *cristero* rebellion), these men plotted and schemed to recover their former power and preeminence.

By the time General Castro arrived in Chiapas, this conflict

156

had already produced considerable violence and bloodshed. Beginning in 1903, Orozco and his collaborators had turned native unhappiness with Liberal administration to their own purposes by inciting the Indians against Porfirista authorities in Tuxtla.[2] For example, one of these men, Manuel Pineda (whose son, Alberto, later waged guerrilla warfare against Carrancista forces), wrote an elaborate and legalistic defense of native *ejidos*—ignoring the role that highland Conservatives had played in usurping indigenous land.[3] Not content to press their case in the courts and the newspapers, however, they also recruited a network of agents—*ladinos* and Indians alike—who organized what in effect constituted an alternative system of regional government. Among these agents, Jacinto Pérez Chixtot (known as "Pajarito") played a particularly significant and tragic role. On May 15, 1911, the interim governor of Chiapas, Dr. Policarpo Rueda, arrived in San Cristóbal to negotiate a truce between lowland officials and highland conspirators. Rather than accept this arrangement, the bishop and his allies "called upon Jacinto Pérez to bring a large number of Indians from Chamula who marched through the streets in ranks of 8 abreast, interspersed every so often with a *ladino* from the city. According to some estimates, as many as 10,000 Indians participated in this parade."[4] Declaring themselves Maderistas (to discredit their rivals in the state capital), Conservative leaders subsequently dispatched Pajarito and 1,000 volunteers from Chamula against a force of lowland militiamen who cut them to pieces near Chiapa. Reluctant to incur the same fate, *voluntarios* from San Cristóbal, who had observed the battle from their encampment in Ixtapa, fought a brief engagement and withdrew.

Having defended themselves successfully against this challenge, authorities in the central valley turned their attention to the wave of genuine Maderista activity which had engulfed the state. In Cintalapa, textile workers in a factory called "La Providencia" went out on strike and were soon followed by the area's carpenters and mechanics.[5] Closer to home, a young landowner and intellectual, Luis Espinosa, broke ranks with Liberal autocrats in Tuxtla and rebelled against the new federal government headed by Victoriano Huerta. Accompanied by a few friends and allies, Espinosa moved into the countryside and harassed Huertista forces (including the state police) for nearly a year.[6] In Tapachula, members of the anarchist Partido Liberal Mexicano and the I.W.W. began to organize among railroad workers, coffee laborers, and artisans.[7] And in Salto de Agua, which lay far beyond the effective range of Liberal control, plantation employees elected their own *jefe político*, Guillermo Ferrer, who assumed his position in the name of Maderismo and Venustiano Carranza.[8] Faced with this situation, cattlemen in the Grijalva basin quickly threw in their lot with Bernardo Palafox, whom Huerta had sent to govern the state. Volunteering their services as *rurales*, they persecuted Carrancistas and other opponents of the regime throughout the region.[9] And finally, in 1912, when peons in the Lacandón jungle revolted against labor conditions in the *monterías* (lumber camps), such men willingly collaborated with Porfirista forces in Tabasco to put down the uprising.[10]

Thus it is not surprising that Castro regarded landowners in the central valley with great uneasiness. Rather than strike a bargain with them, he chose to neutralize their influence and seek political support elsewhere. On October 30, 1914, he promulgated the Ley de Obreros, a far-reaching measure which abolished debt servitude and *tiendas de raya*, established a minimum daily wage, and granted *finca* workers the right to medical benefits, vacations, and free education.[11] Thereafter, ranging the countryside, his soldiers returned many *hacienda* laborers to their native villages—at gunpoint, if they did not leave voluntarily. *Finqueros* in the Grijalva valley were outraged and horrified. One month later, in the rich cattle and cotton country southwest of Chiapa, several prominent landowners signed the Act of Canguí: "In view of the vandalism to which the Chiapanec family has been subjected by the armed band sent by the Carranza government, which has invaded Chiapanec soil with no other purpose than to tread upon our political institutions, we have resolved to rise up in arms in defense of society."[12] Heeding this clarion call, *hacendados* in Comitán soon formed their own revolutionary army, a rag-tag affair which for the next five years controlled the state's international border. In this effort they were eventually joined by Alberto Pineda, who at the end of

1916 organized his Brigada Las Casas which harassed federal garrisons from Ocosingo to Palenque.

Despite their bravery and determination, these guerrilla bands, poorly armed, untrained, torn by internal rivalries, could not overcome Castro's regulars. After driving federal forces from San Cristóbal, Pineda suffered a series of defeats which effectively ended his military campaign. Similarly, Tiburcio Fernández Ruíz, commander of the *mapache* fighters near Chiapa, continued to lose ground until he, too, eventually laid down his arms. And despite the fact that he enjoyed considerable support from coffee planters in Soconusco, he was unable during six years of intermittant combat to interrupt traffic on the heavily guarded Pan-American Railway, which since 1908 had connected Tapachula to the Isthmus of Tehuantepec. By 1920, when Alvaro Obregón became President, both Pineda and Fernández Ruíz had made an uneasy truce with federal authorities. But whereas the *mapaches* soon became enthusiastic Obregonistas, Pineda and his followers, inspired by Adolfo de la Huerta, revolted again four years later. Ironically, this rebellion, in which Pineda came perilously close to capturing Tuxtla, destroyed those hitherto undimmed hopes—still cherished by highland aristocrats—that San Cristóbal might once again become the state's capital city. For the federal general who defended Tuxtla, and who received much of the credit for Pineda's downfall, was none other than Tiburcio Fernández Ruíz, who in the interim had become governor of Chiapas. Having learned to live with the new regime in Mexico City, lowland ranchers and coffee planters retained their control over the area's destiny.

## PEONS AND POLITICS IN THE AGE OF REVOLUTION

As in the rest of Mexico, agrarian reform in Chiapas made little headway during the years that followed Obregón's ascendence to the presidency. On October 3, 1921, Governor Fernández Ruíz signed the state's first revolutionary land law, which allowed *finqueros* to retain 8,000 hectares for their own use.[13] No restrictions were placed upon the number of family members who might exploit contiguous properties in common; predictably, the law encouraged large landowners to divide their holdings among close relatives and thus preserve their original estates intact. As we might expect, coffee production on such estates continued unabated (Figure 7). By this time, however, opposition to don Tiburcio and his associates had acquired a more insistent tone: in 1921, a group of political activists and labor organizers (including Luis Espinosa) founded the Partido Socialista del Soconusco, which later merged with the Partido Socialista Chiapaneco and became affiliated with Felipe Carrillo's Partido Socialista del Sureste. Already in 1918, 20,000 coffee workers, led by the Sindicato Central de Obreros y Campesinos, had struck in Soconusco; two years later, 7,000 more workers threatened to disrupt the coffee harvest.[14] Thereafter, *jornaleros* and peasants throughout the region joined Socialist unions which demanded increased wages, better working conditions, and the redistribution of private farms.

In response, Fernández Ruíz imposed members of his own political following upon *municipio* governments in which dissidents had achieved public office, and accused his opponents of conspiring with de la Huerta.[15] At the same time, using state lands or properties abandoned by foreign owners, he initiated a policy of selective reform designed to transform landless peons into less militant *ejidatarios*. Between 1918 and 1924, therefore, he created 5 *ejidos* for coffee laborers in Soconusco and 4 others in the central basin.[16] The results of this gambit were twofold. On the one hand, by using agrarian reform to reduce labor unrest and social conflict, Fernández established a *modus operandi* which was followed by virtually all of his successors for the next 20 years. Until 1937, in fact, most of the *ejidos* which obtained definitive title to their lands were located in areas where militancy among plantation workers had reached threatening proportions: Cintalapa, Yajalón, Pichucalco, Soconusco.[17] On the other hand, Fernández's uncompromising attitude toward labor organizations and opposition parties—which were also fervent supporters of the new federal regime—and his obvious eagerness to fight a rear-guard action in defense of foreign plantation owners (whose own loyalties were certainly open to question) earned

FIGURE 7.
Coffee Production in Chiapas, 1900–1935

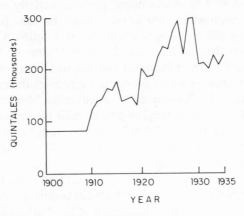

Source: Leo Waibel, *La Sierra Madre de Chiapas.*

him the opprobrium of Obregon's interior minister, Plutarco Elías Calles.[18]

In 1925, after he became president, Calles allowed a Socialist candidate, Carlos Vidal, to become governor of Chiapas. But within two years Vidal was dead: implicated in a conspiracy against the President, his indiscretion provided *la mapachada* with an excuse to massacre Socialist leaders and other opponents of Fernández's rule.[19] Even so, neither don Tiburcio nor his confederates were permitted to regain direct control over the region's affairs: convinced that they were a bunch of dangerous reactionaries, Calles in 1932 appointed a former comrade-in-arms, Colonel Victorico Grajales, to govern Chiapas.[20] As for the Socialists, those few who survived were absorbed into the newly-created Partido Nacional Revolucionario or driven into permanent isolation.[21] As the country prepared to elect Calles' successor in 1934, therefore, landowners in Chiapas had learned another important fact of political life: by cooperating with the official party and accepting its authority in matters of government, they might obtain relief from labor agitation and radical *agrarismo*.

In fact, it was the gubernatorial election in 1936 which ultimately brought agrarian reform to the area and which, paradoxically, put an end to independent political activity among peasants and plantation workers. Loyal to his patron and commanding officer, Grajales nominated a fellow Callista, Dr. Samuel León Brindis, to succeed him as governor of Chiapas.[22] By that time Calles' principal rival, General Lázaro Cárdenas, had become president and set out to reorganize the ruling party, now renamed the Partido de la Revolución Mexicana (PRM). Naturally, Cárdenas refused to give Brindis his *imprimatur*, and sent another candidate, Efraín Gutiérrez, from Mexico City. But Brindis refused to withdraw; instead, he and Grajales assembled an independent campaign organization which they required state employees and *presidentes municipales* to join. Gutiérrez and his personal secretary, Dr. Pascacio Gamboa (who later became governor of Chiapas, president of the Partido Revolucionario Institucional, and secretary of health), organized their own political machine, staffed primarily by federal workers. Realizing that they commanded virtually no support in the central highlands, they recruited a minor customs official from Tapachula, Erasto Urbina, to run their campaign in Indian *municipios*.[23]

As it turned out, Urbina was ideally suited for the job: of humble origins, he had grown up in San Cristóbal, which he left in 1918 to become a railroad worker. Imbued with the sort of radical populism upon which Cárdenas had based his presidential campaign, he also retained a wide range of acquaintances among the *ladino* artisans and peddlers who populated his native *barrio de mexicanos*. And it was precisely these men, who travelled constantly throughout the highlands and traded in Indian communities, that he was to call upon in order to secure Gutiérrez's margin of victory.[24] Once this objective was accomplished, Urbina was rewarded with two positions of political responsibility: in 1937, he was appointed director of a new state agency, the Departamento de Acción Social, Cultural y Protección Indígena (which had been organized to carry forward the work of Cárdenas' Departamento de Asuntos Indígenas), and the following year he was elected to represent San Cristóbal in the

TABLE 38.
Number of Coffee Workers Hired Through the
Oficina de Contrataciones, 1937–1944

| Municipio | 1937 | 1938 | 1939 | 1940 | 1941 | 1942 | 1943 | 1944 |
|-----------|------|------|------|------|------|------|------|------|
| Chamula | 1,737 | 1,508 | 1,613 | 913 | 997 | 1,738 | 2,329 | 236 |
| Chenalhó | 240 | 715 | 243 | 99 | 100 | 238 | 198 | 51 |
| Huistán | 280 | 107 | 247 | 117 | 26 | 225 | 313 | — |
| Mitontic | 1,199 | 204 | 506 | 56 | 70 | 353 | 419 | 79 |
| Oxchuc | 1,689 | 970 | 660 | 62 | 123 | 517 | 810 | — |
| San Andrés | — | 100 | 310 | 71 | 25 | 235 | 308 | — |
| San Cristóbal | — | 29 | 100 | 27 | 27 | 110 | 215 | — |
| Tenejapa | 1,748 | 895 | 1,094 | 881 | 899 | 1,228 | 1,646 | 30 |
| Total | 6,893 | 4,528 | 4,773 | 2,226 | 2,267 | 4,644 | 6,238 | 396 |

Source: Ricardo Pozas, *Chamula, un pueblo indio de los altos de Chiapas*, p. 124.

state congress.[25] As director of Indian affairs, he set out to consolidate the hold which PRM officials exercised over native labor in central Chiapas. To this end he recruited a small but steadfastly loyal group of *agentes montados* (mounted agents), many of whom had formerly worked as fiscal police for the state treasury, in which capacity they had been charged with enforcing an officially sanctioned monopoly against Indian distillers of *aguardiente* and had gained considerable experience with the area's people and terrain.[26] Moreover, in general they too had grown up in the *barrio de mexicanos* and shared Urbina's disdain for what he loosely called *la burguesía* in San Cristóbal.

Armed with this private police force, Urbina created two new agencies, the Oficina de Contrataciones and the Sindicato de Trabajadores Indígenas (STI), which he placed under the nominal direction of a few hand-picked young Indians from Chamula. Thereafter, all peons who were hired to work on plantations in the north or along the coast were required to sign a contract with plantation agents in the Oficina and to join the STI (Table 38).[27] In this way, Urbina assured that coffee laborers were paid the legal minimum wage and treated according to standards established by Cárdenas' ministers in Mexico City. More important, he also asserted his control over the operations of highland *enganchadores*, who by that time had installed themselves in virtually every major Indian town.[28] From that time onward, his agents delivered work gangs to politically understanding planters who accepted their place within Cárdenas' *estado cooperativista*.[29]

By 1938, such cooperation had become imperative in order to assure the success of another important Cardenista project: land reform in Soconusco. According to the government's agrarian policy, coffee plantations such as those in Chiapas were limited to 300 hectares. As in 1921, many growers—whose holdings generally ranged between 5,000 and 8,000 hectares—subdivided their properties among close relatives.[30] But Cárdenas had foreseen such an eventuality and had made *fraccionamientos* of this sort liable to confiscation. As a result, many plantations lost a considerable amount of land—land which was granted to their erstwhile *peones*.[31] At first, of course, resistance to such measures was strong, and tempers quickly wore thin. Within a short time, however, most planters realized that in the end they stood to benefit from these reforms. After all, they were allowed to retain the best parcels as well as their processing facilities, buildings, and other equipment.[32] And in the absence of a major program to build such equipment for the new *ejidos*, they soon found that they could buy or process virtually all of the coffee grown on their former lands without incurring the normal risks of production. What is more, between 1935 and 1938 many *finqueros* had imported additional workers from Guatemala; indeed, it was these people, uncontaminated by Socialist politics and eager to remain in Mexico, who formed the majority of *ejidatarios*.[33] By 1940, in fact, such *ejidatarios* (or their children), unable to make ends meet, frequently returned to the plantations as day laborers or even as foremen.[34] All in all, then, agrarian reform in the region served to surround large landholdings with a protective buffer of underproductive and undercapitalized *ejidos* which contributed to the prosperity of private growers.[35]

Having resolved these issues, Governor Gutiérrez and his collaborators turned their attention to that plaguey old problem

TABLE 39.
Private Fincas in the Central Highlands,
1940

| Municipio | Estates | Land |
|-----------|---------|------|
| Chamula | 2 | 135.0 has. |
| Chanal | 11 | 640.5 |
| Chenalhó | 20 | 3,911.3 |
| Huistán | 121 | 23,366.2 |
| Pantelhó | 163 | 16,380.0 |
| San Andrés | 2 | 13.5 |
| San Cristóbal | 463 | 22,659.5 |
| Tenejapa | 24 | 5,185.2 |
| Teopisca | 96 | 14,177.2 |
| Zinacantan | 26 | 8,665.5 |
| Total | 928 | 95,133.9 has. |

Source: Pozas, Chamula, p. 117.

which had bedeviled their predecessors for over a century: how to contain the power of landowners in San Cristóbal, and especially to limit their influence over Indian communities. And it was here that Urbina used his combined resources as *jefe del departamento* and local deputy to devise a unique and effective solution. By 1936, as Table 39 suggests, these landowners had become particularly vulnerable to agrarian reform: almost without exception, their highland properties were liable to confiscation and redistribution by the state.[36] Under Urbina's tutelage, agrarian committees directed by young bilingual men like those who ran the coffee workers' union were organized in native communities throughout the region.[37] In Chamula, for example, which provided a disproportionate number of the area's plantation laborers, a small group of these men occupied virtually all positions of importance within the STI, the *comisariado ejidal*, and the town government.

Predictably, among the very first properties which *agraristas* in Chamula claimed was the *finca* of San Francisco, a local

TABLE 40.
Ejidos in Central Chiapas, 1944

| Municipio | Number of Ejidos | Amount of Land[a] | Percentage of Total Area |
|---|---|---|---|
| Chamula | 5 | 37,754.0 has. | 99.6% |
| Chanal | 1 | 432,580.7 | 99.8 |
| Chenalhó | 9 | 10,601.7 | 71.5 |
| Huistán | 12 | 12,856.2 | 35.5 |
| Pantelhó | 6 | 4,002.3 | 19.6 |
| San Andrés | 2 | 1,638.0 | 99.2 |
| San Cristóbal | 6 | 7,643.3 | 24.3 |
| Tenejapa | 2 | 1,172.8 | 6.6 |
| Teopisca | 8 | 13,389.8 | 48.5 |
| Zinacantan | 2 | 18,143.2 | 68.0 |
| Total | 53 | 539,782.0 has. | 57.3% (average) |

Source: Pozas, Chamula, p. 117.

[a] Including terrenos comunales (common lands) which had not been entitled as private property.

ranch which had been purchased in 1928 by Pablo Reincke to provide peons for his plantation in Soconusco. By that time, too, Urbina had installed new municipal secretaries in many highland pueblos, selected from among the same small-time peddlers and merchants who served in the Departamento de Protección. During the next three years, Urbina was able to transform the basis of landed wealth in the region—even as he carefully circumscribed the autonomy of native agrarian committees (Table 40). By 1941, in fact, these committees had been fully incorporated into the Liga de Comunidades Agrarias y Sindicatos Campesinos de Chiapas, a branch of the official Confederación Nacional Campesina (CNC).[38] And when in 1938 highland landowners, led by the indomitable Alberto Pineda, tried to have Urbina assassinated, he placed the town under military rule and had himself appointed presidente municipal.[39]

Despite his enthusiasm for reform, Urbina was not altogether uncompromising in his attitude toward these *finqueros*. As in Soconusco, they were generally permitted to retain their buildings and other capital improvements as well as their choicest lands and irrigated parcels (Table 41). By selling these parcels to local Indians, they were often able to realize a reasonable profit, which they were free to reinvest outside of the region. In 1941, for example, Pablo Reincke relinquished his remaining share of San Francisco (355 hectares) to members of the Colonia Agraria Belisario Domínguez, who had delegated the head of their agrarian committee to purchase the property.[40] Similar transactions took place throughout the highlands: in Zinacantan, Tenejapa, Huistán, Mitontic, Chenalhó, San Andrés.[41] Elsewhere, according to the economist Moisés de la Peña, *terratenientes* sold their properties to native tenants or even gave away land in order to protect their more valuable assets. Consider the case of coffee growers near Yajalón who "instead of murdering *agrarista* leaders as their counterparts have done in many other states, have banded together and bought [6,000 hectares of] uncultivated land which they gave to nearby communities."[42] The results of such measures, which were clearly designed both to forestall more radical demands and to facilitate continued production, soon became apparent. De la Peña estimates that by 1940 most of the state's *ejidatarios* owned no more than 5 hectares of seasonally arable land; of the 62,000 families which had benefited from agrarian reform, fully one-third possessed insufficient resources to sustain themselves. And beginning in 1937, government officials began to grant *certificados de inafectabilidad ganadera* (exempting most pasturelands from expropriation) to cattle ranchers in the Grijalva basin and northern lowlands.[43] In this way, many ranchers managed to salvage all but an insignificant portion of their enormous estates (Table 42).

Not surprisingly, by 1942, when federal authorities abandoned most of Cárdenas' so-called *política de masas*, officials in Chiapas were eager to replace Urbina and his subordinates with less diligent functionaries.[44] Through the intercession of Pascacio Gamboa (who by that time had become president of the PRI), a *hueso* was found for Urbina in Guanajuato, then in Tijuana, where in 1947 he was finally made intervenor at the local jai-alai

## TABLE 41.
### Private Property in the Central Highlands, 1944

| Municipio | 100.0–200.0 has. | 200.1–400.0 has. | 400.1–1000.0 has. | Above 1000 has. | Total Number | Total Area |
|---|---|---|---|---|---|---|
| Chenalhó | 3 | 3 | 4 | 0 | 10 | 4,967.4 |
| Huistán | 24 | 11 | 4 | 5 | 44 | 21,270.9 |
| Pantelhó | 14 | 24 | 8 | 0 | 46 | 12,547.8 |
| San Cristóbal | 19 | 26 | 2 | 3 | 50 | 16,431.1 |
| San Felipe | 1 | 6 | 4 | 1 | 12 | 4,920.1 |
| Tenejapa | 2 | 5 | 0 | 2 | 9 | 5,918.0 |
| Teopisca | 16 | 12 | 4 | 3 | 35 | 14,108.9 |
| Zinacantan | 2 | 7 | 1 | 2 | 12 | 7,933.6 |
| Total | 81 | 94 | 27 | 16 | 218 | 88,097.8 |

*Source:* Pozas, *Chamula,* pp. 117–118.

TABLE 42.
Land Tenure in Central Chiapas, 1950

| Municipio | Percentage of Titles | | | Percentage of Farmlands | | |
|---|---|---|---|---|---|---|
| | 0–5 [a] has. | Above 5 has. | 500–2000 has. | 0–5 [a] has. | Above 5 has. | 500–2000 has. |
| Acala | 60% | 40% | 2% | 33% | 67% | 18% |
| Chiapa | 64 | 36 | 0.5 | 36 | 64 | 23 |
| Chiapilla | 85 | 15 | 0 | 70 | 30 | 0 |
| Ixtapa | 49 | 51 | 3 | 88 | 12 | — |
| La Concordia | 12 | 88 | 17 | 24 | 76 | 75 |
| San Lucas | 90 | 10 | 0.5 | 42 | 58 | 14 |
| Socoltenango | 85 | 15 | 14 | 7.5 | 92.5 | 17 |
| Tuxtla | 58 | 42 | 0.2 | 19 | 81 | 10 |
| V. Carranza | 19 | 81 | 13 | 8 | 92 | 29 |
| Villa Flores | 15 | 85 | 3 | 28 | 72 | 22 |

Sources: Secretaría de Agricultura y Ganadería, Censo agrícola, ganadero y ejidal, 1950; Moisés de la Peña, Chiapas económico, vol. 2, pp. 332ff.

[a] Including ejidos.

concession.[45] Here it was expected that he would enrich himself with bribes and other graft and retire to San Cristóbal. To his credit, it seems that he did not avail himself of these opportunities, and he died a decade later in modest circumstances.

Meanwhile, an important landowner, Alberto Rojas, assumed control of the state Departamento de Asuntos Indígenas (which had superceded the Departamento de Protección) and installed his own lieutenants in Indian towns. Among these men, for example, he named Celso Villafuerte, who for many years had been employed by Guillermo Pohlenz as enganchador in Chenalhó, to the post of municipal secretary in Chamula.[46] By that time, too, Mexico had declared war on Germany and had expropriated many of the area's coffee plantations, which were held in trust by the federal Junta de Administración y Vigilancia de la Propiedad Extranjera.[47] In fact, it was this event which finally transformed both the STI and the Liga de Comunidades Agrarias

7

TABLE 43.
Ejido Lands in Zinacantan, 1940

| Hacienda | Area Granted to Ejidatarios (hectares) | | | Retained by Owner | |
|---|---|---|---|---|---|
| | Seasonably Arable | Forest | Total | Area | Percentage |
| Guadalupe Xucun | 501 has. | 930 has. | 1,431 has. | 391 has. | 21.4% |
| San Antonio | 1,858 | 2,272 | 4,130 | 341 | 7.6 |
| San Nicolás | 78 | 0 | 78 | 655 | 89.3 |
| Tierra Colorada | 114 | 267 | 381 | 440 | 53.6 |
| El Pig | 218 | 405 | 623 | 390 | 38.5 |
| Yalemtaiv | 57 | 133 | 190 | 421 | 68.9 |
| Santa Rita Agil | 9 | 21 | 30 | 421 | 91.3 |
| La Lagunita | 60 | 112 | 172 | 205 | 53.9 |
| Jok' Ch'enom | n.a. | n.a. | 5,030 | n.a. | n.a. |
| Total | | | 12,065 has. | | 31.7% [a] (average) |

Source: Matthew Edel, "El ejido en Zinacantan," in E. Z. Vogt, ed., Los Zinacantecos, pp. 171–173.
[a] Excluding Jok' Ch'enom.

into what they remain to this day: minor branches of the state bureaucracy. Nor did this situation change when in 1946 the coffee plantations were returned to their original owners. On the contrary: as *sindicato* members showed signs of renewed militancy during the early 1950s, coffee growers obtained permission from the interior ministry to import as many as 20,000 non-union workers a year from Guatemala.[48] Deprived of the power to organize these *braceros*, STI officials continued to exercise the one function which they might rightfully perform: they served as government-sponsored hiring agents for the coffee *fincas*.

In order to understand how such measures affected Indians in the central highlands, it is useful once again to consider the examples of Zinacantan and Chamula. On April 6, 1940, federal and state agrarian authorities approved Zinacantan's petition to expropriate land from a number of local properties (Table 43).[49]

TABLE 44.
Proportion of Eligible Families Which Received Ejido Land
in Zinacantan, 1961

| Settlements | Ejidatarios | Families | Percentage |
|---|---|---|---|
| Zinacantan, Pat Osil | 160 | 449 | 36% |
| Salinas, Saklum, Petztoj | 44 | 108 | 41 |
| Na Chij | 98 | 230 | 43 |
| Paste', Elan Vo' | 179 | 419 | 43 |
| Nabenchauk | 66 | 307 | 21 |
| Apas | 91 | 176 | 54 |
| Jok' Ch'enom | 231 | 267 | 86 |
| Total | 869 | 1,956 | 44% |
| | | | (average) |

Source: Edel, "El ejido en Zinacantan," p. 172.

As Matthew Edel has pointed out, this marked the midpoint in a long and difficult struggle which since 1925 had pitted many determined Zinacantecos against local landowners. Like peasants elsewhere in Mexico, *agraristas* in Zinacantan finally won their grant only after they had armed themselves (with Urbina's encouragement) and occupied the lands in question. Even so, they waited 17 more years until President Ruíz Cortines confirmed their rights to these fields. In the interim, they lobbied vigorously to extend and expand their claims beyond the modest limits which official surveyors had originally established. In 1944, for example, the state's *delegado agrario* reported that their provisional grant excluded a fairly large portion of the lands to which they were entitled, and that nearly half of those families eligible to receive allotments had been excluded (Table 44). To make matters worse, most landowners retained both their best fields and their control over local water supplies. As a result, fully 60 percent of the town's final grant consisted of forests and hillsides, while only 40 percent contained "seasonally arable" farmlands.[50] Predictably, within a few years population growth had undermined even those slight benefits which land reform had promised. By 1960, therefore, many native *ejidatarios* had realized that their victory over proprietors and bureaucrats, in which they had invested countless time and money, had borne little fruit.[51]

Despite its failure to improve Zinacantan's economic situation, agrarian reform left its stamp upon the *municipio*'s political life.[52] Between 1890 and 1916, a small group of important men— including Antonio Muruch, Antonio Promax, Lorenzo Pérez Jil, and Juan Hernández Zárate (in the *cabecera*), Fabián Santis in Nabenchauk, and Manuel Chuch in Paste'—had limited public office to those Indians who had served in prestigious religious positions and had thus demonstrated their respect for indigenous authority. In this way they hoped to deflect or at least mitigate the effects of *ladino* rule, which was exercised in the community by local *alcaldes* and justices of the peace. During the revolution, most people in Zinacantan—*mestizos* and Indians alike—remained neutral: having suffered considerable hardship at the hands of marauding *mapaches*, their primary concern lay in avoiding requisitions by any of the warring parties.

Finally, in 1918, a number of Zinacantecos, persuaded by Obregón to guide his forces in exchange for promises of land, played a decisive role in ending Pineda's occupation of the highlands.[53] Obregón did not order the immediate expropriation of local farms, as many Indians apparently expected. Nonetheless, he did install one of his former Zinacanteco scouts, Pedro Tzu of Nabenchauk, in the town's presidency. For his part, having attained this office without the consent of "traditional elders," Tzu naturally regarded the notion of mandatory religious service without great enthusiasm. By that time, too, most of the region's priests, including the curate of Zinacantan, had fled to the safety of San Cristóbal or Guatemala—a situation which relieved native *mayordomos* and *alféreces* of their economic obligations. According to one informant, "Tzu was right, in a sense, because many times the people who were given *cargos* couldn't afford them. But for lack of volunteers the *principales* pressed these jobs upon whoever had the most money, or a few animals, or a house with a tile roof, or even upon someone who had gotten out of line and had to be taught his responsibilities."[54] It was precisely against this kind of coercion that Tzu directed his efforts as *presidente*, efforts which aroused the ire of his political rival Fabián Santis. In the end, Santis and his confederates, aided by the indifference of state authorities, where able to regain control of the *cabildo* and perpetuate their rule for another generation.

After removing Tzu from office, elders in Zinacantan governed the community with a much greater degree of autonomy than in previous years. In this respect they were aided by the fact that during the revolution most of the area's *ladinos* had abandoned their homes and did not return after peace was restored. Moreover, following a practice which had been instituted by Jesús Castro, state authorities no longer insisted that Indian *cabildos* include *mestizo* judges and councilors. Of greater importance, however, it must be remembered that for nearly a century native *alcaldes* and *regidores*, ignoring the constitutional separation of Church and State, had supervised the town's principal *fiestas*. When rural *municipios* were reorganized after the revolution, these *alcaldes* lost their official functions, but local *regidores* continued to perform both civil and religious duties. As a result, indigenous *principales* faced few obstacles in selecting presidents and *síndicos* who fulfilled their particular criteria of loyalty, obedience, and honesty. "In those days," according to a man who lived in Zinacantan at the time, "they would call together everyone from the *parajes*, the whole town, to name a new president. For one reason or another, the men they chose didn't work out, so in the end they simply imposed a member of their own group: Juan Zárate."[55]

Recalling Obregón's promise to give them land, in 1925 these men filed a petition with the Comisión Agraria Mixta. As we know, their request was ignored until 1937, when Erasto Urbina appointed Juan Zárate's son, Mariano, to lead Zinacantan's agrarian committee.[56] Simultaneously, Urbina required Indian *ayuntamientos* to name bilingual *escribanos* (scribes)—a measure which was calculated specifically to strengthen the authority of men like Zárate.[57] Thereafter, using his combined powers as *comisariado ejidal* and Urbina's personal representative, don Mariano governed Zinacantan on behalf of the PRM (and later the PRI) for over 20 years.

Many Zinacantecos, of course, understood very well the nature of Zárate's influence in public life. As long as he performed his *ejido* functions adequately, however, and as long as he enjoyed the confidence of government officials, they accepted his rather autocratic political rule. Like his counterparts in Chamula, Zárate carefully served a series of important religious offices. In this fashion, he won the allegiance of traditional elders who in any case found themselves obliged to support him in most matters of general concern. For these reasons, it seems unlikely that Zárate owed his power primarily to economic rivalries between *ejidatarios* and non-*ejidatarios*, as Edel has suggested.[58] In fact, many of Zárate's staunchest supporters included men who never became *agraristas*. These Zinacantecos refused to join the *ejido* movement not, as other investigators have maintained, out of fear or ignorance, but simply because, as one of them explained, "We realized that we had nothing to gain."[59] Even among *agraristas*, economic stature and political sympathies varied widely from hamlet to hamlet. In Salinas, for example, most *ejidatarios* also owned their own land, and were thus able to meet the numerous expenses which *ejido* activity entailed. Among these men, it was the wealthiest *agraristas*, not the poorest, who resented Zárate's leadership and eventually protested against him to state authorities.[60] At the same time, in Elan Vo' both Indian smallholders and landless peasants became *ejidatarios* in equal numbers—primarily because they desired to acquire the nearby *finca* of Guadalupe Xucun. And finally, in Nabenchauk, where highland farming still played a small part in economic life, only one-quarter of those eligible to join the *ejido* solicited land.

In the end, it was not opposition from anti-*agraristas* which brought about Zárate's downfall, but rather an internal dispute among his own followers.[61] In 1961, with Zárate's blessing, a young *ejidatario* from Na Chij, Guillermo Pérez Nuj, became Zinacantan's *presidente municipal*. By that time, the Instituto Nacional Indigenista (INI, successor to the federal Departamento Autónomo de Asuntos Indígenas) had employed Zárate as a community development agent and rural schoolteacher. By that time, too, he had established a brokerage system in which Indians who wished to deal with government agencies paid him for his endorsement. But whereas 20 years earlier his knowledge of Spanish and his political friendships had permitted him to demand such gratuities, by 1960 most Zinacantecos no longer required his intercession. Simultaneously, it seems that INI officials, suspicious that Zárate had secretly sabotaged several of their projects to preserve his own influence, no longer gave him their unconditional support.[62] It was the Pan-American Highway, however, passable in 1947, which in the end sealed Zárate's fate. By providing rapid and efficient transportation to the Grijalva valley, this roadway encouraged *agraristas* to abandon their marginal and unproductive *ejidos* in favor of fields rented from lowland cattlemen. As a result, Zárate found himself deprived of his principal constituencies and abandoned by many of his friends. Upon becoming *presidente*, therefore, Guillermo Nuj—who refused to accept bribes on Zárate's behalf—imprisoned the *cacique* for murder. Although Zárate's allies soon removed Nuj from office, and although they soon procured their leader's release from jail, don Mariano never again recovered his preeminence in municipal affairs.[63]

Much the same conditions prevailed in Chamula, where from 1910 to 1921 native people were left more or less on their own.[64] Previously, the onslaught of forced labor had caught them unprepared and had taught them a lesson which they were determined to remember. In 1911, then, when official labor recruitment was abolished, local elders set out to take command of their municipal government. Thereafter, with the *jefes políticos* in flight and the state government in disarray, these men strengthened their defenses against the day when state authorities might again reassert their control. To this end they received some encouragement from General Castro, who in 1914 conferred positions of official leadership upon men whom he regarded as "traditionalists." Prompted by such actions, community leaders in Chamula subsequently declared that all future town officers—particularly municipal presidents—would henceforth be chosen from among the ranks of monolingual elders. In this way they hoped to forestall the possibility that their own officials would again be compelled to organize work crews for the plantations or *monterías*.

Not surprisingly, the restoration of public order after 1921 permitted coffee planters to resume normal operations and to recruit highland workers. During these years, of course, economic conditions in Chamula remained deplorable: without land or an effective minimum wage, most Indians were reduced to the same miserable conditions they had experienced before the revolution. Even so, freed from direct political interference, local elders consolidated their hold over public affairs. In so doing, they pursued two separate but related courses of action. After consulting with members of the municipal government, they chose the new slates of officers which each year assumed formal leadership of the town council. In order to be eligible for such a post, these officers were required to serve at least one religious cargo. Such cargos were generally filled by young men who owed their appointment to the town's ranking civil authorities. In this way, all positions of importance within the community were in effect controlled by a group of self-defined principales who had worked their way up through a system which in large measure they themselves had devised: the civil-religious hierarchy.

As one might expect, this situation changed rapidly after 1936, when Urbina appointed a group of scribes in Chamula who not only served in the town's cabildo but also presided over the local agrarian reform committee, represented their community in the regional agrarian commission, and assumed direction of the STI. In fact, so successfully did they perform such functions that in 1940 state officials tried to install them formally in the municipal presidency. From that time onward, these officials declared, government agencies would recognize only presidents who spoke Spanish. For their part, principales in Chamula—who in general responded quite favorably to Cardenista programs—viewed this measure as an infringement upon their right to conduct communal affairs, and continued for three more years to name their own presidente. During this period, the community had two mayors: a traditional cargo-holder designated by the elders, and a young scribe who had been named by state authorities. Rather than force the issue, however, local scribes decided for the moment to conciliate the principales. Then in late 1942, the official candidate requested that he be given an expensive religious post—not immediately, but in five years' time. Simultaneously, the state government began to enforce a law, enacted in 1937, which effectively permitted only religious officials (or those who would soon assume such office) to sell liquor in Indian communities—as a way of paying the costs of their service. Essentially, then, this regulation offered traditional authorities a new source of income to compensate for their loss of power—a source of income which depended upon their cooperation with the young presidents.

Having formed an alliance with these elders, Chamula's scribes confidently took their place at the head of both civil and religious government in the community. For the next 30 years, they alternately occupied the municipal presidency and served in important religious positions—a course of action which permitted them to consolidate and legitimate their power. In much the same vein, it was they who first spawned the idea of compiling waiting lists for prestigious *cargos*. By placing their names on such lists, they earned the right to sell liquor—an extremely profitable venture—several years before serving the saints. By the 1950s, in fact, their unorthodox political origins had been all but forgotten. Instead, they had themselves become the town's elders and had displaced those troublesome *principales* whom they had by that time outlived. In this capacity, they played a prominent role in INI's plan to develop the highlands: beginning in 1952, they became the region's first schoolteachers and health workers, the first owners of improved breeding stock and seeds, of "cooperative" stores and communal trucks. With the income derived from these activities, they also lent out money to their less fortunate neighbors at a monthly interest rate of around 10 percent. More important, by carefully husbanding their relationship with state and federal officials, they determined who else might gain access to such resources. And finally, by permitting only loyal followers to pursue religious careers, they continued to decide who might eventually accede to high local office—a decision which they continued to make long after they had retired from active public life.

At this point, one might speculate that after 1942, state authorities directed municipal scribes in Chamula to serve as religious *cargo*-holders. Perhaps these officials had come to appreciate the importance of public ritual—ritual over which Catholic priests no longer exercised any direct influence—in native political life. After all, it is at least suggestive that a similar pattern of events occurred during this period throughout the central highlands. Consider, for example, the question of waiting lists, which appeared in both Zinacantan and Chamula for reasons which have little to do with demographic pressure.[65] Such lists also became a prominent feature of religious life in Huistán, where *ladino* authorities, responding to conflicts over land and labor, intervened to modify the town's political structure. In much the same fashion, it appears that young *caciques* rose to political power in communities as diverse as Cancuc, Mitontic, and Tenejapa.[66] Even in Chenalhó, where *caciquismo* of this sort did not develop, we find evidence that Cardenistas tried to alter existing arrangements for their own purposes.

What all of these *pueblos* have in common, and what distinguishes them from Zinacantan, is that their inhabitants worked on Chiapas' coffee plantations. Not pure coincidence, it would seem, but rather conscious design inspired state authorities to create a group of local leaders, beholden exclusively to the governing party, who would ensure the flow of seasonal laborers to their appointed destinations. And it was entirely logical that these leaders should in turn utilize local religious institutions to enforce public order in the highlands—the kind of order which permitted commercial agriculture in Chiapas to grow and prosper.

## Decline and Recovery in the Grijalva Basin

By 1948, when the Pan-American Highway was completed in central Chiapas, state officials and local landowners had worked out the mechanisms whereby social peace was restored and the appearance of reform might be maintained. As Table 45 indicates, in the Grijalva basin, at least, land remained highly concentrated in the hands of men who had entitled and monopolized it since the 1840s. For these men, whose workers had been returned to the highlands by Jesús Castro in 1914, the problem

TABLE 45.
Distribution of Private Farmlands in Central Chiapas, 1950

| Percentage of Properties (deciles) | Percentage of Land | Percentage of Land (cumulative) |
|---|---|---|
| I | 0.04% | 0.04% |
| II | 0.07 | 0.1 |
| III | 0.2 | 0.3 |
| IV | 0.2 | 0.5 |
| V | 0.4 | 0.9 |
| VI | 2.0 | 2.9 |
| VII | 4.4 | 7.3 |
| VIII | 10.0 | 17.3 |
| IX | 19.7 | 37.0 |
| X | 63.0 | 100.0% |

Source: Secretaría de Agricultura y Ganadería, Censo agrícola, ganadero y ejidal, 1950.

Municipios: Acala, Comitán, Chiapa, Chiapilla, La Concordia, San Lucas, Socoltenango, Totolapa, Venustiano Carranza (San Bartolomé), Villa Corzo, Villa Flores.

now was not land but labor and the changing demand for their products abroad. Terratenientes throughout Mexico now found that they had become increasingly dependent upon a single export market, the United States. As a result, Mexican cotton planters, including those in the southeastern states, watched helplessly when in 1929 their exports declined to the vanishing point.[67] Similarly, between 1931 and 1935 sugarcane production in Chiapas and elsewhere fell sharply. But while hacendados in northern and central Mexico recovered from these disasters during World War II, their counterparts in the Grijalva valley gradually ceased to cultivate such commodities. By 1950, therefore, cotton production in the region had decreased significantly, while throughout the state only 4,400 hectares were planted in sugarcane.[68] In the end, changing patterns of international trade, not conscious design, destroyed that symbiosis of cattle and cotton which for nearly a hundred years had formed the mainstay of agriculture in the central basin.

Under these circumstances, local ranchers experimented with

new crops and cropping systems. In 1922, for example, the German geographer Leo Waibel remarked that Chiapas seemed to be divided into a series of specialized zones whose economic life was shaped largely by their relation to the state's coffee plantations.[69] The central highlands, which produced very little grain, continued to provide the Sierra Madre with its principal source of seasonal laborers, while commercial farmers in the Grijalva valley depended upon the coffee plantations to buy their cattle and corn. As the coffee industry expanded throughout the 1920s, lowland ranchers struggled to increase their production of these two essential commodities. Paradoxically, however, having invested their money in cattle rather than in irrigation or modern equipment, they continued to rely upon the same techniques of swidden agriculture which characterized native farming. In order to combat their declining yields, then, they permitted Indian tenants from highland communities to rent unused or underutilized brushlands (monte). Initially, they also attempted to reimpose those conditions of unpaid drudgery under which in earlier days their laboríos had worked. But within a few years they relinquished such pretensions, and soon acquired a large workforce of native arrendatarios (tenants or sharecroppers) who traveled continuously between highland hamlets and lowland fields. In this way they converted their uncultivated lands to maize at an unprecedented rate. As for older fields (fields which had been planted consecutively for three or four years), these might be left to recover their fertility or they might be used as pasture.

Let us now consider more carefully how this new agro-ecosystem evolved during the years which followed 1920. As Figure 8 shows, between 1930 and 1945 landowners in the Grijalva basin, stimulated by a national economic policy of import substitution, directed their energies toward the production of food grains for sale in local markets.[70] Even so, their progress remained unexceptional: citing contemporary sources, another German geographer, Karl Helbig, noted that as late as 1940 the region still possessed enormous stretches of uncleared monte.[71] After the United States entered World War II, however, this situation changed dramatically. Faced with an enormous increase in in-

FIGURE 8.
Cattle Production and Land Area Planted in Maize, Chiapas, 1930–1970

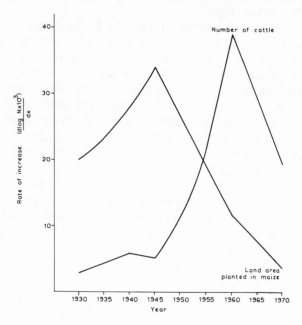

Source: Secretaria de Agricultura y Ganadoria, *Censo Agricola y Ganadero*

ternational commerce, ranchers in northern Mexico withdrew their cattle from national markets. Rather than sell these animals in Mexico City or Veracruz at domestic prices, they preferred to do business in Texas and Chicago. As a result, farmers in southern Mexico, including Chiapas, expanded their production to meet the demands of consumers in the capital.[72] In the Grijalva valley, they redoubled their efforts to attract native tenants, a task which was greatly facilitated after the highway was completed in 1948. As we might expect, this highway, which ran directly through Zinacantan, soon gave rise to a network of secondary roads that linked lowland *haciendas* directly with highland communities. As early as 1949, such developments had begun to change the nature of agricultural production in central Chiapas:

according to de la Peña, the large expanses of *monte* mentioned by Helbig had been replaced in many areas by elephant grass and other forage crops.[73]

At this point, it is useful to ask why lowland ranchers preferred to employ Tzotzil tenants rather than to recruit local men and women to work on their properties. We must recall that the agrarian reform laws encouraged landless peasants to claim territories which lay close to their own communities. Under these circumstances, ranchers in the Grijalva region naturally discouraged such peasants from residing on their holdings—a situation which might lead to legal disputes and expropriation. On the contrary, they benefited directly from the *ejido* grants which were made in highland areas like Zinacantan and Chamula—just as coffee growers benefited from *ejidos* surrounding their plantations. For such grants, far from freeing native people from their dependence upon tenancy arrangements, encouraged them to rent more land in the Grijalva valley. During these years, for example, men in the hamlet of Apas raised only half of what they needed to survive on their own parcels—not enough to live on, but certainly enough to sustain them in the face of a poor lowland harvest.[74] It is perhaps this fact, as much as other differences, that distinguished Zinacanteco renters from their counterparts in Chamula. Unlike Zinacantecos, few of these men received *ejido* plots, a state of affairs which apparently made them less inclined to undertake the risks of lowland farming.

Given these facts, it is not surprising that Zinacantan's population once again underwent a startling and dramatic process of redistribution (Table 46). The rapid growth of such hamlets as Sek'emtik and Apas, of course, reflected the large number of former *baldíos* and *laboríos* who settled there. Nonetheless, the significant thing is that returning Zinacantecos preferred to make their homes in hamlets which overlooked the Grijalva basin, not in such areas as the *cabecera* and Na Chij. In spite of the *municipio's* general growth rate, those *parajes* most isolated from the lowland showed a marked tendency to decline in size. As in Petztoj and Saklum, many Zinacantecos who had formerly engaged in peddling and barter began to rent small parcels of lowland *monte*.[75] For most of these people, the transition to share-

TABLE 46.
Demographic Variation in Zinacantan, 1910-1960
(percentage of increase)

| | 1910-1940[a] | 1940-1950 | 1950-1960 |
|---|---|---|---|
| Entire *municipio* | 76% | 39% | 22% |
| *cabecera* | 34 | 51 | 30 |
| Elan Vo' | 64 | 106 | 8.1 |
| Pat Osil | 76 | −4.5 | 36 |
| Apas | 285 | 28 | 47 |
| Na Chij | −12 | 54 | 224 |
| Nabenchauk | 60 | 36 | 8 |
| Paste' | — | 211 | 200 |
| Sek'emtik | 695 | 32 | −23[b] |
| Salinas | 149 | 43 | 25 |

*Sources:* Gobierno del Estado de Chiapas, *Anuario estadístico*, 1911; Secretaría de Industria y Comercio, *Censos generales de población*, 1940, 1950, 1960.

[a] The censuses of 1920 and 1930 have been omitted because of obvious inaccuracies.
[b] During this period, the Sek'emtik census area was redefined.

cropping occurred gradually and with considerable hesitation. In fact, among Indians as well as *ladinos,* the 1920s and 1930s may perhaps best be viewed as a period of experimentation, a period in which Zinacantecos tried their hand at lowland farming. For this reason, they preferred at first to plant only one or at most two hectares and to maintain their activities as *marchantes.* But by the early 1940s, only young men still occupied themselves primarily in peddling. As soon as they had acquired a horse and a little experience, they too rented land in the central basin.

Stimulated by these arrangements, the internal structure of Zinacantan become more differentiated and stratified. Most Zinacantecos planted only as much land as they needed to feed themselves and their families. In order to clear and cultivate such land, they invested weeks of arduous and painstaking labor which late rains or a plague of insects could quickly invalidate. Furthermore, landlords did not always act in predictable or hon-

TABLE 47.
Maize Harvested by Zinacanteco Arrendatarios
in the Grijalva Valley, 1930–1935

| Parcel Size | Old Fields | New Fields |
|---|---|---|
| 1 ha. | 6¼ fanegas[a] | 12½ fanegas[a] |
| 2 ha. | 12½ | 25 |

[a] 1 fanega = 138 kg.

orable ways. Faced with labor shortages or other difficulties, they often pressed Zinacanteco tenants into service in their own fields or turned their cattle to graze on Indian corn. Even if they avoided such misfortunes, prolonged illness or other troubles might force Zinacantecos so deeply into debt that they withdrew from sharecropping altogether. After several years of relative prosperity, then, even successful *arrendatarios* might suddenly find themselves reduced to complete poverty. Under these circumstances, they preferred to avoid the uncertainties of farming for two or three years and return to peddling.

Despite such obstacles, a few Zinacantecos accumulated more cash and corn than they consumed each year. For the most part, these men converted their surpluses into mules and, to a lesser extent, into highland property. In this way, they often acquired as many as 10 or 12 pack animals, an enterprise in which they invested 5,000 pesos or more. Using these animals, they transported corn from lowland ranches to their native hamlets—not only their own corn, of course, but also that of their neighbors. Furthermore, after 1935, rising land rents and declining yields on farms near the highlands forced many tenants to move their activities farther from Zinacantan (Table 47). Braving high overhead costs, these men cleared virgin territory on such estates as Rosario, Las Limas, and Santo Tomás, all located a full day's walk from highland *parajes*. And whereas Indian sharecroppers who farmed near Chiapa paid only about 10 percent of their harvests in freight charges, those who rented land on more dis-

FIGURE 9.
Distribution of Average Zinacanteco Harvest, 1935[a]

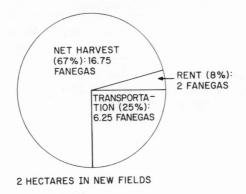

NET HARVEST
(67%): 16.75
FANEGAS

RENT (8%):
2 FANEGAS

TRANSPORTA-
TION (25%):
6.25 FANEGAS

2 HECTARES IN NEW FIELDS

[a] Two hectares in new production areas.

tant properties—including large numbers of men from Nabenchauk, Paste', and Elan Vo'—paid up to 25 percent (Figure 9).
Depending upon the distances involved, native mule-owners
earned between 2 and 3 pesos per day for each animal—enough
to provide them with three times the income of other Zinacantecos. By the late 1930s, therefore, according to informants, many
*arrieros* regarded Zinacanteco corn as their most valuable haul,
and only secondarily engaged in peddling or farming.

By this time, too, many Zinacantecos were eager to assure
their access to unused or particularly fertile lands, a right of
access which they pursued in two different but interrelated
ways. On the one hand, many tenants established semi-permanent leasing arrangements with relatively large landowners—
that is, with those who promised to rent them virgin *monte* every
two or three years. In some cases, these relations (which Indian
farmers periodically reaffirmed with gifts of sheep, fruit, or money) lasted as long as 25 or 30 years. On the other hand, Indians
who did not enjoy such friendships roamed ceaselessly from one
ranch to another. In this way they hoped to find appropriate
fields, which they utilized for short periods of time. At first they
confined their quest to areas which could be reached easily by

TABLE 48.
Agricultural Investment in Chiapas, 1953–1962
(millions of pesos)

|  | 1953 | 1962 | Percentage of Increase |
|---|---|---|---|
| Total investment | 19.5 | 39.7 | 103% |
| Investment in livestock | 15.0 | 37.9 | 152 |
| Investment in agriculture | 4.5 | 1.8 | −60 |

Source: Alvaro de Albornoz, Trayectoria y ritmo del crédito agrícola en Mexico.

mule; but after 1947, the Pan-American Highway permitted them to explore untapped territories far beyond their former zones of operation.

Before we examine these events in greater detail, it is necessary to consider the relationship between commercial agriculture in the Grijalva valley and the development of new roads. As might be expected, landowners and merchants, quick to take advantage of Chiapas' expanding infrastructure, purchased a great many cargo trucks. In 1945 only 1.1 million pesos had been invested in such vehicles, but ten years later this figure had increased to 14.9 million,[76] and private investment in cattle and agriculture had doubled.[77] As Table 48 discloses, it was cattlemen, not crop farmers, who received the bulk of these funds. Between 1953 and 1962, investments in agricultural activities other than stock-raising actually declined. As a result, in the decade after 1950, ranchers expanded their herds by 65 percent—from 480,308 head to 792,070.[78] Nonetheless, a few proprietors, borrowing money from both commercial and government sources, installed new irrigation facilities and purchased agricultural machinery. In this way, cotton and sugarcane—crops which 30 years before had almost disappeared from the region—regained a measure of their former importance (Table 49).[79] And finally, despite the absence of either public or private credit, landowners in Chiapas planted an additional 84,000 hectares of maize.[80]

TABLE 49.
Cotton and Sugarcane Production
in Chiapas, 1950–1960

|  | Area Cultivated | |
|  | 1950 | 1960 |
|---|---|---|
| Cotton | 41 ha. | 6,474 ha. |
| Sugarcane | 4,400 | 5,966 |

Source: José Jiménez Paniagua, *Política de inversiones en el Estado de Chiapas.*

It was precisely this fact, together with the renaissance of cattle-raising after 1950, which modified and reordered social relations throughout the region. According to one anthropologist, Frank Cancian, Zinacanteco tenants, spurred by the quest for higher profits, willingly cleared and cultivated these new fields. In so doing they broke with many of those long-standing patronal relations which they had forged with proprietors closer to Zinacantan. As a result, men from Apas and Na Chij, departing from their usual custom, changed farming locations between 1957 and 1966 approximately every four and a half years. Moreover, in the hopes of increasing their harvests, they hired *jornaleros* from Chamula to cultivate additional land. Using these laborers, many Zinacantecos planted 4, 5, or even 8 hectares—far more land than they had rented in previous years. By 1966, Cancian contends, almost 45 percent of the men from Na Chij and 25 percent of those from Apas seeded 4 or more hectares of *milpa.* By that time, too, two federal commodities agencies, CONASUPO (Compañía Nacional de Subsistencias Populares) and ANDSA (Almacenes Nacionales de Depósito, now merged with CONASUPO), had established receiving stations in the region. Thus many Zinacantecos—or at least those who cultivated large quantities of land—were able to sell part of their harvest at official government prices.[81]

What Cancian does not stress, however, is that Zinacantecos changed their habits only with great hesitation. As late as 1966,

TABLE 50.
Modal Na Chij Harvests in Two Parts of the Grijalva Valley,
1957–1966

|  | Area 1 | | Area 2 | |
| --- | --- | --- | --- | --- |
| Gross yield | 3,036 kilos | 100% | 3,933 kilos | 100% |
| Rent | 690 | 23 | 690 | 18 |
| Labor | 690 | 23 | 552 | 14 |
| Transportation | 276 | 9 | 373 | 9 |
| New yield | 1,380 kilos | 45% | 2,318 kilos | 59% |

most of his informants—56 percent of the renters in Na Chij, 89 percent of the men from Apas—still preferred to rent land within older, more familiar zones of operation. Because sharecroppers from such hamlets, relying upon their collective experience, tended to farm together, Indians from both places continued to farm precisely where they had worked since the late 1930s. Similarly, despite the fact that some men expanded the size of their operations, most renters cleared and planted only 2 or 3 hectares of *milpa*, just as they had done 30 years earlier. If we calculate the area which most Na Chij men seeded (i.e., the mode, 2.0 hectares), we see that their harvests remained modest. More important, much of this corn now found its way into the hands of landlords, truck owners, and Chamula laborers (Table 50). Faced with this situation, many Indians, hopeful that they might reduce their transportation costs, had purchased their own mules and pack animals. Informants recall that possession of these animals encouraged Zinacantecos to farm within familiar territories.

Why did these men eventually turn their backs upon long-standing patterns of work and abandon their established routine? In order to answer this question, it is instructive to examine the behavior of tenants from two closely-related hamlets, Na Chij and Elan Vo'. Between 1940 and 1950, both hamlets grew at the expense of more isolated villages. But when the highway was completed, many Zinacantecos flocked to Na Chij, where they married into local families. They thus placed heavy demands

TABLE 51.
Primary Farming Locations of Na Chij
Arrendatarios, 1973 (N = 180)

| Municipio | Arrendatarios |
|---|---|
| Acala | 4.0% |
| Chiapa | 3.0 |
| Comitán | 0.5 |
| La Concordia | 0.5 |
| San Lucas | 0.5 |
| Socoltenango | 70.0 |
| Totolapa | 8.0 |
| Tuxtla | 1.0 |
| Venustiano Carranza | 6.0 |
| Other | 6.5 |

upon the already diminished stock of lowland *monte* to which
Na Chij men retained access. Unlike their neighbors in Elan Vo',
they began to rent land at great distances from the highlands,
primarily in *municipios* to the southeast (Tables 51 and 52).

Within a few years, however, Na Chij farmers soon found
themselves enmeshed in a very difficult and highly complex
system of economic relations. Although at first their fields were
extraordinarily productive (157 units of maize harvested per unit
seeded, according to Cancian), these yields quickly diminished
by 30 percent. Moreover, several proprietors, realizing that good
lands had become relatively scarce, raised their rents once again.
As a result, Indian tenants paid between 33 and 38 percent of
their harvests in rent—an increase which they could scarcely
afford. In order to offset such costs, and to augment their own
productivity, they pursued the only alternative which remained
available to them. Without credit or technology, they preferred
not to reduce labor and transportation expenses (as Elan Vo' men
did); instead they chose to clear and cultivate extremely large
*milpas* which sometimes covered 15 or 20 hectares. By 1973, in
fact, most Na Chij farmers had expanded their operations from
2.0 to 6.0 hectares (Table 53). Paradoxically, such strategies in-

TABLE 52.
Changes in Primary Farming Locations among Na
Chij Arrendatarios, 1966–1973

| Municipio | Zone[a] | Arrendatarios | |
|---|---|---|---|
| | | 1966 | 1973 |
| Chiapa | 1 ⎫ | | 3.0% |
| Acala | 2 ⎪ | | 4.0 |
| Chiapilla | 3 ⎬ | 35.0% | —0— |
| San Lucas | 4 ⎪ | | 0.5 |
| Totolapa | 5 ⎭ | | 8.0 |
| V. Carranza (north) | 5 | 21.0 | 1.0 |
| V. Carranza (center) | 6 | 12.0 | 2.0 |
| V. Carranza (south) | 7 and 8 ⎫ | 31.0 | 73.0 |
| Socoltenango | 9 ⎭ | | |
| Comitán | | — | 0.5 |
| Tuxtla | | — | 1.0 |
| La Concordia | | — | 0.5 |
| Other | | 1.0 | 6.5 |

[a] According to Cancian's classification.

creased their dependence upon both Chamula laborers and private truck owners (Table 54). For their part, these shippers, eager to capitalize upon local prosperity and the rising price of corn, doubled their passenger and freight rates. By 1973, therefore, despite the fact that *arrendatarios* from Na Chij farmed twice as much land as they had in 1966, their net returns remained virtually unchanged (Table 55).

Clearly, then, the animating spirit behind Zinacanteco sharecropping no longer involved merely a search for higher profits and more productive croplands. Even in relatively unexploited areas of the Grijalva valley, soil fertility declined steadily and inexorably. By the early 1970s, tenants in Socoltenango and southern Venustiano Carranza (San Bartolomé) consistently obtained lower yields than did those men who rented land in tradi-

TABLE 53.
Area Cultivated by Na Chij Arrendatarios,
1973 (N = 180)

| Hectares | Farmers | Farmers (cumulative) | |
|---|---|---|---|
| 1 | 9 | 9 | 5% |
| 2 | 23 | 32 | 18 |
| 3 | 20 | 52 | 29 |
| 4 | 23 | 75 | 42 |
| 5 | 12 | 87 | 49 |
| 6 | 37 | 124 | 68 |
| 7 | 1 | 125 | 69 |
| 8 | 6 | 131 | 73 |
| 9 | 3 | 134 | 74 |
| 10 | 16 | 150 | 83 |
| 11 | 3 | 153 | 85 |
| 12 | 8 | 161 | 89 |
| 13 | 1 | 162 | 90 |
| 14 | 2 | 164 | 91 |
| 15 | 6 | 170 | 94 |
| 16 and above | 10 | 180 | 100% |

Mean 7.07
Median 5.05
Mode 6.00

TABLE 54.
Composition of Lowland Work Groups among Na Chij Arrendatarios,
1973 (N = 179)

| | Work alone | Work with sons | Work with brothers | Work with in-laws | Work with laborers |
|---|---|---|---|---|---|
| Farmers | 7 | 46 | 3 | 2 | 171 |
| Percentage of total | 4% | 26 | 2 | 1 | 95 |

TABLE 55.
Modal Na Chij Harvests in New Cultivation Zones, 1973 (N = 125)

| | | |
|---|---|---|
| Gross yield | 6,555 kilos | 100% |
| Rent | 1,449 | 22 |
| Labor costs | 2,070 | 32 |
| Transportation | 1,311 | 20 |
| Net yield | 1,725 | 26% |

TABLE 56.
Ratio of Surplus Production to Wages, 1957–1966

| Municipio | Cultivated | | | |
|---|---|---|---|---|
| | 2 ha. | 4 ha. | 6 ha. | 8 ha. |
| Totolapa, Chiapilla | 2.3 | 3.7 | 3.7 | 4.0 |
| Venustiano Carranza (north) | 3.7 | 2.5 | 1.9 | 2.0 |
| Venustiano Carranza (center) | 3.6 | 2.6 | 2.7 | 2.9 |
| Venustiano Carranza (south) | 4.2 | 3.0 | 3.2 | 3.6 |

Source: Frank Cancian: Change and Uncertainty in a Peasant Economy.

tional farming zones. Obviously, the success or failure of such enterprises depended less upon capital investment, hard work, and thrift than upon the amount of surplus which might be extracted from Chamula workers. In 1966, taking advantage of landlessness and unemployment in neighboring Tzotzil communities, Zinacanteco tenants had imposed highly unfavorable working conditions upon these men (Table 56). As more and more Chamulas had sought employment elsewhere, however, Zinacanteco employers were forced to offer them higher wages. By 1973, therefore, as Tables 57 and 58 indicate, Chamula laborers in the upper Grijalva basin had transformed a sizable portion of their surplus production into wages.

Faced with such difficulties, Zinacanteco renters once again

TABLE 57.
Change in Ratio of Surplus
Production, 1966–1973

|  | 1966 | 1973 |
|---|---|---|
| Old zone | 3.1 | — |
| New zone | 3.2 | 2.3 |

TABLE 58.
Ratio of Surplus Production to
Wages by Size of Operation, 1973

|  | s/v |
|---|---|
| 4 ha. | 2.1 |
| 6 ha. | 2.5 |
| 8 ha. | 2.0 |
| 10 ha. | 2.0 |

TABLE 59.
Primary Economic Activity of Household Heads in Elan Vo', 1973 (N = 105)

|  | Wage labor | Land rental (has.) | | | | | Farm ejido lands |
|---|---|---|---|---|---|---|---|
|  |  | 1 | 2 | 3 | 4 | 5–7 |  |
| Number | 23 | 38 | 14 | 9 | 2 | 14 | 5 |
| Percentage | 22% | 36 | 13 | 9 | 2 | 13 | 5 |

changed their production strategies and modes of operation: they simply reduced their use of hired hands. In Elan Vo', where most men still rented within older areas, such economies were obtained by refusing to cultivate more land (Table 59). Foregoing those temptations which had seduced their neighbors in Na Chij, they continued by and large to plant 1 or 2 hectares—that is, the amount which a single man might cultivate without *jornaleros*.

FIGURE 10.
Distribution of Elan Vo' Harvests in the Grijalva Valley, 1973 (N=105)

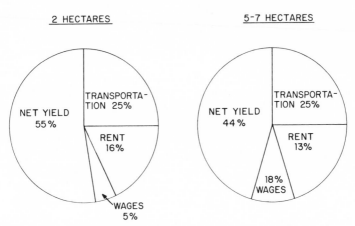

By limiting the number of workers, they harvested enough maize and beans to meet their needs—or at least to meet their basic subsistence requirements. Furthermore, even those few men who cleared larger areas (15 percent) tended to rely more upon the labor of their sons than upon paid fieldhands. Despite higher transportation costs, then, such farmers enjoyed net returns which far exceeded those of equivalent Na Chij enterprises (Figure 10). Even so, increased demographic pressure and a diminution of appropriate farmlands were soon felt among Elan Vo's tenant farmers. By 1973, fully 36 percent of these men had reduced their rented *milpas* to a single hectare, while 27 percent of them had abandoned lowland agriculture altogether.

In contrast to Elan Vo', only 6 percent of Na Chij's adult men had by 1973 become rural or urban laborers. As for those who rented land, these Indians continued to explore both new farming zones and new ways to organize their activities. Not surprisingly, they soon turned to a device which a few years earlier they had virtually rejected: commercial herbicides. According to Cancian, the spray used by Zinacantecos is effective in recently cleared fields . . . where broadleaf weeds rather than grasses are the major problem; but it cannot be used where beans are interplanted with corn. In the early 1960s a good many farmers tried chemical weed-killer, but many of them lost their crops while waiting for [it] to work on old fields, where grasses were the principal competition for the corn.[82]

As long as they farmed within older zones of operation, Zinacantecos had little incentive to utilize such sprays. By 1973, however, they faced renewed and intense competition for their lowland fields from other landless Indians. In order to protect their livelihoods, then, Zinacantecos began once again to search for stands of uncut forest. In 1974 they farmed in the *municipio* of Comitán, more than 80 kilometers from Zinacantan. Pushing onward, in 1975 they arrived at the Guatemalan border, 100 kilometers away. Naturally, they could not pay the prohibitive transportation costs and the high wages which such operations entailed. On the contrary, after clearing and planting enormous plots of ground, they discharged their workers for the duration of the growing season. Thereafter, they applied chemical herbicides to their fields. They thus indirectly encouraged the spread of grasses into such fields—a practice which accelerated the transformation of farmlands to pasture.

The irony is that it may well have been government commodities agencies, together with the new roads, which created this situation. In 1966, Cancian noted that such agencies "provide a stable base for the corn market, lowering the risk to truckers and other private buyers in the fields."[83] Naturally, many Zinacantecos, in particular those who grew large amounts of corn, preferred to sell part of their harvest to these agencies. As a result, they decreased their transportation costs and acquired the cash with which to ship their unsold grain to the highlands. Furthermore, Cancian declares, receiving centers paid 880 pesos (U.S. $70.40) per metric ton, a favorable price compared to other markets. In contrast, many Indians, those who cultivated modest amounts of land, avoided such agencies. Like their wealthier neighbors, they also needed cash to pay for transportation. Frequently, however, they did not possess the means to sell their corn to the government, a procedure which required both time and capital. Instead, they sold their surplus at a 10-percent discount to private haulers who bought corn in the fields and resold it to official warehouses. Because they lacked both cash and credit, in effect, these farmers paid a 10-percent surcharge on their shipping rates. Similarly, lowland proprietors soon realized that they might earn considerable profits simply by reselling the corn which their Indian tenants raised. As a result, they encouraged native men to clear and cultivate even larger *milpas* and to hire more *jornaleros*. And of course, the more workers they hired, the more cash they required at the end of the harvest. By such means, ranchers and private truckers increased their share of Indian harvests until by 1973 they claimed 44 percent of the total crop.

By 1973, too, problems of credit and liquidity had spread even to those tenants who rented relatively large amounts of land. In fact, only 23 percent of these men, primarily those who planted 10 hectares or more, still delivered their grain to the government (Table 60). At first glance, we might attribute this strange phenomenon to a rather simple and straightforward fact: between 1966 and 1973, the annual mean price of corn in San Cristobal rose by 140 percent! Curiously, however, during these same years the amount of maize which renters from Na Chij sold in the city remained relatively modest (Table 61). In fact, they became more dependent upon their landlords to purchase their harvest. Simultaneously, another type of transaction, in which tenant farmers sold part of their prospective harvests to other Indians early in the year, placed a heavy lien on much of the grain that eventually arrived in Na Chij. Faced with this situation, many farmers—almost 10 percent—ceased to cultivate their own lowland parcels. Instead, they became *contratistas*—that is, in exchange for a predetermined fee they organized and directed indigenous work crews on lowland ranches. In a word, economic growth in Chiapas ultimately reduced many sharecroppers to the position of hired hands, itinerant rural foremen who sold their services outright for corn or cash.

At this point it is instructive to examine in detail the position which tenant farmers occupied in the economic life of specific

TABLE 60.
Markets Used by Na Chij Tenants, 1973 (N = 60)

| Area Cultivated | Percentage of Tenants | | | | |
| --- | --- | --- | --- | --- | --- |
| | ANDSA (lowlands) | ANDSA (highlands) | San Cristóbal Market | Private Sale (lowlands) | Private Sale (highlands) |
| 1 ha. | | | 5% | 3% | 2% |
| 2 | | | 7 | 7 | 5 |
| 3 | | | 8 | 8 | 7 |
| 4 | | | 12 | 13 | 10 |
| 5 | 2% | | 5 | 3 | 7 |
| 6 | 3 | | 18 | 15 | 12 |
| 7 | | | 0 | 0 | |
| 8 | | | 3 | 2 | 2 |
| 9 | | | 2 | 2 | |
| 10 | 5 | 2% | 8 | 7 | 2 |
| 11 | 3 | 2 | 3 | 3 | 2 |
| 12 | 3 | | 7 | 3 | |
| 13 | 2 | | 2 | 2 | |
| 14 | 3 | | 2 | 2 | |
| 15 and above | 2 | 2 | 5 | 7 | |
| Total | 23% [a] | 6% | 87% | 77% | 49% |

[a] One-third of these men are full-time intermediaries.

### TABLE 61.
### Maize Sales by Na Chij Tenants, 1973

| Amount Sold | ANDSA (lowlands) | ANDSA (highlands) | San Cristóbal | Private Sale (lowlands) | Private Sale (highlands) |
|---|---|---|---|---|---|
| less than 1 fanega | | | 5 | | |
| 1–5 | | | 63 | 23 | 12 |
| 6–10 | 2 | | 13 | 18 | 15 |
| 11–15 | | | 3 | 10 | 12 |
| 16–20 | | | | 2 | 7 |
| 21–25 | 3 | | 3 | 2 | |
| 26–30 | 8 | 2 | | 12 | |
| 31–35 | | | | 2 | |
| 36–40 | | 2 | 2 | 3 | |
| 41–45 | 3 | | | 2 | |
| 46–50 | | | | 2 | |
| 51–55 | | | | 3 | |
| 56–60 | 3 | | | 2 | |
| 61–65 | | | | | |
| 66–70 | | | | | |
| 71–75 | | 2 | | | |
| Median sale | 28.7 fanegas | 35 fanegas | 3.5 fanegas | 10 fanegas | 19 fanegas |

ranches. To this end, we shall consider a series of facts about one *hacienda* in the *municipio* of Socoltenango, a property representative of farms in the "new" cultivation zones. Finca Espinal contained approximately 300 hectares (the legal limit), on which the owner maintained 200 head of cattle. In addition, he also planted 50 hectares of sugarcane and maize. Except during the cane harvest, he hired no agricultural laborers. Instead, he relied upon his tenants not only to clear overgrown brushlands but also to cultivate his fields. In order to attract a sufficient number of sharecroppers, he regularly rented out almost 100 hectares— nearly one-third of his entire property. As a result, between 1970 and 1974 he acquired a semi-permanent labor force of around 30 men who planted their *milpas* several years in succession on his ranch. Under normal conditions, these men paid the owner 25 percent of their harvests, an amount which in 1974 (a bad year) earned him approximately U.S. $4,200. By comparison, his new 10-ton truck cost $12,000—so that in less than three years he might have paid for it from land rent alone. Moreover, his tenants each agreed to work 12 days preparing his cornfields, repairing his fences, etc., for which he paid them slightly less than half the minimum daily wage. And finally, in 1974, he purchased 7.2 tons of grain from tenants who required cash to meet their own operating expenses—grain which he resold to government agencies.

Not all Zinacantecos accepted such conditions, nor did they become impoverished and discouraged. On the contrary, a few— luckier perhaps than their neighbors—grew enough corn to produce a substantial profit. For the most part, these men spent their earnings not on religious offices (as other investigators have suggested) but on houses, on consumer goods of all sorts, and on land. In this way, for example, Mariano Zárate and his associates, who quietly arranged to purchase most of the land owned by private *finqueros* in Zinacantan, subsequently produced fruit and flowers for sale in such markets as Tuxtla, Arriaga, and Oaxaca. More recently, men along the highway invested considerable sums for the same purpose in places like Na Chij, Nabenchauk, Sek'emtik, and Jok' Ch'enom. At the same time, a very small group of people bought passenger and cargo trucks. Be-

Figure 11.
Number of Trucks Operated by Zinacantecos, 1955-1974[a]

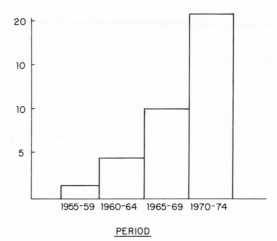

PERIOD

[a] Residents of Zincantan Center, *Stz'elej, Na Chih, Elan Vo'*, and *Pat Osil*. Residents of *Nabenchauk* and *Sek'emtik* are excluded because of the short periods during which they owned trucks.

tween 1957 and 1974, as shown in Figure 11, these men, who numbered around 30, purchased almost 40 separate vehicles. In most cases, such enterprises required more money than individual owners could provide. Unlike lowland farming, then, family groups quickly assumed control of Zinacantan's trucking trade. In fact, such operations permitted a small number of tenant farmers to escape the deteriorating economic conditions which threatened their livelihoods in agriculture. Unfortunately, these incipient corporations remained highly unstable, subject to frequent failure and collapse. As one truck or another broke down or was repossessed by *ladino* creditors, the number of Zinacanteco operators diminished from 20 to 8. By 1974, therefore, one family in Na Chij, that of José K'obyox, owned fully one-third of all the vehicles in Zinacantan.

Events of this sort exerted quite a different effect upon men and women in Chamula.[84] Oddly enough, despite the fact that a

TABLE 62.
Maize Production in Chamula, 1970–1974

| Paraje | Average Parcel Size | Modal Parcel Size | Yield per ha. |
|--------|--------------------|--------------------|----------------|
| Calvario San Juan | 0.71 ha. | 0.25 ha. | 430.3 kg. |
| Lomo' | 0.34 | 0.25 | 527.8 |
| Milpoleta | 0.63 | 0.40 | 331.5 |
| Cruz Ton | 0.33 | 0.25 | 486.2 |
| Petej | 0.34 | 0.25 | 475.8 |
| Chik'omtantik | 0.42 | 0.25 | 579.8 |
| Ni Ch'en | 0.36 | 0.25 | 481.0 |
| K'at'ixtik | 0.19 | 0.25 | 179.4 |
| $\bar{x} =$ | 0.41 ha. | 0.27 ha. | 436.5 kg. |
| $s =$ | 0.16 ha. | 0.05 ha. | 170.7 kg. |

Source: Robert Wasserstrom, *Ingreso y trabajo rural en los altos de Chiapas*.

few of these people received *ejido* grants, by 1970 most of the town's residents cultivated only minute quantities of land—in general, around one-quarter of a hectare (Table 62). From this tiny parcel they obtained a fraction of their food; indeed, many families harvested scarcely enough maize to plant their *milpas* the following year (Table 63). Contrary to much scholarly opinion, however, such facts cannot be explained simply as the unfortunate outcome of population growth or short-sighted cropping techniques.[85] As we know, for nearly a century state authorities and private landowners alike have collaborated to transform the area into a source of abundant and ill-paid seasonal laborers. In order to assure that such conditions prevailed after land reform, they permitted municipal authorities (particularly former scribes) to acquire large tracts of communal land and to amass extensive private estates. In turn, these men, who dominated the town's agrarian committees, allowed a few favored allies in each hamlet to accumulate considerable resources of their own. Similarly, through graft and corruption, *caciques* in Chamula obtained monopoly rights over trucking and the sale of such lucrative commodities as liquor, soft drinks,

TABLE 63.
Proportion of Domestic Maize Requirement Produced
in Highland Milpas[a]

| Paraje | Proportion of Domestic Requirement | |
|---|---|---|
| | Mode | Mean |
| Calvario San Juan | 10.7% | 30.5% |
| Lomo' | 13.2 | 17.9 |
| Milpoleta | 13.3 | 20.9 |
| Cruz Ton | 12.1 | 16.0 |
| Petej | 11.9 | 16.2 |
| Chik'omtantik | 14.5 | 24.3 |
| Ni Ch'en | 12.0 | 17.3 |
| K'at'ixtik | 4.5 | 3.4 |
| $\bar{x}$ = | 11.5% | 18.3% |
| s = | 2.86% | 4.96% |

[a] Family with five members and an estimated annual consumption of 1,000 kg.

and beer. By lending money at usurious rates, they soon extended their hold over most of the community's productive farmlands and all of its commerce. As a result, even those men and women who became *ejidatarios* in 1937 and 1938 were quickly forced to rely upon wage labor as their primary source of income. By 1970, in fact, such conditions had become the common lot of over three-quarters of the *municipio*'s population (Table 64).

If most families in the *municipio* did not engage in subsistence farming, what other means did they devise to make ends meet? Between 1970 and 1974, it seems, 52 percent of the community's family heads worked on the coffee plantations, and 25 percent found jobs as unskilled *peones* in such places as San Cristóbal, Tuxtla, and the La Reforma oilfield. Naturally, such figures included many people who engaged in two, three, or even four activities each year—in fact, during this period they combined a limited number of what might be called primary occupations in no less than 60 different ways. As Table 65 shows, however, not all family heads depended upon wage labor. On the contrary,

TABLE 64.
Wage Labor in Chamula (family heads)

| Paraje | All Types[a] | Seasonal Work in Fincas | Other Types |
|---|---|---|---|
| Calvario San Juan | 88% | 27% | 61% |
| Lomo' | 72 | 47 | 25 |
| Milpoleta | 81 | 59 | 22 |
| Cruz Ton | 60 | 53 | 7 |
| Petej | 88 | 73 | 15 |
| Chik'omtantik | 74 | 72 | 2 |
| Ni Ch'en | 81 | 42 | 39 |
| K'at'ixtik | 69 | 40 | 29 |
| $\bar{x}$ = | 76.62% | 51.62% | 25.00% |
| s = | 9.08% | 14.93% | 18.80% |

[a] Includes those family heads who performed such work during at least three of the years under consideration (1970–1974).

TABLE 65.
Proportion of Chamula Family Heads Engaged
in Horticulture or Tenant Farming

| Paraje | Horticulture | Tenant Farming |
|---|---|---|
| Calvario San Juan | 47% | 12% |
| Lomo' | 62 | 20 |
| Milpoleta | 44 | 37 |
| Cruz Ton | 34 | 30 |
| Petej | 2 | 11 |
| Chik'omtantik | 10 | 29 |
| Ni Ch'en | 63 | 13 |
| K'at'ixtik | 7 | 47 |
| $\bar{x}$ = | 33.62% | 24.88% |
| s = | 24.60% | 13.11% |

nearly two-thirds of them also raised vegetables in their own hamlets, and a quarter of them rented land in the Grijalva valley. Although most of these men and women did not derive their

TABLE 66.
Other Modes of Livelihood
in Chamula

| Occupation | Parajes |
|---|---|
| Peddling | 2 |
| Pottery making | 1 |
| Distilling (aguardiente) | 3 |
| Charcoal production | 1 |

entire livelihood from such enterprises, some—including many
of the town's wealthiest residents—planted extensive gardens of
cabbage and potatoes. Stimulated by the increased demand for
such products in local cities and by the construction of rural
roads throughout the highlands, a few families had during the
past 15 years acquired and consolidated those small parcels
which their poorer neighbors had been forced to relinquish. And
finally, in addition to such occupations, people in several hamlets earned their living by producing *aguardiente* or handicrafts
(Table 66).

If we now examine the relationship between these activities
and patterns of residence in the community, we discover a number of interesting facts. As it turns out, in hamlets where tenant
farmers and coffee growers predominated, few people planted
vegetables. By contrast, in villages where horticulturalists owned
much of the land, dispossessed smallholders avoided lowland
farming and instead sought temporary employment as construction workers (Table 67). Not surprisingly, too, Indians who engaged in similar occupations tended to reside in the same areas
of Chamula (Maps 9 and 10). Unlike their counterparts in Zinacantan, for example, men who rented land in the Grijalva basin
often lacked the time-honored relations with *ladino* ranchers
that gave Zinacantecos a claim to more desirable lowland fields.
Even on more distant *haciendas*, such landlords preferred to
deal with their tenants through a single representative. In turn,
this man, commonly called the *caporal* (foreman), distributed

TABLE 67.
Occupational Structure of Chamula[a]

|  | Seasonal Finca Labor | Tenant Farming | Horticulture |
|---|---|---|---|
| Seasonal finca labor | 1.0 | 0.63 | −0.57 |
| Tenant farming |  | 1.0 | −0.69 |
| Horticulture |  |  | 1.0 |

[a] Spearman's Rank Order Coefficient for *paraje* lists, ranked according to the proportion of family heads who engaged *primarily* in these occupations.

parcels among his companions, negotiated the rent, and managed tenant affairs.

Frequently, of course, landlords obliged such *caporales* to accept extremely poor or rocky land along with flatter or more irrigated parcels. Taking advantage of this situation, Zinacanteco *caporales*, who predominated throughout the region, deliberately included Chamula renters in their work groups—precisely in order to distribute such fields among them. In other words, these Chamulas played an important role not only in preparing new pasturelands for *ladino* ranchers, but also in maintaining the relative prosperity of Zinacanteco sharecroppers. Pressed by such circumstances, they rented smaller parcels, invested less labor, and obtained smaller harvests than did other tenants (Table 68). And unlike vegetable growers, they tended to live in regions where land had not yet become concentrated into a few hands and which did not enjoy direct access to the market in San Cristóbal.

But possession of highland fields itself, although important, did not guarantee the success of lowland sharecropping. An example of this situation may be found in K'at'ixtik, a hamlet which borders Zinacantan. For nearly three generations, men from K'at'ixtik had loaded their mules with provisions and cultivated their fields in the Grijalva basin. More recently, they traveled by truck to San Cristóbal and from there along the Pan-American Highway to their farming sites. Unlike Zinacantecos, however,

MAP 9. The Parajes of Chamula Associated with Lowland Tenant Farming

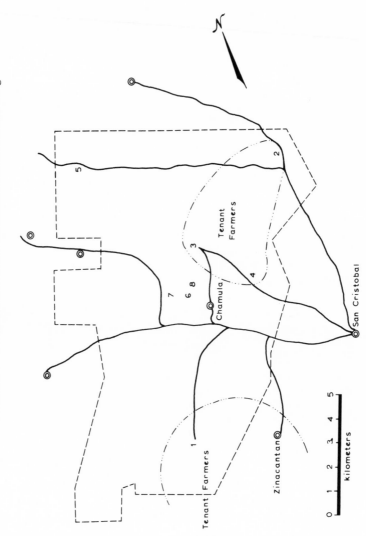

MAP 10. The Parajes of Chamula Associated with Horticulture

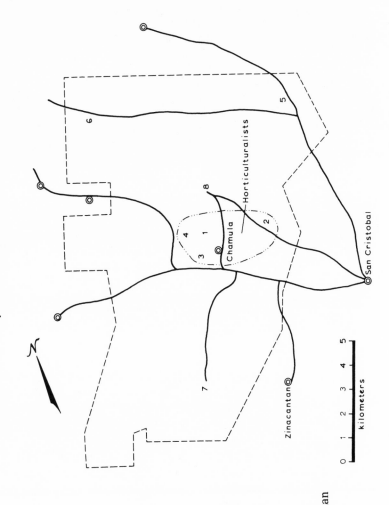

*Key to Hamlets*
(Maps 9 and 10):
1 K'at'ixtik
2 Cruz Ton
3 Lomo'
4 Milpoleta
5 Chik'omtantik
6 Calvario San Juan
7 Ni Ch'en
8 Petej

TABLE 68.
Net Maize Harvests of Chamula Tenants in the Grijalva Valley

| Paraje | Tenants | Parcel Size | Harvest | Percentage of Total Harvest |
|---|---|---|---|---|
| Calvario San Juan | 11 | 2.0 has. | 1,026 kilos | 39.0% |
| Lomo' | 12 | 2.0 | 2,808 | 56.0 |
| Milpoleta | 20 | 3.0 | 1,368 | 33.0 |
| Cruz Ton | 33 | 2.0 | 1,030 | 44.0 |
| Petej | 15 | 2.0 | 4,680 | 52.0 |
| Chik'omtantik | 72 | 2.0 | 686 | 34.0 |
| Ni Ch'en | 11 | 2.0 | 3,528 | 76.6 |
| K'at'ixtik | 69 | 1.0 | 283 | 34.6 |
| $\bar{x} =$ | | | | 39.0% |

these men planted only the amount of land which one man and perhaps a son might work alone. By way of contrast, Chik'omtantik, a hamlet which until 1973 remained isolated from the nearest road, merits our consideration for two reasons: despite their relative isolation, more than 25 percent of the village's adults rented lowland parcels; and like Zinacantecos, these men regularly employed their poorest neighbors as *peones*—which increased their already substantial costs. Such a paradox is resolved when we recognize that during the past few years they paid their *jornaleros* half the wage which day laborers elsewhere in Chamula received. In other words, turning isolation to their advantage, these men lowered their labor costs sufficiently to offset the augmented burden of inadequate transportation. Not only landownership, then, but the availability of cheap labor near at hand proved a decisive factor in determining which men might become *arrendatarios*.

At this point it is useful to examine the position of landless or nearly landless men and women in Chamula—that is, those who lived almost entirely upon unsteady wages. Generally, as we have seen, these people fell into two groups: those who migrated seasonally to Soconusco and those who found temporary work as unskilled laborers elsewhere throughout the state. As for the coffee workers, their lives generally followed a distinct pattern: beginning in early November, when coffee beans were both ripe and plentiful, they traveled to the plantations. In most cases, they remained there for 15 weeks, during which they earned an average wage of $200. At other times, they took whatever employment they could find—employment which rarely added more than $40 to their incomes. Significantly, too, such workers also included many small sharecroppers and horticulturalists—particularly those who did not make ends meet at their primary pursuits. In contrast, a second group of laborers, principally those who lived near San Cristóbal, did not migrate to the plantations. Initially hired as unskilled peons on government and private construction projects, they soon came to form a large mass of underemployed *jornaleros* who circulated from one region to another. It was precisely these men, for example, who hired themselves out for a few weeks now and then to Zinacanteco tenant farmers—a poorly paid occupation which they avoided whenever other work was available. Like coffee workers, therefore, *peones* of this sort performed an essential function in the state's economy: they provided inexpensive labor at moments of intense demand, after which they were left to their own devices.

Underlying these arrangements, we clearly discern a system of social classes which extends far beyond Chamula's borders. Some men not only enjoyed enhanced access to land and other resources, but received vastly greater remuneration. Such men, who included the area's principal vegetable producers, distillers, and truck owners, regularly earned more than $800 per year—in some cases, this figure exceeded $10,000. Below them, in both wealth and power, a group of tenant farmers, small-scale vegetable growers, and peddlers—perhaps 25 or 30 percent of the population—obtained from $400 to $800. Unlike the more prosperous residents, however, men in this category became sharecroppers precisely because they were unable to invest in more intensive forms of agriculture. By and large, the maize which they brought home from their lowland fields represented not a kind of profit, but rather a sort of disguised wage—a wage which moreover might vary dramatically from year to year. Too ambitious to pick coffee and too poor to plant cabbages, such

TABLE 69.
Income Distribution in Chamula, 1970–1974

| Paraje | Average Yearly Income (thousand pesos) | | | | | | | | | Percentage of Family Heads in Each Hamlet | |
| --- | --- | --- | --- | --- | --- | --- | --- | --- | --- | --- | --- |
| | 0–1.9 | 2.0–2.9 | 3.0–3.9 | 4.0–4.9 | 5.0–5.9 | 6.0–6.9 | 7.0–7.9 | 8.0–8.9 | 9.0–9.9 | 10.0–14.9 | 15.0+ |
| Calvario San Juan | 27.5% | 8.8% | 6.6% | 8.8% | 7.7% | 4.4% | 8.8% | 2.2% | 1.1% | 9.9% | 14.3% |
| Lomo' | 2.0 | 2.0 | 17.0 | 10.0 | 12.0 | 5.0 | 8.0 | 15.0 | 17.0 | 2.0 | 9.0 |
| Milpoleta | 12.7 | 17.5 | 12.7 | 6.3 | 15.9 | 6.3 | 3.2 | 4.8 | 3.2 | 2.4 | 15.1 |
| Cruz Ton | —0— | 28.9 | 25.4 | 13.1 | 10.5 | 7.9 | —0— | 0.9 | 3.5 | 1.7 | 7.9 |
| Petej | 6.5 | 10.1 | 59.4 | 10.9 | 5.0 | 5.8 | —0— | 0.7 | 0.7 | —0— | 0.7 |
| Chik'omtantik | 13.0 | 55.0 | 11.0 | 8.0 | 4.0 | 2.0 | 2.0 | 1.0 | 2.0 | 1.0 | 2.0 |
| Ni Ch'en | 11.6 | 25.2 | 22.3 | 7.8 | 7.8 | 1.9 | 10.7 | 1.0 | 3.9 | 4.8 | 2.9 |
| K'at'ixtik | —0— | 42.0 | 28.0 | 7.4 | 6.7 | 2.7 | 2.7 | 2.0 | 3.4 | 3.4 | 2.0 |
| $\bar{x}$ = | 8.9% | 23.3% | 22.6% | 8.9% | 9.1% | 4.7% | 4.5% | 4.4% | 4.4% | 3.0% | 6.3% |

TABLE 70.
The Theil Index for
Each Hamlet[a]

| Paraje | T |
|---|---|
| Calvario San Juan | 0.234 |
| Lomo' | 0.075 |
| Milpoleta | 0.235 |
| Cruz Ton | 0.165 |
| Petej | 0.036 |
| Chik'omtantik | 0.070 |
| Ni Ch'en | 0.126 |
| K'at'ixtik | 0.079 |
| *Municipio* | 0.133 |

[a] For an explanation of the Theil Index
and its application to income distribution
in Mexico, see Wouter van Ginniken, *Socio-Economic Groups and Income Distribution in Mexico* (New York: St. Martin's
Press, 1980).

*campesinos* (whose livelihood depended entirely upon the ebb
and flow of commercial cattle production) belonged in reality to
the rural semi-proletariat. And finally, at the bottom of the economic hierarchy, the majority of Chamulas—about half the total
number—earned around $240—that is, barely enough to survive
(Table 69).

Not only did some social groups earn considerably more than
others, but the degree of inequality among them differed markedly from one part of the *municipio* to another (Table 70). As we
might expect, the distance between rich and poor was most pro-
nounced in *parajes* where commercial horticulture, not tenant
farming or migrant labor, dominated economic life. In hamlets
like Calvario San Juan and Milpoleta, for example—areas in
which new roads had vastly augmented the profitability of vegetable production—such inequities exceeded by three or four
times the moderate differences which existed in Chik'omtantik
and K'at'ixtik. Given this fact, one might well suspect that the

Table 71.
Correlation Between Theil Index, Number of Horticulturalists,
and Traveling Distance From San Cristóbal[a]

|  | Horticulture | Theil Index | Distance from San Cristóbal |
|---|---|---|---|
| Horticulture | 1.0 | 0.76 | 0.29 |
| Theil Index |  | 1.0 | 0.69 |
| Distance from San Cristó- bal |  |  | 1.0 |

[a] Spearman's $r_s$.

expansion of infrastructure in central Chiapas—indeed, the entire program of modernization and transculturation which state and federal agencies had since 1952 put into effect there—had in reality caused living standards to decline. This hypothesis finds tentative confirmation in Table 71: Chamulas who lived close to San Cristóbal and to the town's oldest roads ran a much greater risk of losing their land and becoming itinerant laborers than did their neighbors in more isolated regions. Even more significantly, these facts lead us to a most startling and unanticipated conclusion: despite their enforced residence in areas which, according to Gonzalo Aguirre Beltrán, have been "protected by natural barriers from competition" at the hands of hardier stock, people in Chamula now conform to the very same patterns of socioeconomic stratification which persist throughout Mexico (Figure 12).[86] And although in general they remain much poorer than peasants in other regions, among the *municipio*'s richest families a few men and women enjoy incomes equaled by less than 5 percent of Mexico's rural population. Clearly, highland residents have not remained on the fringes of economic development, at least not in the usual sense. No: modernization in Chiapas has accelerated the differences between rich and poor *campesinos* to a much greater degree than in more prosperous areas.

For these reasons, we may now appreciate the significance of so-called traditional handicrafts and occupations—that is, occu-

FIGURE 12.
The Distribution of Income in Chamula and Among All Agricultural Families in Mexico.

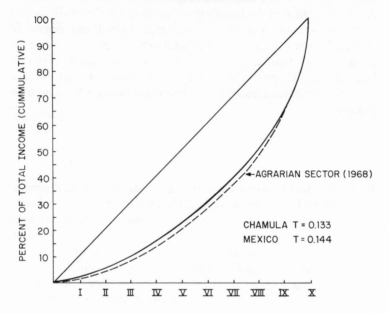

PROPORTION OF TOTAL FAMILIES (DECILES)

pations in which local people engaged when other forms of employment were unavailable. Far from simply supplementing agricultural production or wage labor, as many specialists have suggested, such additional sources of income actually permitted the workforce to reproduce itself. In this way, for example, almost every family in Chamula—nearly 70 percent—owned a small flock of sheep. From such animals, highland women obtained enough wool each year to weave a large part of their clothing and that of their families. Those women who did not possess sheep, or needed more wool, often agreed to clean and spin what other people had clipped. In return for such labor, they demanded not cash or maize, but a portion of their own handiwork. At current prices, then, the fiber produced by an average flock of 7.4 half-starved animals contributed between $40 and $60 each year toward domestic expenses. Adding to such figures the value of home-made clothing itself, we recognize that the poorest third of the town's population derived something like 30 to 40 percent of their total earnings from these beasts. In economic terms, therefore, such animals played a far more essential role in their lives than did their tiny highland *milpas*—a fact which perhaps explains why large areas of Chamula have over the years been transformed from croplands into communal pasture.

## CONCLUSIONS

By 1950 it had become clear that agrarian reform and similar measures had profoundly altered the entire fabric of social relations in central Chiapas. By accepting such measures, lowland ranchers and coffee planters hoped primarily to assure themselves of an adequate labor supply—despite the fact that they were obliged to relinquish some of their (least productive) croplands. After a certain amount of hesitation, cattlemen in the Grijalva basin eagerly embraced a form of sharecropping or tenancy which required native farmers to clear and plant extensive lowland fields. For their part, Indians from Zinacantan and Chamula accepted such arrangements because in so doing they overcame—at least temporarily—the difficult problem of demographic pressure, a problem which itself was derived from the extremely unequal distribution of land and other resources. More important, during the next three decades these arrangements allowed lowland ranchers to employ their capital in ways which now bring them the most substantial benefits: they use their money not to improve their pastures, but rather to increase their holdings in livestock and to expand their own commercial activities.

As we have seen, these practices did not arise in a haphazard or improvised fashion. On the contrary, they evolved in the early 20th century, when a series of semi-isolated regional economies, stimulated by international markets, became joined into an integrated political and economic system. Within this system, Zinacantecos and Chamulas have for many years performed different, indeed complementary functions. Whereas Zinacanteco labor remains essential to cattle ranchers in the Grijalva valley, Chamula has provided seasonal workers to harvest the region's principal export crop, coffee. And finally, in more recent years, many Chamulas have also begun to work as tenants in the lowlands, a phenomenon which not only enlarges the local workforce but also enables Zinacantecos to cultivate the more attractive fields.

If we accept these views, then we need not be surprised by the degree to which Chamulas have themselves become divided into different economic and social groups. As we have seen, the same historical processes which transformed these men and women into migrant laborers during the late 19th century have also given rise to a concomitant process of capital accumulation within the *municipio*. As a result, a handful of rich Indians now possess substantial portions of the town's best farmlands, own its trucks, and control its politics. In most cases, too, the yearly incomes of such people are 5 to 10 times greater than those of coffee workers. Below this elite, both in wealth and stature, numerous small horticulturalists, tenant farmers, and peddlers eke out a modest but adequate living. Indeed, it is the existence of such groups which argues most persuasively for the notion that since 1936 at least, ethnic differences throughout the region have become submerged beneath more fundamental differences of wealth, property, and power. As the nature of agricultural production in Chiapas has itself become more complex and varied, therefore, new social classes have emerged which now span the time-honored division between creole landowners and Indian peasants.

# "OUR FATHERS, OUR MOTHERS"
## Domestic Life and
## Religious Change in Zinacantan
## 1910–1975

The reorganization of work which took place in Chiapas after 1920 and acquired particular intensity in the years following 1936 naturally had a variety of effects upon highland communities. Not only did they become more highly stratified and divided, they also experienced a process of transformation which extended down to the most intimate levels of family life itself. By now, of course, it has become commonplace to observe that domestic activity serves among other things to reproduce and nourish future generations of peasants or rural workers.[1] And yet, the way in which it performs such functions, the way in which ordinary people order their lives to transact domestic affairs, constitutes an important and much-neglected subject of anthropological research. In their work on Apas, for example, George Collier and Victoria Bricker have suggested that Zinacantecos who own sizable parcels of land within the *municipio* are most effective in creating large corporate families and attracting additional dependents.[2] By holding out the prospect of sizable inheritance to their sons, it is said, these men are able to maintain group solidarity and to exploit their lowland fields at lesser cost.

By way of contrast, Collier has argued that in Chamula both cultural tradition and demographic imbalance have reduced the degree to which a "father can retain control over his sons after they marry, for they can readily resort to wage labor or economic specialization [e.g. handicrafts]..."[3] Implicit in this argument is the notion that ethnic differences among *municipios* have themselves given rise to different patterns of livelihood and social intercourse. In the following pages we shall consider an alternative view of these events, one which permits us to unravel the complex web of social fiction that becomes manifest when we turn to the questions of religious belief and secular ideology.

## A Woman's Place in Zinacantan

Let us first review how domestic arrangements in Zinacantan evolved after 1910. Until that time, as we have seen, most Zinacantecos lived either outside of the *municipio* on lowland ranches or in highland *parajes* as seasonal coffee workers. As such people moved from outlying hamlets like Sek'emtik and Joyjel, they gave up their old *apellidos* and were absorbed into larger name groups which anthropologists subsequently called "patrilineages." Naturally, we cannot be certain exactly how these families functioned, but it seems likely that they owed their existence to the unequal distribution of land and other resources within the community. Such difficulties must surely have become even more intense after 1914, when *baldíos* from the Grijalva basin returned to Zinacantan and claimed their right to live in highland settlements. In a few places, it appears, these people were accommodated with little fanfare or disruption. By and large, however, they returned to areas which were already hardpressed to make room for them. As a result, they quickly attached themselves to distant cousins who had become affiliated with one or another of the leading "lineages." Rather than retain their former *apellidos* and surnames, these immigrants soon assumed the names of families in which they claimed direct membership: the Pérez Asientos, Vázquez Xuljols, and López Tzintans.

Given the scarcity of farmlands in Zinacantan, procedures of this sort, rather than enhancing and strengthening the social fabric, might well have caused it to break apart once again. After 1920, however, native fathers discovered that they could provide for all of their children and followers—not in the highlands, as

Collier has suggested, but rather on rented lowland fields. Indeed, they soon realized that for those men who worked with their sons, sharecropping in the Grijalva valley provided an adequate livelihood and perhaps even a handsome surplus. Although one *arrendatario* might clear and plant enough corn to feed his family, three men laboring together could easily produce twice as much grain as they consumed. In other words, given the nature of lowland farming, extended families—not individuals or corporate lineages—enjoyed substantial economic advantages. It was for this reason that Zinacanteco fathers frequently invested a part of their earnings in highland properties and promised to reward obedient sons with a valuable patrimony. So important, in fact, did such arrangements become that by 1940, *cargo* service and other activities depended less upon one's own economic resources than upon the cooperation of one's dependents. And of course, among Zinacantan's richest inhabitants figure men who, like Juan Vázquez Xuljol and Antonio Hernández Nuj, deployed family labor among a variety of undertakings. In the years that followed, as Collier and Bricker have documented, both the cohesiveness of such families and the extent of their fortunes waxed and waned according to the vagaries of tenancy in the central basin.[4]

Given these facts, it is not surprising that the number of surnames used by Zinacantecos (and presumably the number of corporate groups which these names designated) continued to decline (see Appendix). Between 1855 and 1960, this figure dropped from 152 to around 70; at the same time, no less than 9 Spanish *apellidos* disappeared or were transformed into Tzotzil loan-words (e.g., Mandujano; see Table 72). Of the 23 major Indian names which occurred in 1855, 20 still existed in 1960—although the town's population had increased fivefold.[5] As major name groups absorbed or displaced smaller ones, they also came to designate informal *barrios* or sections which some anthropologists later called *snas* (from Tzotzil *sna*, as in *sna Xun Vaskis*, "the house of Juan Vázquez").

One dramatic example of this process involved the Pérez Ok'il family, whose members had abandoned Zinacantan before 1832 and settled on lowland ranches. Like other *baldíos*, these men

TABLE 72.
Name Groups in Zinacantan, 1960

| Spanish Apellido | Tzotzil Apellido | Previous Occurrence | | |
|---|---|---|---|---|
| | | 1749 | 1832 | 1855 |
| Arias | Kelemchitom | yes | yes | yes |
| de la Cruz | Akov | yes | yes | yes |
| | Chamul | yes | yes | yes |
| | Ok'il | Pérez Ok'il | no | no |
| | Tantob | yes | yes | yes |
| de la Torre | Chochov | no | yes | yes |
| García | Noquero | no | yes | yes |
| | Tzu | no | no | no |
| Gómez | Burro | yes | yes | yes |
| | Rodrigo | yes | yes | yes |
| González | Pakanchil | yes | yes | yes |
| | Caten | yes | yes | yes |
| Hernández | Ch'uch'ukun | yes | yes | yes |
| | Gerónimo | yes | yes | yes |
| | Inas | Las? | Las? | Las? |
| | Jol Ch'o | yes | yes | yes |
| | Kiribin | no | no | no |
| | K'o | yes | yes | yes |
| | Lantu | no | yes | yes |
| | Lek'sim | González | González | González |
| | Mentira | yes | yes | yes |
| | Min | no | yes | yes |
| | Muchic | no | yes | yes |
| | Nuj | yes | yes | yes |
| | Promash | yes | yes | yes |
| | Tijilnuk' | no | yes | yes |
| | Zapote | yes | yes | yes |
| | Zárate | yes | yes | yes |
| Jiménez | Maní | yes | yes | yes |
| | Tantiv | no | with de la Cruz, Gómez, Hernández | |

(continued)

TABLE 72. *(continued)*
Name Groups in Zinacantan, 1960

| Spanish Apellido | Tzotzil Apellido | Previous Occurrence | | |
|---|---|---|---|---|
| | | 1749 | 1832 | 1855 |
| López | Chiku | no | a | yes |
| | Kitz' | yes | yes | yes |
| | Tan Chak | yes | yes | yes |
| | Tzintan | no | b | yes |
| Martínez | Capitán | no | yes | yes |
| Méndez | Patistan | no | yes | yes |
| Montejo | Conde | no | with Méndez | no |
| | K'a Mok | no | no | no |
| | Tas Vet | yes | yes | yes |
| | Tijilnuk' | no | no | no |
| Pérez | Amalix | yes | yes | yes |
| | Asiento | yes | yes | yes |
| | Buluch | yes | yes | yes |
| | Chechev | no | no | no |
| | Jiliat | yes | yes | yes |
| | Jolote | no | no | no |
| | Kavrit | no | with de la Torre | |
| | K'obyox | no | yes | yes |
| | Konkoron | yes | yes | yes |
| | Kulantu | no | yes | yes |
| | Mandujano | appears as separate *apellido* | | |
| | Mochilum | yes | yes | yes |
| | Okotz | yes | yes | yes |
| | Pulano | yes | yes | yes |
| | P'uyum | yes | yes | yes |
| | Taki Bek'et | no | no | no |
| | Tanjol | yes | yes | yes |
| | Tasajo | yes | yes | yes |
| | Tzo T'ul | yes | with López | with López |
| | Tzotzil | no | c | d |
| | Votz | yes | ? | yes |
| | Votash | with Sánchez | Sánchez | Sánchez |

*(continued)*

TABLE 72. *(continued)*
Name Groups in Zinacantan, 1960

| Spanish Apellido | Tzotzil Apellido | Previous Occurrence | | |
|---|---|---|---|---|
| | | 1749 | 1832 | 1855 |
| | Xik' Mut | ? | with de la Torre | |
| | Xuk'umte' | no | yes | yes |
| | Xulubte' | no | yes | yes |
| | Xut | yes | yes | yes |
| Ruíz | Rojillo | yes | yes | yes |
| Sánchez | Es | yes | yes | yes |
| | Ne Uch | yes | yes | yes |
| | Pulivok | yes | yes | yes |
| | Velio | yes | yes | yes |
| Vázquez | Xuljol | yes | yes | yes |

a With López and Hernández.
b With López and Pérez.
c Appears as Tzotzilchiquin.
d With Gómez and López.

and women returned to the *muncipio* in 1914 and made their home in an area which was occupied by people named de la Cruz. Within a few years, the new arrivals had shed the surname Pérez and created a novel "patrilineage" known as de la Cruz Ok'il—a designation which their descendents bear to this day. Simultaneously, it seems, pressure to resolve such matters as inheritance and ownership became so intense that virtually all Zinacantecos were divided among a relatively small number of "lineages" which shared a single and exclusive pair of surnames. What is most striking about these groups, of course, is not that they functioned as effective corporations or even as viable extended families. On the contrary, given the uncertainties of lowland farming and the ease with which successful sharecroppers founded new dynasties, such groups represented a sociological fiction that had outlived its usefulness almost at the moment of its inception.

It is this important principle, the principle of sociological fiction, which helps us to unravel another element of life in Zinacantan: the ceremonial subordination of women. In his extensive and detailed ethnography, E.Z. Vogt has described the domestic chores which women commonly perform: preparing meals, weaving clothing, caring for young children, collecting wood and water, etc.[6] At the same time, women appear in public ritual only when their activities as helpmates and homemakers are given special emphasis. During religious processions, for example, the wives of *cargo* officials make a perfunctory appearance to pray with their husbands before retreating once again to domestic chores. Even more dramatic, as Victoria Bricker has pointed out, during the *municipio*'s holiest festivals—those which occur around the turn of the year—women assume virtually no active part at all. On these occasions, she notes, they are replaced by high-ranking *mayordomos* who dress in women's clothing and harangue female onlookers to serve their husbands without complaint.[7] Such restrictions affect even those women who function as curers in their own hamlets: they are excluded from special rituals, conducted each year by male shamans, to pray for collective good fortune. This sort of oversight seems especially odd when we recall that all curers in Zinacantan are ranked according to the number of years which they have served, and that in many hamlets the most senior shamans are women.

In order to understand such paradoxes, we must focus once again upon the major New Year celebrations, and particularly on the roles played by *mayordomos* in a series of dramas which Bricker has called the "bullfight sequence."[8] Commenting upon these dramas, which take place between December 14 (Nativity of the Virgin) and January 22 (San Sebastián), both Bricker and Vogt have stressed the importance of a traditional ideology—accepted by all Zinacantecos—which defines the respective duties of men and women.[9] Of primary significance, Bricker argues, this ideology enjoins women from engaging in men's work or from usurping male prerogatives. Speaking of two players whom she calls the "grandmothers," for example, she writes that

These men do not masquerade as women in order to make fun of the opposite sex, their characteristic attitudes, movements, appearances, and roles. Rather, they perform as Grandmothers with the sole purpose of showing how ridiculous women can be when they try to behave like men. Although costumed like women, the Grandmothers make no attempt to behave like them. . . . They behave like men, and in so doing express most dramatically how incongruous and inappropriate masculine behavior is for those who wear women's clothing.[10]

Interestingly enough, if we compare Zinacantan with other native communities, we notice two startling, indeed profoundly revealing facts. Unlike Zinacantecos, Indians elsewhere in the highlands reserve their most elaborate dramas not for the New Year period but for *Carnaval,* when they perform such time-honored dances as the *moros y cristianos* and the Dance of the Conquest. In these communities, too, ritual dramas place particular emphasis upon conventional themes like the triumph of good over evil, of Christianity over paganism, of civilization over chaos.[11] By way of contrast, *Carnaval* in Zinacantan has become a relatively minor affair, attended only by those officials who play a direct role in the ceremony. And only in Zinacantan, unique among its neighbors, have dramatic themes been transposed to coincide with the yearly investiture of new religious officials and transmuted into the domination of men over women. Obviously, then, whatever forces have modified domestic life there have also transformed the religious beliefs and practices of Zinacantecos.

Let us now consider in more detail the ways in which these people organize and conduct their ritual dramas.[12] In the first of these affairs, which is repeated on several occasions between Nativity and Epiphany (January 6), two players known as the "grandfathers" purchase a bull (in reality a straw dummy) which gores them as they ride with the "grandmothers" on stick horses. Shrieking in mock agony, the "grandfathers" are cured by whatever other officials happen to be available—the *presidente,* for example, or another *mayordomo.* Unlike real shamans, however, these officials improvise obscene prayers which by means of *double entendre* chide the grandfathers for their stupidity and bad judgment. In the second drama (which also takes place four times during this period), the grandmothers put on what Bricker has designated the spinning lesson, in which they simultaneously parody the womanly arts and proclaim their own feminine virtues. Finally, on Christmas and New Year's Day, a variant of the bullfight is performed in which the grandmothers try to tame wild horses and joust with each other. The upshot of this venture, as we might imagine, is that they, too, are soon injured and must be healed by local authorities. All the while they are accompanied by a group of young boys called "angels" who are said to be their children and who serve as models of propriety and obedience.

In her analysis of these events, Victoria Bricker has suggested that such performances serve to instruct young Zinacantecos in their proper roles and responsibilities:

> The behavior of the Angels and that of the Grandmothers seem to serve a similar function: that of showing Zinacantecos what behavior is expected of them. But the means by which they accomplish this are quite different. The Angels teach young boys how to behave by engaging in the ideal behavior themselves. The Grandmothers teach women and young girls how to behave by describing their own behavior as ideal, while at the same time behaving as deviants.

By systematically violating social norms, these performers offer a horrifying example of what women must never do:

> The moral theme of the spinning lesson is concerned with how women ought to work.... This incongruity of men dressed as women pretending to do women's work serves to ridicule women who do not perform the woman's role adequately and who thus seem as awkward as men doing women's tasks. The fact that the Grandmothers are really men serves yet another purpose. It permits men to state how they believe their wives ought to behave.

Moreover, this lesson is reiterated in particularly graphic fashion when the grandmothers are cured after falling off their horses:

> The same fate overcomes the Grandmothers as that which befell their husbands, but the reaction of the "curer" is different in their

case. When the Grandfathers fall off their horses, they are berated for having bought such wild animals. But when the Grandmothers come to grief, the official host tells them that they must not try to do what their husbands do. . . . Riding horses is too dangerous for women—they risk damaging their reproductive organs beyond repair, so that they will not be able to fulfill their main function, that of procreation.[13]

While their husbands are criticized for allowing *ladino* ranchers to cheat them, the grandmothers are admonished to forswear activities of which men do not approve.

Similar themes predominate during the *fiesta* of San Sebastián (January 22–25), where outgoing religious officials impersonate a variety of legendary figures, including two rich *ladinos* and their wives. Like the performers at *Carnaval* in other communities, these officials deliberately offend public decency and invert the normal order of things with a degree of impunity which serves above all to underscore the festival's basic seriousness. Their misbehavior forms a dramatic counterpoint to the stolid demeanor of incoming *cargo*-holders, who throughout the ceremony maintain a posture of stiff-necked rectitude. The contrast between order and chaos, between moral righteousness and sexual excess, between propriety and impropriety, could not be greater. Against this backdrop, the *ladino* women play a very important, albeit largely unheralded role: they represent a darker, more ominous kind of sexuality, the sexuality of betrayal. Consider the way in which they respond to the taunts of official musicians, who accuse them of marrying only for gain and/or of being whores: "He has a lot of money, and he has cattle. That is why I like him, even though he is an old man already. But he is a rich man, and he buys me rings and necklaces. Look—I have a mirror. You would never buy your wives that."[14] Bricker considers the point of this exercise to "make fun of the vain Ladino women, who are always combing their hair and looking at themselves in mirrors." Given the circumstances, however, we might recognize in such characters the more familiar outlines of *La Malinche*, who makes a direct and undisguised appearance elsewhere in the highlands. Rather than admonish women in Zinacantan not to emulate the errant ways of a *ladino* slut (an opportunity which few of them enjoy), such dramas may well recall the days not too long ago when half of the town's population did in fact abandon their homes to become *mestizos*.

The most striking aspect of this injunction lies not in what it intends to rectify but in what it misrepresents: during the 19th century, as we know, Zinacanteco men, not their wives, left the community in large numbers to become wandering *comerciantes* or lowland peons. In their absence, women assumed many of the functions from which they had formerly been excluded: they conducted curing ceremonies, tended highland fields, and engaged in local trade. After 1920, however, when men from Zinacantan returned to their hamlets and rented lowland fields, they devised a series of rituals which were designed to reassert their authority over all public affairs. As successful sharecroppers, for example, they began to perform what Vogt has called "year-renewal" and *k'in krus* ceremonies for their new "patrilineages" and settlements. Although these festivals ostensibly permitted local curers to pray for the health and welfare of their villages, in effect they allowed male shamans to stage a public demonstration of their own prowess and to exclude their more senior female colleagues. Similarly, by reinterpreting traditional dramas like the *baile de la conquista* and the Dance of the Christians and Moors, they portrayed a world in which men commanded the unconditional obedience of their womenfolk—not the world which really was, of course, but a world which they wished to create. And by reordering the annual cycle of celebrations in Zinacantan, they organized their new rituals to coincide with Nativity, the birth of Christ, and the *fiesta* of San Sebastián, whose martial virtues lent themselves more readily to such purposes. After all, what better occasion to reaffirm male superiority than at the very moment when one group of men was handing over the reins of formal power to another?

This interpretation becomes even more convincing when we compare Zinacantecos with their nearest neighbors in Chamula.[15] Like Zinacantecos, these people conduct both public festivals to honor their saints and private rituals to heal the sick. And as in Zinacantan, public festivals are sponsored by *mayor-*

*domos* and *alféreces* who provide all of the food, drink, candles, and fireworks which such celebrations require. Unlike Zinacantecos, however, people in Chamula do not perform special ceremonies in their *parajes*, nor do women play a major role in curing. In some measure, such differences may be due to the fact that since the 1930s municipal authorities (who manipulate religious office to serve their own ends) have not permitted independent ceremonies to occur. But to a large degree they may be traced to the different way in which economic and political forces have affected family life in Chamula. Men from Chamula did not often engage in peddling or mule-driving during the 19th century; when landlessness or forced labor became unbearable, they simply fled with their entire families and became peons on lowland ranches. More recently, as Collier has noted, seasonal migration to the coffee *fincas* has fragmented the *municipio* into a congery of household units which have no need to join even such nominal "patrilineages" as have emerged in Zinacantan.[16] With no highland patrimonies to sanctify or accumulate, rural workers in Chamula have not developed new corporate rituals, nor do they participate extensively in public ceremony. And of course, given the fact that households themselves—not extended families—constitute the basic units of production and consumption within the community, these men have enjoyed little opportunity to emphasize their own superiority and power.

## THE EXCHANGE OF SAINTS IN ZINACANTAN

As men in Zinacantan have altered the substance of their religious life in order to redefine "a woman's place," they have also responded to other pressures by modifying the form which *cargo* service there has assumed. For it is at least worth noting that, alone among their neighbors, Zinacantecos have elaborated the kind of competitive four-tiered structure which anthropologists now consider to be the hallmark of native "civil-religious hierarchies." After all, in virtually every other highland community vestiges of the old *cofradía* system may still be clearly discerned within the functions which *mayordomos* and *alféreces* perform.

In Chamula, San Andrés, Chenalhó, Magdalena, and Mitontic, for example, the position of *mayordomo* remains what it was four centuries ago: a rotating stewardship to which younger Indians are appointed as they assume the duties of manhood. Equally important, such offices are generally ranked not according to the amount which their incumbents spend (which may be quite modest), but according to the importance of the saints these men serve.[17] Like officials in Zinacantan, they may subsequently aspire to such "higher" offices as *alcalde* or *gobernador,* which in former times gave them some measure of political power. But at least since 1920, these offices have offered little more than a form of honorable retirement—just as the post of *alcalde juez* in Zinacantan is today filled by older men who exercise no real civil or religious authority. What all of these examples show, of course, is that religious activity has continued to flourish even as the center of political gravity—which at the turn of the century was occupied by *ladinos* and local *principales*—has shifted elsewhere.

In this light, one cannot fail to be startled by the emergence in Zinacantan of six new chapels (four constructed since 1970), and their effect upon the community's central *cargo* hierarchy. Following Frank Cancian, opinion holds that religious service in Zinacantan both promotes communal solidarity and provides a measure of internal stratification:

> The *cargo* system ranks the members of the community into a single social structure. All sectors of the community accord prestige and respect to the incumbent and past *cargo*-holder, and the public nature of *cargo* service makes it an effective way of ranking all Zinacantecos.[18]

Pursuing this line of argument, Cancian declares that "the few individuals who do not take any roles in public life are usually at the bottom of the social scale in Zinacantan."[19] In contrast to Manning Nash, however, he does not suggest that "the hierarchy is virtually the entire social structure of the Indian *municipio* . . . [and] does for Indians what kinship does for African societies [or] what the social class system does for Ladino society."[20] Cancian

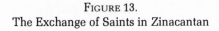

FIGURE 13.
The Exchange of Saints in Zinacantan

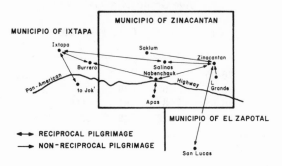

also rejects that body of theory, represented most prominently by Gonzalo Aguirre Beltrán, which regards religious service as the wellspring and motive force of native economic life. Rather, he claims that "participation in the *cargo* system reflects the individual's economic rank and determines, in large measure, his social rank." And finally, Cancian believes that "by allowing and in fact requiring the rich to make the greatest contribution for community ... observances," religious office "legitimates" economic inequalities.[21]

In order to analyze these views, we must first consider the uses to which local people have actually put their chapels. In this respect, it is instructive to examine the activities of men and women in Salinas, where *arrieros* from Jok' Ch'enom built their own church sometime around 1850. During the *fiestas* of San Sebastián in January and San Lorenzo in August, men from Salinas carry an image of the Virgin to the *cabecera*. In like fashion, Zinacanteco *cargo* officials, bearing a statue of Santo Domingo ("deputy" of the town's patron, San Lorenzo) celebrate the fiesta of Rosario in Salinas. At other times, one of the hamlet's two *cargo*-holders, the *mayol*, prepares salt from local wells for authorities in Zinacantan. Twice a month he exchanges this offering for ceremonial gifts of meat, tortillas, sugar, and *aguardiente* (Figure 13). By means of such transactions, hamlet and *municipio* remain united in a round of reciprocity that symbolizes their

TABLE 73.
Cargo Participation in Salinas by
Age Group (N = 114)

| Age Group | Cargos Served | | | |
|-----------|-----|-----|-----|-----|
|           | 0   | 1   | 2   | 3   |
| 26–35     | 94% | 6%  |     |     |
| 36–45     | 62  | 38  |     |     |
| 46–55     | 31  | 61  | 8%  |     |
| 56–65     | 28  | 28  | 28  | 16% |

interdependence and their common heritage. As Vogt has written, they provide a mechanism whereby the municipal center may command "ceremonial and political allegiance from hamlets with chapels and saints of their own."[22] In other words, ceremonial relations between Salinas and the *cabecera* attempt to overcome those forces of geography and history which have undermined *municipio* loyalties.

Despite its role in maintaining bonds of this sort, however, the chapel of Rosario has also created new and unconventional forms of authority which cannot be so easily reconciled with traditional custom and ideology. Although service at home qualifies them for higher office in the *cabecera*, fewer and fewer men from Salinas have in fact pursued such careers (Table 73). In contrast, virtually all of them have performed a *cargo* as *mayor* or as *mayordomo* within their *paraje*; indeed, some have held both offices or have held one of them twice. In effect, such men now become *pasados*—a status customarily reserved for those few officials who serve municipal offices on all four levels. Simultaneously, of course, they undertake other local duties: they may serve on the school or church committees, for example, or as representatives to the land reform committee. In other words, their loyalties to municipal authorities and institutions have been tempered over the years as relations with lowland *finqueros* and politicians have become strengthened. Contrary to what both Cancian and Vogt suppose, then, the municipal hierarchy has

TABLE 74.
Participation Rates among Salinas Residents in
Municipal Hierarchy, 1955–1970 (N = 120)

| | |
|---|---|
| Salinas men in *municipio* population (percentage) | 5 |
| First-level positions held by Salinas men if *cargos* were allocated according to proportion in municipal population | 45 |
| Second-level positions held by Salinas men under same conditions | 11 |
| First-level positions actually held | 30 |
| Second-level positions actually held | 5 |
| Participation rate at first level (actual service as percentage of potential) | 67 |
| Participation rate at second level (percentage) | 45 |

not been extended to incorporate men from Salinas. Instead, the chapel (and its religious offices) have provided a mechanism whereby local bonds find expression at the expense of relations between *paraje* and *cabecera* (Table 74).

In much the same way, it must be noted that the construction of Nabenchauk's chapel in 1952 has not significantly increased the frequency with which its inhabitants served *municipio* office. As we have seen, Nabenchauk—founded in the mid-19th century—grew rapidly after 1930 until it had surpassed Zinacantan Center both in population and in prosperity. Like Na Chij, Nabenchauk's newfound importance was considerably enhanced with the construction of the highway, which transformed it into a sophisticated and highly energetic little town. Flexing their new economic muscles, men in Nabenchauk soon petitioned the state government to grant them limited judicial powers as a semi-autonomous *agencia municipal*. By 1972, Nabenchauk's *agente municipal* settled legal disputes involving not only local residents but also those from *parajes* as far away as Petztoj, Chikinibal Vo', and Sek'emtik. During these years, Nabenchauk's residents remodeled their chapel and added religious images. And beginning in 1957 they appointed two *mayor-*

TABLE 75.
Cargo Participation in Nabenchauk, 1960–1970 (N=384)

| | |
|---|---|
| Nabenchauk men in *municipio* population (percentage) | 16 |
| First-level positions held by Nabenchauk men if *cargos* were allocated according to proportion in municipal population | 49 |
| Second-level positions | 22 |
| First-level positions actually held | 33 |
| Second-level positions actually held | 19 |
| Participation rate at first level (percentage) | 67 |
| Participation rate at second level (percentage) | 86 |

*domos* each year to pay the costs of celebrating a festival in honor of their patron, the *Señora de Guadalupe.* Having asserted their political and economic independence from the *cabecera,* Indians in Nabenchauk appeared anxious to declare their spiritual equality as well. Within a few years, therefore, they had organized religious exchanges not only with the church in Zinacantan but also with towns and villages throughout the region.

Given these practices, it is difficult to accept Cancian's suggestion that Nabenchauk's *cargos* have permitted hamlet residents to further their religious careers in the municipal center. To be sure, it appears that some men have utilized local positions in order to pursue higher office. As Table 75 reveals, Nabenchauk men have become *alféreces* (second-level officials) at a fairly undiminished rate—a rate that accurately reflects their place in the *municipio's* population. Upon closer examination, however, it must be noted that only 67 percent of those Nabenchauk men who might have become *mayordomos* (either in Zinacantan or in their own chapel) accepted such responsibilities. In other words, while they now tend to avoid service in the center, they have not undertaken comparable duties at home. Even the hamlet's *cargo-*holders, despite their relative wealth and their unquestioned civic pride, have pursued further office only with great reluctance. In contrast to men from Nabenchauk who actually served

TABLE 76.
Cargo Histories of Nabenchauk Men, 1957–1972[a]

|  | Cargos Held | | |
| --- | --- | --- | --- |
|  | 2 | 3 | 4 |
| Percentage of Nabenchauk men who served first *cargo* in *municipio* center (N = 11) | 90% | 18% | 9% |
| Percentage of Nabenchauk men who served first *cargo* in Nabenchauk (N = 30) | 17 | 10 | 0 |

[a] Including men who placed their names on waiting lists.

as *mayordomos* in the center, fewer than half of them have become *alféreces* (Table 76). As in Salinas, then, the chapel in Nabenchauk has given birth to a body of *pasados* whose ceremonial experience reflects a profound sense of regional loyalty. Committed as they are to Nabenchauk's increased social and political autonomy, they have performed ceremonial functions not in order to justify their own social position, still less to prepare themselves for municipal service. Rather, they have undertaken such duties because family tradition and religious conviction have demanded pious works.

Not surprisingly, the chapel in Apas owes its origins to similar experiences and sentiments. As we know, Apas survived the demographic catastrophes which in the 19th century decimated other hamlets. More recently, its inhabitants have enjoyed substantial economic advantages not possessed by Indians near the *cabecera*. Even after the highway was completed, for example, local men who rented land in the Grijalva basin avoided high transportation costs by carrying their harvests homeward on muleback. As Apas' population grew, so did the number of residents who wished to celebrate their own festivals. In 1961, three of these men persuaded their neighbors to build a small chapel which they dedicated to the Señor de Esquipulas. Predictably, they soon organized four local *cargos* on the model of Zinacantan's *ermita de Esquipulas* (two *mayordomo-reyes* and two *me-*

*soneros*) and invited religious officials in both Nabenchauk and the *cabecera* to exchange images. In response, *municipio* authorities proposed that *mayordomo-reyes* in Apas celebrate no fewer than five festivals each year in Zinacantan. Angered and offended, these men withdrew their invitation: to this day, they refuse to visit the *cabecera* on ritual occasions. Rather than accept such humiliation and incur such expense, they chose instead to attend the festival of Guadalupe in Nabenchauk, an exchange which might be undertaken without loss of honor. Clearly they felt that what independence and prosperity had wrought, *municipio* elders might not be permitted to cast asunder.

Like Nabenchauk and Apas, three other hamlets (Paste', Elan Vo', and Na Chij), responding both to social change and to demographic growth, have organized their own ceremonies since 1971. In each case, as we know, during the previous 40 years these villages had grown rapidly both in size and in stature. By 1970, in fact, it appeared that they might split into a number of distinctive social and political units. Under these circumstances, prominent men within each community (shamans and former *cargo*-holders, for the most part) encouraged their neighbors to organize local chapels. As they pointed out, several families had already constructed their own small *ermitas*. In Elan Vo', for example, Juan López Chiku had for many years possessed the *t'ent'en* (San Sebastián's drum), which he housed in a small chapel adjacent to his home. Only a few miles away, in Paste', the Pintoletik family guarded Zinacantan's *k'oltixyo* and *varaetik*, a sort of jousting target and lances used during the *fiesta* of San Sebastián. Also in Paste', the Lotriko family kept an image of the Virgen del Rosario in their private hermitage, an image which had been removed years before from Zinacantan. Not surprisingly, it was precisely this chapel that, in 1971, local men refurbished and rededicated in the form of a community church. And finally, the following year, residents of Elan Vo', prompted by their parish priest (who refused to celebrate mass for the *t'ent'en*), built a new *ermita* and added an effigy of San Sebastián himself.

In all of these *parajes*, it is important to note that village residents have taken no steps to establish religious *cargos*. On the contrary, they specifically reject the notion that local saints and images require new *mayordomos*. As in rural towns throughout Mexico, they have formed church committees to look after their chapels and collect funds for major ceremonies. In no way do committee members regard their service as a *cargo*, nor do they hope to assume more important functions in the future. Why, such men frequently ask, should we create elaborate ceremonial obligations which only increase our already substantial economic difficulties? After all, our *ermitas* provide a means whereby we may all participate in religious activities, while at the same time we reduce our personal expenses. Similarly, as might be expected, shamans in Elan Vo' (who before 1968 conducted an annual pilgrimage to the *cabecera*) decided that such journeys had become both costly and unnecessary. Since that time they have abandoned these activities, although they continue to participate in Zinacantan's year-renewal ceremonies. In order to protect their livelihoods from the social, economic, and religious constraints imposed by traditional practices, then, these men altered time-honored ceremonial patterns. In so doing, they created novel religious institutions that more adequately reflect their position in a transformed Zinacanteco social order. Like their neighbors in Salinas and Nabenchauk, they have utilized religious ritual not at all as a means of enforcing municipal solidarity. Ritual now serves as a symbolic means of expressing their hard-won economic independence and their increased political autonomy.

Many of the same themes become apparent when we examine Sek'emtik, where in 1971 a new *ermita* was dedicated to the Virgen de Dolores. As in Paste', Elan Vo', and Na Chij, residents of Sek'emtik shared the costs of this enterprise and continue to bear the expenses necessary to celebrate annual *fiestas*. Even so, it is reasonable to ask why these people, who in many respects resemble their neighbors in Nabenchauk far more than other Zinacantecos, chose not to model their chapel after that of the Señora de Guadalupe. After all, both Sek'emtik and Nabenchauk enjoy close proximity to the Grijalva valley. In the early years of this century, both hamlets experienced substantial immigration which anticipated by 20 years or more the growth of Na Chij, Elan Vo', and Paste'. In the same manner, the highway enhanced their prosperity and transformed both into important regional centers. Rather than pray in the *cabecera*, for example, shamans from hamlets in western Zinacantan have for many years preferred Sek'emtik's sacred mountains and religious shrines. Moreover, several years ago Sek'emtik also became an *agencia municipal*, which permitted its inhabitants to settle their own legal affairs. And yet, despite these similarities, men and women there have not organized religious offices nor have they emulated the almost hierarchical style of ritual life in Nabenchauk. For what reason, then, have they decided to celebrate their festivals in cooperative and un*cargo*-like fashion?

The answer to this question may be found in a study of the tenuous nature of social and political relations between the western *parajes* and Zinacantan Center. Until quite recently, as we have seen, men from this region worked as day laborers or as tenants on adjacent lowland ranches. Long before the highway had been completed, it appears, their ties to the *cabecera* had loosened or perhaps even dissolved. Only a few miles away, the closely related community of Muk'ta Jok' (which in the 19th century had become an *hacienda* and was later expropriated to form an *ejido*) withdrew entirely from Zinacantan. Despite the fact that Indians in Muk'ta Jok' paid religious dues to authorities in the *cabecera*, they were not allowed to serve in the municipal *cargo* hierarchy: in the eyes of Zinacanteco officials, it appears, such people (who live within the *municipio* of Ixtapa) had become outsiders. Insulted and outraged by such attitudes, men and women in Muk'ta Jok' installed two *mayordomos* in their own small chapel. At the same time they affiliated themselves formally with the main church in Ixtapa, to which on important feast days they now bring their saint. Although Sek'emtik itself has not undertaken such dramatic actions, it has experienced many of the same pressures and temptations. And despite the fact that its residents remain Zinacantecos, they nonetheless recognize that they share a common destiny with neighboring Ixtapanecos and *mestizos*. Not surprisingly, therefore, they evince little interest in establishing local *cargo* offices. Why, they reason, should we prepare ourselves for religious careers which we do not intend to pursue?

Under these circumstances, it should not surprise us to learn that neither Sek'emtik in western Zinacantan nor Na Chij, Paste', and Elan Vo' near San Cristóbal have exchanged saints with the *cabecera*. On the contrary, within these *parajes* the egalitarian nature of religious life precludes such rituals. After all, traveling saints require fairly elaborate ministrations, which generally fall upon the shoulders of *mayordomos* and their families. Of course, village elders might propose that local residents contribute the time and money which such pilgrimages entail, but this proposition would invariably undermine the communal flavor that hamlet chapels lend to Indian social relations.

In what way, then, do these four hamlets express their sentimental attachment to municipal saints? In Paste' and Elan Vo', such bonds assume tangible form every year when Zinacanteco *cargo*-holders "borrow" the *t'ent'en* and *k'oltixyo* for the festival of San Sebastián. Formerly, arrangements of this sort involved only a few *municipio* officials and the two families in whose care these objects remained. Since Paste' and Elan Vo' built their chapels, however, both the *t'ent'en* and *k'oltixyo* have become communal property, an arrangement with which *paraje* residents readily concur. Like the Virgen del Rosario in Salinas, therefore, these two images (as Zinacantecos sometimes describe them) receive formal invitations to visit the *cabecera*. And like the saints in Salinas, Ixtapa, and San Lucas, they respond to such invitations in that time-honored Zinacanteco fashion: surrounded by pomp and circumstance, they arrive in a stately and formal embassy.

Still, two important *parajes*, Na Chij and Sek'emtik, steadfastly refuse to send delegations to the *cabecera* or to receive ceremonial visitors. At first glance, it might seem that these hamlets no longer participate in the *municipio's* religious life, that they have withdrawn from its distinct ritual system. Yet this notion is false in that men from both hamlets continue to serve in the town's government and (from time to time) in the *cargo* hierarchy. In order to resolve the issue, we must consider not simply those chapels that exchange ritual objects within Zinacantan, but also the activities of local shamans. Most particularly, it must be recalled that Zinacantecos do not divide their religion into "Catholic" and "native" components, that shamans and saints do not play contradictory or antithetical roles. Although church committees in Na Chij and Sek'emtik do not maintain formal relations with *municipio* officials, shamans from both villages participate in the *cabecera*'s year-renewal ceremonies. As a result, they have avoided the type of spiritual confrontation that disrupted relations with Apas. In other words, contrary to what Vogt has suggested, the exchange of religious images and practitioners between *paraje* and *cabecera* does not "command ceremonial and political allegiance from . . . hamlets with chapels and saints of their own."[23] Certainly, in limited measure, Zinacanteco ceremonial life reflects such notions. Ritual exchanges find their profoundest inspiration, however, in those common historical and ethnic experiences which modern Zinacantecos share. In the end, only time can tell how long these men and women will continue to feel such responsibilities toward a *cabecera* that during the past 30 years has in many respects become the *municipio*'s sleepiest and most isolated hamlet.

## CONCLUSIONS

By 1970, religious life in Zinacantan had undergone a number of significant alterations. Responding to realignments in the social relations of agricultural production, families in the community initially changed their names and joined larger corporate units which controlled access to essential resources. As such units outlived their usefulness, however, these people attached themselves to successful sharecroppers and peddlers whose own fortunes might rise or fall within a relatively short period. Under these circumstances, as George Collier and Victoria Bricker have correctly recognized, "lineage names" themselves soon become quite meaningless. For one thing, literally dozens of men and women might share the same surname pairs such as Hernández Co or Pérez Asiento. For another, shifting alliances and constant movement compelled these people to devise a more flexible naming system which reflected the transformed realities of social and domestic life. Rather than forsake their surnames entirely, they chose instead to do what their ancestors had done a century earlier—that is, they began to use nicknames to designate new family groups. At the same time, Zinacanteco men organized a novel series of "year-renewal" ceremonies by means of which they asserted their authority over precisely those domains that they had relinquished during the previous 150 years. By performing these ceremonies (which may even be conducted by members of a particularly prosperous or successful household), such men in effect nullify the accumulated seniority of women shamans and exclude them from public life. And in order to assure that their message is clearly understood by men and women alike, during major festivals they rewrite their own history and proclaim their new tale from the church door.

In much the same fashion, religious service itself has acquired new meaning and significance as social relations undergo further modification. Of primary importance, as Frank Cancian has suggested, the *cargo* system does not "level" those differences of wealth and power which, he believes, might upset Zinacantan's delicate social balance. According to genealogical information, however, as early as the 1920s and 1930s many well-to-do men avoided religious office altogether or performed only the most perfunctory service. In fact, as Cancian intimates, at most this system encouraged prosperous Indians to devote a significant portion of their incomes to public celebrations. In return, they received the gratitude and approbation of their neighbors, as well as the knowledge that they had filled a sacred trust. By and large, however, it is the nature of agricultural expansion outside of Zinacantan—not, as Cancian would have it, an insufficient number of *cargo* positions—which in recent times has undermined the *municipio's* religious organization. Lowland sharecropping and the Pan-American Highway have created new social divisions and political conflicts that traditional rituals and practices cannot resolve. Since 1940, many hamlets have grown so rapidly that *cargo* service and year-renewal ceremonies no longer provide a common ground on which rich and poor might meet as equals. Under these circumstances, hamlet elders have encouraged local residents to build new chapels and to organize cooperative, not hierarchical, festivals. By creating such institutions, it seems, they hope to restrain and reconcile in some measure those inequalities that modernization has created.

# CONCLUSIONS

In his brief but excellent book *The Fiesta System and Economic Change*, Waldemar Smith argues that religious practice in western Guatemala has undergone fundamental modification within a relatively short period as economic conditions in the region have altered. "The processes of change are numerous," he suggests, "and they interact in various ways to produce what is more a mosaic than a pattern."[1] In highland Chiapas, what anthropologists and historians have called "Indian culture" emerged as native people have both resisted and accommodated themselves to much the same sort of pressures and events. Paramount in this process, religious belief has provided these people with a vantage point from which to take stock of their own past; unique among all aspects of native life, religious traditions represent a body of shared experience whose origins may be found in Las Casas' message that faith in God and freedom from domination were inextricably linked. In recent years, this message has acquired special urgency as modern forms of inequality have replaced the class relations that developed under both Spanish mercantilism and Liberal free trade. To paraphrase Smith once again, such forms are not necessarily better than their predecessors, but they are certainly different—and their effect on Indian communities has been profound.

What is most striking about these events is that they have given rise to a number of myths whose tenacity and resistance to revision have remained virtually unshaken right down to our own day. Let us review briefly how such myths arose and analyze them in the light of our previous discussions.

First, there is the notion that Indians rejected Christianity from the start and continued to practice their own brand of superstition behind the backs of their diligent pastors. In its modern form, this startling concept provides the starting point for much anthropological scholarship on native syncretism, on the "idols behind the altars" to whom Indian prayers are supposedly addressed. Second, modern investigators have generally accepted the Liberal view that native laziness and sloth (or cultural deprivation), not the systematic despoiling of Indian communities, have transformed central Chiapas into an island of backwardness and traditionalism. In what other way, for example, may we interpret George Collier's suggestion that people in Chamula live in "obvious disequilibrium" with their environment, that the perpetuation of ethnic ties has taken precedence over the rational use of their own slender resources? True enough, such people share a body of custom and belief that distinguishes them from their neighbors in other highland communities. But as the events of 1712 and 1869 clearly demonstrate, they are also capable of making common cause with these neighbors to protest against the worst abuses of power—just as they have continually made common cause with *mestizos* of similar class and condition since the revolution to obtain more land or higher wages. And when competition among them has rendered common action unworkable, it has generally fallen to government agencies—not traditional elders—to stress the importance of community interests at the expense of more general concerns.

At this point, it is perhaps useful to compare the religious experience of Indians in central Chiapas with Christian practice and belief among rural people in Europe. In his brilliant work on popular Catholicism during the late Middle Ages, Lionel Rothkrug contends that peasants in France and Germany might enjoy full citizenship in the Church only by submitting to what he calls "the penitential system."

The Europe-wide pilgrimage expansion, the multiplication of indulgences, the proliferation of saints, and the prodigious rise of confraternities must all be seen as different parts of a single penitential system. It was calculated to enroll the dead in a vast network of reciprocal services, the totality of which constituted both the cult of purgatory and, in its widest theological sense, the "communion of saints," that is, the entire Church conceived as "the unity under and in Christ of the faithful on earth, the souls in Purgatory, and the blessed in Heaven."[2]

As a result, popular attention shifted from localized relic cults and miracle-working to an intensified concern with canonized saints. Eventually this movement to democratize the Heavenly Kingdom, to make salvation accessible to "everyone [who] contributed toward the redemption of another," found ultimate expression in a new ideology of collective worship.

In the fourteenth century, the confraternity, not the Church, may have appeared to ordinary folk as the institution outside of which there was no salvation. For to sever one's corporate ties meant to dissolve all the horizontal and vertical expiatory relationships that bound a member to his fellows, both living and dead, through whom alone he had access to an all-powerful patron saint. . . . Thus the widespread adoption of the corporative principle of collective responsibility and its corollary, collective redemption, as a chief tenet of penitential piety made it difficult for men to distinguish religious bonds from communal ones. Every locality, every occupation established some form of local ritual network uniting living and departed souls in common devotional assistance.[3]

Such beliefs underwent considerable modification as the Reformation proceeded. Responding to attacks on the efficacy of saint worship, Church officials substituted new forms of devotion to the Virgin Mary—now anointed "Queen of Heaven and Earth"—and to Christ himself. Confraternities that had previously celebrated local saints now extolled the Blessed Virgin, and particularly her special relationship with God. Under her aegis, regional pieties were woven into national cults upon which, it was believed, the authority of a universal Church might be reestablished.[4] Ronald Finucane has suggested that in England, for example, earlier kinds of veneration were displaced during the 15th and 16th centuries by eucharistic and Marian observances that in most cases remained under the direct control of bishops and priests.[5] And finally, to reassert its primacy in matters of faith and doctrine, the Church expounded new dogmas concerning Mary's own miraculous nature.

Similar events took place in rural Spain, where eucharistic practices displaced relic worship during the 15th century. According to William Christian, this transformation was undertaken largely by secular and regular clergymen, who by 1575 had established themselves throughout Castile.[6] As in England, France, and much of Germany, Spanish peasants had until a few years earlier addressed their prayers to local saints at nearby shrines. Beginning in the 12th century, however, "Marian shrines gradually won preeminence over the bodies of local saints as important sources for practical divine help."[7] Once again, it seems, religious brotherhoods provided the primary medium through which to implore Mary's aid. Although many of these *cofradías* had originally been founded to commemorate saints like San Sebastián, "the newer were penitential brotherhoods like that . . . of the True Cross and the Rosary, which were building chapels in the decade 1570–1580."[8] And within two centuries—that is, by the end of Spanish colonialism in the New World—

there was a kind of reshuffling of Marian devotion: old devotions declined, and less venerated images were accorded more attention. And a new echelon of Marian images was added; more than a third of those accorded special devotion in the 1780s were not even mentioned 200 years earlier. Many of these new Marian devotions were advocations associated with the Passion. . . .[9]

With these facts in mind, I believe it becomes easier to understand how native religion in Mesoamerica assumed its current shape and form. As Robert Ricard has observed, during the 16th century Spanish missionaries took great pains to instill in their followers a highly purified, highly eucharistic form of European Catholicism.

At least in the field of religion, a complete rupture occurred. The very superficial analogies that might be observed between Mexican paganism and Christianity were not used. The missionaries thought that baptism, confession, and communion among the ancient Mexicans had nothing in common with the sacraments of the Church . . . but were only a satanic parody of them. . . . It was held that for the Mexican to become a true Christian he had to break entirely with his past, except . . . in his language, because it was clearly understood that to become a true Christian he did not at all have to become a Spaniard.[10]

In a fundamental way, then, Indian men and women became Christians by enrolling in that same penitential system that had so recently and so forcefully asserted itself in Europe. United to the Blessed Virgin through their ancestors in purgatory, they sought salvation through *collective* devotion—not as a matter of individual conscience or action. As in Europe, too, *cofradías* provided the primary means for accomplishing this task. Indeed, as both Rothkrug and Christian have suggested, "the confraternity, not the Church, may have appeared . . . as the institution outside of which there was no salvation." And since participation in *cofradías* soon became synonymous with residence in established communities, it is not difficult to see how community membership came to stand for incorporation into the *corpus mysticum* itself.

The practical and ideological consequences of this view may be perceived most clearly in the form native devotion assumed during the uprising of 1712. As we have already seen, just before open rebellion broke out in the central highlands Indians in the Tzotzil town of Santa Marta built a chapel for the Blessed Virgin, who had miraculously appeared in the woods nearby. Almost immediately, attendance at mass in communities as far away as Totolapa dropped as native men and women embarked on the sacred journey to Santa Marta. According to Victoria Bricker, such pilgrims arrived there in the evident expectation that they "would go to Heaven, even if they had many sins"—just as rural folk in Europe purchased indulgences and forgiveness at shrines of the Holy Queen.[11] Unlike European peasants, however, Indian pilgrims immediately excited the suspicions of Church officials who, in the spirit of Núñez de la Vega, regarded such practices as paganism and superstition. Not surprisingly, then, these officials arrested two *mayordomos* who attended the Virgin in Santa Marta and put them on trial.

From this event, in fact, we may note the unfortunate disparity between ecclesiastical practice in Spain and in the New World. As William Christian and other scholars have pointed out, votive offerings to images of the Blessed Virgin were commonplace on the continent and represented a focal point of lay devotion in 18th-century Spain. In this case, however, the investigating magistrate, Juan Santander, doggedly insisted that Indian pilgrims had prayed to the image in Santa Marta merely to ask for good health—despite the fact, as Bricker points out, that "none of the testimonies and confessions . . . supported this interpretation." As for the kind of rites native supplicants conducted there, "Dominica López [a *mayordoma*] replied that the ceremonies had been performed with the same pomp and rites used for the patron saint." [12] Of course, such explanations were of little avail: Dominga ("Dominica") and her husband, who also served as *mayordomo*, were sentenced to prison and the image was destroyed. And here we see most dramatically the difficulty colonialism had precipitated within a Church that promised salvation through universal faith. In Europe, where the subordination of Indians to Spaniards was not at issue, these *mayordomos* would probably have been reprimanded for error or excessive zeal; in America, they were condemned for heresy. Still, Indians in Chiapas adhered scrupulously to the penitential creed: a few months later, when open rebellion finally broke out in Cancuc, it was organized at first as an extended *cofradía* dedicated to the Holy Mother.

Perhaps the strongest evidence in favor of this interpretation may be found in the kinds of religious organizations that have survived among native people in Mesoamerica to this day. Beginning with Sol Tax and his students, several generations of anthropologists have proposed that indigenous "civil-religious hierarchies" survived the cataclysm of conquest or emerged shortly thereafter to fill the vacuum left by military disaster. [13] Billie DeWalt has suggested that modern *cofradías* trace their origins to such "traditional hierarchies," that non-hierarchical or relatively unstratified religious offices have evolved as these systems fall apart.[14] In central Chiapas, however, we have seen that highly stratified forms of religious service developed during the late 19th century when Indian communities tried to protect themselves against the depredations of both the Church and civil officials. For the most part, these efforts were unsuccessful and led to the complete dissolution of local *cofradías*. In their place, individual *mayordomos* and *alféreces* assumed the functions which penitential confraternities had performed for nearly 400 years. Only in Zinacantan and a handful of other villages did a true "hierarchy" emerge; elsewhere, civil and religious authority remained in the hands of men who might negotiate some kind of peace with priests and *jefes políticos*.

Arrangements of this kind underwent considerable modification in Guatemala, where pressures against confraternities never reached the same level of intensity. Even today, *cofradías* continue to exist in many Indian communities. Moreover, as Smith has shown, the particular way in which these *cofradías* are structured often provides a sensitive measure of economic difference and political inequality. Despite such diversity, most *cofradías* share a number of common features. Let us consider the religious system described by Manning Nash in the town of Cantel. In 1954, Cantel possessed seven brotherhoods that were ranked according to the importance of their patrons.[15] At any given moment, membership in these organizations was limited to a small number of men who had previously performed certain public functions. According to Nash, such men joined *cofradías* primarily to further their "*cargo* careers"—that is, to assume high office as an *alcalde* or as *mayordomo* of an important saint (see Figure 14). But Nash acknowledges that most men undertook careers of a very different sort: they performed ritual service in a modest way on several occasions throughout their lives. To these men, then, the devotional and penitential aspects of *cofradía* membership apparently transcended a more straightforward desire for power and prestige. One suspects that such motives were much more widespread among *cofrades* than the kind of self-promotion that attracted the attention of anthropologists. In fact, the

### Figure 14.
### Cofradías in Cantel, 1954

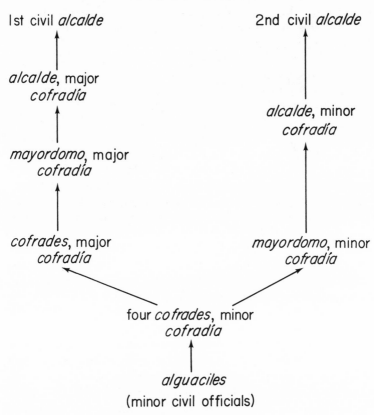

Source: Manning Nash, *Machine Age Maya*, pp. 126–127.

ethnographic literature provides abundant confirmation of this view.[16]

Curiously, what most anthropologists seem to miss in their accounts of native political and religious organization is that, before 1945, Indian officials enjoyed neither power nor prestige in rural Guatemala. Rather, such power was vested in a group of low-level functionaries called *alcaldes* or *intendentes* who were appointed by government officers in Guatemala City and who were invariably *ladinos*. The origins of this situation are not hard to find. "In order to provide land and labor for the coffee plantations," writes Robert Carmack, "Liberals dispossessed the Indians of their lands (only 7.3% of the population owned land in 1926), shattered their villages, and instituted forced labor (through debt peonage)."[17] One prominent effect of these measures was to create within Indian communities new divisions that were reflected in the nature and variety of *cofradía* functions. As I have discussed elsewhere, by 1944, when the Ubico dictatorship collapsed, religious affiliation—including affiliation with Protestant sects and the Acción Católica—appears to have become a proxy for direct political action.[18] Consider once again the case of Cantel, where service in confraternities was by and large monopolized by a new elite of factory workers who took elaborate measures to exclude their more "traditional" peasant neighbors. In response, many rural people in the area converted to Protestantism; others joined opposition political parties. Similar events took place throughout the country: in the Quiché region, in the towns around Lake Atitlán, and even on the outskirts of Guatemala City. Whatever functions *cofradía* membership may have served in the 19th and 20th centuries, therefore, it did not provide Indians with an avenue of social mobility.

Must we conclude, then, as Judith Friedlander has proposed, that Indian culture—devised by missionaries as an instrument of oppression—is now fed mainly by anthropologists and politicians who maintain a professional interest in keeping alive the "Indian question"? On this score, she believes, "Indian-ness is more a measure of what the villagers are not or do not have vis-à-vis the Hispanic elite than it is of what they are or have."[19] Like their venerable forebears, however, ideas of this sort tell us more about the poverty of anthropology than about how native people have responded to the strains of social transformation. Rather than revising conventional wisdom, in fact, such theories seem merely a radical restatement of Redfield's original views, a restatement in which "Indian communities" appear today only as a poor version of what *we* were yesterday. As a result, it is said, these communities have failed to become part of class society because they retain the customs and traditions that arose under colonialism, because in some sense they remain encapsulated to this day within the feudal social order. A few specialists even claim that such customs themselves now provide the mechanism whereby native people in rural Mexico suffer economic and political exploitation.[20] And yet surely the time has come to accord Indian history the same respect with which we treat our own: anthropology may then take its rightful place as the history of the Indian present—not as a substitute for historical inquiry.

One recent effort in this direction is Victoria Bricker's *The Indian Christ, The Indian King*, in which historical evidence is employed to decode what she calls the "paradigm of ethnic conflict" underlying native ritual and custom. In this view, Indians in Chiapas (like their cousins in Yucatan and Guatemala) share a cyclical concept of time that allows them to assimilate distinct chronological events into a general theory of history. Essential to this theory is the conviction that antagonism between Indians and *ladinos* remains timeless and permanent, so that native reenactments of the Passion during Easter week also connote the conquest of Chiapas, the 1712 rebellion, the events of 1869, and the Mexican revolution. Or as Bricker puts it,

> The heterogeneity of elements in Maya folklore is the product of syncretism and temporal distortion. Syncretism integrates beliefs and practices of different origin and meaning and makes them part of Maya history. Temporal distortion brings events into the timeless paradigm of myth and ritual.[21]

Of course, no one could reasonably disagree with the idea that native traditions compress a wide variety of incidents into a small number of symbols. But as Bricker herself admits, little consensus has existed among native people, even during such cataclysmic events as the 1712 uprising. We have already seen how rituals performed in Zinacantan each year at the festival of San Sebastián represent an attempt to reassert the authority of men over women, not a generalized recognition that male authority in such matters is a time-honored right. Pilgrimages among outlying chapels in the *municipio* accomplish a very similar purpose. At any moment, then, the paradigm of ethnic conflict is subject to considerable modification and manipulation by different constituencies within native communities. And, of course, the nature of those constituencies is intimately related to the political requirements of *ladino* society at large.

Along these lines, it is instructive to examine a number of works like David Ronfeldt's *Atencingo* and Arturo Warman's . . . Y *venimos a contradecir*. What these books have in common, and what distinguishes them from more conventional research, is that they focus on the relationship between peasants in Mexico and their most important social antagonists, including the state itself. As the state acquired its present functions in postrevolutionary society, it undertook a series of measures to guarantee peace in the countryside and at the same time to encourage production. For this reason, Warman writes, "conflict in the countryside inevitably leads to conflict with the State"—a fact that gives such events "a political significance far beyond the importance of the specific issues at hand."[22] Similarly, in *Atencingo*, Ronfeldt has argued that successive administrations carefully transformed revolutionary disaffection in southern Puebla into the struggle for lawful reform and finally into a highly localized and fragmented competition for bureaucratic patronage. Such events cannot help but recall that control over *agraristas* and coffee workers in Chiapas permitted federal authorities to impose their will on political rivals and the state's major landowners. In fact, as we have seen, it is measures of this sort, not the nature of the Indian worldview or community organization, that set the limits for action in places like Zinacantan and Chamula and form the backdrop against which their economic, political, and religious institutions evolve.

What I think becomes clear from this discussion is that, beginning in colonial times, some Indians in central Chiapas have refused adamantly to submit to *ladino*-ization, to the ultimate indignity of transculturation. Instead, they have managed to preserve an independent sense of their own destiny—occasionally by rebelling against their rulers, more often through the less vulnerable mechanism of corporate religious ritual. How unsurprising it is, after all, that *cargo* systems should "define community membership" (as Frank Cancian has written) in response to the exigencies of *mestizo* priests and politicians. How unsurprising, too, that this system of community service, forged in the crucible of liberal economics and forced labor, should give way in the 20th century to more decentralized and less rigid religious ways. And yet, to a large degree, these new institutions preserve the aims and intentions of their original creators—that is, they allow native people to withstand the pressures of social and economic change without sacrificing what they hold most sacred and dear. However much the chapels in Salinas, Nabenchauk, and Sek'emtik may resemble their counterparts in non-Indian communities, they remain Zinacanteco churches, repositories of Zinacanteco history, where Indian men and women may still address their saints in the same language in which their forefathers first prayed to a new and vengeful god nearly five centuries ago.

# APPENDIX

## Indian Surnames in Zinacantan, 1749–1855

| Spanish and Tzotzil surname pairs | | |
| --- | --- | --- |
| | 1749 | 1855 |
| Alarcón | | |
| Alvaro | | |
| Arias | Cotin | Fortuna |
| | Fortuno | Jiliat |
| | Kolonchiton | Quelemchitom |
| de la Cruz | Biquet | Biquil |
| | Chalmul | Chanmul |
| | Chanchac | Jolakov |
| | Chanmut | Manic |
| | Contachiton | Saquiloquil |
| | Jolaco | Tantiv |
| | Tonton | Tontom |
| de la Torre | Julbac | Cabrito |
| | Panchi | Chach |
| | Penitencia | Chanmul |
| | Quilan | Chocho (v) |
| | Sopilote | Penitencia |
| | | Tzopilote |
| | | Xicmut |
| | | Zalea |

Spanish and Tzotzil surname pairs

| | 1749 | 1855 |
|---|---|---|
| Díaz | Tuilmedio | |
| | Tzot | |
| García | Jolchic | Jolchig |
| | Manjo | Manzo |
| | Peut | Noquero |
| | Puxantzum | Pojantzuc |
| | Yatpux | |
| Gómez | Abetar | Abela |
| | Burro | Bastian |
| | Castellanos | Burro |
| | Chuiatel | Cabranegra |
| | Izcumilco | Culpa |
| | Lencin | Jolchoc |
| | Nachi | Monte |
| | Natzin | Osol |
| | Rodrigo | Rodrigo |
| | | Tantiv |
| | | Tzotzil |
| | | Zapote |
| González | Cantero | Caten |
| | Catten | Co |
| | Cunuc | Cutnuc |
| | Lencin | Cutunui |
| | Pacanchib | Lecsim |
| | Pisnail | Pacanchil |
| | Pixnuit | Pisnail |
| Gutiérrez | Chot | Sotz |
| | Nichuch | |
| | Tzot | |
| Hernández | Bonette | Bocio (Rosillo) |
| | Castuli | Chailal |
| | Casuilo | Chamula |
| | Cogho | Chiuc |
| | Coljol | Chojonuc |
| | Cot | Chucchum |

Spanish and Tzotzil surname pairs

| 1749 | 1855 |
| --- | --- |
| Chamu | Chutcun |
| Chat | Co |
| Chaylaquei | Cox |
| Chuchum | Cul |
| Chuixhum | Gerónimo |
| Chuizt | Jolcho |
| Gerónimo | Lantu |
| Guitarra | Las |
| Ichinin | Maltin |
| Isbatlajan | Melelcop |
| Jolchoc | Memela |
| Jonton | Mentira |
| Laz | Min |
| Lantebente | Muchic |
| Lechat | Nuj |
| Marín | Padesuan |
| Melolcop | Pisante |
| Memela | Pisnail |
| Memira | Promas |
| Minero | Rico |
| Nichat | Rodrigo |
| Nijo | Saquiloquil |
| Nog | Tantiv |
| Pinacho | Tijilnuc |
| Rico | Totom |
| Samayut | Viejo |
| Sayun | Zapote |
| Sica | Zárate |
| Solis | |
| Tizinuc | |
| Tolol | |
| Tonquich | |
| Tuilmedio | |
| Tuzninuc | |
| Zapote | |
| Zazate (Zárate) | |
| Zet | |

Spanish and Tzotzil surname pairs

| | 1749 | 1855 |
|---|---|---|
| Jiménez (Ximénez) | Calbequet Chajan Chato Ibalmet Ical Maní Manos | Iblemit Jolchitom Maní |
| López | Bet Caporal Cendal Chic Cochog Mtuluc (Me' tuluk') Quiz Sibalat Sintan Sotul Tanchac Tutupajel Zelan | Cabranegra Caporal Chacharron Chacho Chiuc Chogchoc Cocho Guet Nacalchitom Quitz Tanchac Tuitz Tzelan Tzibalat Tzintan Tzotul Tzotzil |
| Martínez | | Capitán |
| Méndez | Conde | Conde Culig Patistan |
| Montejo | Iman Tazuet | Chojonuc Iman Tasquet |
| Pérez | Amalis Ampros Asiento Biquil Bojero | Alvarez Amalix Asiento Biquilchij Buluch |

## Spanish and Tzotzil surname pairs

| 1749 | 1855 |
| --- | --- |
| Buluch | Chojonuc |
| Buquitzan | Chuccum |
| Conchabe | Chut (Xut) |
| Conchauc | Cocoron |
| Coscorron | Comyos |
| Chicaguac | Culantro |
| Chilchil | Hiccaltzi |
| Chito | Jiliat |
| Chiy | Jualcum |
| Chucum | Mochilum |
| Guitarrin | Mortial |
| Ical | Ocotz |
| Icaltzi | Obeja |
| Jiliat | Pulano |
| Jojolbequet | Puyum |
| Joltuluc | Tambec |
| Luctzin | Tanjol |
| Maneltenu | Tasajo |
| Mectaluc (Me'tuluk') | Totom |
| Monja | Tulis |
| Mortial | Tzanchug |
| Muchilum | Tzintan |
| Negro | Tzotzilchiquin |
| Obeja | Tzuquipan |
| Ocot | Tzut |
| Oquil | Xucumté |
| Oquit | Xulumte |
| Pochiquin | Zanu |
| Puium | Zapote |
| Pulano | |
| Risca | |
| Silibet | |
| Soquil | |
| Sotanjol | |
| Sotul | |
| Suquipan | |
| Sut | |
| Tazajo | |

### Spanish and Tzotzil surname pairs

|  | 1749 | 1855 |
|---|---|---|
|  | Toncocou |  |
|  | Tulabel |  |
|  | Tulis |  |
|  | Tziquin |  |
|  | Tzitz |  |
|  | Vhoz |  |
|  | Vilquini |  |
|  | Viquilobic |  |
|  | Vizcaíno |  |
|  | Yacanzgo |  |
| Rúiz | Roxillo | Bocío |
|  | Viejo | Portuno |
| Sánchez | Ala | Acbal |
|  | Balu | Es |
|  | Bello | Escribano |
|  | Botas | Governador |
|  | Etz | Guetio |
|  | Garabatto | Meuch |
|  | Izco | Nuch |
|  | Neus | Pulivoc |
|  | Sixnum | Velio (Bello) |
|  | Tochililan | Votas |
|  | Urdemales |  |
| Vázquez | Soljol | Fiscal |
|  | Soquian | Shuljol |

### New Spanish surnames in 1855

Bautista
Bocío (Roxillo)
Chailal
Lunes        } paired with various Indian *apellidos*
Mandujano
Patistán
Surián
Xilón (Girón)

### Major Surname Groups in 1749 which Decline or Disappear in 1855

| Surnames | | Frequency in 1855 | |
| --- | --- | --- | --- |
| Spanish | Tzotzil | Expected[1] | Observed |
| Arias | Fortuna | 5 | 3 |
| Hernández | Memela | 7 | 0 |
| López | Tanchac | 10 | 3 |
| Pérez | Ampros | 9 | 0 |
| | Icaltzi | 5 | 2 |
| | Jiliat | 9 | 3 |
| | Ocotz | 10 | 9 |
| | Tasajo | 10 | 9 |
| Ximénez | Maní | 10 | 7 |

*Sources:* "Padrón y nueva cuenta de Zinacantan, . . . 1749," AGGG, Serie Chiapas, A3.16.4509.353; "Padrón del pueblo de Zinacantan, . . . 1855," AHDSC.

[1] Calculated on the basis of frequency in 1749, increasing at the rate of 153%/year.

### Tzotzil Surnames Which Occur with More Than One Spanish Surname, 1749 and 1855

| 1749 | | 1855 | |
| --- | --- | --- | --- |
| Tzotzil | Spanish | Tzotzil | Spanish |
| Lencin | Gómez | Bocio | Hernández |
| | González | | Rúiz |
| | Pérez | Cabranegra | Gómez |
| Metuluc | López | | López |
| | Pérez | Chanmul | de la Cruz |
| Tzot | Díaz | | de la Torre |
| | Gutiérrez | Chiuc | Hernández |
| Tzotul | López | | López |
| | Pérez | Chucchum | Hernández |
| | | | Pérez |

Tzotzil Surnames Which Occur with More Than
One Spanish Surname, 1749 and 1855

| 1749 | | 1855 | |
|---|---|---|---|
| Tzotzil | Spanish | Tzotzil | Spanish |
| | | Co | González |
| | | | Hernández |
| | | Cohonuc | Hernández |
| | | | Montejo |
| | | | Pérez |
| | | Fortuna | Arias |
| | | | Rúiz |
| | | Jiliat | Arias |
| | | | Pérez |
| | | Jolcho | Gómez |
| | | | Hernández |
| | | Maní | de la Cruz |
| | | | Jiménez |
| | | Padesuan | Hernández |
| | | | Méndez |
| | | Pisnail | González |
| | | | Hernández |
| | | Rodrigo | Gómez |
| | | | Hernández |
| | | Saquiloquil | de la Cruz |
| | | | Hernández |
| | | Tantiv | de la Cruz |
| | | | Gómez |
| | | | Hernández |
| | | Tzotzil | Gómez |
| | | | López |
| | | Zapote | Gómez |
| | | | Hernández |
| | | | Pérez |

# GLOSSARY

*Agrarista.* In Mexico, a peasant who petitioned to receive land under the agrarian reform law.

*Aguardiente.* Cheap rum manufactured from distilled cane.

*Alcalde (ordinario).* Mayor of a colonial town, the chief presiding officer of its town council and magistrate of the first instance in the colonial legal system.

*Alcalde mayor.* Provincial governor before 1790, and appellate judge in the colonial legal system.

*Alcaldía (mayor).* A province or district governed by an *alcalde mayor.*

*Alférez.* Among Spanish colonists, an honorary title of military distinction purchased from the Crown; among Indians, the sponsor of important religious festivals in conjunction with *cofradía* officials.

*Altiplano.* The central highlands of Chiapas.

*Apellido.* Surname.

*Arrendatario.* A sharecropper or tenant farmer.

*Arriero.* Muledriver.

*Arroba.* A colonial measure of cotton, cochineal, etc., equivalent to 25 pounds.

*Audiencia.* The royal court in Guatemala, highest administrative body in Central America and highest court of appeals in the colony.

*Ayuntamiento.* Town council; replaced the term *cabildo* in 19th-century Chiapas in referring to municipal officers.

*Baldío.* In the 19th century, a kind of sharecropper, usually one whose lands were absorbed by newly-formed estates and who was required to work 3 or 4 days each week for the landlord.

*Cabecera.* Head village, usually with several villages under its jurisdiction.

*Cabildo.* Town council, and by extension its officers.

*Cacicazgo.* At conquest, territory governed by a native *cacique.*

*Cacique.* At conquest, the native ruler of a locality; later, its leading political figure.

*Caja de comunidad.* A sort of community fund established in Chiapas by the Dominicans, from which unpaid taxes and other dues were deducted.

*Capellanía.* Perpetual endowment in behalf of a designated chaplain, usually to celebrate annual masses for the donor or his descendants.

*Cargo.* Religious office such as *mayordomo* or *alférez.*

*Clérigo.* Secular priest.

*Cofrade.* Member of a *cofradía.*

*Cofradía.* Religious brotherhood founded to honor an important patron saint.

*Comisariado ejidal.* Local land reform committee which administers an *ejido* grant. Among Indians in Chiapas, it also refers to the head of that committee.

*Conquistador.* Spanish soldier who participated in the conquest of America.

*Consejo de las Indias.* The Council of the Indies in Spain, the highest royal body for colonial affairs.

*Corregidor.* Royal official appointed during the early colonial period to govern principal towns and districts; replaced by *alcaldes mayores.*

*Cura.* Incumbent curate of a royal benefice or parish; also used to refer to Dominican *doctrineros.*

*Derecho.* Fee charged by parish priests and their superiors for such services as baptism, marriage, confirmation, etc.

*Doctrina.* Mission district administered by Dominican or Franciscan friars. Such districts supposedly became parishes when secular clergy were available to administer them. Given the reluctance of friars to relinquish their benefices, by the 18th century many *doctrinas* were simply Dominican parishes.

*Ejidatario.* A peasant who received land under the agrarian reform law, member of an *ejido* (land-grant) community.

*Ejido.* A grant of land made under the agrarian reform laws.

*Encomendero.* Holder of a royal grant to collect tribute from designated Indian towns.

*Encomienda.* Royal grant of right to collect tribute from designated Indian towns.

*Enganchador.* Hiring agent for coffee plantations or *monterías;* often accused of using compulsion or chicanery to recruit Indian labor.

*Ermita.* A small chapel, generally dedicated to a minor saint.

*Escribano.* Scribe; in the 20th century, a younger Indian appointed by state authorities to supervise the activities of other members of Indian *cabildos.*

*Estancia (de ganado).* Cattle ranch; replaced by the term *finca* in 19th-century Chiapas.

*Finca.* In colonial times, any rural estate; since the 19th century, this term has come to refer more specifically to cattle ranches or coffee plantations.

*Fiscal.* The royal prosecutor in colonial Guatemala; also used to describe an Indian who served as assistant to parish priests.

*Fundo legal.* An expanse of inalienable public land belonging to Indian communities during the colonial period, generally determined by measuring 500 yards in every direction from the church door.

*Gobernador.* In many colonial communities, the chief presiding officer of an Indian *cabildo.*

*Hacendado.* Owner of a rural estate.

*Hacienda.* A rural estate; in Chiapas, the term refers to any kind of estate except coffee plantations.

*Hermano.* Brother; member of a *cofradía.*

*Hidalgo.* Minor Spanish nobility (pl. *hijosdalgo*).

*Ingenio.* Sugar mill.

*Intendente.* From 1790 to 1811, the royal governor of a province; replaced the *alcalde mayor* during the last years of colonial rule.

*Jefe político.* Administrative officer in 19th-century Chiapas responsible for 10–15 separate *municipios.*

*Jornalero.* Day laborer.

*Juez de milpa.* Royal district judges appointed in a few areas of Chiapas at the beginning of colonial rule.

*Juez real.* Royal judge.

*Justicias.* Officers of a recognized town, the *alcalde* and *regidores* of its *cabildo.*

*Labor.* A highland farm, usually for producing wheat.

*Laborío.* A kind of sharecropper in the Grijalva basin, generally one who settled on the margins of large estates and contributed labor to the landlord when it was needed. Similar to the *arrimado* found in the Andes.

*Ladino.* In Chiapas and Guatemala, a non-Indian.

*Limosna.* Literally, "alms"; in colonial Chiapas, a fee extorted by priests and bishops for *cofradía* celebrations or other public functions.

*Macehaules.* Early colonial term for Indian commoners.

*Mapache.* Member of the guerrilla band led by Tiburcio Fernández Ruíz in 1914.

*Mayordomía*. Principal office in a *cofradía*, involving a sort of steward-ship of its patron saint.

*Mesón*. A sort of inn or traveler's lodge available to Spanish authorities in colonial Indian towns.

*Milpa*. Native cornfield.

*Montería*. Lumber camp in the eastern jungle.

*Motín*. Riot.

*Mozo*. Servant, generally a peon on rural estates.

*Nagualismo*. Superstition, usually a belief in animal spirits.

*Natural*. Indian.

*Oidor*. Judge of the royal court (*audiencia*) in Guatemala.

*Ordenanzas*. Royal regulations, including those which were devised by visiting judges and members of the *audiencia*.

*Padrón*. Colonial census.

*Patronato real*. Royal right to appoint all members of the Catholic Church in Spain and the colonies.

*Peste*. Any disease or epidemic.

*Presbítero*. Secular cleric.

*Presidente*. Chief magistrate of the *audiencia* in Guatemala and chief administrative officer of the Crown in Central America.

*Presidente municipal*. A local mayor, the head of a *municipio*. Formerly called *alcalde* or *alcalde ordinario*.

*Principal*. At conquest, a native lord (usually inferior to the ruler of a locality); later, simply an elder in Indian communities.

*Pueblo*. A legally recognized town chartered to elect its own council.

*Real cédula*. A royal order having the force of law.

*Realenga*. Crown lands.

*Regidor*. Town councilman in colonial *cabildo*. The number of *regi-dores* varied according to the size of the community.

*Repartimiento*. A temporary grant of Indian labor made to Spanish settlers at the beginning of colonial rule.

*Repartimiento de mercancías* (or *efectos*). Forced sale of merchandise or goods to Indian communities by the *alcalde mayor*.

*República de españoles*. A legal concept referring to all Spanish settlers and their governors in the New World.

*República de indios*. A legal concept which includes all native inhabit-ants of the New World and their natural lords.

*Residencia*. Examination of an outgoing *alcalde mayor*, generally by his successor, to uncover any wrongdoing or malfeasance in office.

*Sarampión*. Measles.

*Señorío*. Pre-Columbian fiefdom or *cacicazgo*.

*Sustento.* During the 18th and 19th centuries, rations received by parish priests above their legal salary.

*Teniente.* Assistant to the *alcalde mayor*, generally responsible for administering his economic affairs in a given district.

*Tienda de raya.* Company store on coffee and cotton plantations.

*Trapiche.* Sugar mill, sometimes also a distillery.

*Vecino.* Legal resident and householder in an official town.

*Viruela.* Smallpox.

*Visita.* Official inspection tour by a royal judge; also refers to visits made by bishops every two or three years to Indian communities.

*Vista de ojo.* Visual inspection.

# NOTES

NOTES TO CHAPTER 1

1. Among the most significant of these works are the following ethnographies: Ricardo Pozas, *Chamula, un pueblo indio de los altos de Chiapas* (Mexico City: Instituto Nacional Indigenista, 1959); Calixta Guiteras Holmes, *Perils of the Soul: The World View of a Tzotzil Indian* (New York: Free Press, 1961); William Holland, *Medicina maya en los altos de Chiapas: un estudio del cambio socio-cultural* (Mexico City: Instituto Nacional Indigenista, 1963); Fernando Cámara Barbachano, *Persistencia y cambio cultural entre los Tzeltales de los altos de Chiapas* (Mexico City: Escuela Nacional de Antropología e Historia, 1966); Frank Cancian, *Economics and Prestige in a Maya Community* (Stanford, Calif.: Stanford University Press, 1965); and *Change and Uncertainty in a Peasant Economy* (Stanford, Calif.: Stanford University Press, 1973); Henning Silverts, *Oxchuc: una tribu maya de Mexico* (Mexico City: Instituto Indigenista Interamericano, 1969); E. Z. Vogt, *Zinacantan: A Maya Community in the Highlands of Chiapas* (Cambridge, Mass.: Harvard University Press, 1969); and *Tortillas for the Gods: A Symbolic Analysis of Zinacanteco Ritual* (Cambridge, Mass.: Harvard University Press, 1976); June Nash, *In the Eyes of the Ancestors* (New Haven, Conn.: Yale University Press, 1970); Norman McQuown and Julian Pitt-Rivers, eds., *Ensayos de antropología en la zona central de Chiapas* (Mexico City: Instituto Nacional Indigenista, 1970); Henri Favre, *Changement et continuité chez les mayas du Mexique* (Paris: Anthropos, 1971); Ester Hermitte, *Pinola* (Mexico City: Instituto Indigenista

Interamericano, 1973); Horacio Fabrega and Daniel Silver, *Illness and Shamanistic Curing in Zinacantan: An Ethnomedical Analysis* (Stanford, Calif.: Stanford University Press, 1973); Victoria R. Bricker, *Ritual Humor in Highland Chiapas* (Austin: University of Texas Press, 1973); Nancy Modiano, *Indian Education in the Chiapas Highlands* (New York: Holt, Rinehart, and Winston, 1973); Jane Collier, *Law and Social Change in Zinacantan* (Stanford, Calif.: Stanford University Press, 1973); Gary Gossen, *Chamulas in the World of the Sun: Time and Space in a Maya Oral Tradition* (Cambridge, Mass.: Harvard University Press, 1974); George A. Collier, *Fields of the Tzotzil: The Ecological Bases of Tradition in Highland Chiapas* (Austin: University of Texas Press, 1975); Francesca Cancian, *What Are Norms? A Study of Beliefs and Action in a Maya Community* (Cambridge, Eng.: Cambridge University Press, 1975); Jacinto Arias, *El mundo numinoso de los mayas* (Mexico City: SepSetentas, 1975); Ulrich Köhler, *Cambio cultural dirigido en los altos de Chiapas* (Mexico City: Instituto Nacional Indigenista, 1975); Virginia Molina, *San Bartolomé de los Llanos* (Mexico City: SEP-INAH, 1976); John Haviland, *Gossip, Reputation, and Knowledge in Zinacantan* (Chicago: University of Chicago Press, 1977); Victoria R. Bricker, *The Indian Christ, the Indian King* (Austin: University of Texas Press, 1981).

2. Eric Wolf, "Closed Corporate Peasant Communities in Mesoamerica and Central Java," *Southwestern Journal of Anthropology* 13 (1957): 1–18; Sol Tax, ed., *The Heritage of Conquest: The Ethnology of Middle America* (Glencoe, Ill.: Free Press, 1952).

3. Sol Tax, "The Municipios of the Midwestern Highlands of Guatemala," *American Anthropologist* 39 (1937): 423–444, and "World View and Social Relations in Guatemala," ibid. 43 (1941): 27–42.

4. This correspondence has been deposited in the archives of the University of Chicago Library. Dr. Tax has kindly permitted me to examine his copy of the relevant documents.

5. Robert Redfield, "Culture Changes in Yucatan," *American Anthropologist* 36 (1934): 69.

6. Tax, "World View and Social Relations," p. 41.

7. Ibid., p. 42.

8. For an enlightening discussion of this phenomenon, see Morton Fried, *The Notion of Tribe* (Menlo Park, Calif.: Cummings, 1975).

9. Robert Wauchope, ed., *Handbook of Middle American Indians* (Austin: University of Texas Press, 1964–1969).

10. Frank Cancian, *Economics and Prestige in a Maya Community*; see also Pedro Carrasco, "The Civil-Religious Hierarchy in Meso-American Communities: Pre-Spanish Background and Colonial Development," *American Anthropologist* 63 (1961): 483–497.

11. George Collier, *Fields of the Tzotzil.*

12. Haviland, *Gossip, Reputation, and Knowledge in Zinacantan,* p. 56.

13. Ibid., p. 124.

14. Francesca Cancian, *What Are Norms?*, Chaps. 8 and 9.

15. Vogt, *Tortillas for the Gods*; Gossen, *Chamulas in the World of the Sun.*

16. Favre, *Changement et continuité*; Bricker, *Ritual Humor in Highland Chiapas.* See also Victoria Bricker's more recent articles: "Algunas consecuencias religiosas y sociales del nativismo maya del siglo XIX," *América Indígena* 33 (1973): 327–348; "Historical Dramas in Chiapas, Mexico," *Journal of Latin American Lore* 3 (1977): 227–248; "Movimientos religiosos indígenas en los altos de Chiapas," *América Indígena* 39 (1979): 17–46.

17. It is interesting that much of Tax's paradigm has found its way into the work even of social scientists who do not share his theoretical and political views. Examples of this work, I think, include Gonzalo Aguirre Beltrán's book *Regiones de Refugio* (Mexico City: Instituto Indigenista Interamericano, 1967); Rodolfo Stavenhagen's book *Las clases sociales en las sociedades agrarias* (Mexico City: Siglo XXI, 1969); and the various books and articles published recently by Roger Bartra. For a fuller discussion of this matter, see my article "La investigación regional en ciencias sociales," *Historia y Sociedad,* ser. 2, no. 9 (1976): 58–73.

18. Carlos Navarrete, *The Chiapanec History and Culture* (Provo, Utah: New World Archaeological Foundation, no. 21, pub. 16, 1966); Peter Gerhard, *The Southeast Frontier of New Spain* (Princeton, N.J.: Princeton University Press, 1979).

19. Gerhard, p. 147.

20. Edward E. Calnek, "Highland Chiapas Before the Spanish Conquest" (Ph. D. diss., University of Chicago, 1962), p. 9.

21. Ibid., pp. 17–18; J. Eric S. Thompson, *Maya History and Religion* (Norman: University of Oklahoma Press, 1970).

22. Donald McVicker, "Cambio cultural y ecología en el Chiapas

central prehispánico," in McQuown and Pitt-Rivers, eds., *Ensayos de antropología en la zona central de Chiapas,* pp. 77–104; Robert M. Adams, "Changing Patterns of Territorial Organization in the Central Highlands of Chiapas, Mexico," *American Antiquity* 26, no. 3 (1961): 341–360.

23. Quoted in A. Cardos de Méndez, *El comercio de los mayas antigüos* (Mexico City: Escuela Nacional de Antropología e Historia, 1959), p. 74.

24. Murdo J. MacLeod, *Spanish Central America: A Socioeconomic History, 1520–1720* (Berkeley and Los Angeles: University of California Press, 1973), pp. 68–79.

25. Donald McVicker, quoted in Robert Wasserstrom, "Our Lady of the Salt" (B.A. Honors Thesis, Harvard University, 1970), p. 10.

26. Navarrete, *Chiapanec History and Culture,* pp. 99–103.

27. Bernal Díaz del Castillo, *Historia verdadera de la conquista de la Nueva España* (Mexico City: Porrua, 1955), p. 210.

## NOTES TO CHAPTER 2

1. For a comparative examination of the conquest in eastern Chiapas (i.e., the Lacandón jungle), see Jan de Vos, *La paz de Dios y del rey: la conquista de la Selva Lacandona* (Tuxtla Gutiérrez: Fonapas Chiapas, 1980).

2. Antonio de Remesal, *Historia general de las Indias Occidentales, y particular de la gobernación de Chiapa y Guatemala* (Guatemala City: Biblioteca "Goathemala" de la Sociedad de Geografía e Historia, 1932), vol. 1, p. 380.

3. For comparative information, see William B. Taylor, *Landlord and Peasant in Colonial Oaxaca* (Stanford, Calif.: Stanford University Press, 1972), p.72; MacLeod, *Spanish Central America,* pp. 138–139; Charles Gibson, *The Aztecs Under Spanish Rule* (Stanford, Calif.: Stanford University Press, 1964).

4. Remesal, vol. 2, p. 399.

5. For an account of the cacao industry in Soconusco, see MacLeod, pp. 68–80.

6. Remesal, vol. 2, pp. 73–74.

7. Ibid., pp. 76–79.

8. Ibid., p. 113. A more detailed description of Rogel's activities may be found in William L. Sherman, *Forced Native Labor in Sixteenth-Century Central America* (Lincoln: University of Nebraska Press, 1979).

9. Remesal, pp. 236–237. In the following pages I present an account of missionary labor in Chiapas which differs substantially from standard discussions of the subject in New Spain. For a different perspective, see Robert Ricard, *La "Conquête Spirituelle" du Mexique* (Travaux et Memoires de l'Institut d'Ethnologie, Paris: Université de Paris, 1933); John L. Phelan, *The Millennial Kingdom of the Franciscans in the New World* (Berkeley and Los Angeles: University of California Press, 1956).

10. Remesal, pp. 239–240; Francisco Ximénez, *Historia de la provincia de San Vicente de Chiapa y Guatemala de la Orden de Predicadores* (Guatemala City: Biblioteca "Goathemala" de la Sociedad de Geografía e Historia, 1929–1931). MacLeod, following Ximénez, mentions 17 *encomenderos*; but Ximénez takes their names from Remesal, who lists 16. To further confuse matters, Ximénez omits one name from his list and thus enumerates only 15 affected colonists.

11. Remesal, p. 243. According to Remesal, "In Ostutla, 3 towns were brought together. In Ixtapa, 5, not counting many other Indians who live among their fields and salt springs, plantings and canyons. In Chamula, 3. In Tecpatán, 5 without the people who lived amidst their fields, wells, and farms."

12. MacLeod, p. 113.

13. According to Juan Friede in his work *Bartolomé de Las Casas, precursor del anticolonialismo* (Mexico City: Siglo XXI, 1974), the bishop arrived in Ciudad Real with 40 of the original 50 monks who had departed with him from Spain. In contrast, Remesal mentions only 33 friars in his account of these early years.

14. Remesal, vol. 1, p. 459.

15. Friede, p. 72.

16. Ibid.

17. Ibid., p. 118.

18. Ibid., p. 119.

19. Ibid., p. 130.

20. Ibid., p. 128.

21. Remesal, vol. 1, p. 407.

22. Manuel B. Trens, *Historia de Chiapas* (Mexico City: Talleres Gráficos de la Nación, 1957), p. 23.

23. Remesal, vol. 1, p. 400.

24. Ibid., pp. 465–501. He often slept with these women before their marriages—in spite of the fact that such practices had been specifically forbidden in royal *cédulas* of 1539 and 1546.

25. Ibid., p. 490.

26. Taylor, *Landlord and Peasant*, p. 37, reports that the Dominicans in Oaxaca followed much the same procedures. For information about Guatemala, see Remesal, vol. 2, p. 54.

27. Remesal, vol. 1, p. 421.

28. An excellent account of administration in Chiapas during these years may be found in Peter Gerhard's recent book, *The Southeast Frontier of New Spain*, pp. 152–154.

29. Remesal, vol. 2, p. 119.

30. Ibid., pp. 119–120.

31. In 1560, for example, the *audiencia* ordered that surviving *caciques* and *principales* in two Tzotzil communities, Santa Marta and Magdalenas, organize such a *cabildo* and prepare a report describing the territory over which they had exercised jurisdiction at the time of Mazariegos' arrival. A typescript copy of this document, entitled "Probanza de Magdalenas, 1560," is in the library of Prudencio Moscoso, San Cristóbal, Chiapas.

32. Remesal, vol. 2, p. 139.

33. In Remesal's words (ibid., p. 368), they should be "acquainted with the most common things of the faith so that . . . if they are asked, they may show some consent in them. . . . But with the children, let greater care be taken. And if they perceive, however rudely, these common articles of faith, and know the commandments, and the Paternoster, and the Credo, it is enough." Similarly, on the subject of the Eucharist, the friars also opted for moderation (ibid., p. 402): "The Indians must be exhorted to confess . . . but in no manner are they to be compelled to do so . . . and in no manner are they to be denied absolution if they say that they do not dare to accept communion."

34. Juan de Pineda, "Descripción de la provincia de Guatemala, año 1594," in *Relaciones histórico-geográficas de América Central* (Colección de Libros y Documentos Referentes a la Historia de América, Madrid, Spain, 1908), vol. 3, pp. 442–444.

35. Francisco Orozco y Jiménez, *Colección de documentos inéditos relativos a la Iglesia de Chiapas* (San Cristóbal: Imprenta de la Sociedad Católica, 1905 and 1911), vol. 2, p. 145.

36. Ximénez, vol. 1, pp. 536–538.

37. Orozco y Jiménez, vol. 2, p. 145; "Extracto de un título de Chiapa de los Indios probando su antigüedad y legitimidad de posesión de sus tierras, 1571" (unpublished typescript in the Biblioteca Fray Bartolomé de Las Casas, San Cristóbal, Chiapas).

38. Remesal, vol. 2, pp. 490–491.

39. Ibid., p. 144.

40. Ximénez, vol. 2, p. 197.

41. Remesal, vol. 2, p. 490.

42. Ibid., vol. 1, p. 393.

43. AHDSC, *Libros de las Cofradías*. For further discussion of these organizations, see Chapter 4.

44. According to Remesal, for example, in 1596 Guatemala boasted separate *cofradías* of *Rosario, Santísimo Sacramento,* and *Asunción* for Spaniards, Indians, and black slaves. For this reason, he wrote (vol. 2, p. 246), both the quality of religious life and the quantity of ceremonial objects had increased with gratifying speed over the previous eight years.

45. Ximénez, vol. 2, p. 197.

46. Ibid., p. 176.

47. Remesal, vol. 2, p. 498.

48. Fray Andrés de Ubilla, "Memoria de los pueblos y beneficios que hay en el obispado de Chiapa" (1592?) (typescript in the Biblioteca Fray Bartolomé de Las Casas, San Cristóbal, Chiapas).

49. Remesal, vol. 2, p. 534.

50. Ibid., p. 490.

51. MacLeod, p. 99.

## NOTES TO CHAPTER 3

1. J. Eric S. Thompson, ed., *Thomas Gage's Travels in the New World* (Norman: University of Oklahoma Press, 1958), pp. 138–139.

2. Ibid., pp. 147–148.

3. "Carta del obispo de Chiapa, Fr. Juan Sandoval Zapata, a Su Magestad" (1619[?]) in Hermilio López Sánchez, *Apuntes históricos de San Cristóbal de Las Casas, Chiapas, México* (Mexico City: published by author, 1960), vol. 2, pp. 641–642.

4. "El obispo de Chiapa, Illmo. Bernardino de Salazar y Frías, sobre la excomunión que impuso al alcalde mayor" (1624), AGCh, *Boletín* 4 (1955): 9–26.

5. "Carta del alcalde mayor de Chiapa, Gabriel de Ugarte y Ayala, a Su Magestad" (no date), in López Sánchez, vol. 2, p. 638; "Petición del alcalde mayor de Chiapa, Juan Ruíz de Contreras, a Su Magestad" (no date), ibid., p. 648.

6. "Informe del juez real, Francisco Dávila, sobre la residencia del alcalde mayor de Chiapa, Juan Ruíz de Contreras" (no date), ibid., p. 651.

7. "Informe de la audiencia de Guatemala sobre el encuentro violento entre don Francisco Dávila y Lugo, alcalde mayor de Chiapa, y don Diego Vaquero, alcalde ordinario de la misma ciudad y tesorero de la Santa Cruzada" (no date), ibid., p. 652.

8. "Petición del cabildo de Ciudad Real a Su Magestad" (1693), ibid., pp. 679–680. In 1709, the *cabildo* asked royal judges in Guatemala to conduct a special *residencia* of the *alcalde mayor,* whom in effect they accused of having excluded them from the cochineal trade: "Petición del alférez mayor y el alcalde ordinario de Ciudad Real, para que se examine la conducta del alcalde mayor de Chiapa, Don Martín González de Vergara" (1709), ibid., p. 695.

9. Thompson, *Thomas Gage's Travels,* pp. 140–142.

10. Sociedad Económica de Ciudad Real, "Informe rendido por la Sociedad Económica de Ciudad Real sobre las ventajas y desventajas obtenidas con el implantamiento del sistema de intendencias" (1819), AGCh, *Boletín* 6 (1956): 27–28; "Provisión de la Real Audiencia sobre los capítulos que el alcalde mayor de esta ciudad puso al obispo y curas" (1779), AHDSC, Asuntos Secretos, ff. 1–81; "El cura de Chamula se queja del alcalde mayor; también el de Teopisca" (1779), AHDSC.

11. Letter from Fr. Eugenio Saldivar to Dominican Provincial, August 23, 1770, in AGCh, *Boletín* 4 (1955): 126–132.

12. "Hambre y explotación indígena en 1771," AGCh, *Boletín* 4 (1955): 113–155; "Autos en que consta la despoblación de varios pueblos de la provincia de Chiapa" (1734), AGGG, Serie Chiapas, A1.1.3.1; "Los

nativos de Yajalón informan de que sus sementeras han sido destruidas por la langosta" (1769), ibid., A1.1.10.1; "Autorización a los indios de Zinacantan para que del fondo de sus comunidades tomen lo necesario para el fomento de sus siembras" (1788), ibid., A3.40.4343.334; "Los indígenas del pueblo de Zinacantan piden se les rebaje la asignación de tributos" (1734), ibid., A3.16.4636.359. See also note 50 below.

13. Francisco Ximénez, *Historia de la provincia de San Vicente de Chiapa y Guatemala*, vol. 3, p. 257. This passage has been reprinted in María Teresa Huerta and Patricia Palacios, comps., *Rebeliones indígenas de la época colonial* (Mexico City: SEP–INAH, 1976), pp. 136–173. A fuller account of the rebellion (which is discussed in the next chapter) is given by Kevin Gosner, "Soldiers of the Virgin: An Ethnohistorical Account of the 1712 Rebellion in Highland Chiapas" (Ph.D. diss., University of Pennsylvania, Philadelphia, 1983).

14. Thompson, *Thomas Gage's Travels*, pp. 142–143. For a more extensive discussion of the colonial Church, see Nancy Farriss' masterful study, *Crown and Clergy in Colonial Mexico, 1759–1821* (London: Athlone Press, 1968). Another useful work on this subject is Francisco Morales, *Clero y política en México, 1767–1834* (Mexico City: SepSetentas, 1975).

15. Sherman, *Forced Native Labor in Sixteenth-Century Central America*, pp. 357–358. In 1610, according to the royal *visitador* Manuel de Ungría Girón, the province contained 230 Spanish *vecinos* and 60 *encomenderos*: "Informe del visitador real, Lic. don Manuel de Ungría Girón, a Su Majestad," in López Sánchez, vol. 2, p. 650. It is significant that both demographic and economic patterns in Chiapas differed somewhat from those which have been described in New Spain: see Woodrow Borah's classic work, *New Spain's Century of Depression* (Berkeley: University of California Press, 1951); and Charles Gibson's more recent study, *The Aztecs Under Spanish Rule* (1965).

16. Gerhard, *The Southeast Frontier of New Spain*, p. 159; MacLeod, *Spanish Central America*, pp. 98–100. For New Spain, comparable information may be found in Sherburne F. Cook and Lesley Byrd Simpson, *The Population of Central Mexico in the Sixteenth Century* (Berkeley: University of California Press, 1948); and Sherburne F. Cook and Woodrow Borah, *The Indian Population of Central Mexico, 1531–1610* (Berkeley and Los Angeles: University of California Press, 1960) and *Essays in Population History: Mexico and the Caribbean* (3 vols.; Berkeley and Los Angeles: University of California Press, 1971, 1974, and 1979).

17. Edward E. Calnek, "Los pueblos indígenas de los altos de Chiapas," in McQuown and Pitt-Rivers, Ensayos de antropología; Calnek, "Highland Chiapas Before the Spanish Conquest"; Remesal, Historia; Ximénez, Historia. According to Remesal, for example (vol. 2, pp. 76–79), in Zinacantan only a handful of people survived the first decades of conquest.

18. Gerhard, The Southeast Frontier, p. 152: "In 1611 there were just 58 encomenderos, of whom 6 received an annual tribute income of about 2,500 pesos each, one-third received approximately 1,000 pesos, and the others had annuities of less than 500 pesos. In 1637 the tribute of 5 pueblos that had originally been assigned to one person was divided among 9 holders. Those who could not qualify as encomenderos were often assigned pensions paid from the tributes of Crown or privately-held pueblos. Perhaps because there were so many aspirants to this income among the local Spaniards, relatively few encomiendas in Chiapa were granted to European absentee holders. . . . However, in 1630 the cabildo of Ciudad Real complained that more than half of the privately-controlled tributaries were held by wealthy merchants and others in Guatemala City." See also "Petición del cabildo de Ciudad Real para que las encomiendas vacantes en Chiapa no se proveyan en vecinos de Guatemala," in López Sánchez, vol. 2, pp. 645–646; "Tasación y encomienda del pueblo de San Bartolomé" (1656), AGGG, A3.16.3905.290; "Vacante de la encomienda que fue del capitán don Juan de Cárdenas y Mazariegos" (1666), ibid., A3.16.3910.290; "Cuenta general del ramo de tributos de la provincia de Chiapa" (1679), ibid., A3.16.3914.290.

19. Thomas Gage, The English-American (Guatemala City: El Patio, 1946), pp. 158–159.

20. Robert Chamberlain, The Governorship of Adelantado Francisco de Montejo in Chiapas, 1539–1544 (Washington, D.C.: Carnegie Institution, pub. 574, contribution 46, 1947); Orozco y Jiménez, Colección de documentos, vol. 1, p. 8; Thompson, Thomas Gage's Travels, pp. 138–159; Remesal, vol. 2, p. 119.

21. Orozco y Jiménez, vol. 2, pp. 212–229.

22. "Título de dos caballerías de tierra situadas en términos del pueblo de Chamula, jurisdicción de Chiapa, 22 de mayo de 1591," AGGG, A1.57.4588.157; "Título de dos caballerías de tierra en los llanos de Huistán en el arroyo de Cisintiq, a favor de Carlos de Estrada, vecino de Ciudad Real de Chiapa, 23 de abril de 1592," ibid., A1.57.4588.207;

"Título de dos caballerías de tierra en términos de Zinacantan y Chamula en el paraje nombrado Los Corrales a favor de Diego de Mesa, vecino de Ciudad Real de Chiapa, 5 de junio de 1592," ibid., A1.57.4588.210; "Título de una caballería de tierra y de un ejido de agua en términos del pueblo de Chamula a favor de Pedro de Solórzano, vecino de Ciudad Real, 27 de julio de 1592," ibid., A1.57.4588.214; "Título de un sitio de estancia de ganado mayor en términos del pueblo de Zinacantan a favor del indígena Cristobal Arias, 27 de mayo de 1599," ibid., A1.57.4588.270. A total of 22 such documents are listed in the *juzgado de tierras.*

23. Juan Manuel García de Vargas y Rivera, "Relación de los pueblos que comprehende el obispado de Chiapa" (1774) (Madrid: Biblioteca del Palacio, ms. 2840, misc. de Ayala XXCI), f. 282; Francisco Polanco, "Estado de los vasallos que tiene su Magestad en este obispado de Ciudad Real," in Trens, *Historia de Chiapas,* pp. 221–224.

24. Orozco y Jiménez, vol. 1, p. 8; vol. 2, pp. 179–180.

25. Ibid., vol. 2, pp. 212–229.

26. "Acta del cabildo de Ciudad Real, 26 de marzo de 1684," in López Sánchez, vol. 2, pp. 677–678; also "Información sobre la necesidad de instruir un curato en el pueblo de las Chiapas de Indios" (1682), AGGG, Serie Chiapas, A1.4.686.69.

27. "Nómina de todos los vecinos españoles del obispado de Chiapa" (1735), AGGG, A1.52.185.13.

28. Thompson, *Thomas Gage's Travels,* pp. 146–148.

29. García de Vargas y Rivera.

30. Ibid.; also "Libro de Nuestra Señora de la Luz de Huistán" (1790), Instituto Nacional de Antropología e Historia, microfilm collection; Serie Chiapas, roll 20.

31. Orozco y Jiménez, vol. 2, pp. 179–180.

32. Thompson, *Thomas Gage's Travels,* p. 140.

33. Wenceslao Domínguez, "Fundaciones," in Cámara Nacional de Comercio, Agricultura e Industria de San Cristóbal Las Casas, Chiapas, *Boletín,* special issue (1926).

34. Orozco y Jiménez, vol. 1, p. 8.

35. Ibid., pp. 187–188. In 1684, Bishop Francisco Núñez de la Vega ordered these parishes to pay a total of 280 pesos each year to the

*colegio.* Only the Franciscans seem to have avoided activities of this sort. For a description of their place in provincial society, see ibid., vol. 2, pp. 137–143.

36. Juan de Pineda, "Descripción de la provincia de Guatemala, año 1594."

37. "Informa el alcalde mayor de Chiapa que además de la extinción de varios pueblos la baja de tributos se debe a que no han sido empadronados los indígenas" (1734), AGGG, A3.16.4635.359; and "Autos en que consta de la despoblación de varios pueblos de la provincia de Chiapa" (1734), ibid., A1.1.3.1.

38. Trens, p. 146; López Sánchez, vol. 2, p. 679. A few years earlier, in 1693, Zoque people in Tuxtla, infuriated by a similar set of circumstances, had killed the province's governor, Manuel de Maisterra: "Carta del Sor. Obispo al Presidente don Fernando López Vecino y Orbaneja," AGCh, *Boletín* 2 (1953): 37–51.

39. Favre, *Changement et continuité chez les Mayas du Mexique,* p. 43.

40. "El obispo de Chiapa informa a V.M. sobre los remates de maíz, frijol y chile que tributan los naturales de aquellas provincias y dice juzga conveniente se observe el estilo que se ha tenido en ellos con las calidades que expresa" (1716), López Sánchez, vol. 2, pp. 699–701. In fact, it was by means of such devices that in 1709 a previous *alcalde mayor,* Martín González de Vergara, had monopolized the local trade in cochineal (see note 8 above).

41. "Autos sobre secularización en Chiapas" (1735), AHDSC. Interestingly, a few years later, one *alcalde mayor,* Francisco de Elias y Saldivar, occupied the *cabildo* with his followers to prevent municipal counselors from auctioning off the right to supply meat to Ciudad Real, Chiapa, and San Bartolomé. In the ensuing melée, one *regidor* received a pistol wound and a servant of the *alcalde mayor* was stabbed to death: "Zafarrancho en el cabildo de Ciudad Real entre el alcalde mayor y los capitulares" (1751), AGCh, *Boletín* 4 (1955): 69–112. For a description of Elias' position within Guatemalan society, see "Título de alcalde mayor de Chiapa a favor de don Francisco de Elias Saldivar para cuando cumpla don Juan B. de Garracín Ponce de León, 1747," López Sánchez, vol. 2, p. 796.

42. In 1738, for example, the post was occupied by Antonio Zuazua y Múgica, who was subsequently imprisoned for defrauding the Crown of 152,000 pesos: "El ex-alcalde mayor de Ciudad Real, don Antonio de

Zuazua, sigue autos contra los justicias de San Lucas por el incendio de dho. pueblo en que perdió varias pacas de algodón" (1744), AGGG, A1.15.341.22; "Autos seguidos contra el ex-alcalde mayor, Antonio de Zuazua, por esconder bienes de Su Magestad" (1742), ibid., A1.15.342.22; "Embargo de los bienes del ex-alcalde mayor Antonio Zuazua (1742), ibid., A1.15.344.22; "Juicio de tercería interpuesto por el prior del hospital de Ciudad Real en el juicio de embargo que se sigue al Pbro. José Linares, fiador del alcalde mayor Antonio de Zuazua" (1743), ibid., A1.15.345.22; "Informe del obispo de Ciudad Real al virrey de Nueva España" (1744), López Sánchez, vol. 2, p. 790. Zuazua was followed by Juan Bautista Garracín Ponce de León, who according to one historian was "examined, and upon being vindicated returned to Spain. But after his death it was learned that he owed 30,000 pesos of tribute collected in Chiapas, and by royal order his bondsmen forfeited the property which they had pledged in his behalf": López Sánchez, ibid., p. 795.

43. López Sánchez, vol. 2, pp. 829–834; "Expediente sobre restablecer el cabildo o ayuntamiento de Ciudad Real" (1781), AHDSC.

44. López Sánchez, vol. 2, p. 810.

45. AGGG, *Boletín* 2, no. 4 (1937): 474–479.

46. Francisco Polanco, in Orozco y Jiménez, vol. 2, p. 80.

47. "El rey manda que se le informe por el alcalde si será conveniente que se divida en varias alcaldías la alcaldía mayor de Chiapa" (1760), in Flavio Antonio Paniagua, *Documentos y datos para un diccionario etimológico, histórico y geográfico de Chiapas* (San Cristóbal: Tipografía de Manuel Bermúdez R., 1911), vol. 3, pp. 17–26; "Real cédula para que se divida la alcaldía mayor de Chiapas en dos" (1768), López Sánchez, vol. 2, pp. 811–812; "Real cédula sobre el nombramiento de Juan de Oliver como alcalde mayor de Tuxtla en la provincia de Chiapa" (1770), ibid., p. 812.

48. Letter from Fray Eugenio Saldivar to the Dominican Provincial, August 23, 1770, AGCh, *Boletín* 4 (1955): 126–127.

49. Letter from Don Bartolomé Gutiérrez to the President of the Audiencia, January 14, 1771, ibid., pp. 113–114.

50. "Cordillera a los padres curas para que animen a sus feligreses a que fomenten sus sementeras" (1771), and "Carta de don Fray Juan Manuel García de Vargas y contestaciones" (1771), AHDSC.

51. Ibid.

52. Ibid.

53. Ibid.

54. Ibid.

55. "Fundación del pueblo Sabana de Tulijá, año 1816," AGCh, *Boletín* 6 (1956): 103; "El real acuerdo pide los autos acerca de la fundación del pueblo de La Sabanilla, jurisdicción de Ciudad Real" (1777), AGGG, A1.12.267.19.

56. López Sánchez, vol. 2, p. 813.

57. Ibid.

58. Ibid., p. 815; "Una representación hecha por el cabildo al rey de España sobre la necesidad de esta santa iglesia agregando cinco curatos" (1759), AHDSC.

59. "Informe del obispo de Chiapa, Dr. Don Marcos Bravo de la Serna Manrique, al rey" (1677), López Sánchez, vol. 2, pp. 664–665.

60. "Sobre si los indios deben pagar los derechos de visita del sor. obispo" (1770), AHDSC; "Providencia del superior gobierno prohibiendo a los curas del obispado de Chiapa el sistema de derramas y otras contribuciones so pretexto de visitas" (1771), AGGG, A1.11.28.744.80.

61. Trens, pp. 123–134; "Información recabada a solicitud del fiscal de la audiencia acerca de la manera en que los frailes dominicos administran las doctrinas de los tzendales" (1642), AGGG, A1.11.12.707.72; "El obispo de Chiapa, Fr. Mauro de Tovar, sobre que el R. P. Provincial del Convento de Santo Domingo no ha cumplido con lo ordenado por cédula de 1603 sobre servicio de curatos por religiosos" (1656), ibid., A1.11.12.708.72; "Sobre administración eclesiástica en la provincia de Chiapa" (1665), AHDSC.

62. Ximénez, vol. 2, p. 454; "Autos sobre secularización" (1735), AHDSC; "El Dr. Fr. Mauro Bravo de la Serna Manrique, obispo de Chiapa, expone que el vicario general, Fr. Sebastián Mejía, de la Orden de Predicadores no cumple con sus deberes" (n.d.), AGGG, A1.11.13.710.72; "El provincial de la provincia de San Vicente de Chiapa y Guatemala protesta por el Venerable Dean y Cabildo Eclesiástico de Ciudad Real sedevacante nombró un clérigo para el servicio de cura de almas en el pueblo de Chiapa de los Indios" (1707), ibid., A1.11.13.712.72; "Certificación en que consta que los PP. dominicos que sirven en las doctrinas de Totolapa, San Lucas, el Barrio de Mexicanos, Cerrillo y Cuctitali han desempañado cumplídamente" (1705), ibid., A1.11.160.13.

63. "Autos sobre la secularización de las doctrinas servidas por regulares en la jurisdicción de obispado de Chiapa" (1733), AGGG, A1.11.52.890.115.

64. "Autos sobre secularización" (1735), AHDSC.

65. Ibid.

66. Ibid.

67. López Sánchez, vol. 2, pp. 683–684.

68. Trens, p. 138.

69. López Sánchez, vol. 2, p. 793; "Autos sobre la secularización de las doctrinas..." (1733), AGGG; "Informe rendido por el alcalde mayor de Chiapa acerca de los siete curatos del partido de zendales" (1735), ibid., A1.11.185.13.

70. "Autos fechos en la secularización de curatos vacantes que poseían los regulares de Nuestro Padre Santo Domingo proveídos en clérigos interinos" (1771), AHDSC.

71. Ibid.

72. "Una representación hecha por el cabildo al rey de España sobre la necesidad de esta santa iglesia agregando cinco curatos" (1759), AHDSC.

73. "Real cédula sobre la agregación de los cinco curatos" (1762), AHDSC.

74. "Auto del cabildo eclesiástico" (1762), AHDSC.

75. "Real cédula sobre... los cinco curatos" and "Pedimento al Sor. Fiscal" (1762), AHDSC.

76. "Informe al rey sobre la secularización de los curatos de la religión de Santo Domingo" (1774), AHDSC; also "Copia simple de una real cédula y los informes hechos a su continuación sobre doctrinas administradas por los religiosos dominicos" (1764), AHDSC.

77. "Autos fechos en la secularización de curatos vacantes..." (1771), AHDSC.

78. Ibid.

79. "Informe al rey sobre la secularización de los curatos de... Santo Domingo" (1774).

80. "Testimonio de real provisión sobre que a los padres del convento de Chiapa no se les secularizara el curato de dho. pueblo por... Dr. D. Fr. Manuel García de Vargas" (1771) and "Diligencias practicadas

en la secularización de las doctrinas... en la provincia de Zoques" (1771), AHDSC.

81. "Testimonio de real provision."

82. "Los frailes dominicos del pueblo de Chiapa de la Real Corona despojan a los naturales del templo de Santo Domingo" (1776), AGCh, *Boletín* 1 (1953): 21–58.

83. "Informe al rey sobre la secularización de los curatos de... Santo Domingo" (1774); "Testimonio del Padre Roca del expediente instruido a consulta del discreto provisor... sobre secularización de doctrinas..." (1784), AHDSC.

84. "Carta del Sor. Polanco al rey" (1779), AHDSC, Asuntos Secretos.

85. "Carta del alcalde mayor al presidente" (1778); also "Provisión de la Real Audiencia sobre los capítulos que el alcalde mayor de esta ciudad puso al obispo y curas" (1779), AHDSC.

86. "Carta del Sor. Polanco al rey" (1779) and "Informe del. R. P. Fr. Tomás Luis Roca, cura de Zinacantan" (1779), AHDSC.

87. "Carta del Sor. Polanco al rey," "Cuentas presentadas por el Br. don Joseph Ordoñez y Aguiar" (1783), and "Informe que yo, don Bartolomé Gutiérrez,... doy al Sr. don Agustín de las Cuentas Zayas..." (1793), AHDSC.

88. "Juicio contra Josef Ordoñez y Aguiar, vicario perpetuo de Chamula" (1775), AHDSC. Significantly, these disputes dragged on for more than 20 years and filled several hundred pages of documentation. In 1764, for example, Ordóñez y Aguiar persuaded the *audiencia* to grant him a *repartimiento de indios* in order to establish his personal properties; 20 years later, his enemies prepared a dossier in which they accused him of both exaggerating his needs and abusing his trust: "Auto del repartimiento de indios a favor del Pbro. José Ordoñez y Aguiar" (1764), AGGG, A3.12.1981.240; "Cuaderno en que constan los vicios con que el pbro. vicario de Chamula, Joseph Ordoñez y Aguiar, alcanzó la gracia de un repartimiento de indios" (1785), ibid., A3.12.2983.240.

89. "Juicio contra Josef Ordoñez y Aguiar."

90. Ibid.

91. "Expediente sobre restablecer el cabildo o ayuntamiento de Cuidad Real" (1781), AHDSC; "Nómina de los vecinos hombres de bien que pueden entrar en el cabildo de esta ciudad como vecinos que son de ella" (1781), López Sánchez, vol. 2, pp. 839–840; "El cabildo de Ciudad

Real pide su restablecimiento, explicando los motivos que tuvo para hacer nueva elección de alcaldes y demás miembros" (1782), AGGG, A1.2.67.5. In 1778, according to a petition filed by these *vecinos*, Ortíz had torn down the *cabildo* and adjacent jails so that the *ayuntamiento* could not meet in public. Moreover, they continued, on the slightest pretext he imprisoned them "in a run-down adobe hut on the edge of the city, which in general was occupied by a large number of Indians who had not met their *repartimientos* and which, being extremely uncomfortable, made such imprisonment insufferable for a resident of higher station, which was one of his principal reasons for destroying the town hall that had been provided with jails for both Spaniards and Indians . . .": "El común de Ciudad Real acusa de arbitrario al alcalde mayor, don Cristóbal de Avilés" (1778), AGCh, *Boletín* 10 (1960): 13-18.

92. López Sánchez, vol. 2, p. 837. Within two years, in fact, the *fiscal* in Guatemala was able to report that "the office of *alférez real* was auctioned to don Juan Oliver for 500 pesos, that of *alcalde provincial y regidor* to don Antonio Gutiérrez de Arce for 550 pesos, that of *alguacil mayor* and *regidor* to don Nicolás Coello for 500 pesos, that of *depositario general* and *regidor* to don José de Robles y Mazariegos for 350 pesos. Don Agustín de Tejada, don Bartolomé Gutiérrez, don José Antonio Domínguez, and don Blas Gorris y Zuza were also named *regidores sencillos* for 300 pesos each." See "Informe del fiscal de la real audiencia de Guatemala al Consejo de Indias" (1783), ibid., p. 845.

93. "Remate de diezmos" (1774-1785), AHDSC.

94. Ironically, it was precisely by these means that he was also able to enforce the cooperation of his Dominican colleagues. As the province's largest landowners, they paid the largest amount of tithes for newborn cattle and other products. In addition to sharing such revenues with local *vecinos*, then, Polanco dramatically limited the Order's economic power and brought their enterprises under some measure of episcopal control.

95. "Respuesto del obispo de Chiapa al informe de don Esteban Gutiérrez, con documentos de apoyo" (1779), AHDSC. Gutiérrez was Ortíz's *teniente* in Ciudad Real.

96. "Instancia de los indios de Chamula . . . sobre que su cura . . . los grava con dros. y contribuciones excesivas" (1779) and "Fallo de la Real Audiencia" (1779), AHDSC.

97. "Pleito entre el alcalde mayor de Ciudad Real y el vicario de Chamula" (1785), AGCh, *Boletín* 6 (1956): 75-100.

98. "Padrones de los tributarios" (1816–1819), AGGG, A3.16.3.4168.308.

99. Sociedad Económica de Ciudad Real, "Informe rendido . . ." (1819), AGCh, *Boletín* 6 (1956): 17.

100. Taylor, *Landlord and Peasant.*

101. "El padre procurador de los dominicos solicita 10,000 pesos del fondo de comunidades para la conducción de religiosos de España," (1819), AGGG, A3.40.4382.336.

### Notes to Chapter 4

1. "Motín indígena de Tuxtla" (1693), AGCh, *Boletín* 2 (1953): 25–52.

2. "Motín indígena de Ocozocuautla" (1722), ibid, pp. 53–66.

3. "Libro de la cofradía de San Andrés" (1649), AHDSC.

4. E.g., "El doctor don Diego de Valverde y Orozco, juez fiscal defensor de indios, expone los agravios que reciben en jurisdicción de Chiapa en los repartimientos y otros empleos" (1662), AGGG, Serie Chiapas, A3.12.3975.240; "Instancia de los indios de Escuintenango de la jurisdicción de Chiapa acerca de que se les modere en el repartimiento destinado al padre cura doctrinero. Este expediente tiene importantes referencias acerca de la despoblación de Escuintenango y otros pueblos" (1685), ibid., A3.12.2976.240; "El capitán Sebastián de Olivera Ponce de León solicita un repartimiento de indios para el cultivo de milpas" (1706), ibid., A3.12.2977.240; "Real ejecutoria librada a favor de los padres mercedarios de Chiapa acerca de que gocen de repartimientos de indios" (1752), ibid., A3.12.2978.240; "Provisión otorgando a Francisco Mateo un repartimiento de indios para los trabajos de campo de sus haciendas" (1796), ibid., A3.12.2979.240; "Auto de repartimiento de indios a favor del presbítero José Ordoñez y Aguiar" (1764), ibid., A3.12.2982.240.

5. Gosner, "Soldiers of the Virgin."

6. Facultades concedidas por el santísimo señor nuestro Alejandro por la Divina Providencia papa séptimo al reverendo padre don Mauro de Tovar, obispo de Chiapa en las indias occidentales" (1664), López Sánchez, vol. 2, pp. 662–663.

7. "Ordenanzas del visitador Don Jacinto Roldán de la Cueva" (1674), document in the municipal archive of Oxchuc, Chiapas.

8. "Carta pastoral de su ilustrísimo . . . Dr. don Marcos Bravo de la Serna" (1679), AHDSC. (Typed copy in Biblioteca Fray Bartolomé de Las Casas, San Cristóbal, Chiapas.)

9. "Proceso contra indio de Tenejapa por hechicero" (1678), AHDSC.

10. López Sánchez, vol. 2, p. 683; Trens, *Historia de Chiapas,* p. 181.

11. Fray Juan Podas, "Arte de la lengua tzotzlem o tzinacanteca" (1688), Bibliothèque Nationale, Paris, Collectione Americana Domini Brasseur de Bourbourg, série E3, no. 67, ms. mexicain 411, R27.746—this handbook was recopied and reissued in 1723. Also Fray Luis Barrientos, "Doctrina cristiana en lengua chiapaneca" (1690), in Alphonse-Lucien Pinart, ed., *Bibliothéque linguistique et d'ethnographie américaines* (Paris: Ernest Leroux, 1875), vol. 1.

12. P. Manuel Hidalgo "Libro en que se trata de la lengua tzotzil . . ." (1735), Bibliothèque Nationale, Paris, ms. mexicain 412, R27.747.

13. Trens, p. 131.

14. "Provincia de Chiapa, dada por D. José Descals, caballero de la Orden de Santiago, del Consejo de Su Magestad su oidor, alcalde de la corte en la audiencia de Santiago de Guatemala, visitador de la provincia de Chiapa" (1690), in López Sánchez, vol. 2, p. 684.

15. Francisco Núñez de la Vega, "Carta IX pastoral," in *Constituciones diocesanas del obispado de Chiapa* (Rome, Italy, 1702).

16. With characteristic disdain, for example, Ximénez (*Historia,* vol. 3, p. 261) wrote that "The Indians are for the most part very malicious and deprived of understanding, very inclined toward idolatry, and averse to everything that is sacred and serious; of all religious matters they participate willingly in those which are ceremonious, in those which include public spectacle, trumpets and noise, cymbals and dances; and they prefer to celebrate those saints which are on horseback and those which are accompanied by animals, like the evangelists. . . ." And yet, a few pages later, Ximénez describes how for nearly 200 years native people had been denied religious instruction and excluded from communion on the grounds that they might not understand what was being explained to them.

17. "Resolución del Santo Oficio sobre lo dispuesto por el visitador don José Descals" (1691), López Sánchez, vol.2, pp. 684-685.

18. "Carta pastoral de . . . Bravo de la Serna."

19. López Sánchez, vol. 2, p. 714.

20. Ximénez, vol. 3, p. 266.

21. Ibid., p. 263.

22. Ibid., p. 268.

23. Ibid., p. 270.

24. Ibid., p. 271.

25. Ibid., p. 280.

26. López Sánchez, p. 720; Ximénez, vol. 3, pp. 281–282.

27. Ibid., p. 284.

28. Ibid., p. 287.

29. López Sánchez, vol. 2, p. 716.

30. Orozco y Jiménez, vol. 2, p. 152.

31. Ximénez, vol. 3, pp. 282–283.

32. Ibid., pp. 333–334.

33. Hidalgo, "Libro."

34. Henri Favre, *Changement et continuité*, p. 43; Herbert Klein, "Rebeliones de las comunidades campesinas: la república tzeltal de 1712," in McQuown and Pitt-Rivers, eds., *Ensayos de antropológia*, p. 153.

35. "Petición del alcalde ordinario de Ciudad Real, Capitán José de Azcaray, a favor de los naturales de San Felipe, provincia de Chiapa" (1713), López Sánchez, vol. 2, pp. 687–688.

36. "Sentencia dictada por el presidente de la real audiencia, don Toribio Cosio, contra el sargento mayor de Chiapa, Pedro de Zabaleta" (1716), ibid., pp. 688–689; also "Informe rendido por Jacinto, obispo de Chiapa, al rey" (1717), ibid., p. 689.

37. "Auto sobre la disposición del asunto de don Pedro de Zabaleta" (1721), ibid., p. 689.

38. "Informe del fiscal de V. S. en la causa de don Pedro de Zabaleta" (1721), ibid., p. 690.

39. "Sentencia dictada por el Consejo Supremo de Indias en la causa de don Pedro de Zabaleta" (1722), ibid., pp. 690–691.

40. "Sobre reducción de misas" (1769), AHDSC.

41. Hidalgo,"Libro"; Josef de la Barrera, *Libro de lengua tzotzil* . . . (Washington, D.C.: Library of Congress, 1782); Anonymous, "Breve ex-

plicación de la lengua tzotzil para los pueblos de la provincia de Chiapas" (1804), AHDSC.

42. "Libro de la cofradía del Santísimo Sacramento de Amatenango" (1729), AHDSC.

43. "Despoblación de Jiquipulas, Tecoasintepec, Las Pitas, Coneta, Suchjltepeque, Popocatepeque, Ecatepec, Bachajón, San Andrés, Ixtapilla, Zacualpa" (1733), AGCh, *Boletín* 4 (1955): 27–68.

44. "Los indígenas del pueblo de Zinacantan piden se les rebaje la asignación de tributos" (1734), AGGG, A3.16.4643.359. Part of this petition reads as follows: "Lorenzo Vásquez, Miguel Mártir, Nicolás Vásquez, Juan Santos González, Miguel Lázaro, Valeriano Barroquín, and Martín Hernández, *alcaldes, regidores,* and *principales* of the town of Zinacantan, in our own right and in the name of the other Indians of our town appear before Your Highness in the person of our lawyer and declare that because of the epidemics which we have suffered, our town has lost many of its tributaries and many others have fled because of hunger and other necessities. For these reasons, we are now paying tribute for those who have died or are absent...." Similar petitions were filed on behalf of Indians in Comitán, Tila, and Ocosingo.

45. "Padrón y nueva cuenta de los tributarios del pueblo de Zinacantan, provincia de Chiapa" (1749), ibid., A3.16.4509.353; also "Autos tramitados en cumplimiento de la cédula de 25 de Septiembre de 1740 en que su magestad ordena que a los indígenas que están en las montañas se les extraiga y paguen tributos" (1742), ibid., A3.16.4643.359. According to López Sánchez (vol. 2, pp. 789–790), in 1743 the King commended his administrators in Guatemala for having "returned a large number of Indians (in Chiapas) to their towns and increased my royal revenues by 8,000 pesos."

46. Chamberlain, *The Governorship of Montejo;* "Sobre restitución de bienes de don Luis Alfonso de Estrada" (1601), AHDSC.

47. Ibid.; "Título de un sitio de estancia para ganado mayor en términos del pueblo de Zinacantan a favor del indígena Cristóbal Arias" (1599), AGGG, A1.57.4588.270.

48. "Escritura de venta del sitio del Burrero" (1651), AHDSC.

49. García de Vargas y Rivera, "Relación de los pueblos que comprehende el obispado de Chiapa" (1744), Biblioteca del Palacio, Madrid, ms. 2840 (Misc. de Ayala, XXVI, ff. 282–322. A typescript copy of this document is also available in the Biblioteca Fray Bartolomé de Las Casas, San Cristóbal, Chiapas.

50. "Escritura de venta de San Nicolás, pueblo de Zinacantan" (1750), AHDSC.

51. "Los alcaldes y común de los pueblos de Chamula y Zinacantan de la provincia de Chiapa exponen que el actual alcalde mayor durante la visita oficial que esta efectuando impone repartimiento en efectivo hasta por 200 pesos" (1742), AGGG, A3.12.40.163.2776; "Informe rendido por la Sociedad Económica de Ciudad Real sobre las ventajas y desventajas obtenidas con el implantamiento del sistema de intendencias" (1819), AGCh, *Boletín* 5 (1955): 98–112, and 6 (1956): 7–54.

52. "Los alcaldes y demás común de Zinacantan piden se les asigne una parte de su tributo para reedificar su iglesia" (1749), AGGG, A1.11.25.

53. "Autos acerca de la reconstrucción del edificio del cabildo y mesón de Zinacantan" (1788), ibid., A1.1.20.2; "Autorización a los indios de Zinacantan para que del fondo de sus comunidades tomen lo necesario para el fomento de sus siembras" (1788), ibid., A3.40.4343.334.

54. "Padrón y nueva cuenta . . . de Zinacantan" (1749), ibid., A3.16.4509.353.

55. "Sobre reducir a poblado los oriundos de la zona de Zinacantan que viven dispersos por los montes" (1819), ibid., A1.12.274.19.

56. "Auto de repartimiento de indios a favor del presbítero José Ordoñez y Aguiar" (1764), ibid., A3.12.2981.240.

57. "Instancia de los indios de Chamula de la provincia de Ciudad Real sobre que su cura, don Josef Ordoñez, los grava con derechos y contribuciones excesivas" (1779), AHDSC.

58. "Petición del ministro compañero de Chamula, Don Nicolás Morales, al cabildo eclesiástico pur su sueldo" (1778), and "Testimonio de la demanda de Don Josef Ordoñez, vicario de Chamula, contra los partícipes a los productos de dha. vicaría" (1788), AHDSC. This controversy, which continued for nearly 20 years and involved at least a dozen members of the Church in Chiapas, fills several hundred pages of documentation in the AHDSC and AGGG.

59. "Resolución de la real audiencia en la consulta que se hizo acerca de la causa instruida contra don Josef Ordoñez" (1784), AHDSC.

60. "Instancia de los indios de Chamula" (1779).

61. Ibid. As a result, Ordoñez was forced to reconstruct this list—

upon which he based both his parish accounts and his *repartimientos*—with the help of his native lieutenants: "Padrón de casados, viudos y solteros de Chamula," included in "El vicario de Chamula se queja del alcalde mayor" (1779), AHDSC.

62. "Sobre idolatrías en San Andrés" (1778), AHDSC.

63. Ibid.

64. Ibid.

65. Ibid.

66. Ibid.

67. According to López Sánchez (vol. 2, p. 843), "Chiapas was divided into 3 *partidos* and later into 12 *subdelegaciones*. Ciudad Real was the center of the first *partido*, which contained 56 towns, assigned to 20 parishes. The second *partido* was based in Tuxtla and consisted of 33 towns divided among 13 parishes; the third *partido* included all of the Soconusco, with 20 towns divided into 5 parishes. The *subdelegaciones* were Palenque, Ocosingo, Tila, Huistán, Comitán, Simojovel, Ixtacomitán, San Andrés, Tapachula, Tonalá, and Llanos [San Bartolomé]."

68. "Informe rendido por la Sociedad Económica de Ciudad Real," part 1, p. 99.

69. Trens, p. 233.

70. "Instancia de los indígenas del pueblo de Chamula sobre que se les autorice tomar de los fondos de comunidades para la compra de terrenos y aumentar sus ejidos" (1798–1801), AGCh, *Boletín* 5 (1955): 77–94.

71. "Sobre reducir a poblado."

72. Francisco Polanco, "Estado de los vasallos que tiene Su Magestad . . . " (1778), in Orozco y Jiménez, vol. 2, pp. 74–79; "Informe rendido por la Sociedad Económica de Ciudad Real," part 2, pp. 13–15. For an instructive contrast with *mestizos* in urban Oaxaca, see John Chance, "On the Mexican Mestizo," *Latin American Research Review* 14, no. 3 (1979): 153–168, and his book, *Race and Class in Colonial Oaxaca* (Stanford, Calif.: Stanford University Press, 1978). Comparative information on other areas of Mexico may be found in Cook and Borah, "Racial Groups in the Mexican Population Since 1519," in *Essays in Population History: Mexico and the Caribbean*, vol. 2, pp. 180–269.

73. "Padrón general que yo, don Manuel Ruíz, cura propio de este

beneficio de Ocosingo, formo de orden de mi ilustrísimo señor obispo Dr. don Fermín Josef de Fuero, del consejo de Su Magestad, etc." (1797), ADHSC.

74. "Real cédula y autos relativos a la información elevada a Su Magestad del estado en que se encuentra la escuela de hilados y tejidos establecida en Teopisca" (1794), AGCh, *Boletín* 10 (1960): 67–152.

75. "Sobre reducir a poblado."

76. "Sobre un motín en Yajalón" (1819), AHDSC.

## Notes to Chapter 5

1. John L. Stephens, *Incidents of Travel in Central America, Chiapas, and Yucatan* (New York: Dover, 1969; originally published 1841), vol. 1, p. 250. For a discussion of the independence movement in Chiapas, see Flavio Guillén, *La federación de Chiapas a México* (Tuxtla Gutiérrez: Gobierno del Estado, 1972); and Manuel Larraínzar, *Noticia histórica de Soconusco y su incorporación a la República Mexicana* (Mexico City: Imprenta de J. M. Lara, 1843). More recently, Roderic Ai Camp has taken up this subject in his article "La cuestión chiapaneca: revisión de una polémica territorial," *Historia Mexicana* 23, no. 4 (1975): 579–606.

2. Gobierno del Estado de Chiapas, *Anuario estadístico del Estado de Chiapas, 1909* (Tuxtla Gutiérrez: Tipografía del Gobierno, 1911), pp. 95–102.

3. *Informes de los párrocos del Estado al Gobierno del mismo, sobre la situación de los pueblos, dados en cumplimiento de la orden circular de 23 de junio de 1830* (San Cristóbal: Imprenta de la Sociedad dirigida por Secundino Orantes, 1830), pp. 1–2. Reflecting these same sentiments, in 1827 the state's *secretario de gobierno*, José María Escuinca (quoted in Trens, *Historia de Chiapas*, p. 305), informed the congress that, "With the exception of a few municipalities, [the *ayuntamientos*] are composed in such a way as to render them virtually useless, especially among the Indians, who surely do not even comprehend the purpose of such institutions. Accustomed in the past to oppression and slavery at the hands of colonial administrators, their intelligence now qualifies them only for such a destiny." Similarly, during the conservative administration which followed (1835–1846), municipal corporations were organized only in towns with 8,000 inhabitants or more: San Cris-

tóbal, Comitán, San Bartolomé, and Chamula. Elsewhere, local affairs were managed directly in each *partido* by subprefects who were in turn responsible to 5 district prefects and *jueces de primera instancia*. Finally, according to Trens (pp. 390–392), such districts also possessed their own *ayuntamientos*, composed exclusively of creoles from the district capitals (San Cristóbal, Comitán, Chilón, Tuxtla, and Ixtacomitán).

4. For an extensive discussion of civil administration in Chiapas, see Jan Rus, "Great San Juan, Great Patron: Social History of a Maya Community, 1800–1976" (Ph.D diss., Harvard University, 1983).

5. In 1827, the clergy in Chiapas included 66 secular priests and 39 Dominicans affiliated with 4 monasteries. Of the 42 parishes in the state, only 9 were served by monks; the others had been placed in the hands of *clérigos*. By this time, the *frailes* owned 11 *fincas* worth 11,320 pesos which yielded an annual profit of around 9,900 pesos. By contrast, their revenues from parish administration represented only about 2,000 pesos—a fact which may explain their subsequent hostility toward Liberal authorities. This situation did not change appreciably during the next 20 years; in 1846, 12 of the state's 41 parishes were occupied by Dominicans and the remainder were held by secular curates who, together with members of the cathedral chapter and seminary staff, numbered 60 men: Gobierno de los Estados Unidos Mexicanos, "Memoria que en cumplimiento del Artículo 120 de la Constitución Federal . . . leyó el Secretario de Estado y del Despacho Universal de Justicia y Negocios Eclesiásticos . . ." (1828) and "Estado que manifiesta el número de eclesiásticos y parroquias que hay en este obispado" (1846), AHDSC.

6. Stephens, p. 327.

7. *Informes*, pp. 17–18.

8. E. Pineda, "Descripción geográfica del Departamento de Chiapas y Soconusco," *Boletín de la Sociedad Mexicana de Geografía y Estadística* 3, ser. 1 (1852). Similar events occurred around San Bartolomé. Already by 1828, nearly 1,100 people resided as servants on 10 local *haciendas*; 525 *mozos* lived on a single property: letter from P. Venances Espinoza to *Provisor General*, Dec. 15, 1828, AHDSC, Correspondencia Parroquial.

9. Gobierno del Estado de Chiapas, "Memoria del estado en que se hallan los ramos de la administración pública . . ." (1830) (San Cristóbal: Imprenta de la Sociedad dirigida por Secundino Orantes, 1830), in Instituto Nacional de Antropología e Historia (INAH) microfilm collection, Documentos de Chiapas; Trens, pp. 550–551.

10. E. Pineda, passim.

11. Trens, pp. 331–451. A complete compilation of these measures is contained in Gobierno del Estado de Chiapas, *Colección de leyes agrarias y demás disposiciones que se han emitido con relación al Ramo de Tierras* (Tuxtla Gutiérrez: Imprenta del Gobierno, 1878).

12. Gobierno del Estado de Chiapas, *Anuario estadístico*, p. 52. In 1885, for example, the curate of Las Margaritas, located between Comitán and the Lacandón jungle, reported that his parish contained 5,591 inhabitants, of whom 1,260 (including 400 *ladinos*) lived in the town of Margaritas, and the rest were employed as *mozos* on 46 nearby *haciendas*!. See "Informe que el Presbítero Eligio Velasco, cura interino de la parroquia de Margaritas, presenta al . . . Obispo acerca de los puntos que determina la superior circular de 10 de Abril de . . . 1885," AHDSC.

13. Stephens, pp. 252–253.

14. Gobierno del Estado de Chiapas, *Anuario estadístico*, p. 52.

15. Ibid.

16. Enrique Santibáñez, *Geografía regional de Chiapas* (Tuxtla Gutiérrez: Gobierno del Estado, 1907), p. 64.

17. Gobierno del Estado de Chiapas, *Anuario estadístico*, p. 52.

18. Ibid., pp. 95–102; W. W. Byam, *A Sketch of the State of Chiapas, Mexico* (Los Angeles: Geo. Rice and Sons, 1897), pp. 25–30, 41–62.

19. By way of comparison, in the years 1855–57 this area was divided among approximately 55 small *fincas* which raised cattle and maize; the tithe collector in Tapachula estimated that such activities yielded a total annual profit of 2,000 pesos: "Demonstración que forma el que subscribe como Colector de Diezmos de la parroquia de Tapachula para mostrar al ingreso de granos y pagos en numerario habidos en el año actual" (1855, 1856, 1857), AHDSC.

20. U.S. Department of Commerce, *Rubber Statistics, 1910–1937* (Washington, D.C.: Government Printing Office, 1938); *The India Rubber World and Gutta-Percha Trades Journal* (London, various years beginning in 1880); *The India Rubber World* (New York, various years beginning in 1885).

21. "Troubles of the Ubero Plantation Companies," *India Rubber World,* May 1, 1905, pp. 278–281; "Affairs of the Ubero Companies," ibid., June 1, 1905, pp. 301–302. By 1897, in fact, the Mexican Land and Colonization Company, Ltd., had obtained the following concessions in Chiapas:

| District | Hectares |
|---|---|
| Pichucalco | 248,256 |
| Tuxtla and Chiapa | 380,423 |
| Libertad and Comitán | 584,814 |
| Tonalá | 342,815 |
| Soconusco | 251,061 |
| Total | 1,807,369 ha. |

From Moisés T. de la Peña, *Chiapas económico* (Tuxtla Gutiérrez: Departamento de Prensa y Turismo del Estado, 1952), vol. 2, p. 336.

22. "'Castilloa' Rubber in Chiapas (Mexico-I)," *India Rubber World,* Feb. 1, 1910, pp. 163–166. In 1903, Harrison ran an advertisement in this journal which proclaimed: "RUBBER AND COFFEE LANDS: The Mexican Land and Colonization Company owns several hundred thousand acres of land suitable for Rubber and Coffee in the State of Chiapas, Mexico. The majority of the coffee plantations in Soconusco now producing largely were originally purchased from this company, also La Zacualpa and other rubber plantations."

Among the lumbering concessions which were registered in the Lacandon jungle, federal records show the following titles:

| Year | Area | Titleholder |
|---|---|---|
| 1903 | 24,761 ha. | Eduard Hartmann |
| | | Angel López Negrete |
| | | Hiram Smith |
| 1904 | 107,854 | Luis Martínez de Castro |
| 1908 | 35,743 | Policarpo Valenzuela |
| 1909 | 117,115 | Federico Schindler |
| | | Manuel Gabucio |

As late as 1960, however, such records suggested that the real number of concessions had been much greater. According to an official survey in the area, for example, the following titles were still in effect:

| District | Area | Titleholder |
|---|---|---|
| Palenque | 118,765 ha. | Dorantes, Romano and Co. |
| | 27,636 | Doremberg Estate (sold to Javier Martínez del Río) |
| Tulijá | 41,766 | Doremberg Estate (sold to Manuel Rinfrull) |
| Valenzuela and Santo Domingo | 224,891 | various owners |

| Monte Líbano | 107,633 | Martínez de Castro Co. |
|---|---|---|
| | 50,000 | Arizpe Amador and Co. |
| | 40,051 | Hartmann, López Negrete, and Smith |
| | 21,943 | Hiram G. Smith |
| Jataté | 27,463 | various owners |
| Miramar | 29,949 | Taide A. de Hartmann |
| | 29,537 | Eduard Hartmann |
| | 24,760 | López, Hartmann, and Smith |
| | 10,000 | Sociedad Explotadora de Chiapas |
| Lacandona | 102,275 | various owners |
| | 29,537 | López Negrete |
| | 67,413 | Agua Azul Mahogany Co. |
| | 148,374 | Romano and Co. |

| Total | 1,091,700 ha. |
|---|---|

In addition, one large area, known as the Marqués de Comillas (130,914 ha.), had already reverted to the state treasury: Secretaría de Agricultura y Ganadería, Subsecretaría de la Forestal, "Memoria económico-justificativa sobre la Selva Lacandona" (1975), pp. 125–165.

23. Manuel Carrascoa, *Apuntes estadísticos del Estado de Chiapas* (Mexico City: Sociedad Mexicana de Geografía y Estadística, 1883), p. 11. In 1895, according to a prospectus published in Spanish and English by the state government, several German coffee planters had established themselves in Palenque, but little other development had occurred: Oficina de Informaciones de Chiapas, *Chiapas, su estado actual, su riqueza, sus ventajas para los negocios* (Mexico City: Imprenta de la Escuela Correccional, 1895). Apparently it was not until around 1903 that American rubber growers acquired a major interest in the area.

24. *India Rubber World*, 1901–1911; also Chacamas Plantation Co., "Inspection Report by Frank R. McKinstry, Gen. Mgr., and Charles M. Roe, Director" (Chicago, 1903).

25. *India Rubber World*, March 1, 1903, Mutual Rubber Production Co. advertisement, p. xxxviii.

26. Chacamas Plantation Co.; "Operaciones eccas. sobre San Quintín Monterías de Bulnes" (1889), AHDSC. It was this situation, of course, that inspired B. Traven to write a number of his best-known novels, including *March to Caobaland* and *General from the Jungle*. In their report to the Chacamas Plantation Co., McKinstry and Roe estimated that mahogany from this area might be cut and delivered in New York for $14 (in gold) per ton and sold for $45.

27. Carrascoa, p. 10.

28. Gobierno del Estado de Chiapas, "De la vagancia" (Tuxtla Gutiérrez: Tipografía del Gobierno, June 1, 1880). For a discussion of these
laws and their effects upon highland Indians, see Jan Rus and Robert
Wasserstrom, "Civil-Religious Hierarchies in Central Chiapas: A Critical Perspective," American Ethnologist 7, no. 3 (1980): 466-478.

29. Gobierno del Estado de Chiapas, "La contribución personal"
(Tuxtla Gutiérrez: Tipografía del Gobierno, Sept. 14, 1892); "Ley Orgán-
ica del Partido de Chamula, March 24, 1896." Such measures, which
were felt almost immediately by native people in the municipios around
San Cristóbal, produced a rather dramatic effect. In 1892, for example,
the curate of San Felipe resigned from his parish because "the poverty
of this place is so great that nearly everyone has gone off to the plantations, and now three months go by without a single baptism": letter from
P. Cristóbal Martínez to bishop, Oct. 24, 1892, AHDSC.

30. Quoted in "Coffee and Rubber in Chiapas," India Rubber World,
July 10, 1896, p. 290.

31. Gobierno del Estado de Chiapas, Anuario estadístico, p. 52; Santibáñez, Geographía regional, p. 41. According to another estimate, the
population of this area in 1885 was 17,973: "Cuadro estadístico de la
provincia 3a ecca. del Soconusco que forma el cura vicario para conoci-
miento del ... Obispo" (1885), AHDSC. Finally, in 1895, the state government (Oficina de Informaciones, Chiapas) published the following
figures in a pamphlet designed to attract foreign investment:

| Department | Indians | Ladinos | Total |
| --- | --- | --- | --- |
| Soconusco | 7,872 | 13,056 | 20,928 |
| Tonalá | 0 | 10,032 | 10,032 |
| Tuxtla | 6,948 | 14,007 | 20,955 |
| Chiapa | 9,241 | 13,243 | 22,484 |
| La Libertad | 6,920 | 7,109 | 14,029 |
| Las Casas | 42,213 | 11,555 | 53,768 |
| Comitán | 33,029 | 16,830 | 49,859 |
| Chilón | 16,285 | 4,166 | 20,451 |
| Palenque | 10,449 | 3,376 | 13,825 |
| Simojovel | 14,645 | 5,375 | 20,020 |
| Pichucalco | 3,302 | 18,089 | 21,391 |
| Mescalapa | 8,162 | 885 | 9,047 |
| Total | 159,066 | 117,723 | 276,789 |

32. "Libros de bautizmos" and "Estados trimestres" (1816–1910), AHDSC. Much of this discussion was taken from my article, "Population Growth and Economic Development in Chiapas, 1524–1975," *Human Ecology* 6, no. 2 (1978): 127–143; permission to include it here is gratefully acknowledged.

33. *Informes*, pp. 13–14.

34. E. Pineda, passim.

35. Carlos Cáceres López, *Historia general del Estado de Chiapas* (Tuxtla Gutiérrez: published by author, 1958), pp. 59–60. Such measures merely served to outrage landowners, however, and within two years they were repealed: Trens, pp. 496 and 513.

36. There is a fascinating discussion of *desamortización* in Chiapas in "Contestaciones habidas entre el...Gobernador del Estado de Chiapa, don Angel Albino Corzo, y el...Obispo,...Dr. don Carlos María Colina, con motivo de la venta jurídica y en asta pública que el segundo ha hecho de la hacienda llamada 'Trapiche de la Merced,' perteneciente al Seminario Conciliar de su misma diócesis" (Guatemala: Imprenta de la Paz, 1857); also Carlos María Colina, "Sexta pastoral del Obispo de Chiapas" (Guatemala City: Tipografía de la Paz, 1856).

37. Interestingly enough, Liberal governments consistently upheld the right of Conservatives to entitle native lands. In 1855, for example, Indians from Mitontic, Abasolo, Chenalhó, Cancuc, and Tenejapa complained that former *santanistas* had defrauded them of communal territories. Despite the fact that many of these officials were actively involved in royalist intrigues against the Liberal regime, however, state authorities refused to consider the claim, which they regarded as invalid. There is an extended discussion of this affair in *La Voz del Pueblo* (the official newspaper), Nov. 30, Dec. 3, and Dec. 8, 1855. Trens (p. 596) also mentions the ensuing debate.

38. The best description of these events may be found in Jan Rus' essay, "El mito de la guerra de castas en Chamula, 1869," in Jan Rus and Robert Wasserstrom, *Los Indios de Chiapas: historia y antropología* (Mexico City: Editorial Nueva Imagen, forthcoming).

39. Much of the following discussion is based on my article, "A Caste War That Never Was: The Tzeltal Conspiracy of 1848," *Peasant Studies* 7, no. 2 (1978): 73–85. Permission to use this material here has been graciously given by the editors. There is another version of these events in *El Noticioso Chiapaneco* (San Cristóbal), June 25, 1848.

40. In fact, so involved were these officials in their own variety of

intrigue that they even tried to make political capital of the conspiracy. "To test the loyalty of Liberals in Chiapa," writes Cáceres López (p. 52),"Colonel Escudero, aide to Cardona [the Conservative state governor] asked them to send their militia to Palenque, noting that he had already ordered 100 members of the regular army to the scene. . . . The municipal authorities of Chiapa complied, but when their forces had arrived in Zinacantan, they received a counterorder because rumors about the Indian uprising had turned out to be false."

41. An excellent account of this uprising, certainly the most important Indian revolt in modern Mexican history, may be found in Nelson Reed, *The Caste War of Yucatan* (Stanford, Calif.: Stanford University Press, 1964), from which the following information is taken. For Oaxaca, similar events are described by John Tutino in his essay "Indian Rebellion at the Isthmus of Tehuantepec: A Socio-Historical Perspective," given at the XLII International Congress of Americanists, Paris, 1977.

42. Stephens, p. 255.

43. Ibid., pp. 257–258.

44. Ibid., p. 267.

45. "Inventario de los expedientes del ramo de tierras que corresponden al Departamento de Las Casas, 1831–1891," AHDSC.

46. Letter from Fray José Mariano Guerrero to *Provisor General*, June 25, 1848, AHDSC, Correspondencia Parroquial.

47. "Inventario, 1831–1891."

48. Letter from Luis Beltrán Villatoro to *Provisor General*, June 5, 1848, AHDSC, Correspondencia Parroquial; "Estado trimestral del movimiento que ha tenido la población de la Villa de Ocosingo, 1838–1850," AHDSC.

49. Letter from Mariano Ramírez de Páramo to *Provisor General*, June 30, 1848, AHDSC, Correspondencia Parroquial.

50. *Informes*, pp. 1–3.

51. Letter from Ramírez de Páramo. Indeed, even those communities which had not been overwhelmed by *ladino* immigrants fell victim to such exploitation. In the Tzotzil town of San Andrés, 30 miles away from Ocosingo, the presence of four *mestizos*, "two of whom exercise no particular trade," proved to be sufficiently disruptive to bring about a state of general drunkenness and disorder: letter from Pedro José Cruz to *Provisor General*, June 13, 1848, AHDSC, Correspondencia Parroquial. Nor did such complaints cease after the supposed uprising; as late

as 1857, the curate of Tenejapa and Huistán remarked that "The same group of *ladinos* from the capital has continued to exercise its immoral influence over [the Indians], but—God be praised—I have been able to convince them that only ordained ministers are commissioned to teach the Holy Gospel": letter from Manuel José López to *Provisor General*, June 30, 1857, AHDSC, Correspondencia Parroquial.

52. Stephens, p. 269.

53. Letter from Manuel José Roxas to *Gobierno Eclesiástico*, 1825, AHDSC, Correspondencia Parroquial.

54. "Diligencia practicada . . . por el Fray Mariano Lazo," Feb. 4, 1846, AHDSC.

55. Letter from Patricio Correa to *Provisor General*, June 6, 1849, AHDSC, Correspondencia Parroquial.

56. Letter from Ramírez de Páramo.

57. Letter from Guerrero.

58. Letter from Bartolomé Gutiérrez to *Provisor General*, June 30, 1848, AHDSC, Correspondencia Parroquial.

59. Significantly, as Stephens (p. 327) noted, many of these men embraced Liberal views, even as they attempted to perpetuate traditional social relations within Indian communities. Like other creoles and rich *mestizos*, they often owned ranches and occasionally accepted political office in Liberal administrations. Naturally, this served to further compromise the position they occupied. As we might expect, they sought to remedy their plight in a variety of (generally unsatisfactory) ways. Among such schemes, it is interesting to note that in 1838, ecclesiastical authorities contemplated the possibility of appointing their own tax collectors in native towns. In this way, they hoped to circumvent uncooperative *ayuntamientos* which had become increasingly unwilling to collect Church dues. But apparently, this idea was never put into practice; local pastors were uncertain that anyone in their parishes could be persuaded to fill the new office: letter from anonymous friar to *Provisor General*, Jan. 12, 1838, AHDSC, Correspondencia Parroquial.

60. Letter from Manuel Gutiérrez to *Provisor General*, June 28, 1848, AHDSC, Correspondencia Parroquial.

61. By 1847, in fact, the state government, aware that many Indians had fled to remote areas such as the jungle, sought to close off this avenue of escape. In a *proclama* dated January 7, 1847, it proposed to reduce all such men and women to new settlements under the direct

control of both civil and religious authorities. Like much of the legislation of the day, however, this decree was never carried out. Apparently, the condition which it was intended to rectify had already grown to such proportions that local officials found themselves incapable of applying the new law. In 1852, for example, the *cura* of Tila reported enthusiastically about his visit to a number of hamlets founded by his parishioners along the Tulijá river: letter from P. Cristóbal Gutiérrez to *Provisor General*, May 27, 1852, AHDSC, Correspondencia Parroquial.

62. Wasserstrom, "Population Growth and Economic Development," pp. 136–137.

63. "Padrón de los tributarios de San Juan Bautista Ocozocuautla" (1817), AGGG, A3.13.3.4188.309.

64. *Informes*, p. 18.

65. "Padrón de la Parroquia de Zinacantan hecho para el cumplimiento de los preceptos de Nuestra Santa Madre Iglesia, de confesión sagrada comunión" (1832) and "Padrón del pueblo de Zinacantan formado por el infrascripto cura interino de la Parroquia del mismo nombre, a solicitud de la superior orden del Obispo de la Diócesis de 10 de Marzo de 1855," AHDSC. Not surprisingly, during this period a number of observers reported that Zinacanteco men occasionally married several wives: letters from Roberto García to *cura* of Zinacantan, Feb. 17, 1823, and Patricio Correa to *Vicario General*, Aug. 22, 1835, AHDSC, Correspondencia Parroquial. Moreover, the census of 1855 lists at least four marriages which took place between men and women who possessed the same set of *apellidos*—a situation which did not occur in 1749 and which suggests that possibly such marriages were now contracted between first cousins.

66. Mariano Jacinto López, "Informe trimestre de Zinacantan" (July 5, 1855), AHDSC.

67. "Padrón del pueblo de Zinacantan . . ."(1855), AHDSC. Interestingly enough, the names of two such men—José Pérez Mochilum and Antonio González—have survived in Zinacanteco oral tradition regarding the settlement of Salinas (interview with Mariano Hernández Nuj, Zinacantan, July 1, 1974).

68. "Cuentas parroquiales, Zinacantan, 1856," AHDSC.

69. Interview with Chavel Martínez, San Cristóbal, July 21, 1976.

70. Flavio Antonio Paniagua, *Catecismo elemental de historia y estadística de Chiapas* (San Cristóbal: Tipografía del Porvenir, 1876), pp. 55–60; Santibáñez, pp. 60–62.

71. "Inventario de los expedientes, 1831-1891."

72. Letter from Patricio Correa to *Provisor General,* Nov. 11, 1848, AHDSC, Correspondencia Parroquial.

73. George Collier, *Fields of the Tzotzil,* pp. 144-145.

74. "Informe del párroco de Zinacantan, don Patricio Correa, al Provisor General," Nov. 11, 1848, AHDSC.

75. Letter from Mariano Jacinto López to *Provisor General,* June 6, 1855, AHDSC, Correspondencia Parroquial.

76. Mariano Jacinto López, "Informe trimestre de Zinacantan," Oct. 1, 1856, AHDSC. Similarly, in 1850 the *cura* of Chamula reported that none of his flock wished to serve in the church, nor would the local prefect compel them to do so. A few years later, in 1859, the *mayordomos* and *alféreces* of Mitontic protested to this officer that their new curate wished to be compensated promptly for his services—in violation of "established custom" which permitted them to pay in lengthy installments: letters from Manuel Cruz y Aguilar to *Provisor General,* Nov. 6, 1850, and Andrés Díaz, *mayordomo* of Mitontic, to *Prefecto del Centro,* Dec. 22, 1859, AHDSC, Correspondencia Parroquial.

77. "Cuentas parroquiales, Zinacantan, 1855," AHDSC.

78. Letter from Francisco Gordillo to *Provisor General,* Aug. 31, 1857, AHDSC, Correspondencia Parroquial.

79. For an excellent discussion of these events, see Rus, "El mito de la guerra de castas."

80. Indeed, Church officials collaborated willingly and directly with the French invaders, who established a small garrison in San Cristóbal. In late 1863, for example, the *cura* of Huistán congratulated his superior for using these forces to reestablish good order in the region, and suggested that local authorities be compelled to provide intelligence information to their priests for military purposes: letter from J. Agustín Velasco to *Provisor General,* Oct. 12, 1863, AHDSC, Correspondencia Parroquial.

81. Examples of this process may be found in "Sobre excesos en las capillas de las fincas Bochil, Naranjo, Chavarría, de la comprensión de la Parroquia de Jitotol" (1862), AHDSC. Similar documents exist from Zinacantan, Pantelhó, Ocosingo, and Tila.

82. Letter from Manuel María Suárez to *Provisor General,* March 28, 1862, AHDSC. Correspondencia Parroquial.

83. Rus, "El mito."

84. "Sobre excesos en las capillas"; "Fallo del ministerio fiscal" (1862), AHDSC. In addition, this matter is discussed in an abundant series of letters between lowland *hacendados* and ecclesiastical authorities.

85. Rus, "El mito."

86. "Cuentas parroquiales de Zinacantan, 1855–1881," AHDSC.

87. In 1865, for example, the *cura* of Oxchuc was proud to report that he had compelled *vecinos* in all of the towns of his *vicaría* (Oxchuc, Chanal, Huistán, Abasolo, and Tenejapa) to recant their oaths of loyalty to the 1857 constitution. And although he had succeeded in bringing almost all of the area's *ladinos* back to confession, he lamented that his Indian parishioners, "deprived in part or in whole of intelligence," refused to accept the sacraments: letter from Francisco Gordillo to Cathedral Chapter, Dec. 6, 1865, AHDSC, Correspondencia Parroquial.

88. Letter from Bruno Domínguez to *Provisor General,* June 4, 1867, AHDSC, Correspondencia Parroquial.

89. Rus, "El mito."

90. Letter from Bruno Domínguez to *Provisor General,* Feb. 26, 1868, AHDSC, Correspondencia Parroquial.

91. Letter from Vicente Anselmo Guillén to *Provisor General,* March 12, 1869, AHDSC, Correspondencia Parroquial.

92. Rus, "El mito." As late as 1880, the vicar of Yajalón reported that "In this town, the parish center, neither religion nor morality exist: the former, because they do not celebrate a single function in the church; the latter, because not even in their own homes do they say the Holy Rosary.... Without exception, marriages are a civil affair, and to my knowledge there is not a single Catholic school in the entire region": letter from Vicar of Yajalón to Cathedral Chapter, Nov. 22, 1880, AHDSC, Correspondencia Parroquial.

93. Standard works on these events include Vicente Pineda, *Historia de las sublevaciones habidas en el Estado de Chiapas* (San Cristóbal: Tipografía del Gobierno, 1888), and Cristóbal Molina, "War of the Castes: Indian Uprisings in Chiapas, 1867–70" (New Orleans: Tulane University, Middle American Series, pamphlet 8, pub. 5, 1937). According to Rus, however, such accounts were written by conservative leaders, who were under considerable pressure to justify their own improvident (and in some cases, blatantly illegal) actions.

94. Rus, "El mito."

95. In the years following 1848, this pretext was often invoked to justify various kinds of policy against native people. In 1881, for example, *ladinos* in Yajalón who wished to move to Tabasco asked the parish priest for permission to remove the town's image of Guadalupe—"persuaded," as they wrote, "of the immense danger which surrounds us involving a great and horrible caste war." Their request was forwarded to the vicar general, who responded with scorn that "this matter merely shows the duplicity of such *ladinos* against the Indians, who at present have not even thought of an uprising, as even I am aware": "Varios vecinos de Yajalón piden se les conceda llevar a Teapa la imagen de Nuestra Señora de Guadalupe, donde intentan irse a radicar, por temor de la sublevación de indígenas," AHDSC.

96. "Queja del ayuntamiento de Zinacantan contra su cura" (1870), AHDSC.

97. Letter from Patricio Correa to *Provisor General*, Nov. 11, 1848.

98. Mariano Jacinto López, "Informe trimestre de Zinacantan," Oct. 1, 1856. Similar complaints were registered in Huistán and Tenejapa, among other communities: letters from Manuel José López to *Provisor General*, Sept. 30 and Dec. 31, 1856, AHDSC, Correspondencia Parroquial.

99. Between 1871 and 1880, the bishop and his assistants drafted a series of *circulares* and orders in which these measures were formulated and put into practice. Among the most important of these documents are the "Circular sobre institución de Vicarías Provinciales," Dec. 15, 1871; "Pastoral," Feb. 21, 1871, and "Circular," July 3, 1872 (San Cristóbal: Tipografía del Porvenir, 1872), all in AHDSC. Reactions to such orders by parish priests are also recorded in the AHDSC.

100. Interview with Mariano Hernández Nuj, Zinacantan, July 1, 1974.

101. It was during this period, for example, that *ladino* merchants moved back into towns like Chenalhó and San Andrés (abandoned after the 1869 disorders) and reestablished their claims to Indian land: interview with Celso Villafuerte, Chenalhó, Nov. 6, 1975; "Lista de las personas que poseen bienes y causan los santos diezmos, según el Art. 5 de la Superior Circular expedida con fecha 8 de mayo de 1885, Tenejapa, Cancuc, Guaquitepec," AHDSC.

102. Interview with Chavel Martínez, San Cristóbal, Jan. 21, 1976.

103. Chester Lloyd Jones, *Mexico and Its Reconstruction* (New York: Appleton, 1922), pp. 119–120.

104. Gobierno del Estado de Chiapas, *Anuario estadístico,* p. 52.

105. Byam, *A Sketch,* p. 69.

106. "A Sensationalist Writes on Rubber," *India Rubber World,* March 1, 1910, p. 217. See also Herman Witaker, "Barbarous Mexico: The Rubber Slavery of the Mexican Tropics," *American Magazine* 69, no. 4 (1910): 546–554, and "Three Months in Peonage," ibid., no. 5: 633–638.

107. Jones, p. 121.

108. Byam, p. 24.

109. Ibid. Early in the 19th century, state authorities had assumed control of the *escuelas de primeras letras* in Indian towns, through which they hoped to provide native people with instruction in the duties of citizenship. Predictably, these efforts reached a peak in 1857 during the administration of Governor Angel Albino Corzo, who established the first normal school in San Cristóbal to train native teachers. According to Corzo's plan, the school was to open with 39 students elected by their *ayuntamientos* or *agentes municipales* and supported with communal funds. The curriculum consisted of arithmetic, reading, writing, and ethics. After one year of instruction, pupils were expected to return to their towns, where they would take charge of a reorganized system of primary education. And to insure that such plans were not sabotaged by local authorities or worried parents, penalties were provided for Indians who refused to cooperate or carry out their assigned roles: Gobierno del Estado de Chiapas, "Memoria presentada al Honorable Congreso Constituyente, Constitucional del Estado Libre y Soberano de Chiapas" (San Cristóbal: Imprenta del Gobierno, 1857).

110. David J. McCreery, "Coffee and Class: The Structure of Development in Liberal Guatemala," *Hispanic American Historical Review* 56, no. 3 (1976): 438–460.

111. In fact, native attitudes toward Liberals and Conservatives (including priests) bear a striking resemblance to those which T. G. Powell describes among Indians elsewhere in Mexico. For a more detailed discussion, see her excellent article, "Priests and Peasants in Central Mexico: Social Conflict during 'La Reforma,'" *Hispanic American Historical Review* 57, no. 2 (1977): 296–313.

## NOTES TO CHAPTER 6

1. For a general description of the revolution in Chiapas, see José Casahonda Castillo, *50 años de revolución en Chiapas* (Tuxtla Gutiérrez: Instituto de Ciencias y Artes de Chiapas, 1974); Antonio García de León, "Lucha de clases y poder político en Chiapas," *Historia y Sociedad* 22 (1979): 57–88; Prudencio Moscoso Pastrana, *El pinedismo en Chiapas* (Mexico: published by author, 1960). Alicia Hernández Chavez, in "La defensa de los finqueros en Chiapas, 1914–1920," *Historia Mexicana* 28, no. 3 (1979): 335–369, claims that Castro's superior, Venustiano Carranza, was particularly anxious to prevent the southeastern states (which shared a long and unpatrolled border with Central America) from becoming a haven for reactionaries. Not only had Félix Díaz chosen this region as his theater of operations, but Carranza also doubted the loyalty of federal troops there. One of Castro's first acts, then, was to discharge these troops and occupy their garrisons. Whether they had in fact planned to rebel against *constitucionalista* rule remains a subject of speculation; in any case, several discharged officers subsequently found their way into the anti-government forces which soon began to operate there.

2. Francisco Orozco y Jiménez, "Edicto diocesano," Dec. 29, 1903, and "Nombramiento de colector de los santos diezmos," Nov. 12, 1903, AHDSC.

3. Manuel Pineda, *Estudio sobre ejidos* (San Cristóbal: Tipografía Juana de Arcos, 1910).

4. Prudencio Moscoso Pastrana, *Jacinto Pérez "Pajarito," último líder Chamula* (Tuxtla Gutiérrez: Gobierno del Estado de Chiapas, 1972), pp. 37–38. More details concerning Orozco's involvement in the tragic events which followed are in his letter to the President of the Republic, Francisco L. de la Barra, Oct. 1, 1911, "Un viejo liberal," and "El señor obispo Don Francisco Orozco y Jiménez y la rebelión habida en Chiapas: Una carta pastoral que no hace honra al prelado," January 1912, AHDSC.

5. García de León, p. 66. It is possible that these events were precipitated in part by the presence of ex-*zapatistas* who formed their own agrarian colonies in the area: Gen. Rafael Cal y Mayor, "Establecimiento de colonias militares en Chiapas" (Mexico City (pamphlet), 1920).

6. Casahonda, p. 22.

7. García de León, pp. 66–68.

8. Interview with Celso Villafuerte, San Pedro Chenalhó, Nov. 6, 1975, in Robert Wasserstrom, *Ingreso y trabajo rural en los altos de Chiapas* (final report of project "Minifundismo y trabajo asalariado; estudio de caso II: San Juan Chamula, 1975–1977," San Cristóbal: Centro de Investigaciones Ecológicas del Sureste, 1980).

9. Casahonda, pp. 52–55; also see Luis Espinosa's own account of these events, *Rastros de sangre* (Mexico City: Editorial Indoamericana, 1944).

10. García de León, pp. 66–68.

11. Casahonda, pp. 43–47.

12. Ibid., p. 49.

13. Moisés T. de la Peña, *Chiapas económico,* vol. 2, p. 350.

14. García de León, pp. 69–70. For a general discussion of labor during the revolutionary period, see Ramón Eduardo Rúiz, *La revolución mexicana y el movimiento obrero, 1911–1923* (Mexico City: Editorial Era, 1978).

15. García de León, p. 70.

16. De la Peña, vol. 2, p. 375.

17. Ibid., pp. 375–379.

18. García de León, pp. 71–72; Casahonda, pp. 73–75. The best account of political events in Mexico during these years is Arnaldo Córdova's masterful work *La ideología de la revolución mexicana: la formación del nuevo régimen* (Mexico City: Editorial Era, 1973); see also his *La formación del poder político en México* (Mexico City: Editorial Era, 1972).

19. García de León, pp. 72–73.

20. Casahonda, p. 74.

21. García de León, pp. 74–75.

22. Casahonda, pp. 112–116.

23. Interviews in San Cristóbal with Francisco Liévano, Oct. 28, 1975, and Carlota viuda de Urbina, Sept. 9, 1975.

24. Interview with Francisco Porras, San Cristóbal, Oct. 24, 1975.

25. Interview with Carlota viuda de Urbina.

26. Interview with Francisco Liévano.

27. There is a more extensive description of these events, and of

Indian policy in general, in Jan Rus, "Managing Mexico's Indians: The Historical Context and Consequences of *Indigenismo*" (unpublished ms., Harvard University, 1976).

28. Interview with Celso Villafuerte.

29. Interview with Francisco Liévano.

30. Leo Waibel, *La Sierra Madre de Chiapas* (Mexico City: Sociedad Mexicana de Geografía y Estadística, 1946); Carlos Helbig, *El Soconusco y su zona cafetalera* and *La cuenca superior de Río Grijalva* (both Tuxtla Gutiérrez: Instituto de Ciencias y Artes de Chiapas, 1964).

31. Waibel, passim; Helbig, *El Soconusco*, passim.

32. Interviews with *administrador* of Finca Monte Perla, March 12, 1976; Erwin Velázquez, *subgerente*, Banco de Crédito Rural del Istmo, Huixtla, Feb. 18, 1976; Manuel Martínez, *jefe de operaciones*, Zone A, Banco de Crédito Rural del Istmo, Tapachula, Feb. 17, 1976; *administrador* of Finca Hamburgo, Feb. 17, 1976.

33. "Resolución y antecedentes del problema agrario en la zona del Soconusco, Chiapas" (Tuxtla Gutiérrez: Liga de Comunidades Agrarias y Sindicatos Campesinos de Chiapas, 1942).

34. Interview with Isais García and Plácido Alfaro, Ejido Mixcum, Soconusco, March 12, 1976; interview with *administrador* of Finca Monte Perla.

35. Waibel, passim; interviews with Manuel Martínez and Erwin Velázquez.

36. Ricardo Pozas, *Chamula, un pueblo indio de los altos de Chiapas*, vol. 8, pp. 114–118.

37. Much of the following discussion was presented in Jan Rus and Robert Wasserstrom, "Civil-Religious Hierarchies in Central Chiapas: A Critical Perspective," and "Evangelization and Political Control: The SIL in Mexico," in Søren Hvalkof and Peter Aaby, eds., *Is God an American?* (London: Survival International, 1981).

38. "Resolución y antecedentes."

39. Interviews with Francisco Liévano and Carlota viuda de Urbina.

40. "Testimonio de la escritura de compra venta de parte de la finca rústica San Francisco de Paula, otorgada por el apoderado de don Pablo Reincke en favor de 99 personas representadas por su apoderado Salvador López Castellanos" (1941), Municipio de Chamula archives.

41. Pozas, pp. 114–118; Matthew Edel, "El ejido en Zinacantan," in

E. Z. Vogt, ed., *Los Zinacantecos* (Mexico City: Instituto Nacional Indigenista, 1966), pp. 163-177.

42. De la Peña, p. 353.

43. Ibid., p. 380.

44. For an excellent discussion of Cárdenas and his administration, see Arnaldo Córdova, *La política de masas del Cardenismo* (Mexico City: Editorial Era, 1974) and *La formación del poder político en Mexico.*

45. Interview with Carlota viuda de Urbina, Sept. 10, 1975.

46. Interview with Celso Villafuerte.

47. "Breve memoria de su actuación durante el período comprendido entre el 15 de junio de 1942 y el 15 de junio de 1943" (Mexico: La Junta de Administración y Vigilancia de la Propiedad Extranjera, 1943).

48. Interview with president of the Unión de Asociaciones de Cafeticultores, Tapachula, February 1976.

49. Edel, p. 165. Much of the description which follows will seem familiar to students of the agrarian movement in Mexico. Without providing detailed references to similar events elsewhere in the country, I would recommend such excellent works as John Womack's classic study *Zapata and the Mexican Revolution* (New York: Knopf, 1969); Arturo Warman's *Y venimos a contradecir* (Mexico City: Ediciones de la Casa Chata, 1976); and David Ronfeldt's *Atencingo* (Stanford, Calif.: Stanford University Press, 1973).

50. Edel, pp. 168-171.

51. Interviews in Zinacantan with Mariano López Chiku, Sept. 20, 1973; José Pérez Nuj, June 25, 1974; Lorenzo Sánchez Velio, Sept. 13, 1973; Antonio Hernández González, Sept. 25, 1973.

52. Much of the information which follows was obtained during an extensive series of interviews with Chavel Martínez in San Cristóbal, Jan. 21-25, 1976. Don Chavel is a *mestizo* who was born in Zinacantan around 1903 and lived there until the 1950s.

53. Interviews in Zinacantan with Juan Vázquez Xuljol, July 1972, and Pedro Vázquez Xuljol, July 25-27, 1972.

54. Interviews with Chavel Martínez.

55. Ibid.

56. Edel, p. 176.

57. Rus and Wasserstrom, "Civil-Religious Hierarchies," p. 474.

58. Edel, p. 177.

59. Interview with Mariano Hernández Nuj, Zinacantan, Aug. 10, 1974.

60. Interview with Manuel Hernández Tijilnuk, Zinacantan, Sept. 15, 1973.

61. This information was obtained in an extensive series of interviews with José Pérez Nuj, Zinacantan, July 7–12, 1974.

62. Edel, p. 176.

63. Interviews with José Pérez Nuj.

64. The following information was taken from Rus and Wasserstrom, "Civil-Religious Hierarchies," pp. 473–475; a more detailed account of sources is given in the notes to that article.

65. The argument that waiting lists represented an effort to keep up with growing population was first advanced by Frank Cancian in *Economics and Prestige in a Maya Community*, p. 183, and repeated by such authors as Victoria Bricker, Gary Gossen, and E. Z. Vogt.

66. For details about Cancuc, see Henning Silverts, "The Cacique of K'ankujk," *Estudios de Cultura Maya* 5 (1965): 339–360. Information on Mitontic from interview with Vicente López Méndez, San Cristóbal, Sept. 29, 1975; on Tenejapa, from material provided by Pablo Ramírez, *secretario general*, Departamento de Asuntos Indígenas del Estado de Chiapas, San Cristóbal, 1976.

67. Sergio Reyes Osorio et al., *Estructura agraria y desarrollo agrícola en México* (Mexico City: Fondo de Cultura Económica, 1974).

68. José Jiménez Paniagua, *Política de inversiones en el Estado de Chiapas* (Mexico City: UNAM, 1963), p. 62.

69. Waibel, *La Sierra Madre*, pp. 146–147. Much of the following discussion was published in preliminary form in my article "Land and Labour in Central Chiapas: A Regional Analysis," *Development and Change* 8, no. 4 (1977): 441–463.

70. For a discussion of this process, see Clark Reynolds, *The Mexican Economy: Twentieth-Century Structure and Growth* (New Haven, Conn.: Yale University Press, 1968).

71. Helbig, *La cuenca superior*, p. 52.

72. Comisión Económica para América Latina, *La industria de la carne de ganado bovino en México* (Mexico City: Fondo de Cultura Económica, 1975), pp. 9–17.

73. De la Peña, p. 372.

74. George Collier, *Fields of the Tzotzil*, pp. 34–37.

75. The following information is based upon extensive interviews with sharecroppers, muledrivers, and peddlers in a number of hamlets: Salinas, Na Chij, Elan Vo', Vo' Ch'o Vo', Paste', Nabenchauk, Apas, Sek'emtik, Pat Osil, Joyjel, and the *municipio* center. As indicated below, it also includes large surveys of production and marketing among farmers from Salinas, Na Chij, and Elan Vo'.

76. Jiménez Paniagua, pp. 104–105.

77. Alvaro de Albornoz, *Trayectoria y ritmo del crédito agrícola en México* (Mexico City: Instituto Mexicano de Investigaciones Económicas, 1966), pp. 236–255.

78. De la Peña, pp. 470–472; Jiménez Paniagua, p. 60.

79. Jiménez Paniagua, p. 62.

80. Jorge Vivó Escoto, *Estudio de geografía económica y demográfica de Chiapas* (Mexico City: Escuela de Economía, UNAM, 1960), pp. 52–55.

81. Frank Cancian, *Change and Uncertainty in a Peasant Economy*, pp. 1–5, 44, 85–88, 99.

82. Ibid., p. 60.

83. Ibid., p. 85.

84. The following discussion is based upon a survey of household income and employment conducted during 1974–75 in 10 separate *parajes* distributed throughout the *municipio*. All local families were interviewed; the total sample (968 households) represents approximately 10% of the *municipio*'s population.

| Hamlet | Families |
|---|---|
| Calvario San Juan | 91 |
| Cruz Ton | 114 |
| Chik'omtantik | 251 |
| K'alch'entik | 19 |
| K'at'ixtik | 148 |
| Lomo' | 60 |
| Milpoleta | 63 |
| Ni' Ch'en | 60 |
| Petej | 138 |
| Yaxalumiljo' | 24 |
| Total | 968 |

$\bar{x} = 96.8$; $s = 66.2$

For the sake of simplicity, K'alch'entik and Yaxalumiljo' are included with the adjacent hamlet of Ni' Ch'en in subsequent tables and figures. An excellent account of highland farming practices in Chamula, Mitontic, and Tenajapa is given by Ronald B. Nigh in his doctoral dissertation, "Evolutionary Ecology of Maya Agriculture in Highland Chiapas, Mexico" (Stanford University, 1976).

85. George Collier, ch. 5.

86. A description of income distribution in Mexico is given in Banco de México, *La distribución del ingreso en México* (Mexico City: Fondo de Cultura Económica, 1974).

## NOTES TO CHAPTER 7

1. See, for example, Annette Kuhn and AnnMarie Wolpe, eds., *Feminism and Materialism* (London: Routledge and Kegan Paul, 1978); Naomi Quinn, "Anthropological Studies on Women's Status," *Annual Review of Anthropology* 6 (1977): 181-225; Susan Carol Rogers, "Woman's Place: A Critical Review of Anthropological Theory," *Comparative Studies in Society and History* 20, no. 1 (1978): 123-162.

2. Victoria R. Bricker and George A. Collier, "Nicknames and Social Structure in Zinacantan," *American Anthropologist* 72, no. 2 (1970): 289-302.

3. George Collier, *Fields of the Tzotzil*, p. 71.

4. Bricker and Collier, p. 291.

5. E. Z. Vogt, *Zinacantan: A Maya Community in the Highlands of Chiapas*, appendix 3.

6. Ibid., pp. 35-70.

7. Victoria Bricker, *Ritual Humor in Highland Chiapas*, pp. 12-67.

8. Ibid., pp. 16-45.

9. Ibid., pp. 219-224; Vogt, *Zinacantan*, passim. Similar arguments have been advanced by Francesca Cancian in *What Are Norms?*

10. Bricker, *Ritual Humor*, p. 15.

11. Ibid., pp. 84-144; see also Gary Gossen, *Chamulas in the World of the Sun: Time and Space in a Maya Oral Tradition*.

12. The following discussion is based upon Victoria Bricker's descriptions in *Ritual Humor*, pp. 13-67.

13. Ibid., pp. 38-39.

14. Ibid., p. 64.

15. Gossen; Ricardo Pozas, *Chamula*.

16. George Collier, *Fields of the Tzotzil*, pp. 121–123.

17. For San Andrés Larraínzar, see William Holland, *Medicina maya en los altos de Chiapas*. Information for Mitontic is from interview with Vicente López Méndez; for Magdalena, from interview with Melchor Méndez Gómez, San Cristóbal, March 4, 1977. For western Guatemala, see my article, "Revolution in Guatemala: Peasants and Politics under the Arbenz Government," *Comparative Studies in Society and History* 17, no. 4 (1975): 443–478; Waldemar R. Smith, *The Fiesta System and Economic Change* (New York: Columbia University Press, 1977).

18. Frank Cancian, *Economics and Prestige in a Maya Community*, p. 135.

19. Ibid., p. 27.

20. Manning Nash, "Political Relations in Guatemala," *Social and Economic Studies* 7 (1958): 65–75.

21. Frank Cancian, *Economics and Prestige*, pp. 107, 135.

22. Vogt, *Zinacantan*, p. 365.

23. Ibid. Part of the material used in this chapter first appeared in *Ethnology* 17, no. 2 (1978): 197–210. Permission to reproduce it here is gratefully acknowledged.

## NOTES TO CHAPTER 8

1. Waldemar R. Smith, *The Fiesta System and Economic Change*, p. 5.

2. Lionel Rothkrug, "Popular Religion and Holy Shrines," in James Obelkevich, ed., *Religion and the People, 800–1700* (Chapel Hill: University of North Carolina Press, 1979), p. 33.

3. Ibid., pp. 39–40.

4. Lionel Rothkrug, "Religious Practices and Collective Perceptions: Hidden Homologies in the Renaissance and Reformation," *Historical Reflections* 7, no. 1 (1980): 15–48.

5. Ronald C. Finucane, *Miracles and Pilgrims* (Totowa, N.J.: Rowman and Littlefield, 1977), p. 38.

6. William A. Christian, Jr., *Local Religion in Sixteenth-Century Spain*, (Princeton, N.J.: Princeton University Press, 1981), p. 14.

7. Ibid., p. 8.

8. Ibid., p. 51.

9. Ibid., p. 182.

10. Robert Ricard, *The Spiritual Conquest of Mexico* (Berkeley and Los Angeles: University of California Press, 1966), pp. 286–288.

11. Victoria R. Bricker, *The Indian Christ, the Indian King* (Austin: University of Texas Press, 1981), p. 57.

12. Ibid., pp. 57–59.

13. See, for example, Sol Tax, ed., *The Heritage of Conquest*; Pedro Carrasco, "The Civil-Religious Hierarchy in Meso-American Communities"; Frank Cancian, "Political and Religious Organization," in Robert Wauchope, ed., *Handbook of Middle American Indians*, vol. 6.

14. Billie R. DeWalt, "Changes in the Cargo Systems of Mesoamerica," *Anthropological Quarterly* 48 (1975): 87–105.

15. Manning Nash, *Machine Age Maya* (Chicago: University of Chicago Press, 1958), p. 80.

16. Works containing such material include Richard Adams, ed., *Political Change in Guatemalan Indian Communities* (New Orleans: Middle American Research Institute, Tulane University, pub. 24, 1957); Douglas Brintnall, *Revolt Against the Dead* (New York: Gordon and Breach, 1979); Ruth Bunzel, *Chichicastenango: A Guatemalan Village* (American Ethnological Society Publications, vol. 23, 1948); Benjamin Colby and Pierre L. van den Berghe, *Ixil Country* (Berkeley and Los Angeles: University of California Press, 1969); John Gillin, *San Luis Jilotepeque* (Guatemala City: Seminario de Integración Social, 1958); M. Michael Mendelson, *Escándolos de Maximón* (Guatemala City: Seminario de Integración Social, 1965); Alexander Moore, *Life Cycles in Atchalán* (New York: Teachers College Press, 1973); Maude Oakes, *The Two Crosses of Todos Santos* (New York: Bollingen Foundation, 1951); Ruben Reina, *The Law of the Saints* (New York: Bobbs-Merrill, 1966); Melvin Tumin, *Caste and Class in a Peasant Society* (Princeton, N.J.: Princeton University Press, 1952); Charles Wagley, *The Social and Religious Life of a Guatemalan Village* (Menshasa, Wisc.: American Anthropological Society Memoir no. 71, 1949): Kay B. Warren, *The Symbolism of Subordination* (Austin: University of Texas Press, 1978).

17. Robert M. Carmack, "Spanish–Indian Relations in Highland Guatemala, 1800–1944," in Murdo J. MacLeod and Robert Wasserstrom, eds., *Spaniards and Indians in Southeastern Mesoamerica: Essays on*

the *History of Ethnic Relations* (Lincoln: University of Nebraska Press, 1983), pp. 13–14.

18. Wasserstrom, "Revolution in Guatemala."

19. Judith Friedlander, *Being Indian in Hueyapan* (New York: St. Martin's Press, 1975), p. 71.

20. See Ricardo Pozas and Isabel H. de Pozas, *Los indios en las clases sociales de México* (Mexico City: Siglo XXI, 1971); Gonzalo Aguirre Beltrán, *Regiones de refugio*; Mercedes Olivera, "The Barrios of San Andres Cholula," in Hugo Nutini et al., eds., *Essays on Mexican Kinship* (Pittsburgh, Pa.: University of Pittsburgh Press, 1976), pp. 65–96.

21. Bricker, *The Indian Christ*, p. 180.

22. Arturo Warman, *Ensayos sobre el campesinado en México* (Mexico City: Editorial Nueva Imagen, 1980), p. 142.

# BIBLIOGRAPHY

## A NOTE ON THE SOURCES

Historical research on native communities in Chiapas is both an exciting and a frustrating enterprise. Documentation on some subjects is embarrassingly abundant, while on others it remains notably paltry. Even when such material may be found in a single location, it tends to possess large gaps which make systematic investigation difficult. A case in point involves research on highland demography. Almost all existing baptismal registers have been deposited in the Archivo Histórico Diocesano de San Cristóbal (AHDSC), which is housed at the cathedral in San Cristóbal. Unfortunately, an equal number of these books have been lost over the years, so that it is virtually impossible to study the population of any given community accurately. Such shortcomings might be overcome by extrapolating certain information from tribute lists and other census materials, many of which have been located in the Archivo General de Indias (AGI) in Sevilla, Spain, and the Archivo General del Gobierno de Guatemala (AGGG) (now called the Archivo de América Central) in Guatemala City. Like baptismal registers, however, these documents often present contradictory testimony on questions of population size; and in any case, they are notoriously incomplete for the 16th and 17th centuries. In contrast, the problem of checking these sources against each other has now been at least partially resolved through the offices of Dr. Jan de Vos at the Centro de Investigaciones Ecológicas del Sureste, who has microfilmed the Chiapas collection in AGI and made it available to scholars at the Archivo Histórico del Estado de Chiapas

315

(AHE) in Tuxtla Gutiérrez. Since the 1950s, this archive has also possessed a partial copy of the Serie Chiapas in AGGG. For the first time, then, it is possible to consult virtually all major documentary sources on Chiapas either in Tuxtla or in San Cristóbal.

What do these sources contain? Let me begin with the collections in which I conducted the major part of my own research, AHDSC and AGGG. During the colonial period, these archives served complementary functions: they formed the main repositories of ecclesiastical and civil matters concerning the province, and thus allow us to view many aspects of colonial life from two sharply contrasted perspectives. One colorful example involves the voluminous and sordid affairs of Father José Ordoñez y Aguiar, vicar of Chamula from around 1765 to about 1790. On various occasions throughout his long career, don José abandoned his parish for the safety of Guatemala, where he produced a steady outpouring of petitions, demands and other legal instruments. From the documents in AHDSC, we may assemble a detailed picture of how his antagonists in Chiapas—including the *alcalde mayor,* members of the cathedral chapter, and his own parishioners—responded to these initiatives. Even so, it becomes difficult to understand how this man (who violated virtually every judicial norm regarding clerical conduct and systematically ignored the orders of his own bishop) rose unobstructed in the local hierarchy until he died peacefully in his own bed. The answer to this question may be found not in ecclesiastical sources but rather in civil documents which reveal his extensive relations with colonial authorities.

Perhaps a more significant case involves such matters as land titles, tribute lists, and censuses. With few exceptions, enumerations of this kind are much more plentiful in AGGG than in AHDSC, which in any case contains little of value for the years before 1750. By way of contrast, AHDSC is particularly rich in material about native *cofradías,* social conditions in Indian communities, and ecclesiastical politics. Such information may be supplemented by catechismal manuals and other doctrinal handbooks in the Bibliothèque Nationale (Paris), the Biblioteca Fray Bartolomé de las Casas (San Cristóbal), the Library of Congress, and the Butler Library of Columbia University. For a day-to-day view of life in the highlands during the final years of colonial rule, then, the *correspondencia parroquial* in AHDSC (now classified by town and period) provides a unique source of documentation. Indeed, for much of the 19th century, when civil archives in Chiapas were routinely destroyed, it is virtually the only view we now have.

Despite such limitations, our vision of the years which followed independence may be broadened by consulting two additional sources: AHE and the private collection of don Prudencio Moscoso in San Cristóbal. Thomas Benjamin has recently published a description of AHE (see below), which currently houses most of the state's official publications and decrees. It also contains what he describes as "a scattering of periodicals which reach back into the mid-19th century" and a reasonably good selection of newspapers published since 1880. By far the best collection of newspapers and other documents from this period, however, may be found in Moscoso's personal library, which he generously opens to qualified scholars. The core of this collection was obtained from descendants of Flavio Paniagua, a redoubtable conservative publicist who dominated political life in San Cristóbal in the years around 1875. To this nucleus, Moscoso has added a considerable range of manuscripts from colonial times to the present; of particular significance, it remains an important source of information on the revolutionary period.

For these difficult years, it is possible to consult the Archivo General de la Nación (AGN) and the Archivo de la Defensa Nacional (ADN) in Mexico City. In general, however, information in these archives tends to reflect what politicians in the capital thought and said about Chiapas rather than what actually took place there. By way of contrast, such sources become increasingly valuable in the 1920s and 1930s, when other collections like AHE and AHDSC fall completely silent (documents from this period in AHDSC are generally stamped "To be burned," and undoubtedly escaped some more general holocaust). My own view of these years was formed primarily by recording the personal recollections of active participants in post-revolutionary politics and by reviewing whatever private correspondence they have salvaged. A much more extensive treatment of the years since 1880 is currently being prepared by Jan Rus of Harvard University and will undoubtedly shed considerable light on interethnic relations in the present century. Finally, both Rus and I have occasionally uncovered a number of pamphlets, brochures, and miscellaneous materials on Chiapas during the Porfiriato and thereafter in the New York Public Library, the Bancroft Library at the University of California, Berkeley, and the general libraries at UCLA, Columbia University, Harvard University, and the University of Texas.

## Abbreviations

| | |
|---|---|
| AGI | Archivo General de Indias, Sevilla, Spain |
| AGCh | Archivo General de Chiapas (now AHE), Tuxtla Gutiérrez, Chiapas |
| AGGG | Archivo General del Gobierno de Guatemala (now |

Archivo de América Central), Serie Chiapas, Guatemala City

AHDSC   Archivo Histórico Diocesano de San Cristóbal, Chiapas
AHE   Archivo Histórico del Estado de Chiapas, Tuxtla
Gutiérrez, Chiapas
INAH   Instituto Nacional de Antropología e Historia, Colec-
ción Microfilmada, Serie Chiapas, Mexico City

### References

Adams, Richard, ed. *Political Change in Guatemalan Indian Communities.* Middle American Research Institute, New Orleans: Tulane University, pub. 24, 1957.

Adams, Robert M. "Changing Patterns of Territorial Organization in the
Central Highlands of Chiapas, Mexico." *American Antiquity* 26, no.
3 (1961): 341–360.

Aguirre Beltrán, Gonzalo. *Regiones de refugio.* Mexico City: Instituto
Indigenista Interamericano, 1967.

Ai Camp, Roderic. "La cuestión chiapaneca: revisión de una polémica
territorial." *Historia Mexicana* 23 (1975): 579–606.

Albornoz, Alvaro de. *Trayectoria y ritmo del crédito agrícola en
México.* Mexico City: Instituto Mexicano de Investigaciones Económicas, 1966.

Arias, Jacinto. *El mundo numinoso de los mayas.* Mexico City: SepSetentas, 1975.

Banco de México. *La distribución del ingreso en México.* Mexico City:
Fondo de Cultura Económica, 1974.

Barrera, Josef de la. *Libro de lengua tzotzil. . . .* Washington, D.C.: Library of Congress, 1782.

Barrientos, Fray Luis. "Doctrina cristiana en lengua chiapaneca." In
Alphonse-Lucien Pinart, ed., *Bibliothèque linguistique et d'ethnographie americaines,* vol. 1. Paris: Ernest Leroux, 1875.

Borah, Woodrow. *New Spain's Century of Depression.* Berkeley: University of California Press, 1951.

Brachet de Márquez, Viviane. *La población de los Estados Mexicanos
en el Siglo XIX (1824–1895).* Mexico City: Instituto Nacional de Antropología e Historia, Departamento de Investigaciones Históricas,
Colección Científica, no. 35, 1976.

Bricker, Victoria, R. "Algunas consecuencias religiosas y sociales del
nativismo maya del siglo XIX." *América Indígena* 33 (1973): 327–348.

———."Historical Dramas in Chiapas, Mexico." *Journal of Latin American Lore* 3 (1977): 227–248.

———. *The Indian Christ, the Indian King*. Austin: University of Texas Press, 1981.

———. "Movimientos religiosos indígenas en los altos de Chiapas." *América Indígena* 33 (1973): 17–46.

———. *Ritual Humor in Highland Chiapas*. Austin: University of Texas Press, 1973.

———, and George A. Collier. "Nicknames and Social Structure in Zinacantan." *American Anthropologist* 72, no. 2 (1970): 289–302.

Brintnall, Douglas. *Revolt Against the Dead*. New York: Gordon and Breach, 1979.

Bunzel, Ruth. *Chichicastenango: A Guatemalan Village*. American Ethnological Society Publications, vol. 23. New York, 1948.

Byam, W. W. *A Sketch of the State of Chiapas, Mexico*. Los Angeles: Geo. Rice and Sons, 1897.

Cáceres López, Carlos. *Historia general del Estado de Chiapas*. Tuxtla Gutiérrez: published by author, 1958.

Cal y Mayor, Rafael. "Establecimiento de colonias militares en Chiapas." Mexico City (pamphlet), 1920. (A copy is in the Butler Library of Columbia University.)

Calnek, Edward E. "Highland Chiapas Before the Spanish Conquest." Ph.D. dissertation, University of Chicago, 1962.

Cámara Barbachano, Fernando. *Persistencia y cambio cultural entre los Tzeltales de los altos de Chiapas*. Mexico City: Escuela Nacional de Antropología e Historia, 1966.

Cancian, Francesca. *What Are Norms? A Study of Beliefs and Action in a Maya Community*. Cambridge, Eng.: Cambridge University Press, 1975.

Cancian, Frank. *Change and Uncertainty in a Peasant Economy*. Stanford, Calif.: Stanford University Press, 1973.

———. *Economics and Prestige in a Maya Community*. Stanford, Calif.: Stanford University Press, 1965.

———. "Political and Religious Organization." In Robert Wauchope, ed., *Handbook of Middle American Indians*, vol. 6. Austin: University of Texas Press, 1967.

Cardos de Méndez, A. *El comercio de los mayas antiguos*. Mexico City: Escuela Nacional de Antropología e Historia, 1959.

Carmack, Robert M. "Spanish–Indian Relations in Highland Guatemala, 1800–1944." In Murdo J. MacLeod and Robert Wasserstrom, eds., *Spaniards and Indians in Southeastern Mesoamerica: Essays on the History of Ethnic Relations*. Lincoln: University of Nebraska Press, 1983.

Carrasco, Pedro. "The Civil-Religious Hierarchy in Meso-American Communities: Pre-Spanish Background and Colonial Development." *American Anthropologist* 63, no. 4 (1961): 483–497.

Carrascoa, Manuel. *Apuntes estadísticos del Estado de Chiapas*. Mexico City: Sociedad Mexicana de Geografía y Estadística, 1885.

Casahonda Castillo, José. *50 años de revolución en Chiapas*. Tuxtla Gutiérrez: Instituto de Ciencias y Artes de Chiapas, 1974.

Chacamas Plantation Company. "Inspection Report by Frank R. McKinstry, Gen. Mgr., and Charles M. Roe, Director." Chicago: Chacamas Plantation Co., 1903.

Chamberlain, Robert. *The Governorship of Adelantado Francisco de Montejo in Chiapas, 1539–1544*. Washington, D.C.: Carnegie Institution, pub. 574, contribution 46, 1947.

Chance, John. "On the Mexican Mestizo." *Latin American Research Review* 14, no. 3 (1979): 153–168.

————. *Race and Class in Colonial Oaxaca*. Stanford, Calif.: Stanford University Press, 1978.

Christian, William A., Jr. *Local Religion in Sixteenth-Century Spain*. Princeton, N.J.: Princeton University Press, 1981.

Colby, Benjamin, and Pierre L. van den Berghe. *Ixil Country*. Berkeley and Los Angeles: University of California Press, 1969.

Colina, Carlos María. "Sexta pastoral del Obispo de Chiapas." Guatemala City: Tipografía de la Paz, 1856.

Collier, George A. *Fields of the Tzotzil: The Ecological Bases of Tradition in Highland Chiapas*. Austin: University of Texas Press, 1975.

Collier, Jane. *Law and Social Change in Zinacantan*. Stanford, Calif.: Stanford University Press, 1973.

Comisión Económica para América Latina. *La industria de la carne de ganado bovino en México*. Mexico City: Fondo de Cultura Económica, 1975.

*Constituciones diocesanas del obispado de Chiapa*. Rome, Italy, 1702.

"Contestaciones habidas entre el exmo. Sr. Gobernador del Estado de Chiapa, Don Angel Albino Corzo, y el Illmo. Sr. Obispo de la Propia Diócesis, Dr. D. Carlos María Colina, con el motivo de la venta jurídica y en asta pública que el segundo ha hecho de la hacienda llamada 'Trapiche de la Merced,' perteneciente al Seminario Conciliar de su misma diócesis." Guatemala City: Imprenta de la Paz, 1857.

Cook, Sherburne F., and Woodrow Borah. *Essays in Population History: Mexico and the Caribbean*. 3 vols. Berkeley and Los Angeles: University of California Press, 1971, 1974, and 1979.

————, and————. *The Indian Population of Central Mexico, 1531–1610*.

Berkeley and Los Angeles: University of California Press, 1960.

Cook, Sherburne F., and Lesley Byrd Simpson. *The Population of Central Mexico in the Sixteenth Century*. Berkeley: University of California Press, 1948.

Córdova, Arnaldo. *La formación del poder político en México*. Mexico City: Editorial Era, 1972.

———. *La ideología de la revolución mexicana: la formación del nuevo régimen*. Mexico City: Editorial Era, 1973.

———. *La política de masas del Cardenismo*. Mexico City: Editorial Era, 1974.

de Vos, Jan. *La paz de Dios y del rey: la conquista de la Selva Lacandona*. Tuxtla Gutiérrez: FONAPAS Chiapas, 1980.

DeWalt, Billie R. "Changes in the Cargo Systems of Mesoamerica." *Anthropological Quarterly* 48 (1975): 87–105.

Díaz del Castillo, Bernal. *Historia verdadera de la conquista de la Nueva España*. Mexico City: Porrúa, 1955.

Domínguez, Wenceslao. "Fundaciones." *Boletín de la Cámara Nacional de Comercio, Agricultura e Industria de San Cristóbal Las Casas, Chiapas*, special issue (1926).

Edel, Matthew. "El ejido en Zinacantan." In E.Z. Vogt, ed., *Los Zinacantecos*. Mexico City: Instituto Nacional Indigenista, 1966.

Espinosa, Luis. *Rastros de sangre*. Mexico City: Editorial Indoamericana, 1944.

Fabrega, Horacio, and Daniel Silver. *Illness and Shamanistic Curing in Zinacantan: An Ethnomedical Analysis*. Stanford, Calif.: Stanford University Press, 1973.

Farriss, Nancy. *Crown and Clergy in Colonial Mexico, 1759–1821*. London: Athlone Press, 1968.

Favre, Henri. *Changement et continuité chez les mayas du Mexique*. Paris: Anthropos, 1971.

Finucane, Ronald C. *Miracles and Pilgrims*. Totowa, N.J.: Rowman and Littlefield, 1977.

Flores Ruíz, Eduardo. "Fundación de la parroquia de Comitán." Typescript. San Cristóbal, Chiapas: Biblioteca Fray Bartolomé de Las Casas, 1956.

Fried, Morton. *The Notion of Tribe*. Menlo Park, Calif.: Cummings, 1975.

Friede, Juan. *Bartolomé de Las Casas, precursor del anticolonialismo*. Mexico City: Siglo XXI, 1974.

Friedlander, Judith. *Being Indian in Hueyapan*. New York: St. Martin's Press, 1975.

Gage, Thomas. *The English-American*. Guatemala City: El Patio, 1946.

García de León, Antonio. "Lucha de clases y poder político en Chiapas." *Historia y Sociedad* 22 (1979): 57–88.

García de Vargas y Rivera, Juan Manuel. "Relación de los pueblos que comprehende el obispado de Chiapa." (Madrid: Biblioteca del Palacio, ms. 2840, misc. de Ayala XXCI, 1774).

Gerhard, Peter. *The Southeast Frontier of New Spain*. Princeton, N.J.: Princeton University Press, 1979.

Gibson, Charles. *The Aztecs Under Spanish Rule*. Stanford, Calif.: Stanford University Press, 1964.

Gillin, John. *San Luis Jilotepeque*. Guatemala City: Seminario de Integración Social, 1958.

Gobierno del Estado de Chiapas. *Anuario estadístico del Estado de Chiapas, 1909*. Tuxtla Gutiérrez: Tipografía del Gobierno, 1911.

———. *Censo General*. Tuxtla Gutiérrez: Tipografía del Gobierno, 1910.

———. *Colección de leyes agrarias y demás disposiciones que se han emitido con relación al Ramo de Tierras*. Tuxtla Gutiérrez: Imprenta del Gobierno, 1878.

———. "La contribucion personal." Tuxtla Gutiérrez: Tipografía del Gobierno, Sept. 14, 1892.

———. "De la vagancia." Tuxtla Gutiérrez: Tipografía del Gobierno, June 1, 1880.

———. "Memoria presentada al Honorable Congreso Constituyente, Constitucional del Estado Libre y Soberano de Chiapas." No. 7. San Cristóbal: Imprenta del Gobierno, 1857.

Gosner, Kevin, "Soldiers of the Virgin: An Ethnohistorical Account of the 1712 Rebellion in Highland Chiapas." Ph.D. dissertation, University of Pennsylvania, Philadelphia, 1983.

Gossen, Gary. *Chamulas in the World of the Sun: Time and Space in a Maya Oral Tradition*. Cambridge, Mass.: Harvard University Press, 1974.

Guillén, Flavio. *La federación de Chiapas a México*. Tuxtla Gutiérrez: Gobierno del Estado, 1972.

Haviland, John. *Gossip, Reputation, and Knowledge in Zinacantan*. Chicago: University of Chicago Press, 1977.

Helbig, Carlos. *La cuenca superior del Río Grijalva*. Tuxtla Gutiérrez: Instituto de Ciencias y Artes de Chiapas, 1964.

———. *El Soconusco y su zona cafetalera*. Tuxtla Gutiérrez: Instituto de Ciencias y Artes de Chiapas, 1964.

Hermitte, Ester. *Pinola*. Mexico City: Instituto Indigenista Interamericano, 1973.

Hernández Chávez, Alicia. "La defensa de los finqueros en Chiapas, 1914-1920." *Historia Mexicana* 28, no. 3 (1979): 335-369.

Hidalgo, P. Manuel. "Libro en que se trata de la lengua tzotzil." Bibliothèque Nationale, Paris, Ms. Mexicain 412, R27.747. 1735.

Holland, William. *Medicina maya en los altos de Chiapas: un estudio del cambio socio-cultural.* Mexico City: Instituto Nacional Indigenista, 1963.

Holmes, Calixta Guiteras. *Perils of the Soul: The World View of a Tzotzil Indian.* New York: Free Press, 1961.

Huerta, María Teresa, and Patricia Palacios, comps. *Rebeliones indígenas de la época colonial.* Mexico City: SEP-INAH, 1976.

*The India Rubber World.* New York, various years beginning in 1885.

*The India Rubber World and Gutta-Percha Trades Journal.* London, various years beginning in 1880.

*Informes de los párrocos del Estado al Gobierno del mismo, sobre la situación de los pueblos, dados en cumplimiento de la orden circular de 23 de junio de 1830.* San Cristóbal: Imprenta de la Sociedad dirigida por Secundino Orantes, 1830.

Jiménez Paniagua, José. *Política de inversiones en el Estado de Chiapas.* Mexico City: Universidad Nacional Autónoma de México, 1963.

Jones, Chester Lloyd. *Mexico and Its Reconstruction.* New York: Appleton, 1922.

Junta de Conciliación y Vigiliancia de la Propiedad Extranjera. "Breve memoria de su actuación durante el período comprendido entre el 15 de junio de 1942 y el 15 de junio de 1943." Mexico City, 1943.

Köhler, Ulrich. *Cambio cultural dirigido en los altos de Chiapas.* Mexico City: Instituto Nacional Indigenista, 1975.

Kuhn, Annette, and AnnMarie Wolpe, eds. *Feminism and Materialism.* London: Routledge and Kegan Paul, 1978.

Larrainzar, Manuel. *Noticia histórica de Soconusco y su incorporación a la República Mexicana.* Mexico City: Imprenta de J. M. Lara, 1843.

López Sánchez, Hermilio. *Apuntes históricos de San Cristóbal de Las Casas, Chiapas, México.* 2 vols. Mexico City: published by author, 1960.

McCreery, David J. "Coffee and Class: The Structure of Development in Liberal Guatemala." *Hispanic American Historical Review* 56, no. 3 (1976): 438-460.

MacLeod, Murdo J. *Spanish Central America: A Socioeconomic History, 1520-1720.* Berkeley and Los Angeles: University of California Press, 1973.

McQuown, Norman, and Julian Pitt-Rivers, eds. *Ensayos de antropo-*

logía en la zona central de Chiapas. Mexico City: Instituto Nacional Indigenista, 1970.

McVicker, Donald. "Cambio cultural y ecología en el Chiapas central prehispánico." In Norman McQuown and Julian Pitt-Rivers, eds., Ensayos de antropología en la zona central de Chiapas, pp. 77–104. Mexico City: Instituto Nacional Indigenista, 1970.

Mendelson, M. Michael. Escándalos de Maximón. Guatemala City: Seminario de Integración Social, 1965.

Modiano, Nancy. Indian Education in the Chiapas Highlands. New York: Holt, Rinehart, and Winston, 1973.

Molina, Cristóbal. "War of the Castes: Indian Uprisings in Chiapas, 1867–70." New Orleans: Tulane University, Middle American Series, Pamphlet 8, pub. 5, 1937.

Molina, Virginia. San Bartolomé de los Llanos. Mexico City: SEP-INAH, 1976.

Moore, Alexander. Life Cycles in Atchalán. New York: Teachers College Press, Columbia University, 1973.

Morales, Francisco. Clero y política en México, 1767–1834. Mexico City: SepSetentas, 1975.

Morales Avendaño, Juan M. Rincones de Chiapas: ensayo monográfico sobre San Bartolomé de los Llanos. Tuxtla Gutiérrez: published by author, 1974.

Moscoso Pastrana, Prudencio. Jacinto Perez "Pajarito," último líder Chamula. Tuxtla Gutiérrez: Gobierno del Estado de Chiapas, 1972.

———. El Pinedismo en Chiapas. Mexico City: published by author, 1960.

Nash, June. In the Eyes of the Ancestors. New Haven, Conn.: Yale University Press, 1970.

Nash, Manning. Machine Age Maya. Chicago: University of Chicago Press, 1958.

———. "Political Relations in Guatemala." Social and Economic Studies 7 (1958): 65–75.

Navarrete, Carlos. The Chiapanec History and Culture. Provo, Utah: New World Archaeological Foundation, no. 21, pub. 16, 1966.

Nigh, Ronald B. "Evolutionary Ecology of Maya Agriculture in Highland Chiapas, Mexico." Ph.D. dissertation, Stanford University, Stanford, Calif., 1976.

El Noticioso Chiapaneco. San Cristóbal, 1848.

Oakes, Maude. The Two Crosses of Todos Santos. New York: Bollingen Foundation, 1951.

Oficina de Informaciones de Chiapas. Chiapas, su estado actual, su riqueza, sus ventajas para los negocios. Mexico City: Imprenta de la Escuela Correccional, 1895.

Olivera, Mercedes. "The Barrios of San Andres Cholula." In Hugo Nutini et al., eds., *Essays on Mexican Kinship*, pp. 65–96. Pittsburgh, Pa.: University of Pittsburgh Press, 1976.

Orozco y Jiménez, Francisco. *Collección de documentos inéditos relativos a la Iglesia de Chiapas*. 2 vols. San Cristóbal: Imprenta de la Sociedad Católica, 1905 and 1911.

Paniagua, Flavio Antonio. *Catecismo elemental de historia y estadística de Chiapas*. San Cristóbal: Tipografía del Porvenir, 1876.

———. *Documentos y datos para un diccionario etimológico, histórico y geográfico de Chiapas*, vol. 3. San Cristóbal: Tipografía de Manuel Bermúdez R., 1911.

Peña, Moisés T. de la. *Chiapas económico*. 2 vols. Tuxtla Gutiérrez: Departamento de Prensa y Turismo del Estado, 1952.

Phelan, John L. *The Millenial Kingdom of the Franciscans in the New World*. Berkeley and Los Angeles: University of California Press, 1956.

Pineda, E. "Descripción geográfica del Departamento de Chiapas y Soconusco." *Boletín de la Sociedad Mexicana de Geografía y Estadística* 3, primera época. Mexico City, 1852.

Pineda, Juan de. "Descripción de la provincia de Guatemala, año 1594." In *Relaciones histórico-geográficas de America Central*, vol. 3. Colección de Libros y Documentos Referentes a la Historia de América, Madrid, Spain, 1908.

Pineda, Manuel. *Estudio sobre ejidos*. San Cristóbal: Tipografía Juana de Arcos, 1910.

Pineda, Vicente. *Historia de las sublevaciones habidas en el Estado de Chiapas*. San Cristóbal: Tipografía del Gobierno, 1888.

Podas, Fray Juan. "Arte de la lengua tzotzlem o tzinacanteca." Bibliothèque Nationale, Paris, Collectione Americana Domini Brasseur de Bourbourg, série E3, no. 67, ms. mexicain 411, R27.746. 1688.

Powell, T. G. "Priests and Peasants in Central Mexico: Social Conflict during 'La Reforma.'" *Hispanic American Historical Review* 57, no. 2 (1977): 296–313.

Pozas, Ricardo. *Chamula, un pueblo indio de los altos de Chiapas*. Mexico City: Instituto Nacional Indigenista, 1959.

———, and Isabel H. de Pozas. *Los indios en las clases sociales de México*. Mexico City, Siglo XXI, 1971.

Quinn, Naomi. "Anthropological Studies on Women's Status." *Annual Review of Anthropology* 6 (1977): 181–225.

Redfield, Robert. "Culture Changes in Yucatan." *American Anthropologist* 36 (1934): 69.

Reed, Nelson. *The Caste War of Yucatan.* Stanford, Calif.: Stanford University Press, 1964.

Reina, Ruben. *The Law of the Saints.* New York: Bobbs-Merrill, 1966.

Remesal, Antonio de. *Historia general de las Indias Occidentales, y particular de la gobernación de Chiapa y Guatemala.* 2 vols. Guatemala City: Biblioteca "Goathemala" de la Sociedad de Geografía e Historia, 1932.

"Resolución y antecedentes del problema agrario en la zona del Soconusco, Chiapas." Tuxtla Gutiérrez: Liga de Comunidades Agrarias y Sindicatos Campesinos de Chiapas, 1942.

Reyes Osorio, Sergio, et al. *Estructura agraria y desarrollo agrícola en México.* Mexico City: Fondo de Cultura Económica, 1974.

Reynolds, Clark. *The Mexican Economy: Twentieth-Century Structure and Growth.* New Haven, Conn.: Yale University Press, 1968.

Ricard, Robert. *La "Conquête Spirituelle" du Mexique.* Travaux et Memoires de l'Institut d'Ethnologie. Paris: Université de Paris, 1933.

———. *The Spiritual Conquest of Mexico.* Berkeley and Los Angeles: University of California Press, 1966.

Rogers, Susan Carol. "Woman's Place: A Critical Review of Anthropological Theory." *Comparative Studies in Society and History* 20, no. 1 (1978): 123–162.

Ronfeldt, David. *Atencingo.* Stanford, Calif.: Stanford University Press, 1973.

Rothkrug, Lionel. "Popular Religion and Holy Shrines." In James Obelkevich, ed., *Religion and the People, 800–1700,* Chapel Hill: University of North Carolina Press, 1979.

———. "Religious Practices and Collective Perceptions: Hidden Homologies in the Renaissance and Reformation." *Historical Reflections* 7, no. l (1980): 15–48.

Ruiz, Ramón Eduardo. *La revolución mexicana y el movimiento obrero, 1911–1923.* Mexico City: Editorial Era, 1978.

Rus, Jan. "Great San Juan, Great Patron: Social History of a Maya Community, 1800–1976." Ph.D. dissertation, Harvard University, 1983.

———. "Managing Mexico's Indians: The Historical Context and Consequences of *Indigenismo.*" Unpublished ms., Harvard University, 1976.

———, and Robert Wasserstrom. "Civil-Religious Hierarchies in Central Chiapas: A Critical Perspective." *American Ethnologist* 7, no. 3 (1980): 466–478.

——and——. "Evangelization and Political Control: The SIL in Mexico." In Søren Hvalkof and Peter Aaby, eds., *Is God an American?*, pp. 163–172. London: Survival International and the International Work Group for Indigenous Affairs, 1981.

——and——. *Los indios de Chiapas: historia y antropología.* Mexico City: Editorial Nueva Imagen, forthcoming.

Santibáñez, Enrique. *Geografía regional de Chiapas.* Tuxtla Gutiérrez: Gobierno del Estado, 1907.

Secretaría de Agricultura y Ganadería. *Censo agrícola, ganadero y ejidal.* Mexico City, 1920–1970.

——, Subsecretaría de la Forestal. "Memoria económico-justificativa sobre la Selva Lacandona." Unpublished document, Mexico City, 1975.

Secretaría de Comercio e Industria. *Censo general de habitantes.* Mexico City, 1924.

Sherman, William L. *Forced Native Labor in Sixteenth-Century Central America.* Lincoln: University of Nebraska Press, 1979.

Silverts, Henning. "The Cacique of K'ankujk." *Estudios de Cultura Maya* 5 (1965): 339–360.

——. *Oxchuc: una tribu maya de México.* Mexico City: Instituto Indigenista Interamericano, 1969.

Smith, Waldemar R. *The Fiesta System and Economic Change.* New York: Columbia University Press, 1977.

Sociedad Económica de Ciudad Real. "Informe . . . sobre las ventajas y desventajas obtenidas con el implantamiento del sistema de intendencias." AGCh, *Boletín* 6 (1956): 27–54.

Stavenhagen, Rodolfo. *Las clases sociales en las sociedades agrarias.* Mexico City: Siglo XXI, 1969.

Stephens, John L. *Incidents of Travel in Central America, Chiapas, and Yucatan.* New York: Dover, 1969. (Originally published 1841).

Tax, Sol. "The Municipios of the Midwestern Highlands of Guatemala." *American Anthropologist* 39 (1937): 423–444.

——. "World View and Social Relations in Guatemala." *American Anthropologist* 43 (1941): 27–42.

——, ed. *The Heritage of Conquest: The Ethnology of Middle America.* Glencoe, Ill.: Free Press, 1952.

Taylor, William B. *Landlord and Peasant in Colonial Oaxaca.* Stanford, Calif.: Stanford University Press, 1972.

Thompson, J. Eric S. *Maya History and Religion.* Norman: University of Oklahoma Press, 1970.

——, ed. *Thomas Gage's Travels in the New World.* Norman: University of Oklahoma Press, 1958.

Trens, Manuel B. *Historia de Chiapas*. Mexico City: Talleres Gráficos de la Nación, 1957.

Tumin, Melvin. *Caste and Class in a Peasant Society*. Princeton, N.J.: Princeton University Press, 1952.

Tutino, John. "Indian Rebellion at the Isthmus of Tehuantepec: A Socio-Historical Perspective." XLII International Congress of Americanists, Paris, 1977.

Ubilla, Fray Andrés de. "Memoria de los pueblos y beneficios que hay en el obispado de Chiapa, 1592 (?)." A copy of this manuscript is in the Biblioteca Fray Bartolomé de Las Casas, San Cristóbal, Chiapas.

United States Department of Commerce. *Rubber Statistics, 1910–1937*. Washington, D.C.: Government Printing Office, 1938.

Van Ginneken, Wouter. *Socio-Economic Groups and Income Distribution in Mexico*. New York: St. Martin's Press, 1980.

Vivó Escoto, Jorge. *Estudio de geografía económica y demográfica de Chiapas*. Mexico City: Escuela de Economía, Universidad Nacional Autónoma de México, 1960.

Vogt, E. Z. *Tortillas for the Gods: A Symbolic Analysis of Zinacanteco Ritual*. Cambridge, Mass.: Harvard University Press, 1976.

———. *Zinacantan: A Maya Community in the Highlands of Chiapas*. Cambridge, Mass.: Harvard University Press, 1969.

———, ed. *Los Zinacantecos*. Mexico City: Instituto Nacional Indigenista, 1966.

*La Voz del Pueblo*. San Cristóbal, 1855–1858.

Wagley, Charles. *The Social and Religious Life of a Guatemalan Village*. American Anthropological Society Memoir no. 71. Menshasa, Wisc., 1949.

Waibel, Leo. *La Sierra Madre de Chiapas*. Mexico City: Sociedad Mexicana de Geografía y Estadística, 1946.

Warman, Arturo. *Ensayos sobre el campesinado en México*. Mexico City: Editorial Nueva Imagen, 1980.

———. *Y venimos a contradecir*. Mexico City: Ediciones de la Casa Chata, 1976.

Warren, Kay B. *The Symbolism of Subordination*. Austin: University of Texas Press, 1978.

Wasserstrom, Robert. "A Caste War That Never Was: The Tzeltal Conspiracy of 1848." *Peasant Studies* 7, no. 2 (1978): 73–85.

———. "The Exchange of Saints in Zinacantan: The Socioeconomic Bases of Religious Change in Southeastern Mexico." *Ethnology* 17 (1978): 197–210.

———. *Ingreso y trabajo rural en los altos de Chiapas.* Final report of project "Minifundismo y Trabajo Asalariado; Estudio de Caso II: San Juan Chamula, 1975–1977." San Cristóbal: Centro de Investigaciones Ecológicas del Sureste, 1980.

———. "La investigación regional en ciencias sociales." *Historia y Sociedad,* ser. 2, no. 9 (1976): 58–73.

———. "Land and Labour in Central Chiapas: A Regional Analysis." *Development and Change* 8, no. 4 (1977): 441–463.

———. "Our Lady of the Salt." B.A. Honors Thesis, Harvard University, 1970.

———. "Population Growth and Economic Development in Chiapas, 1524–1975." *Human Ecology* 6, no. 2 (1978): 127–143.

———. "Revolution in Guatemala: Peasants and Politics under the Arbenz Government." *Comparative Studies in Society and History* 17, no. 4 (1975): 443–478.

Wauchope, Robert, ed. *Handbook of Middle American Indians.* Austin: University of Texas Press, 1964–1969.

Witaker, Herman. "Barbarous Mexico: The Rubber Slavery of the Mexican Tropics." *American Magazine* 69 (1910): 546–554.

———. "Three Months in Peonage." *American Magazine* 69, no. 4 (1910): 633–638.

Wolf, Eric. "Closed Corporate Peasant Communities in Mesoamerica and Central Java." *Southwestern Journal of Anthropology* 13 (1957): 1–18.

Womack, John. *Zapata and the Mexican Revolution.* New York: Knopf, 1969.

Ximénez, Francisco. *Historia de la provincia de San Vicente de Chiapa y Guatemala de la Orden de Predicadores.* 3 vols. Guatemala City: Biblioteca "Goathemala" de la Sociedad de Geografía e Historia, 1929–1931. (Originally published about 1720.)

# INDEX

Abasalo, 73, 296 n.37, 310 n.87

Acala: cofradías in, 29; curato, 52map; 65map; denuncias in, 122–23; laboríos and tenant farmers in, 94–95, 110, 135, 189, 190; land tenure, 169; population, 121map; visitas and limosnas, 57

Acción Católica, 248

Acculturation, discussed, 248–51

Act of Canguí, 158

Agrarian legislation, 108, 110, 115, 118–19, 123–24, 125–26, 132, 139, 141, 159–60

Agrarian reform, 159–67, 170–74

Agrarismo, 161, 165–66, 171, 174, 250

Agriculture, precolonial, 7

—, pre-20th century: clergy's involvement in, 26–27; early colonial period, 13, 26–27; in 16th and 17th century, 35, 37–39; 19th century, 110–27, 117; and repartimiento system, 35; and social change, 116–27

—, 20th century: in Chamula, 200–20, 205, 213; changing production patterns, 179–82, 217–18, 238–39; commercial, expansion of, 186–200; government subsidies of, 187; income distribution from, 213fig.; investments in, 186; labor used by tenant farmers, 187–88, 192–96, 208–09; mechanization of, 186; in Zinacantan, 186–200, 217–18, 238–39

—: See also Baldiaje and baldíos; Coffee, labor and laborers; Labor; Tenant farmers and farming

Aguacatenango: Indian cofradías in, 29, 88; denuncias in, 122; female-headed households, 97; native tributaries, 73; and 1712 rebellion, 84

Aguardiente. See Liquor

Aguirre Beltrán, Gonzalo, anthropologist, 212, 228–29

Albino Corzo, Angel, governor of

Albino Corzo (cont.)
  Chiapas, 303 n.109
Alcaldes mayores: and repartimientos and regional trade,
  44–47, 54, 66, 68; replaced by
  intendentes, 64
Alcaldía mayor: office abolished,
  103; office purchased, 33, 44–
  45
Alféreces. See Mayordomos and
  alféreces
Alguaciles, 21
Almacenes Nacionales de Depósito, 187, 197, 198
Alvarez de Toledo, Juan Bautista,
  bishop, 36, 52, 76, 79–81
Amatán, 134
Amatenango: cofradías in, 29, 88–
  89; denuncias in, 122; ejido
  petitions, 123–24; female-
  headed households, 97; Indian lands appropriated, 129;
  ladinos in, 104–05; mayordomos flee, 89; native tributaries, 73; and 1712 rebellion, 84
Amazon basin, 113
Amber, production and trade, 9
ANDSA. See Almacenes Nacionales de Depósito
Anexos. See Curatos
Annexation of Chiapas, 107
Anthropology in Chiapas, 1–6, 216,
  239–41, 244–51
Apas (Zinacantan): anthropological research on, 216; civil religious activities, 233–34; families with ejidos, 171;
  female-headed households,
  138; food production in, 182;
  population, 96; tenant farmers
  from, 187–88; mentioned, 136,
  138, 238, 309 n.75

Apellidos. See Surnames, Spanish
  and Tzotzil
Arias, Cristóbal, Zinacantan landowner, 90
Arizpe Amador and Company,
  lumbering concessionaire,
  293–94 n.22
Arrendatarios. See Tenant farmers and farming
Arriaga, 199
Artisans, unionization of, 158
Atonal, Juan, alcalde of Chiapa,
  25–26, 69
Auctions: of public office, 45, 283
  n.92; of products collected as
  tribute, 44
Audiencias, colonial courts, 14, 51
Ayuntamientos, town councils: of
  Ciudad Real, 19, 45, 63; in native towns, 290–91 n.3; stop
  collecting taxes, 103; in Zinacantan, 173; mentioned, 108

Bachajón, 52map, 53map, 72, 73,
  89–90
Baldiaje and baldíos, 104, 119, 125,
  182, 217
Barrientos, Pedro de, priest, 23, 26
Beans, 43, 113, 117; precolonial
  production of, 7; produced by
  Elan Vo' farmers, 193–94; for
  tribute and repartimientos,
  44, 47–48, 91
Beef trade, 46. See also Cattle
Belisario Domínguez, Colonia
  Agraria, 167
Belize, 111–12
Bilingualism, politics and, 165,
  173, 175–76
Blacks: in Guatemalan cofradias,
  273 n.44; slaves, 17, 33
Blanes, Tomás, bishop, 33

Bochil, 91, 119, 146
Bravo de la Serna Manrique, Marcos, bishop, 51, 69, 74–75, 77–78
Bread trade, 136. See also Wheat
Bricker, Victoria, anthropologist, 5, 216, 218, 222–24, 238, 244–45, 249–50
Brigada Las Casas, 158–59
Brindis, Samuel León, governor of Chiapas, 162
Burial, Church fees for, 100
Byam, W. W., writer, 152–53

Cabbage, 203–04. See also Horticulture
Cabildos, 19, 31, 83; ethnic composition of, 173
Cacao: commercial production of, 112–15, 117; in precolonial period, 7, 9, 11; plantations, 39, 42; and tribute and repartimientos, 13, 35, 36, 47–48, 63–64, 103; trade, 12, 32, 33, 35, 44, 46, 60, 130, 135
Caciques, native rulers, 12, 17, 19, 31
Cajas de comunidad, community chests, 43, 60, 62, 68
Calles, Plutarco Elías, interior minister, 161
Calvario San Juan (Chamula): income distribution, 210, 211; maize production, 201, 202, 208; occupations of residents, 203; socioeconomic stratification, 211–12; tenant farming and horticulture in, 206, 207; mentioned, 309–10 n.84
Calvo, Pedro, priest, 15–30
Camino Real, 93
Cancian, Francesca, sociologist, 5

Cancian, Frank, anthropologist, 4, 187, 189, 194–95, 228–30, 232, 239, 251
Cancuc (Chamula): curato and anexo, 53map, 65map, 66map; female-headed households, 97–98; Indian lands entitled, 296 n.37; native tributaries, 73; politics in, 178; and 1712 rebellion, 78, 80–82, 84; visitas and limosnas, 57; mentioned, 146
Cantel (Guatemala), 246–48
Caporales, hacienda foremen, 204–05
Capitación. See Taxes and taxation
Cárdenas, Lázaro, president of Mexico, 162, 164, 167
Cardenistas, 176, 178
Cargos. See Civil-religious system
Carrillo, Felipe, political organizer, 160
Carmack, Robert, historian, 248
Carmen, el, Zinacantan ranch, 139
Carrancistas, 157–58
Carranza, Venustiano, president of Mexico, 158, 304 n.1
Casillas, Tomas, bishop, 12
Caste wars, 150. See also Rebellions: Indian
Castes, 1–2, 108
Castro, Jesús Agustín, general, 156, 157–58, 173, 175, 178
Catholic Action, 248
Catholic Church. See Church
Cattle: in early colonial period, 13, 26–27; 1590–1821, 32, 37–39, 43, 46, 64, 90; post-Independence, 108, 112, 125, 158, 167, 179–82, 186–87, 199, 211, 214–15; in Chamula, 90, 214–15;

Cattle (cont.)

    and civil warfare, 158; com-
mercial production of, 180–82,
186–87; diseases, 38; in Grijalva valley, 13, 37–38, 42,
110–11, 126; and labor, 71,
120, 125–26, 214–15; and peasant dislocation, 125; ranches
owned by clergy, 26–27, 37,
40–42; ranches owned by cofradías, 40–41; and tenant
farming, 196, 199, 214–15; in
Zinacantan, 37–38

Central America, smuggling in, 64

Chalchihuitán, 73, 85, 147, 149

Chamula: anthropological research on, 4–6, 241; anti-
Church activity in, 146, 149–
50, 300 n.76; Church revenues
collected from, 57, 62–63, 99,
100; curato and anexo, 52map,
53map, 65map, 66map; de-
nuncias in, 123; ethnicity in, 6;
family organization and residential patterns, 97–98; 204–
05, 216–17; female-headed
households, 97–98; income
distribution in, 210; land ap-
propriation and land tenure,
104, 129, 165, 166, 182, 296
n.37; maize production, 201,
202; municipal administration, 271 n.11, 290–91 n.3; native tributaries, 73; occupations and economic activities
of residents, 105, 200–05,
206map, 207map, 208–09, 211–
14; and organized labor, 165–
66, 169; population, 120,
125fig.; religion and politics
in, 58–59, 102–03, 131, 157,

169, 175–78, 226–28; and 1712
rebellion, 84–85; social and
economic life, 90–91, 96, 98,
101–02, 208–14, 216–17, 226–
27; as source of agricultural
labor, 87, 115, 163, 187–90,
192, 214–15; mentioned, 108,
134

Chanal, 124, 165, 166, 301 n.87

Chapultenango, 57, 65map

Charcoal production, 204

Charles V, 17, 18

Chenalhó: agricultural laborers
recruited from, 163, 169; denuncias in, 122; ladinos in,
302 n.101; land tenure in, 123–
24, 129, 165, 166, 167, 168, 302
n.101; native tributaries, 73;
religion and politics in, 80,
147, 149, 178, 228; and 1712 rebellion, 85; mentioned, 82

Chiapa: agricultural laborers and
tenant farmers in, 91, 95, 126,
189, 190; agricultural production, 117; Church revenues
collected from, 38, 44, 56, 57;
cofradías in, 29; commerce
with San Cristóbal, 135; curato, 52map, 65map; demo-
graphic trends in, 27, 67, 120,
121fig.; Dominican convent
in, 40, 41map, 56; in early colonial period, 23–24, 43; foreign capital in, 114; Indians
and ladinos in, 295 n.31; land
tenure in, 39, 40, 110, 111, 169;
rubber concessions in, 292–93
n.21; sugar ingenios, 33, 40;
and wheat trade, 32, 136;
mentioned, 11, 32–33, 135,
296–97 n.46

Chiapaneca peoples and region, 9–10, 19, 94, 95fig., 110

Chiapas: anthropological research in, 1–6, 239–41, 244–51; doctrinas, 24map; early colonial period, 8map; population, 67, 118fig.; precolonial period, 7–10

Chiapilla, 29, 110, 169

Chickens (as tribute), 13

Chicomuselo, 57, 65map

Chikinibal Vo', 231

Chik'omtantik (Chamula): income distribution, 210; maize production, 201, 202; occupations of residents, 203; socioeconomic stratification, 211–12; tenant farming and horticulture in, 206map, 207map, 208; mentioned, 309–10 n.84

Children: in households, 94, 97–98; socialization of, 223–25

Chile (as tribute), 43–44

Chilón: agriculture in, 113, 117; cofradías in, 29, 88; curato and anexo, 65map, 66map; described by Stephens, 128; famine and mortality in, 49–50; female-headed households, 97–98; fincas rústicas in, 111; Indians and ladinos in, 129, 295 n.31; and native rebellions, 82, 132–33; native tributaries, 73; visitas and limosnas, 57; mentioned, 127, 291 n.3

Chit, Tomas, governor of Oxchuc, 132

Chol peoples, language, and region, 10, 30, 78, 81, 119

Cholera. See Disease and Epidemics

Chontal dynasty, 9

Christian, William, historian, 244–45

Church: administration of, reorganized, 82–83; conflict with civil authorities, 51, 54–55, 60–64, 132–33, 142, 146–51; conflict within, 51–54, 69–70; and Indian rights, 17; denounces liquor trade, 130; relations with Indians, mid-18th century, 145–51; role in native rebellion, 19th century, 131–33; sides with Conservatives, 126. See also Clergy; Secularization; Civil-religious system; Religion

—revenues, 27, 36–37, 43, 50–58, 75, 87, 89, 126, 277–78 n.35; collected from Chamula, 99, 100; collected from cofradías, 71, 74, 76, 92; collected from Zinacantan, 92, 135, 142, 145; Indians demand abolition of, 84; investigated and regulated, 55; Liberal opposition to, 147; native communities unable to pay, 61, 141; remate de diezmos, 63; and secularization, 58, 64; shortage of, 71; 1668–1808, 75

Cintalapa, 65map, 91, 157, 160

Ciudad Real: agriculture and economic activities, 13, 32–33, 39, 87; ayuntamiento considers secularization, 54; ayuntamiento forbids non-vecinos to trade slaves, 19: ayuntamiento suspended and reinstated, 45, 63; ayuntamiento

Ciudad Real (cont.)
    debates clergy's activities, 53–
    55; cabildo debates control of
    cochineal trade, 274 n.8; ca-
    bildo constructs convent, 22;
    curatos, 52map, 65map; de-
    scribed, 102–03; Dominicans
    in, 38, 40–41, 56, 57, 58; in ear-
    ly colonial period, 18–19, 21–
    23, 34, 37; and food shortages,
    49; Franciscan monastery in,
    79; and 1712 rebellion, 79; Jes-
    uits in, 39; Mercedarians in,
    26–27, 39, 41–42; tribute and
    repartimientos from, 14, 38,
    44, 47; visitas and limosnas,
    57; mentioned, 28, 42, 48,
    53map, 55, 66map, 80, 289
    n.67
Civil-religious system, 119, 218,
    223, 225, 245–46; in Chamula,
    176–78, 250–51; in Salinas,
    230, 231; in Nabenchauk, 232,
    233; in Zinacantan, 172–73,
    177–78, 227–39, 250–51. See
    also Cofradías; Religion
Clergy, 12–16, 291 n.5; ask to leave
    Zinacantan, 145, 172; attitudes
    toward Indians, 22–23, 130–
    32; economic activities and
    income of, 27, 30, 35–37, 39–
    42, 128, 145 fig., 277–78 n.35,
    298 n.59; Indians ordained as,
    82–83; political activities and
    involvement of, 18, 20–23, 82,
    107, 109, 132–34, 298 n.59; sec-
    ular, 28, 30, 37, 51–56, 58–60,
    64, 68, 109. See also Church;
    Dominicans; Jesuits; Merce-
    darians; Religious orders;
    Secularization of native par-
    ishes
Cochineal: for tribute and reparti-
    mientos, 13, 34–35, 36, 47;
    trade, 33, 35, 44, 46, 274 n.8,
    278 n.40; precolonial produc-
    tion of, 7, 9; production col-
    lapses, 103. See also Dyestuffs
Coffee: and Chiapas economy,
    180; growers, 157, 159; lands
    and land reform, 164, 167,
    169–70, 248; and politics, 178;
    production, 112–13, 117, 160,
    161fig.
—Labor and laborers: Chamula,
    202, 208–09, 227; demand and
    recruitment of, 115–16, 120,
    163, 170, 175–76; income of,
    215; and strikes and unioniza-
    tion, 158, 160, 163–65; Zina-
    canteco, 217; mentioned, 250
Cofradías: in early colonial peri-
    od, 23, 25, 27–31; decline of,
    mid-19th century, 146–47;
    18th century, 87–89; com-
    pared with European confra-
    ternities, 242–48; fees paid by,
    39, 71, 74, 98; festivals cele-
    brated by, 71, 76; in Guatema-
    la, 247, 273 n.44; ladino, 105,
    273 n.44; land ownership by,
    40–41; and religious life, 70–
    71, 76–77, 227–28; in Zinacan-
    tan, 92, 142, 145, 227–28; men-
    tioned, 31
Collier, George, anthropologist, 4,
    216–18, 227, 238, 241
Comalapa, 89–90
Comisión Agraria Mixta, 173
Comitán: agricultural production,
    117; cattle ranches in, 64; and
    civil warfare, 158; cofradias

in, 29; curato, 52map, 65map; disease and epidemics in, 27–28, 72; Dominican convent in, 40, 41map, 56, 57; Indian population, 67, 295 n.31; laboríos and mozos in, 91; ladino population, 128, 295 n.31; land and land tenure, 39, 40, 41map, 64, 110, 111, 128, 189, 190; organized as municipal corporation, 290–91 n.3; rubber concessions in, 292–93 n.21; and 1712 rebellion, 84; and smuggling, 111–12; tribute paid by residents, 38, 44, 287 n.44; vecinos of, required to sell food, 49; visitas and limosnas, 57; and wheat trade, 32; Zinacanteco tenant farmers in, 189, 190, 195; mentioned, 23, 32, 112, 138, 289 n.67

CONASUPO (Compañía Nacional de Subsistencias Populares), 187

Concepción, Zinacantan ranch, 139

Concordia, la, 169, 189, 190

Coneta, 89–90

Confederación Nacional Campesina, 166

Confraternities. See Cofradías

Conservatives, 126, 149–50, 157. See also Political parties; Politics

Constituciones diocesanas, 76

Construction workers, Chamula, 204

Conversion, religious. See under Religion

Copainala, 29, 57, 65map, 70

Copanaguastla, 11, 27; disease in, 72; as Dominican parish, 23, 28; tribute paid by residents of, 38, 44

Corn. See Maize

Correa, Patricio, priest, 142, 150

Corregidores, royal officials, 25

Cotton: colonial production and trade, 11, 13, 32–35, 43–44, 46; commercial production (post-Independence), 112, 117, 126, 179, 186–87; for tribute and repartimientos, 34, 36, 43, 47, 54, 62

Council of the Indies, 16, 18, 58–60, 74–75, 87

Council of Trent, 16, 30

Coxoh peoples and language, 10

Credit, agricultural, 186, 196

Cruz Ton (Chamula): income distribution in, 210; maize production, 201, 202, 208; occupations of residents, 203; tenant farming and horticulture, 206map, 207map, 208; Theil Index for, 211; mentioned, 309–10 n.84

Cuba, 16

Culture change, as subject of anthropological research, 2–5

Curatos and anexos: 52map, 53map, 65map, 66map

Curers, 222, 226, 234–35, 237–39

Cuxtepeques, 91, 120, 121fig.

Cuxtepeques, Valley of, curato, 65map

Dávila y Lugo, Francisco, provincial governor, 34

De Feria, Pedro, bishop, 24–26, 30, 51, 69

De la Peña, Moisés, economist, 167, 181–82

De la Torre, Miguel, escribano of San Bartolomé, 54

De la Tovilla, Manuel, landowner, 54

De Laguna, Gabriel, colonial official, 54–56

De las Cuentas Zayas, Agustín, intendente of Ciudad Real, 103–04

De Tovar, Mauro, bishop, 51, 69

Demography: 17th century, 275 n.15; 18th century, 50; and excessive tribute, 89–90; and labor, 94–95, 115–16, 119–20, 208–09; mortality and Spanish conquest, 276 n.17; and religious change, 231–34; of Zinacantan, 93, 136–38, 182–83, 231–34

—, population trends: general, 116, 118fig., 276 n.17; in Grijalva River basin, 121fig.; in highlands, 116, 118–19; Indian, 27, 37, 43, 67, 94–95, 295 n.31; among labor force, 95, 115–16; ladino, 295 n.31; among Spaniards, 39–40; in Zinacantan, 136, 136fig. 137, 171–72. See also Diseases and epidemics; Sex ratio

Denuncias, 122–23

Departamento de Acción Social, Cultural y Protección Indígena, 162, 166, 169

Departamento de Asuntos Indígenas (DAI), 162, 169, 174

Desamortización, 68, 126, 296 n.36

Descals, José, judge, 55, 76

Devil worship, 25

DeWalt, Billie R., anthropologist, 245–46

Díaz Cuzcat, Pedro, fiscal of Chamula, 149

Díaz del Castillo, Bernal, chronicler, 9

Díaz, Felipe, alférez of San Andrés, 102

Díaz, Félix, military leader, 304 n.1

Diseases and epidemics, 72, 119; among Chiapanecas, 94; and cofradía decline, 71; in Comitán, 27; and decline in Indian tribute, 43; demographic consequences of, 37, 118; and locust plague, 50; in Zinacantan, 13, 27, 287 n.44

Doctrinas, parish seats, 23, 24map

Domínguez, Bruno, priest, 147

Dominicans (religious order): accused of misconduct, 54; administration of native towns, 14–15, 21, 51–53, 271 n.11; agricultural and economic activities of, 16, 26–27, 30, 33, 37, 40, 41map, 43, 283 n.94; Bravo de la Serna acts against, 74; collection of revenues by, 55, 57, 58; in early colonial period, 14–15, 21–22; income of, 56; loans made to landowners by, 39; and native religion, 28, 69, 74–77; and politics, 21, 51–53, 55, 61; and secularization, 58–60, 68, 291 n.5

Dorantes, Romano and Company, lumbering concessionaire, 293–94 n.22

Doremberg Estate, lumbering concessionaire, 293–94 n.22

Dyestuffs, 7, 11, 46. *See also* Cochineal; Indigo

Ecological change, in Grijalva basin, 179–82
Ecological zones, precolonial, 7
Economic development, 196–99, 211–12. *See also* Social change
Edel, Matthew, economist, 171–74
Education, Indian, 154
Ejidos: after agrarian reform, 167; in Central Chiapas, 166; in Chamula, 121map, 200–02; and coffee production, 164; entitled by creole landowners, 110; farmed by Elan Vo' residents, 193; in Muk'ta Jok', 236; petitions for, 123–24, 128; and policies of Fernández Ruíz, 160; and political conflict, 157, 174; sold to ladinos, 141; and tenant farmers, 182; in Zinacantan, 139, 141, 170, 171, 174–75
Elan Vo' (Zinacantan): agricultural production by residents of, 188, 193–94, 194fig.; economic activities of household heads from, 193; land tenure, 171, 174; religion in, 234–37; tenant farmers from, 184–85; mentioned, 136, 309 n.75
Encomenderos: and collection of tribute, 13–14, 37; conflict with royal officials, 33–35; and Indian slavery, 19; relations with clergy, 12, 19, 21–25; relations with native rulers, 12

Encomiendas, legal restrictions upon, 17
Enganche. *See* Labor: recruitment
England, religious change in, 243
English investors in Chiapas, 108, 113
Epidemics. *See* Diseases and epidemics
Espinosa, Luis, political leader, 157–58, 160
Esponda, Salvador, teniente of Ixtacomitan, 47–48
Esquintenango, 57, 65map
Estrada, Luis Alfonso de, Zinacantan landowner, 90
Estrada, Pedro de, encomendero of Zinacantan, 12, 20–21, 90
Ethnic groups and ethnicity: anthropological perspectives on, 1–10; in Chamula, 6, 215, 241; changing boundaries, 104–05, 215; conflict between, 126–27, 204–05, 241, 249–50; and Guatemalan cofradías, 273 n.44; precolonial, 3–6, 9–10; and religion, 244, 249–50; and socioeconomic patterns, 216–17. *See also* Chol; Coxoh; Ladinos; Tzeltal; Tzotzil
Ethnography, 5–6
Evangelization among Indians, 22–31. *See also* Church; Clergy
Exports, agricultural, 108, 179

Family life, 227
Family organization: in highland communities, 223; in Zinacantan, 92–96, 135–39, 140, 142. *See also* Kinship

Famine, 35, 43, 48–50, 72, 92, 118, 119

Favre, Henri, anthropologist, 5, 44, 87

Feathers (quetzalli), as articles of trade, 9

Fernández Prieto, Joaquín, provincial governor, 46, 87

Fernández Ruíz, Tiburcio, political leader, 159, 161

Festivals: and changing civil-religious structure, 173; Church income from, 55, 71, 76, 99; decline in celebrations of, 147; discouraged by Church, 105–106; and Indian religious life, 132; in Zinacantan, 148–49, 151, 222

Fincas: and estancias, 39; rústicas, 111. See also Land

Finucane, Ronald, historian, 243

Flowers, commercial production of, 199

Food shortages, 47–50

Foreign investments in Chiapas, 108, 113–15, 294 n.23

Foreigners: attitudes of, toward Indians, 152–54; plantation owners, 160–61

Frailesca, la (Comitán), 91, 126

France: armed forces of, in Mexico, 146; religious change in, 241–43

Franciscans (religious order), 79, 90

French investors in Chiapas, 108, 113

Friedlander, Judith, anthropologist, 248

Frijoles. See Beans

Fruit, commercial production of, 199

Gabucio, Manuel, lumbering concessionaire, 293–94 n.22

Gage, Thomas, Dominican monk, 32–33, 35, 36, 37, 42

Gamboa, Pascacio, politician, 162, 167

García, Juan, Indian military commander, 84

García de Vargas y Rivera, Juan Manuel, bishop, 48–49, 51, 59

Garracín Ponce de León, Juan Bautista, alcalde mayor of Ciudad Real, 46, 68, 278–79 n.42

Germans, and Chiapas coffee industry, 113, 294 n.23

Germany: religious change in, 241–43; war with Mexico, 169

Gold, 11

Gómez, Sebastián, religious leader, 82–86, 87

Gosner, Kevin, historian, 71

Gossen, Gary, anthropologist, 5

Government, Mexican: and agricultural change, 195; and social problems, 241

Gracias a Dios, 13–15

Grajales, Victorico, governor of Chiapas, 161–62

Grijalva, Sebastián de, priest, 70

Grijalva River basin: agriculture and livestock production in, 13, 37–38, 40, 42, 64, 98, 112, 119, 126, 167, 184, 194fig.; described, 7, 11; ecological and economic change, 178–82; land and land tenure, 40, 42, 90, 110, 160; population growth in, 120; ranchers and civil warfare, 158; soil fertility in, 190; tenant farmers in, 194fig., 203–05, 208, 218; mentioned, 156, 214, 215, 217

Guadalupe Xucun (Zinacantan), ejidos in, 170

Guaquitepec: cofradias in, 88–89; curato and anexo, 53map, 65map, 66map; visitas and limosnas, 57; female-headed households, 97–98; native tributaries, 73; population decline in, 89–90; mentioned, 130

Guardianías (district), 50

Guatemala: cofradías in, 273 n.44; laborers imported from, 164, 170; political and religious organization in, 240, 246–48; royal authorities in, 13, 46; source for smuggled goods, 111–12; mentioned, 33, 35, 42, 109, 154, 195

Guerra, Baltazar, encomendero of Chiapa, 12, 15, 19–20

Guerrero, José Mariano, priest, 131–32

Guerrilla fighters, 158–59

Guillén, Vicente Anselmo, priest, 62, 147, 150

Gur (Zinacantan), 96

Gutiérrez, Bartolomé, Oxchuc priest, 132

Gutiérrez, Bartolomé, treasurer of Ciudad Real cathedral, 48

Gutiérrez, Efraín, politician, 162, 164

Gutiérrez, Joaquín, governor of Chiapas, 109

Hamlets, Zinacanteco, 95, 96, 135, 182

Handicrafts: produced by Chamulas, 204; role in regional economy, 212–14

Harrison, O. H., American businessman, 114–15

Hartmann, Eduard, lumbering concessionaire, 293–94 n.22

Hartmann, Taide A. de, lumbering concessionaire, 293–94 n.22

Haviland, John, anthropologist, 4

Helbig, Karl, geographer, 180–82

Herbicides, agricultural, 194–95

Hernández Caña, Martín, alférez of Oxchuc, 132

Hernández Nuj, Antonio, Zinacantan resident, 218

Hicalahau, native deity, 101–02

Hidalgo, Manuel, priest, 86

Hidalgo de Montemayor, Gonzalo, royal judge, 14–15, 22

History, and anthropological research, 241–51

Horses. See Mules and horses

Horticulture and horticulturalists, 202–05, 207map, 209, 211–12

Households and household composition, 94–95, 97–98, 138–39, 140; female-headed, 138. See also Kinship

Huerta, Adolfo de la, military leader, 159

Huerta, Victoriano, president of Mexico, 157

Huertistas, 157–58

Huistán: coffee workers hired from, 163; cofradías in, 29, 88; curato and anexo, 53map; denuncias in, 122–23; female-headed households, 97; land and land tenure in, 40–41, 120, 124, 128, 165, 166, 168; native tributaries, 73; occupational change in, 105; population growth in, 120, 125fig.;

Huistán (cont.)
  religion and politics in, 147, 149, 178, 301 n.87; and 1712 rebellion, 84, 131–32; tribute paid by residents of, 43; mentioned, 289 n.67, 297–98 n.51, 300 n.80, 302 n.98
Huitiupán: cofradías in, 29; curato and anexo, 52map, 65map, 66map; fincas and estancias in, 39; tribute paid by residents of, 38, 43, 44; mentioned, 83

Ibes (Zinacantan), 136
Imperialistas, 126
Import substitution, 180
Imprisonment of Indians, 282–83 n.91
Income: distribution among Mexican agriculturalists, 213fig.; of Chamulas, 209–11, 213fig., 215; from Zinacantan harvests, 185fig.
Independence movement, 107
Indigo, 46, 112, 117. See also Dyestuffs
Ingenios. See Sugar
Inquisition, in Guatemala, 55
Instituto Nacional Indigenista, 174–75, 177
Intendentes and intendencia, 64, 103
Intermarriage between Spaniards and Indians, 85–86
Investments: agricultural and livestock, 186; foreign, 108, 113, 114
Iron and steel trade, 46, 87
Irrigation, 186
Istapilla, 89–90

Isthmus of Tehuantepec, 113–14, 159
Ixtacomitán: curato, 65map; plantations in, 38, 39, 42; repartimiento system in, 47–48; visitas and limosnas, 57; mentioned, 135, 289 n.67, 291 n.3
Ixtapa: agricultural laborers in, 91, 95; cofradias in, 29; curato, 65map; female-headed households, 97; land tenure, 40–41, 65, 169; native tributaries, 73; in precolonial trade, 9; religion in, 236–37; towns consolidated, 271 n.11; visitas and limosnas, 57; mentioned, 157

Jai-alai and Urbina, 167, 169
Jatate, lumbering concessions in, 293–94 n.22
Jesuits, 39, 42–43. See also Church
Jipuyum (Zinacantan), 96
Jiquipulas: conceded by Dominicans, 30; curato, 52map; disease in, 72; land and land use in, 38, 39; population of, 67, 89–90; tribute paid by residents of, 38, 44
Jitogtig (Zinacantan), 96
Jitotol, 65map, 146
Jok' Ch'enom (Zinacantan): land tenure and land use, 170, 171, 199; population, 96; mentioned, 136, 142, 229
Joyjel (Zinacantan), 135, 136, 217, 309 n.75
Judges, intendentes as, 103
Jueces de milpa, 33
Junta de Administración y Vigilancia de la Propiedad Ex-

tranjera, 169

K'alch'entik, 309–10 n.84

K'at'ixtik (Chamula): income distribution in, 210; maize production, 201, 202, 208; occupations of residents, 203; socioeconomic stratification, 211–12; tenant farmers in, 205, 206map, 207map, 208; Theil Index for, 211; mentioned, 309–10 n.84

Kinship: and rights to land, 141–42; in Zinacantan, 217–18, 221–22, 238, 299 n.65. See also Family organization; Households and household composition

Klein, Herbert, historian, 85, 87

K'obyox, Jose, Na Chij resident, 200


Labor: and Chamulas, 201–02; used by Church and clergy, 22–23, 62, 64, 101; coffee (See Coffee: labor and laborers); and commercial agriculture, 115–16, 125–26, 151–53; in early colonial period, 12, 14, 22–23, 33, 35, 38, 43, 64, 66; forced, 62–64, 70, 87, 91, 101, 103, 127; granted to Spanish settlers, 71; in Grijalva basin, 90, 178–79, 183–84; imported from Guatemala, 170; legislation and regulation of, 14, 158, 163–64; on lowland estates, 61, 104, 125–26; and oil, 202; and politics, 126, 163; and politics in Guatemala, 247–48; recruitment, 152, 163–64, 169,
175; and repartimientos, 35, 61, 91; slave, 12, 14–15, 17, 19, 33; supply and demand, 38, 64, 94–96, 170, 183–84; unrest, 70, 157–58, 160, 162, 170; in Zinacantan, 189–94. See also Agriculture; Baldiaje and Baldíos; Tenant farmers and farming

Laboríos and mozos, 90, 91, 94–95, 110, 119, 138

Lacandón jungle, 50, 115, 129, 152, 158

Lacandón peoples, 10

Lacandona, lumbering concessions in, 293–94 n.22

Ladinos: appropriate Indian lands, 127–28, 302 n.101; colonize highlands, 128–29; conflict with Indians, 126–27, 204–05, 241, 249–50; leave San Cristóbal, 151; and liquor trade, 129–30; merchants, 132–33; and politics, 132–33, 162, 228, 247–48; population trends, 104–05, 295 n.31; recruited for agricultural labor, 115; religious participation of, 301 n.87; in Yucatán, 127; in Zinacantan, 172–73, 225–26; mentioned, 200, 302 n.95

Laguna, Gabriel de, alcalde mayor of Ciudad Real, 45, 68

Lagunita, la (Zinacantan), 170

Land: in Chamula, 90–91, 96, 201; owned by Church and religious orders, 40–43, 126, 291 n.5; Indian, acquired from creole landowners, 167; Indian, expropriation of, 38, 65, 108, 110, 120, 127–30, 132–34,

Land (cont.)
296 n.37, 302 n.101; and political conflict, 125–27, 132–34, 156–59, 174; shortages of, 104–05, 188–90, 192–95, 217; tenure, 111, 164, 165, 167, 169, 178–79; use, 90–91, 96, 111, 185–86, 189–90, 201; in Zinacantan, 26, 90–91, 139, 141, 185–86, 188–90, 192–95, 217. See also Agrarian reform; Agrarismo; Ejidos

Lara, Simon de, priest, 80–84

Larraínzar, Ramón, politician, 120, 150

Las Casas, Bartolomé de, bishop, 12, 14–21, 23, 26, 31

Las Casas (district), 111, 114, 117, 295 n.31

Ley de Obreros, 158

Liberals, 125–26, 132–34, 146–47, 151–52, 157. See also Political parties; Politics

Libertad, la, 110, 111, 114, 117, 292–93 n.21, 295 n.31

Liga de Comunidades Agrarias, 167, 169–70

Limas, las (estate), 184

Limosnas. See Church: revenues

Lineages. See Kinship

Liquor: ceremonial exchange of, 229–30; production, 112–13, 117, 204, 209; trade and regulation of, 130, 133, 163, 176–77, 201

Livestock: investments in, 186. See also Cattle; Mules and horses

Llanos district. See San Bartolomé

Locust plagues, 48–50, 72

Lomo' (Chamula): income distribution in, 210; maize production in, 201, 202, 208; occupations of residents of, 203, 206map, 207map; Theil Index for, 211

López Negrete, Angel, lumbering concessionaire, 293–94 n.22

López Tzintan, Zinacantan family, 217

Lumber: production, 115, 293–94 n.22; workers revolt, 158

McCreery, David, historian, 154

Macehuales, 21

MacLeod, Murdo, historian, vii, 15

Macuilapa, 32

Maderistas, 157–58

Madero, Francisco, president of Mexico, 156

Magdalena (Chamula): civil religious office in, 228, 100; curato, 65map; denuncias, 123; female-headed households, 97; indigenous government suspended, 272 n.31; native tributaries, 73

Mahogany. See Lumber

Maisterra, Manuel de, alcalde mayor, 34, 70

Maize: grown by baldíos, 126; grown by Chamula farmers, 201, 202, 208; grown by Zinacanteco farmers, 136, 184, 188, 192, 193–94, 198, 218; paid as tribute, 13, 44, 47–48, 54, 91; in precolonial period, 7; production and marketing, 43, 46, 113, 117, 180, 181fig., 186, 188–90, 195–99; ratio of surplus production to wages, 192; shortages, 40, 47–50; sold to purchase cacao, 35; mentioned, 133

Maldonado, Fernando Nicolás, Santa Anna administrator, 110
Malinche, la, 225
Mapaches, 159, 161, 172
Margaritas, las, 292 n.12
Marín Luis, 11
Mariscal, 111, 117
Markets, 9, 197. *See also* Trade and trading
Marqués de Comillas, lumbering concession, 294 n.22
Marqués del Valle, 12
Marriage, 19, 85–86, 299 n.65. *See also* Kinship
Marroquín, Francisco, bishop, 28
Martínez de Castro Co., lumbering concessionaire, 293–94 n.22
Martínez del Río, Javier, lumbering concessionaire, 293–94 n.22
Mavití, native deity, 26
Maya, 10, 127, 153–54
Mayordomías, 27
Mayordomos and alféreces, 71, 74, 106, 142, 145, 147, 150, 245–46, 226–28, 230–37, 246
Mazariegos, Diego de, colonial official, 11
Measles. *See* Diseases and epidemics
Meat, 46, 229–30, 278 n.41. *See also* Cattle
Mechanics, strike by, 157
Merced (la), Zinacantan trapiche, 96
Mercedarians, religious order, 26–27, 39, 41–42
Mérida, 127
Mescalapa. *See* Mezcalapa
Mestizos. *See* Ladinos

Mexican Land and Colonization Company, Ltd., 114–15, 292 n.21, 293 n.22
Mexico, income distribution in, 213fig.
Mezcalapa, 111, 117, 295 n.31
Michoacán, 59
Migration: and agricultural labor, 110; Indian, 89–90, 129, 298–99 n.61; ladino, 127–30; of Zinacantecos, 134–36, 137, 151. *See also* Demography
Milpoleta (Chamula): income distribution in, 210; maize production, 201, 202, 208; occupations of residents, 203, 206map, 207map; socioeconomic stratification in, 211–12; mentioned, 309–10 n.84
Miracles, religious, 28, 78–81
Miramar, lumbering concessions in, 293–94 n.22
Missionaries, 14–15. *See also* Church; Clergy; Dominicans; Jesuits; Mercedarians; Religion
Mitontic (Chamula): coffee laborers hired from, 163; female-headed households, 97–98; land and land tenure, 97–98, 100, 123–24, 167, 296 n.37; native tributaries, 73; religion and politics in, 147, 149, 178, 228; revenues paid to Church by residents, 100; mentioned, 300 n.76
Money lending: in Chamula, 177, 201–02; by religious orders, 38–39, 42, 92
Monroy, José, priest, 79–80, 85
Monte Libano, lumbering concessions in, 293–94 n.22

Morales, Nicolás, colonial official, 101–03

Mortality. See Diseases and epidemics; Demography

Motines. See Rebellions

Mozos. See Laboríos and mozos

Muk'ta Jok' (Zinacantan), 95, 96, 135, 137, 138, 236

Mulattoes, 105

Mules and horses, 38, 46, 64, 90, 136, 184–85, 188

Murga, Pedro Tomás de, teniente, 46

Muruch, Antonio, Zinacantan politician, 172

Na Chij (Zinacantan): agriculture and land tenure in, 171, 187–92, 194, 199; population, 96; religion in, 234–38; tenant farmers from, 187, 197, 198; mentioned, 136, 138, 174, 182, 231, 309 n.75

Nabenchauk (Zinacantan): agriculture and land tenure in, 171, 174, 199; civil religious system in, 172, 231–33; population characteristics, 138; religious activities, 233–35; tenant farmers from, 184–85; mentioned, 136, 309 n.75

Nagualismo. See Spiritism

Nahualoztomeca, merchants, 9

Nandayageli, Zinacantan hacienda, 96

Nash, Manning, anthropologist, 228, 246

New Laws, 15, 17, 21

Ni Ch'en (Chamula): income distribution in, 210; maize production, 201, 202, 208; occupations of residents, 203, 206map, 207map; Theil Index for, 211; mentioned, 309–10 n.84

Ni Vo' (Zinacantan), 103

Nicaragua, 15

Nichim (Zinacantan), 96

Norms, as exemplified in Zinacantan ritual, 223–26

Notí, Pedro, governor of Chiapa, 19–20

Nuestra Señora, religious cult, 30

Nuevo Eden, finca, 120, 121map, 126

Nuj, Guillermo Pérez, Zinacantan official, 174–75

Nuñez de la Vega, Francisco, bishop, 52, 55, 74–76, 101–02, 153

Oaxaca: Indian rebellion in, 297 n.41; Indians in, 64–65, 276 n.26; ladinos in, 289 n.72; market in, 199; mentioned, 12, 138

Obregón, Alvaro, president of Mexico, 159, 161, 172, 173

Obregonistas, 159

Ocosingo: cofradías in, 29, 88; community disruption, 96; curato and anexo, 52map, 53map, 65map, 66map; female-headed households, 97; and Indian rebellions, 82, 132; labor shortage in, 126; laboríos and mozos in, 91; ladinos in, 105, 128–29; land and land tenure in, 39, 41map, 65, 128; liquor in, 130; native tributaries, 73; tribute collected from, 38, 44, 57, 287 n.44; mentioned, 23, 25, 115, 289 n.67, 300 n.81

Ocosingo valley, 38, 40–41

Ocotepeque, 25

Ocozocuautla, 29, 65map, 70, 135

Offices, political: auction and purchase of, 33, 44–45, 283 n.92; controlled by landowners, 169; Zinacantecos in, 172. See also Civil-religious system; Political Parties; Politics

Oficina de Contrataciones, 163

Oil fields, 202

Olivares y Benito, bishop, 105

Oliver, Juan de, alcalde mayor of Tuxtla, 47–48, 51, 59, 87

Olivera y Pardo, Jacinto de, bishop, 44

Ordoñez y Aguiar, Joseph, vicar of Chamula, 61–63, 68, 98, 100–03

Ordoñez y Aguiar, Ramón, priest, 61, 63–64

Orozco y Jiménez, Francisco, bishop, 156–57

Ortíz de Avilés, Cristóbal, alcalde mayor, 60–62, 101

Ostutla, 271 n.11

Oxchuc: coffee workers hired from, 163; curato and anexo, 53map, 65map, 66map; female-headed households, 97; and food shortage, 48–49; and Indian rebellion, 132; native tributaries, 73; occupational change in, 105; population growth in, 120, 125fig.; religion and politics in, 58–59, 75, 147, 149, 301 n.87; tribute collected from, 43, 57; mentioned, 115

Ozocotlán, 52map

"Pajarito" (Jacinto Pérez Chixtot), 157

Palafox, Bernardo, governor of Chiapas, 158

Palenque: agricultural development and production in, 111, 113, 115, 117; female-headed households, 97; fincas rústicas in, 111; foreign capital in, 114; Indians and ladinos in, 295 n.31; lumbering concessions in, 293 n.22; religion and politics in, 109; and 1712 rebellion, 84; mentioned, 289 n.67, 296–97 n.46

Pan American Highway: and agricultural expansion, 175, 186; and social change, 231, 233, 235–36; in Zinacantan, 175, 239; mentioned, 178, 205, 208

Pan American Railway, 159

Pantelhó: disease in, 119; land tenure in, 165, 166, 168; native tributaries, 73; Santa Catarina, revenues paid to Church, 100

Parish seats. See Doctrinas

Partido de la Revolución Mexicana, 162–63, 173

Partido Nacional Revolucionario, 161

Partido Revolucionario Institucional, 162, 167, 173

Partido Socialista Chiapaneco, 160

Partido Socialista del Soconusco, 160

Partido Socialista del Sureste, 160

Pasté (Zinacantan), 136, 171, 172, 184–85, 234–37, 309 n.75

Pat Osil (Zinacantan), 171, 309 n.75

Patrilineages. See Kinship

Peanut production, 112

Peddlers and peddling, 91, 182–85, 204

Peru, 15

Pérez, Lucas, native priest, 83

Pérez, Nicolás, Tenango official, 84

Pérez Asiento, Zinacantan family, 217

Pérez Chixtot, Jacinto ("Pajarito"), 157

Pérez Dardon, Marcos, Mercedarian superior, 26–27

Pérez Jil, Lorenzo, Zinacanteco politician, 172

Petalcingo, 50, 73, 97

Petej (Chamula): income distribution in, 210; maize production, 201, 202, 208; occupations of residents, 203; tenant farming and horticulture, 206map, 207map, 208; Theil Index for, 211; mentioned, 309–10 n.84

Petztoj (Zinacantan), 136, 171, 182, 231

Pichucalco: agricultural development and production in, 112–13, 117; fincas rústicas in, 111; foreign capital in, 114; Indian labor in, 152; Indians and ladinos in, 295 n.31; labor unrest and land reform in, 160; rubber concessions in, 292–93 n.21; mentioned, 135

Pig, el (Zinacantan), 170

Pineda, Alberto, guerrilla leader, 157–59, 166, 172

Pineda, Juan, Spanish judge, 43

Pineda, Manuel, Liberal politician, 157

Pinola, lowland community, 97

Plagues. See Diseases and epidemics

Plantation workers, unionization of, 158

Pohlenz, Guillermo, landowner, 169

Polanco, Francisco, bishop, 60–61, 63–64, 101

Police, private, 163

Political organization and authority: administration of native municipios, 108–09; early colonial, 11–12, 21; precolonial, 7, 9–10. See also Church; Offices, political; Politics

Political parties: 19th century, 107–09, 125, 145–47, 154–55, 157, 296 n.37; 20th century, 157, 160–63, 173. See also Conservatives; Liberals

Politics: conflict between settlers and royal officials, 33–35; conflict over agricultural labor, 125–27; and Indian life, 154–55; municipal level, 230–33; and religion in Indian communities, 227–39, 246–51. See also Church; Clergy: political activities and involvement of; Offices, political

Polygamy, 299 n.65

Population. See Demography

Porfiristas, 156–59

Potatoes, 203–04

Potogtig (Zinacantan), 96

Potolán, native deity, 101–02

Pottery making, 204

Poverty, 91–93, 103–04, 128–29, 142, 145, 295 n.29. See also Famine; Repartimiento system

Poxlom, native deity, 101–02

Presbíteros. See Clergy: secular

Principales, native leaders, 12, 18–19, 24, 26, 31

Promax, Antonio, Zinacantan pol-

itician, 172
Protestantism, in Guatemala, 248
Provincial governors, 35, 42–46, 54–55, 62–63
Puebla, 250

Quechula, 29, 57, 65map
Quelenes, 10

Rabasa, Emilio, proconsul of Díaz, 156
Railroad workers, unionization of, 158
Real, el (Ocosingo), 129
Real patronato, 18, 55
Realengas, royal lands, 40
Rebellions: cristero, 156; by Spanish colonists, 15
—, Indian: and agrarian reform, 171; and Dominicans, 81–82, 84; of 1848, against ladinos, 126–27, 129, 130–34; of 1911, anti-Porfirista, 157; against repartimientos, 70; of 1712, 36, 40, 43, 53, 76–86, 244–45; mentioned, 106, 241, 249
Redfield, Robert, anthropologist, 2, 248
Reforma, la, oilfield, 202
Regidores, councilmen, 173
Reincke, Pablo, landowner, 165–66
Religion: Church's opposition to native practices, 25–26, 69–71, 74–82, 86, 101–03, 130–32, 147, 149–51; in early colonial period, 22–28, 30, 36; European, compared to Indian, 241–44; Indian conflicts with Church, 101–03, 105–06, 131–32, 145–51; Indian conversion to Ca-

tholicism, 20–25, 69–70, 272 n.33; and 19th century politics, 127, 132–33, 142, 145–47, 149–51; and social change, 222–51. See also Church; Clergy; Civil-religious system; Cofradías; Rebellions
Remate de diezmos, 63
Remesal, Antonio de, Dominican chronicler, 12, 19, 20, 26
Repartimiento system: and agriculture, 34–35, 47–48, 91; alcaldes mayores' profits from, 46–48; commodities obtained through, 36; decline in, 60–64; and Dominicans, 54, 63; effects on native communities, 65–68, 70, 80–94; and food shortages, 48–50; and forced labor, 62–63, 65–66; Indian failure to pay, 282–83 n.91; Indian revolt against, 70; political and religious conflict over, 48–51; and secular clergy, 37, 68. See also Cacao; Taxes and taxation; Tribute
Residencias, judicial reviews, 46
Restitution, 16
Revolution, Mexican, 156–59, 249
Ricard, Robert, historian, 243–44
Rice, 112–13, 117
Rights, political, of Indians, 11, 17, 21
Rinfrull, Manuel, lumbering concessionaire, 293–94 n.22
Ritual, social meaning of, 222–27
Roca, Tomás Luis de, priest, 101–03
Rogel, Juan, audiencia judge, 14
Rojas, Alberto, head of DAI, 169
Roldán, Jacinto, royal official, 74
Romano and Company, lumber-

Romano and Company (*cont.*) ing concessionaire, 293–94 n.22

Ronfeldt, David, anthropologist, 250

Rosario, Grijalva basin estate, 184

Rothkrug, Lionel, historian, 241–42, 244

Rubber industry, 113, 115–16, 153, 292–93 nn.21–22

Rueda, Policarpo, governor of Chiapas, 157

Ruíz Cortines, Adolfo, president of Mexico, 171

Rus, Jan, anthropologist, 147

Sagchaguo (Zinacantan), 96

Saints, exchange of, 229fig.

Saklum (Zinacantan), 136, 171, 182

Salazar y Frías, Bernardino de, bishop, 33

Salinas: civil-religious system in, 229–231; female-headed households in, 138; land tenure in, 171, 174; population, 95, 137, 138; re-founded, 135; religious life in, 103, 235, 237; mentioned, 92, 309 n.75

Salt, ceremonial exchange of, 229–30

Salto de Agua, 156, 158

San Andrés (Chamula): church revenues paid by, 100; civil-religious office in, 228; denuncias in, 122–23; disease in, 119; female-headed households in, 97–98; land and land tenure, 123–24, 165, 166, 167, 302 n.101; native tributaries, 73; mentioned, 71, 101, 102, 163, 289 n.67, 297 n.51

San Antonio (Zinacantan), 170

San Antonio, Zinacantan hacienda, 96

San Bartolomé: agriculture and land use in, 39, 64, 190, 192, 291 n.8; cofradías in, 29; disease in, 118, 119; Indian population in, 67; and Indian rebellions, 78, 84; ladinos in, 104–05; political and religious organization in, 58–59, 290–91 n.3; population growth in, 121fig.; tribute paid by, 38, 54; visitas and limosnas, 57; mentioned, 289 n.67. See *also* Venustiano Carranza

San Cristóbal: Chamula laborers in, 202; coffee workers hired from, 163; denuncias in, 122–23; disease in, 119; land and land tenure in, 123–24, 165, 166, 168; as municipal corporation, 290–91 n.3; normal school in, 303 n.109; political conflict in, 131, 156–57, 300 n.80; as trading and market center, 135–36, 197, 212; mentioned, 127, 150–51, 159, 163

San Felipe: cofradías in, 29, 88–89; denuncias in, 122–23; disease in, 72; effects of taxation on, 295 n.29; and forced labor of residents, 87; private property in, 168

San Lucas: denuncias in, 122; disease in, 118; female-headed households, 97; land and land tenure in, 110, 123–24, 169, 189, 190; native tributaries, 73; religious life, 237

San Martín, 97

San Martín y Cuevas, bishop, 106
San Miguel Mitontic. *See* Mitontic
San Nicolás (Zinacantan), 170
San Pablo, 97, 100
San Pedro, Zinacantan ranch, 96
San Pedro Chenalhó. *See* Chenalhó
San Pedro Martir, Zinacantan Ranch, 139
Sandoval Zapata, Juan, bishop, 33
Santa Catarina Pantelhó, 100
Santa María, Pedro de, Dominican priest, 28
Santa María Magdalena, 123–24
Santa Marta (Chamula): Church revenues paid by residents, 100; denuncias in, 122–23; ejido petitions, 123–24; female-headed households, 97; indigenous government suspended in, 272 n.31; native tributaries, 73; religion in, 103; mentioned, 79, 244, 245
Santa Rita Agil (Zinacantan), 170
Santa Teresa, Zinacantan ranch, 139
Santander, Juan, colonial magistrate, 245
Santiago (Chamula), 73, 97, 100, 103, 122–23
Santiago de Guatemala, 28
Santis, Fabián, Zinacantan politician, 172–73
Santo Domingo, lumbering concession, 293 n.22
Santo Domingo (Zinacantan), 79
Santo Tomás, estate, 184
Saraes, Gerónimo, native priest, 83
Schools, Indian, 303 n.109

Schindler, Federico, lumbering concessionaire, 293–94 n.22
Secularization of native parishes, 16, 28, 30, 51–56, 58–60, 64, 68–69, 76, 109
Sek'emtik (Zinacantan), 136, 142, 182, 199, 217, 231, 309 n.75; religion in, 235–38
Seminary, founded in Chiapas, 51
Señoríos, precolonial fiefdoms, 6
Servants, household, 140
Sex ratio, in Zinacantan, 135, 136fig., 138
Sex roles, 222–27
Shamans. *See* Curers
Sheep. *See* Wool
Sibacá, 29, 73, 88, 97
Sierra Madre mountain range, 7
Simojovel: agriculture in, 113, 117; curato and anexo, 53map; fincas rústicas in, 111; foreign capital in, 114; and Indian rebellions, 78, 84; Indians and ladinos in, 295 n.31; native tributaries, 73; mentioned, 135, 289 n.67
Sindicato Central de Obreros y Campesinos, 160
Sindicato de Trabajadores Indígenas, 163–65, 169–70, 176
Sisal, 127
Sitalá, 73, 97, 130
Skins, trade in, 9
Slavery: black, 17, 33; Indian, 12, 14–15, 19
Smallpox. *See* Diseases and epidemics
Smith, Hiram, lumbering concessionaire, 293–94 n.22
Smith, Waldemar, anthropologist, 240, 246

Smuggling, 54, 111–12

Snas, residential sections, 220

Social change: and agricultural expansion, 116, 118–20, 125–27; and colonization, 19, 43, 64–66; and modernization, 211–12; and religious change, 240–51; as subject of anthropological research, 2–5

Social stratification. See Socioeconomic stratification

Socialists, politicians and labor unions, 160–61

Sociedad Económica de Ciudad Real, 103

Sociedad Explotadora de Chiapas, 293–94 n.22

Socioeconomic stratification, 183–86, 208–15, 228–29, 239–41, 246–51

Socoltenango: agriculture in, 190, 192, 199; cofradías in, 29; curato, 65map; female-headed households in, 97; land use and land tenure in, 169, 189, 190, 199; population growth in, 121fig.; visitas and limosnas, 57; mentioned, 28

Soconusco: agricultural production, 1909, 117; cacao plantations, precolonial, 9; coffee industry and labor in, 115–16, 117; disease in, 119; foreign capital in, 114; Indian labor in, 120, 151–52, 208; land tenure and agrarian reform in, 111, 160, 164, 167; population in, 118fig., 295 n.31; rubber production and concessions in, 115, 292–93 n.21; as trade center, 32; tribute collected

from, 13; mentioned, 12, 156, 166

Soil fertility, 190

Solís, Father, priest, 109, 128, 130–31

Sotaná, 109

Soyaló, 40

Soyatitán, 29, 57, 65map, 97

Spain: religion in, 243, 245; 16th century political situation, 18

Spaniards: agricultural and economic activities of, 12–16, 35, 90, 113; clergy executed, 82; forced to sell food surpluses, 49; in Guatemalan cofradías, 273 n.44; political rights and activities of, 17, 22, 33–35, 45–46; population in Chiapas, 37, 39–40; and secularization, 51–52

Spices, 7

Spiritism, 70, 75. See also Religion

Stephens, John L., American traveler and writer, 107, 109, 111–12, 127–29, 130

Strikes. See Labor: unrest

Suchiapa, 57

Suchitepequez, 32

Sugar: ceremonial exchange of, 229–30; in early colonial period, 7, 12–13, 24; ingenios near Chiapa, 32–33; produced in Grijalva River valley, 37–38, 110–11; produced in Ixtacomitán and Jiquipulas, 38; produced by clergy and religious orders, 26–27, 33, 37, 40–42, 98; produced on Socoltenango hacienda, 199; produced in Zinacantan, 37–38, 90; production trends, 112–15, 117,

127, 179, 186-87; trade, 35; trapiches and native labor, 71

Surnames, Spanish and Tzotzil, 94, 139, 141, 253-60; in Zinacantan, 143-44, 217-21, 238-39, 253-60

Tabasco: Chiapas ladinos in, 127; Dominican landownership in, 40; refugees from Chiapas famine in, 50; role in trade and marketing, 38, 87, 127; mentioned, 42, 78, 112, 134, 135, 138, 158, 302 n.95

Tapachula, 158, 159, 289 n.67, 292 n.18

Tapalapa, 57, 65map

Tapilula, 65map

Tapisculapa, 57

Tax, Sol, anthropologist, 1-5, 245, 269 n.17

Taxes and taxation, 65-66, 103, 110, 129, 135; capitación, head tax, 108, 115. *See also* Church: revenues; Repartimiento system; Tribute

Taylor, William B., historian, 64

Teachers, trained for Indian schools, 303 n.109

Tecpatán: becomes parish seat, 23; cofradiás in, 29; Indian towns consolidated, 271 n.11; curato, 52map; Dominican income from, 56, 57; Dominican monastery in, 39; tribute paid by residents of, 38

Tehuantepec, 70

Tenango, 73, 84, 97

Tenant farmers and farming: Apas residents, 233; Chamulas, 203, 204-05, 206map, 208, 209, 214-15; Elan Vo' residents, 193; and family organization, 217-18, 221; farming locations, 189, 190; maize harvests, 184, 198, 208; markets used by, 197; Na Chij residents, 189, 190, 191, 198; and social and economic change, 196-99, 217-18, 221, 226, 239; Zinacanteco, 180-94, 205, 214-15, 217-18, 221, 226, 239

Tenejapa: civil-religious conflict in, 301 n.87; coffee workers from, 163; cofradías in, 29; curato, 52map; denuncias in, 122-23; Dominican landholdings in, 40; ejidos and ejido petitions in, 123-24, 166; female-headed households in, 97; land and ownership in, 40, 120, 129, 165; native tributaries, 73; occupational change in, 105; population in, 119, 120, 125fig., 168; religion and politics in, 147, 149, 178; mentioned, 74, 115, 296 n.37, 297-98 n.51, 302 n.98

Tenientes, 33-34

Teopisca: cofradías in, 29, 88-89; curato, 52map, 65map; denuncias in, 122-23; disease in, 118-19; ejido and ejido petitions, 123-24, 166; female-headed households in, 97-98; ladinos in, 104-05; land and land ownership in, 65, 123-24, 129, 165, 166, 168; native tributaries, 73; and 1912 rebellion, 84; school of spinning in, 105; visitas and limosnas, 57

Theil Index, 211, 212

Tierra Colorada (Zinacantan), 170

Tijuana, 167–68

Tila: cofradías in, 89; curato and anexo, 52map, 53map, 65map, 66map; famine and mortality in, 50; female-headed households in, 97–98; fincas and estancias in, 39; and Indian tribute, 38, 44, 287 n.44; and religious rebellion, 78; secularized, 30; mentioned, 289 n.67, 298–99 n.61, 300 n.81

Tlamames, Indian bearers, 14

Tobacco, 7, 47, 113

Tojolabal peoples and language, 10

Toldillo. See Cotton

Tonalá: agricultural production in, 117; foreign capital in, 114; fincas rústicas in, 111; Indians and ladinos in, 295 n.31; rubber concessions in, 292–93 n.21; and wheat trade, 136; mentioned, 112, 135, 289 n.67

Topolguó (Zinacantan), 96

Tortillas, ceremonial exchange of, 229–30

Totolapa: curato, 65map; disease in, 118; estates founded in, 110; female-headed households, 97–98; and Indian religious uprising, 80; ladinos in, 104–05; Na Chij tenants in, 189, 190; native tributaries, 73; ratio of surplus agriculture to wages, 192; visitas and limosnas, 57

Tovar, Mauro de, bishop, 74

Trade and trading: of agricultural products, 12, 32–35, 44; Indian, controlled by alcaldes mayores, 44–47; Indian, controlled by provincial governors, 35; between Indians and colonial officials, 43; international, 179–81; partners of provincial governors from Spain and Guatemala, 35; precolonial, 7, 9, 12; Zinacantecos in, 135. See also Cacao; Cochineal; Cotton; Maize; Wheat production and trade.

Transportation, truck, 184–85, 188–90, 194–96, 199–201, 200fig., 209

Trapiches. See Sugar

Treaty of Córdova, 107

Trens, Manuel, historian, 76

Tributaries, native, 38, 73, 95fig.

Tribute: collected by Dominicans, 54; collected by intendentes, 103; collected by provincial governors, 43–44; collected from refugees in Lacandon jungle, 50; collected from Soconusco, 13; collected from Zinacantecos, 13; demanded by Ordoñez, 98–101; in early colonial period, 12–14, 34, 37; and enslavement of Indians, 19; excessive collection of, 13, 35, 65–66, 87, 89–90; inability of native communities to pay, 60–61; Indians demand abolition of, 84; and population decline, 37; requirements loosened, 50. See also Church: revenues; Repartimiento system; Taxes and taxation

Trujillo, Miguel, Chamula schoolteacher, 62

Tulijá: lumbering concessions in, 293 n.22

Tulijá River, 299 n.61

Tumbalá: curato and anexo, 53map, 65map, 66map; described by Stephens, 128, 130; famine and mortality in, 50; female-headed households, 97–98; refugees from, in Lacandón jungle, 50

Tuxtla: agricultural production in, 117; and cacao trade, 47–48, 60; Chamula laborers in, 202; and civil warfare, 159; cofradías in, 29; curato, 52map, 65map; foreign capital in, 114; Indians and ladinos in, 295 n.31; land tenure in, 111, 169, 189, 190; market, 199; Na Chij tenants in, 189, 190; and native rebellions, 70, 278 n.38; rubber concessions in, 292–93 n.21; visitas and limosnas, 57; mentioned, 49, 58, 289 n.67, 291 n.3

Tzajaljemel (Chamula), 149

Tzeltal: peoples and language, 10, 25–26, 40, 75, 78–79, 126–27; region, 32, 50, 81, 104, 119, 128

Tzihuitzín, native deity, 101–02

Tzon, Bartolomé, alguacil of Zinacantan, 20–21

Tzotzil: peoples and language, 10, 75, 86, 89; region, 47, 71, 81, 90, 104, 128, 134, 150

Tzu, Pedro, Zinacantan official, 172–73

Ubero Plantation Company, 113

Ubico, Jorge, president of Guatemala, 248

Unions, labor, 160, 163–65, 176

United States: agricultural products exported to, 179–81; citizens' investments in Chiapas, 108, 113–15, 294 n.23

Urbina, Erasto, politician, 162–67, 169, 171, 173, 176

Usumacinta River region, 115, 153

Vagrancy laws, 115

Valenzuela (district), 293 n.22

Valenzuela, Policarpo, lumbering concessionaire, 293–94 n.22

Vázquez Xuljol, Zinacantan family, 217–18

Velasco, Cristóbal de, encomendero, 34

Venustiano Carranza (town), 169, 189, 190, 192. See also San Bartolomé

Vidal, Carlos, governor of Chiapas, 161

Villa Flores, 169

Villaescusa y Ramírez de Arellano, Domingo, bishop, 71

Villafuerte, Celso, labor agent, 169

Villahermosa, 111–12

Villalpando, Bernardino, secular priest, 28

Visitas, 36, 57–58. See also Church: revenues

Vital de Moctezuma, José, bishop, 58

Vo' Ch'o Vo', 309 n.75

Vogt, E. Z., anthropologist, 5, 222, 226, 230, 238

Wage labor: in Chamula, 203; by Elan Vo' residents, 193

Wages, agricultural, ratio of surplus production to, 192, 193

Waibel, Leo, geographer, 180

Waiting lists for civil-religious office, 178

Warman, Arturo, anthropologist, 250

Water supply, Zinacantan, 171

Wax trade, 46

Wheat production and trade, 32, 38, 42, 90, 126, 128, 133, 136

Whippings: to increase cacao production for repartimientos, 47–48; of Indians by priest, 54; of Indian children, alleged, 62; self-flagellation among Indians, 102

Witchcraft, 74

Wolf, Eric R., anthropologist, 1

Women: in Chamula, 227; as curers, 222, 239; household heads, 97–98, 135, 138; in Zinacantan, 135, 138, 222–27

Wool, 46, 213–14

World War II, 169, 180–81

Ximénez, Francisco, Dominican chronicler, 26, 36, 83, 86

Xucun, Guadalupe, landowner, 174

X'ukun (Zinacantan), 96

Yajalón: cofradías in, 29, 88–89; curato, 53map, 65map, 66map; famine and death in, 50, 72; female-headed households in, 97–98; labor unrest and land reform, 160; ladinos in, 302 n.95; native tributaries, 73; religion and politics in, 106, 109, 301 n.82; visitas and limosnas, 57

Yalchitóm, 91, 104, 121map

Yalemtaiv (Zinacantan), 170

Yaxalumiljo', 309–10 n.84

Ycalum (Zinacantan), 96

Year renewal ceremonies, 226, 238–39

Yucatán, 107–08, 127–28

Zabaleta, Pedro de, sargento mayor, 87

Zacualpa (town), 89–90

Zacualpa, la, rubber plantation, 293 n.22

Zapaluta, 29, 91

Zárate, Juan Hernández, Zinacantan politician, 172–73

Zárate, Mariano, Zinacantan politician, 173–75, 199

Zeldal. See Tzeltal

Zendal. See Tzeltal

Zinacantan: agriculture, land, and land tenure in, 37–38, 65, 104–05, 123–24, 165, 166, 167, 168, 170–72, 181–83, 187–200, 205; anthropological research on, 4–6, 239–41, 245–51; cofradías in, 29, 88–89, 92; conflicts between encomenderos and missionaries, 21; culture and ethnicity in, 5–6; curato and anexo, 52map, 53map, 65map, 66map; demography, 93, 96, 110, 119, 120, 125fig., 136fig., 137, 151, 183; denuncias in, 122–23; disease and epidemics, 13, 27, 72; and excessive tribute, 13, 89–90; household composition and family organization, 97–98, 135, 138, 140; and Indian rebellions, 78–80, 85; as a source of labor, 95; native tributaries, 73; priests' attitudes toward Indian religion, 106, 131; precolonial trade center, 9; relations between cabecera and villages, 233–38; religion and politics in, 103, 146–67, 172–75, 222–39, 229fig., 246–51; religious festivals celebrated in, 106, 146, 148–49; social and economic organization and change, 90–96, 134–51, 182–86; surnames in, 143–44, 217–21, 238–39, 253–60; truck owners in, 200fig.; women in, 97–98, 138, 222–27; mentioned, 11, 20, 22, 26, 62, 214–15, 250–51, 296–97 n.40, 300 n.81, 309 n.75

Zoques people: as cacao growers, 12, 15; cofradía participation, 25–26; and Indian rebellions, 84, 134, 278 n.38; in precolonial period, 9–10; mentioned, 23, 38, 40

Zoques region: disease in, 72, 119; fincas and estancias in, 39; Indian population of, 67; Jiquipulas parish secularized, 30; laboríos and mozos in, 91; locust plague in, 48–49; mentioned by Gage, 32; tribute and repartimientos collected from, 38, 44, 47

Zuazua y Múgica, Antonio, alcalde mayor of Ciudad Real, 278–79 n.42

Designer: Nancy Benedict
Compositor: TriStar Graphics
Text: APS-5 Melior
Display: Phototypositor Melior